THE THREE WAVES OF VOLUNTEERS
AND THE NEW EARTH

By Dolores Cannon

OZARK MOUNTAIN PUBLISHING

PO Box 754, Huntsville, AR 72740
800-935-0045 or 479-738-2348; fax 479-738-2448
www.ozarkmt.com

For permission, serialization, condensation, adaptions, or for our catalog
of other publications, write to Ozark Mountain Publishing, Inc., P.O. Box
754, Huntsville, AR 72740, ATTN: Permissions Department.

Library of Congress Cataloging-in-Publication Data
Cannon, Dolores, 1931 - 2014
    The Three Waves of Volunteers and the New Earth, by Dolores Cannon
The three waves of volunteers that have come from other dimensions, planets,
spacecraft and the Source to assist in elevating the Earth's energies to ascend
into the next dimension.

1. New Earth   2. 2012   3. Ascension   4. Volunteers   5. Metaphysics
I. Cannon, Dolores, 1931- 2014 II. New Earth   III. Ascension   IV.
Metaphysics IV. Title

Library of Congress Catalog Card Number: 2011906783
ISBN: 978-1-886940-15-4

Cover Art and Layout: Victoria Cooper Art
Book set in: Times New Roman
Book Design: Julia Degan

OZARK
MOUNTAIN
PUBLISHING

Huntsville, AR 72740

WWW.OZARKMT.COM
Printed in the United States of America

Table of Contents

Disclaimer

The author of this book does not dispense medical advice nor prescribe the use of any technique as a form of treatment for physical or medical problems.   The medical information included in this book was taken from Dolores Cannon's individual consultations and sessions with her clients. It is not intended for medical diagnosis of any kind, or to replace medical advice or treatment by your physician. Therefore the author and the publisher assume no responsibility for any individual's interpretation or use of the information.

Every effort has been made to protect the identity and privacy of the clients involved in these sessions. The location where the sessions were held is accurate, but only first names have been used, and these have been changed.

PART ONE

THE VOLUNTEERS

INTRODUCTION

Since my first venture into this world of the unknown over forty years ago I have considered myself the reporter, the investigator, the researcher of "lost knowledge." In reality I am a hypnotherapist specializing in past life therapy and tracing the cause of people's problems to other lifetimes rather than the present one. As my work grew and expanded I developed my own hypnotic technique that allows instant healing, so I am now teaching that all over the world. The results have been astounding. When I first felt the urge to teach my method I didn't know if it would be possible, because when you develop something yourself, you know how it works. *However,* would I be able to teach it to others in an understandable way? That was the dilemma. But I knew I would never know if I didn't try. Too many people (and some of my clients) are so afraid of failing that they never try. So I began teaching it in 2002 and it has now spread all over the world, and to my satisfaction my students are reporting the same miracles that I have experienced. Some of them are even attempting ways of using the technique that I would never have thought of. What better gratification could a teacher have than to have her students take what they have been taught and not be afraid to go beyond and explore unknown pathways. My method is not like those other outdated hypnosis methods that teach that you must do exactly as they say. That you cannot deviate even one word from the script. In my teaching I want the student to understand what is being done so they can think for themselves. As long as the client is not being harmed they are free to experiment. I have found the method to be extremely flexible. It is a living and evolving thing. Many times, after all these years, I still come home and tell my daughter, Julia, "Guess what I learned I can do today!" "They" have told me many times that there are no limitations, unless you create them yourselves. Anything is possible. You are only limited by your own imagination.

I think fear of the unknown is what holds many therapists back. They are afraid to try something new, to think for themselves. The main thing that makes my technique different is that I work in the deepest possible level of trance, the somnambulistic level. Most of the other techniques keep the client in the lighter levels of trance where the conscious mind can cause interference. When you take the person to the deepest level we are able to communicate directly with the greatest source of power and healing that there is. I have found a way to contact the Source of all knowledge. This is where the information that I write about comes from, and this is the part that performs the instant healings. It is extremely loving and forgiving. I call it the Subconscious because I didn't know what else to call it when I first began. When I am asked to define it, I say you can call it the Higher Self, the Higher Consciousness or the Oversoul. It is so big and so huge that it has the answers to everything. "They" say they don't care what I call them because they don't have a name anyway. Some of my students have suggested calling it the "Superconscious" rather than the "Subconscious." I don't know if that would be more effective or not. I just know that what I do works, so "If it's not broke, don't fix it." For the purpose of this book I will shorten it to "SC" for easier reading.

In the early years of my work it came through sporadically and subtlety, and I didn't really know what I was speaking to. It took several years of working with it before I realized what I had discovered. Then came the process of working out a method to call it in during every session. This has proved invaluable to my work. People say, "Don't you know you are performing miracles?" I tell them, "*I* am not doing anything! *They* are! I am just the facilitator, they are doing the work." This magnificent and wonderful part knows everything about everyone. And it cares deeply for every single person. There are no secrets, "they" know you better than you know yourself. So when a client comes to see me, I know they will get whatever they need to know. Whatever the Subconscious thinks is appropriate for them to understand. I never know what will happen, so I can't control or manipulate the session. I have been working with them for so long that I usually know what some of the answers will be because they are always the same, yet it is never what I would have thought logically. "They" have a logic all of their own. So I tell the client I never know what will come out during the session. It is different each time, but it will never be more than they can handle. I never know if the answer will relate to karmic problems or something else. Now the answers seem to be more focused on the "something else," and my concept of the Three Waves of Volunteers was formed. I am the first to admit that this view of planetary transformation is both mind-bending and awe-inspiring.

For twenty-five years I have also been investigating UFO sightings and suspected abduction cases. Much of this has been reported in my books, mainly *The Custodians*, and I have found a great deal of information and answers to questions that the other investigators have only been able to skirt around. The ETs have generously given me the answers to any questions I could possibly imagine. I thought there was nothing left to explore in this field. Yet again "they" have surprised me. During the last few years I began to see glimpses of a much bigger story behind the sightings and examinations, etc. I thought I had finally solved the riddle of their involvement with the human race. But during a session in 2009 I was finally given, what I consider to be, the "missing piece" to the entire UFO puzzle. The proverbial "light bulb" went on, and things began to fall together. I soon realized that I had had all the pieces all along. They were scattered throughout my work, especially *The Custodians* and *The Convoluted Universe* series. They had come through many thousands of clients during our regression therapy sessions. I had put some of the story together, and thought I had the whole picture. Now, suddenly, I discovered that there was more and it had been staring me in the face for years. I probably still don't have the entire story. I'm sure there will continue to be surprises along the way, but at last the time has arrived for the veil to lift. The veil has been getting thinner over the last several years, and I have noticed it in my therapy practice. More people are becoming aware that the mundane life they are drudging through is not the reason they came to Earth. The answers keep coming through session after session: "It is time to awaken!" "You have a mission! It is time to begin!" "Stop wasting time! Time is growing short for you to accomplish what you came to Earth to do!"

Over the forty years I have been involved in past-life regression and therapy the pattern was always the same. Of course, there was always the exception to the rule, and that was what I wrote my books about. But, as a rule, the client would go back to the appropriate past life to explain the problems they were having in their present lifetime. Whether it was relationship problems, work-associated problems, or health problems, the answer could usually be traced back to a single past life or a series (pattern) of similar lifetimes where they were repeating the same karma with the same people. I knew the answer was to break the cycle, and this could be done by their subconscious showing them the connection. Then they could have healing and closure. However, during the last few years the pattern of my work began to change, and I was continually encountering a different type of client. It must be strongly stressed that, on the surface, there is nothing unusual about these people. They are perfectly normal human beings living life just like everyone else. They come to me for help in finding solutions to their problems. The answers that have come forth in these sessions were the last thing their conscious minds could possibly imagine. It appears that we truly are multi-faceted humans. We see our lives through one perspective, never knowing the other layers that lie just below

6

the surface. Unknown to our conscious minds, yet they have great influence over our lives. There is much more to us than we can ever imagine. Therein lies the illusion. We think we know ourselves, but do we?

CHAPTER ONE

THE DISCOVERY OF THE THREE WAVES

M y research in the field of hypnosis has taken me on unimaginable journeys through time and space to explore the history of the past and the possibilities of the future. When I first began my investigations through past life therapy, I thought I would only find people remembering lives on Earth because naturally that was all we knew about. My belief system has really been stretched and extended over the past forty years. As my work progressed, I was given a great deal of information about the beginning of life on Earth. I was told that this is the time for this knowledge to come forth. We are moving into a new world, a new dimension, where this information will be appreciated and applied.

During my work, I have heard much about everything being composed of energy; the shape and form is only determined by the frequency and vibration. Energy never dies; it only changes. I have been told that the Earth is changing its vibration and frequency and preparing to rise into a new dimension. There are countless dimensions surrounding us all the time. We cannot see them because as their vibrations speed up, they are invisible to our eyes. It is important for us to know more about this shift to a new dimension because we are in the middle of it now, and its culmination is coming soon.

Earth is a school that we attend and learn lessons, but it is not the only school. You have lived on other planets and in other dimensions. You have done many, many things you cannot even imagine. Many of the people I have worked with in the last few years have regressed to lifetimes where they were light beings living in a state of bliss. They had no reason to come into the Earth's density and negativity. They *volunteered* to come to help mankind and the Earth at this time. I have encountered what I consider to be three waves of these new souls who are living on Earth. They have come at this time because most of those people who have been here for lifetime after lifetime have become bogged down in karma and are not advancing. They have lost sight of their purpose of living on the Earth.

In the early days of my work (and in my early books) I thought that it would be impossible for a person to be experiencing their first life on the planet Earth during our present time. I thought it had to be a gradual process: going through the various life forms before becoming human: air, rocks, soil, plants, animals, nature spirits, and eventually humans. I thought that when a soul decided it was ready to attempt life as a human, it would be in a primitive society so it could adjust slowly. I thought that it could never be suddenly dropped into our hectic modern society with all its chaotic energy. It would be absolutely too much for a newly evolving soul to endure. But then in 1986 I wrote the book *Keepers of the Garden*, about a gentle soul that was experiencing his first life on Earth. He had always had lives on other planets and dimensions. Yet in our first sessions he described several apparent past lives on Earth. So I wondered what was going on. Either reincarnation was true or it wasn't. But then I was given my first explanation of the "imprint" theory. People who have lived on Earth through countless lifetimes have the memories of these experiences in their subconscious memory banks. Unknown to the conscious mind of the individual these buried memories are essential to helping them steer their way through the morass of living as a human. Without some type of background they would not be able to function. The newborn baby appears to come in fresh with nothing to relate to, until taught by its parents and society. But this is far from true. The so-called "baby" is actually a very old soul that has

10

had hundreds of journeys into the complicated scenario we call "life." This gives it something to use as a reference (unconsciously) on how to live as a human. But new souls to Earth do not have that background and would be totally lost. Except for an ingenious concept that has been developed on the spirit side called "imprinting." When the soul is on the spirit side it is shown the type of life it will be entering next, and it makes a plan of what it *hopes* it will be able to accomplish. It also makes contracts with various souls to work out any lingering karma. If the soul has no Earth experience to fall back on, they are taken to the Library. Many, many of my clients have described this Library the same way. It is where all knowledge is kept, everything that is known and will ever be known. It also has the Akashic Records, which are the records of every life that has ever been lived since the creation. Through much discussion and advice with the Librarian, the soul picks out lifetimes that it wants to be imprinted upon its soul pattern. These have been compared to an overlay or a film. It is rather like going to a library to do research and pouring over countless volumes or books to find the correct information. This imprinting becomes an essential part of the new soul's memory. I asked how I would be able to tell, when working with a client, whether the memories that come forth during regression were "real" or an imprint. I was told that I would not be able to tell the difference because *everything,* not only memories, but emotions and everything that made up the lifetime would also be imprinted. They said, because it was only being used as a reference for the soul, that it didn't matter anyway. Since many famous people's lives are often used as an imprint, this explains the skeptics' criticism that reincarnation does not exist because many people claim to be the same important person. Imprinting answers that argument. I asked them, "Does that mean that reincarnation does not exist, if anyone can imprint a life rather than living the actual experience?" They said, no because there have to be lives being lived in order to have material or memories to put into the records.

This made perfect sense, and was a method developed so pure, innocent souls could adapt to a foreign, chaotic world. It would be impossible to come to Earth without some preparation. The tender soul would not have anything to relate to, and would be totally unable to cope. After my first experience with Phil, the young man in *Keepers of the Garden*, I began to encounter these new souls more frequently. These cases are described in *The Convoluted Universe* books. So what I had thought was a rare occurrence was now becoming more common. They had been hiding behind their imprints of other lifetimes, and this was what was being presented to other hypnotists and investigators (especially those who only work in the light levels of trance). Because the imprints are chosen for a purpose to be used during their lifetime, the "apparent" past life will answer some questions, but not the most important. The SC, in its infinite wisdom, will only give the client what they can handle. And the same is true of the hypnotist, if they are only taking their "baby steps" into the unknown they will not be given complex answers. I was not given this information until I was ready to stretch my curiosity. Until recently, I still thought these pure, innocent "first-timers" were rare. But now they are becoming the norm. The SC is not even bothering to cover it up any more. Many times the client has not been able to find a past life, no matter how many variations of my technique I try. Then when I contact the SC for clarification, I always ask why we weren't able to find anything. It will sometimes say, "We could have shown him something, but it would have only been an 'imprint.'" Then it goes on to tell them where they have come from, and their purpose on the planet Earth at this time. There have been a few cases where the Subconscious said that the person refused the imprints just before entering the baby's body. And it has caused a chaotic life without a plan or purpose. So it seems that "they" really do know what they are doing. It is we, the humans, who do not understand, or are not capable of comprehending.

To fully understand the theory (and "missing piece") that I am about to propose, it is necessary to go back to the beginning, to the "seeding" of the human race.

HOW LIFE ON EARTH BEGAN

In order to understand why these three waves of volunteers have come at this time, we have to go back to the beginning—the beginning of life on our world. I know this information is controversial, but when the same information has come to me over and over in thousands of regressions, I feel we cannot ignore it.

Eons ago there was no life on Earth. There were many volcanoes and the atmosphere was full of ammonia. The planet had to be changed for life to begin. In my research I learned that there are Councils that make the rules and regulations for creating life throughout the universe. There are Councils over the solar system, Councils over the galaxy, and Councils over the universe. It is a very ordered system. These higher beings go throughout the universe looking for planets that are suitable for life. They say that when a planet reaches the point where it can sustain life, it is a very momentous occasion in the history of that planet. It is then given its Life Charter.

Then various groups of ETs or higher beings are given the assignment to go and begin life on that planet. These beings are called the Archaic Ones or the Ancient Ones. They have been doing this since the beginning of time. This does not put God out of the picture at all—He is very much in the whole picture. These beings first bring in single-celled organisms to get them to divide and form multi-celled organisms. It depends upon the conditions on each planet which organisms form. After they have seeded a planet, they come back to check on the cells from time to time over the eons. Often the cells do not survive, and they find the planet lifeless again. These beings have told me, "You have no idea how fragile life is."

So down through time they did this on Earth, and after a time plants began to form because you have to have plants before you can introduce animals. As life began to develop, they kept coming back to see and care for it. They formed the oceans and cleansed the air so that various life forms could evolve. Eventually the higher beings began to create an intelligent being. This has happened on every planet; this is the way life is formed.

In my books I have called these beings "keepers of the garden" because we are the garden; we are their children. Now in order to create an intelligent being they had to take an animal with a large enough brain that would have the capacity to learn, and one that had hands so it could develop tools. This is why they chose the ape. Some people don't agree with this, but the truth is that we are 98% genetically compatible. You could give blood to an ape and it would live; that's how close we are genetically. But even so, creating the human being required genetic manipulations and mixing in other cells and genes brought from all over the universe. They said we will never find the missing link; it doesn't exist. Our evolution jumped generations. It did not happen by random chance.

Over time, whenever something needed to be given to humanity, these beings would come and live with humans and give them what they needed. Every culture in the world has legends of the "culture bringer." The Indians have the corn woman who taught them how to plant. There are legends of the ones who taught us about fire and how to develop agriculture. In all the legends of the world these beings come from the sky or from across the sea. These were the teachers, and they could live as long as they wanted. They are the ones who have come down to us as legends of gods and goddesses. It is still happening now, but they cannot live among us; they would be too conspicuous. So when they want to give us new ideas to speed up our evolution, they now put them into the atmosphere. Whoever picks up on that idea is the one who will invent it. They don't care who invents it as long as it is in the timeline. We all know of different people working on the same invention at the same time. An example of this is free energy, which I am hearing about in my travels, that many people are developing all over the world.

THE LOST GARDEN OF EDEN

When an intelligent being was created on Earth, the Council decided to give us free will and see what we do with it. There are planets where there is no free will. The Star Trek directive of non-interference is very, very real. This is part of the Council's directives: they cannot interfere with the development of an intelligent species. They can help by teaching us and giving us knowledge, but they cannot interfere. I asked, wasn't it considered interference when they came and gave us the next thing we would need in our evolution (fire, planting, etc.)? They said, "No, it is a gift we give to you one time to help you in the next stage of your development. What you do with it is your free will." Many times we have taken their gift and used it for something negative or destructive, which was not their intention. I said, "Then couldn't you come back and tell them they were not using it in the correct way?" They said, "No, *that* would be interference. We give it to you. What you do with it is your free will. We can only stand by and shake our heads in wonderment at the complexities of humans, but we cannot interfere." The only exception to this rule would be if we reached the stage of development that we could destroy the world. This could not be allowed because it would reverberate throughout the galaxies, disturbing too many planets and even life on other dimensions. You would not think that a small planet deliberately isolated in this part of our solar system would have that much impact. But they said the results would be extremely far-reaching and devastating.

We were supposed to be a perfect species that would never get sick and could live as long as we wanted. Earth was supposed to be like a Garden of Eden, a perfect place, but something unexpected happened and changed the whole plan. When life was beginning to develop nicely, a meteorite hit the Earth and it brought bacteria that caused disease. This was the first time disease was introduced to the Earth. When this happened the beings overseeing Earth's evolution went back to the Council. They asked what to do now that their perfect experiment was spoiled. There was great sadness. The question was whether to destroy everything and start over, or to allow life to continue to develop. The Council decided to let it go ahead and evolve because so much time and effort had been involved. They allowed it even though they knew, because of disease, that life on Earth would never be perfect as originally planned.

These higher beings continued to observe our evolution from afar, but something happened in 1945 that *really* caught their attention: the explosion of the atomic bomb at the end of World War II. We were not supposed to have atomic power at that stage in our evolution. They knew we would not be able to control it, that we would use it for destruction.

When atomic power was supposed to be introduced into our time line, it was intended to be used for good. I said that we were using it for good, electricity and such as that. They explained that because it was first created as a weapon it would always carry that negative aura, and never have the great benefit it was supposed to have. We had just come through the horrible World War II, so they knew we would never be able to control something as powerful as atomic power. It was just human nature, and they were extremely worried that this could lead to destruction. During the development of the atomic bomb the scientists didn't really know what they were experimenting with. It was an unknown element. They were told that they could conceivably ignite all of the hydrogen atoms in the atmosphere and cause a massive explosion that could destroy our world. But the scientists ignored this advice and their curiosity kept them experimenting. All of this is told in my book, *A Soul Remembers Hiroshima*, where I did years of research on the development of the bomb. Also after the war ended, there was much distrust among the countries that caused a buildup of nuclear stockpiles. So the worries of the higher beings were well founded. We didn't know what we were playing with. It was an extremely dangerous and volatile time period.

It was during this time, at the end of the 1940s and beginning of the 1950s, that UFO sightings began to be publicized. The higher beings went back to the Council and asked what to do since they are not allowed to interfere with mankind's free will. That is when the Council came up with what I think is a brilliant plan. They said, "We cannot interfere from the outside, but what about if we help from the inside?" It is not interfering when you ask for volunteers to come in and help. This is how the call was given throughout the universe for souls to come to help the Earth.

The people on Earth have been caught in the cycle of reincarnation, on the wheel of karma, for hundreds and hundreds of lives, returning and making the same mistakes over and over again. We are supposed to be evolving but we are not. This was the main reason Jesus and the other great Prophets came to Earth: to teach people how to get off the wheel of karma, to help humanity to evolve. But we are still making the same mistakes over and over again: creating wars and so much violence. So the people on Earth were not going to be able to save the Earth. How could they help the Earth when they couldn't even help themselves? It needed pure souls who were not caught in the wheel of karma, who have never been to Earth before.

In the last five years of my work, I have been finding more and more souls who have come directly from God, and have never been in *any* type of physical body. I have had people go back to where they were ETs living in spaceships or on other planets, to where they were on other dimensions, to where they were light beings and did not need a body. The volunteers come in with a sheath or cover over their souls so they cannot accumulate karma because once they accumulate karma they have to be reborn again and again. Now there are tens of thousands of these new souls all over the world, and the higher beings have said they don't have to worry about us destroying the Earth. They say we have finally tipped the balance. We *are* going to be able to save the world.

The purist and most innocent of all are those souls that come directly from the Source or God. I have asked to know what God is. They said that our conception is just a tiny thread of what He truly is. We cannot even *begin* to conceptualize what He is. They all describe God in the same way: He is not a man—if anything He would have been a woman because women are the creative force. But God is neither man nor woman. He is a huge Source of all energy, described as an immense Fire or Light. Some call God the Great Central Sun, a huge energy Source, and yet so full of love, total love. One client described the Source as "The heart of the Sun. The heart of God." When the pure beings who have come directly from God go back to the Source during the session, they do not want to leave. This is where we all began; we were originally one with this Source. The souls who have come directly from God say that there is no separation; it is all one. I have asked, "If you loved it so much, why did you leave?" They all said the same thing: "I heard the call. Earth is in trouble. Who wants to go and help?" Even the ones who are ETs have said the same thing. And when they come into the body, like all of us, their memories are erased. I have asked, "Wouldn't it be easier if we remember why we have come?" They said it wouldn't be a test if you knew the answers.

THE THREE WAVES

So the purpose of the three waves is two-fold. One: to change the energy of the Earth so it can avoid catastrophe. And two: to help raise the energy of the people so they can ascend with the Earth into the next dimension. Estimating the approximate ages of the three waves came about while having sessions with many hundreds of people. They all said the same things about their present lives, and they all went back to the same situations during the session. So I began to roughly categorize them according to their present age.

18

The first wave of these souls, in their late 40s to early 60s (after the dropping of the bomb at the end of the 1940s) now, have had the most difficult time adjusting. They don't like the violence and ugliness they find in this world and want to return "home"—even though they have no idea, consciously, where that might be. Emotions disturb and even paralyze them, especially strong ones like anger and hate. They cannot handle being around people expressing them. These dramatically affect them, as though emotions are foreign to them. They are used to peace and love because that was what they experienced where they came from. Even though these people seem to have a good life, loving family and a good job, many of them try to commit suicide. There seems to be no logical reason, yet they are so unhappy they don't want to be here.

The second wave are now in their late 20s and 30s. They are moving through life much more easily. They are generally focused on helping others, creating no karma, and normally going unnoticed. They have been described as antennas, beacons, generators, channels of energy. They have come in with a unique energy that greatly affects others. They don't have to *do* anything. They just have to *be*. I have been told that just by walking through a crowded mall or grocery store their energy affects everyone they come in contact with. It is that strong, and of course, they do not realize this consciously. The paradox is that although they are supposed to be affecting people by their energy, they really don't feel comfortable being around people. So many of them stay home secluded, to avoid mixing with others; even working from their homes. Thus they are defeating their purpose. Many of the first and second wave do not want to have children. They unconsciously realize that children create karma, and they don't want to have anything tie them here. They just want to do their job and get out of here. Many of them do not marry, unless they are lucky enough to find another of their own kind.

The third wave are the new children, many of whom are now in their teens. They have come in with all the knowledge needed, on an unconscious level. The DNA of everyone on

Earth is being altered at the present time and changed in order to adjust to the new vibrations and frequencies. But the DNA of the new children has already been altered and they are prepared to proceed with little or no problems. Of course, many of these children are misunderstood by the schools and are sadly being medicated. A recent medical report has now announced that 100 million children have been *mis*diagnosed with ADHD, and put on Ritalin and other drugs. There is nothing wrong with these children. They are just more advanced and operating on a different frequency. Because they are so intelligent they become easily bored at school. I have been told that they need challenges to keep them interested. This group have been called the "hope of the world." Some of these children are only nine or ten years old and have already graduated from college. They are forming organizations, and amazingly, these are organizations to help the children of the world!

I asked "them" one time why the first wave had the most difficulty. They said that someone had to be the pioneers, the trail blazers, the ones to show the way. They carved the path that would make it easier for the others who followed them.

In the last few years (2008 to 2010) I have been interviewed on the popular radio show "Coast to Coast" several times. I have also done Project Camelot and other popular internet shows. Also I have had my own radio show on BBSradio.com for almost six years that goes all over the world. The amount of emails and snail mail that I receive after each of these shows is unbelievable. My office is inundated after each airing. Also my books have now been translated into over twenty languages. The mail comes from all over the world, and is always the same. They are so grateful for the information. They thought they were the only ones in the world who had these feelings of not wanting to be here, of not understanding the violence in the world, of wanting to go "home," of seriously entertaining thoughts of suicide in order to get out. It has helped them tremendously to know they are not crazy, that they are not alone. That they are one of many who volunteered to come and help the Earth through its crisis mode. They just were not prepared for the repercussions on their gentle souls.

From the letters there may have been a scattering of a few souls who are older (born in the 1930s and 1940s) who came in before the onslaught after the end of the 1940s and the beginning of the 1950s. Their letters say that they are older, yet they have all the symptoms of the First Wave. It is possible that some were sent as pioneers before the mass insurgence at the end of the 1940s. I have always believed the theory that an increase of births always follows a war or catastrophe where many are killed, as nature's way of replacing and adjusting the population. But this other theory could also be an explanation for the Baby boomers. They are composed of many of the volunteers.

The letters all say the same thing, they are grateful for an explanation that makes sense to them. I have even had them come up to me after one of my lectures, crying, and saying, "Thank you. Now I understand." Even though they still don't like the violence and vibration of Earth, now that they know they have a mission, they are determined to stay and complete it. It has made a vast difference in their lives.

I want to quote from one of thousands of emails I received in 2010 after one of my radio shows. "I'd like to thank you for speaking about the '3 waves' because I believe I am one of the people from the First Wave, born in 1961. My much younger brother, I believe, is from the Second Wave, born 1980. We have talked about this many times, and have agreed that we were in fact Extraterrestrials and were not from Earth! I had an extreme vision once about the actual planning session for the 3 waves that took place before I incarnated. It was quite detailed and interesting. You might also be interested to know that this plan was in fact tried once before, and failed because the numbers of volunteers were not high enough! It was then that 'we' decided to open the flood gates and 'stack the deck' with as many high souls as could possibly be gathered. This time I think the plan is working!"

CHAPTER TWO

A FIRST TIMER

A s I have said, over the years I have discovered many new and pure souls who are coming to Earth at the present time with a different agenda from those who have been trapped on the karmic wheel for countless lifetimes. Because they have no accumulated karma they are free to pursue their real mission. The main problem is the forgetting or amnesia process that affects souls when they come to Earth. "They" have said that ours is the only planet in the universe that forgets their connection with God. And we have to stumble through life with blinders on until we discover it again. The other civilizations remember their connection and their contracts and plans. They greatly admire us for taking on this challenge of forgetting and thinking we are all alone. And having to rediscover it all on our own.

I think it would be so much easier if *we* could come in with full knowledge of our mission, our task, but the powers that be do not agree. They say it is best to have all memory erased and to allow us to rediscover ourselves, as well as our mission. They said it would not be a test if we knew the answers. So even those who come with the purist motives and intentions are bound by the same rules as the rest of us. They must forget why they have come, and where they have come from. All that is left is a secret longing that there is something else that they can't quite grasp. That there is something missing. They have to find themselves again, and stumble through life just like the rest of us until light and memory begins to seep through the blinders. That is where this process of hypnosis helps bring the memories to the forefront. It is time now to remember, to push aside the veil and rediscover our reason for coming to this troubled planet at this precise time in history.

Those that I classify as the Second Wave seem to be observers rather than participants. They are here to facilitate changes without their conscious knowledge or participation. They are to be channels of energy. They are just to *be.* They don't have to *do* anything. This can sometimes be aggravating to some of my clients. On their list of questions that they bring with them to be asked during the session is always what I call the "eternal question." "What is my purpose? Why am I here? What am I supposed to be doing? Am I on the right path?" Everyone who comes to see me wants to know the same thing. The only ones who don't have this question on their list say, "Oh, I don't need to ask that. I know what I am supposed to be doing." Those individuals are rare. The majority are still searching, knowing there is something just out of reach of their conscious mind. When I have those that I have classified as the Second Wave they are usually told by the SC that they don't need to be *doing* anything. They are accomplishing their goal by *being.* After one session, a male client became upset, "But I want to be doing something!" They don't realize that they *are* doing their mission, just by *being* here.

There are many cases of first-timers in my other books. An entire section in *Convoluted Universe, Book Three* is devoted to those who unearthed memories of coming directly from the God Source. In this book are some portions of recent (2009-2010) sessions that illustrate just how complex this decision process was that brought them here to Earth.

MARIE

In my hypnosis technique I use a method of having the client drift down from a cloud into an appropriate past life. I have found it to be 98% effective, so I use it often. When Marie was in deep trance she didn't want to come *down* off the cloud. Instead she wanted to go *up*. When that happens I allow the client to do whatever they wish. I never know where it will lead. As she moved upward she found herself in black space surrounded by many stars. "I see how little I am, and how big it is out there." She seemed to be hovering, suspended in mid-air. "It's all around me and I feel like I'm a part of it all. I'd like to get closer to the stars. Just get closer to the closest star I can, and see if I can look inside of it."

D: *Which direction do you want to go?*
M: The star came to me. I didn't have to go to it. It's right there. I'm looking through it and I'm seeing inside of it, I guess. It's like gases. It's like vapors. Nothing is staying still. All vapor, gas and colors. Like iridescent water, like an oil slick on water. I'm not in the black of the sky anymore. I'm in colors. It's just flashing lights.
D: *So the star is not at all like you thought it would look like.*
M: No, I thought it would be like the big stars going to make me blind, but it's not.
D: *Do you want to see if it has a surface?*
M: It feels right just the way it is because it's encircling me, encompassing me. Just floating through the gases. And my head is moving all around so I can see behind me and around. To see if I can see its outside... but I'm just seeing its inside.
D: *So it doesn't have to have a solid surface?*
M: No. I feel perfect in it. I'm one with it. (Laugh) I don't feel alien to it. It accepts me as part of it. No rejection. I am part of that star, and it hasn't been disrupted because of my appearance. It's still going on and I'm just part of it. No structure. No form.
D: *Do you feel you have a body, or what does it feel like?*
M: Encompassed. I feel like it's whispering all around my body. Very pleasant, very content, very cushioned... part of the vapors. Suspended. I feel suspended, so do

you feel you have a body when you're suspended? You just feel like you're hanging. It's all around me.

D: *Do you feel alone?*

M: I'm all alone. Well, I don't feel like I'm alone because I'm with *it*. I don't feel alone.

D: *I meant, there are no others.*

M: No, nobody besides me. No people at all. Not even the thought of people. I'm in the cosmos. I feel one with it. Not separate from it. If I try to float out and see it I might feel separate of it. I don't know.

D: *Do you have any desire to do anything else?*

I was trying to get her to move on with the story.

M: No, I don't need to do anything but be right there. (Laugh) I don't want to go anywhere else. (Laugh)

This could have gone on for quite a while, so I moved her forward to a time when she decided to leave that place and go somewhere else that was appropriate. When I did she was no longer in space. She saw herself on a very high cliff. There was an overhang, a piece that jutted out over a huge chasm.

M: I can see down there. It's like I can see lots of little ants. (Laugh) It might be people. But they're so tiny. I see little dots that could be trees. They could be cars. They could be people. They're moving so it's like I'm seeing something from far away. I think I might be on top of a mountain... yes. It's not scary. I'm above everybody. They probably are people. The first thing I thought of was ants... little ants. It's distant.

D: *Become aware of your body. What does your body feel like?*

M: I don't feel like I'm in a body.

D: *Do you want to stay there or do you want to go out?*

M: I need to just be there a little longer instead of coming down the mountain. (Laugh) I feel like I'm kind of in the heavens, like the ground is just one little thin layer and then I'm above everything else. So it's like everything else is around me. But I feel I'm more in the sky than the rock I'm on. I feel I could just fly off of there if I wanted to.

D: *No restrictions. No responsibilities. Total freedom.* (Yes)

I decided to move her again, so I had her leave that place and go somewhere else that was appropriate. This time we were in for another surprise. She was still not in a physical body.

M: It's like bare rock. There's no grass. There are no flowers. It's just sheer rock. I'm in the granite. There are colors in the rock. There's gray and black, but I don't see any other colors. I'm surprised.

D: *What does that feel like to be part of a rock?*

M: That same feeling of being encompassed like it's all around me. Yet I'm free. I can get up and go anytime.

D: *It sounds like you can be a part of anything.*

M: Yes. I don't feel rejected. It's accepting me, supporting or cradling me. I'm just part of it.

D: *It sounds like you can just choose any form you want to be and experience it.* (Yes) *That's interesting. Do you feel you learn anything when you become these different objects?*

M: I feel just part of one, and that's a comfort to me that I am just accepted and loved and part of it. No digression between the two. No separation. Not a separateness, but a distinctive difference in the feeling of being encompassed. When I am part of something, I learn to feel one with it instead of separate.

D: *Do you think you're going to be in a physical body some day?*

M: Not unless you tell me to. (Laugh.) It feels limiting to be in a body. (Laugh.) I feel surrounded and it feels like to put a body on it would ground it and stop it from the flow that's going on.

I spent quite a bit of time moving her to try to find a life that we could examine. Instead she kept finding herself as *part* of something solid: a rock, a tree, a flower. Or she saw herself flying from place to place being the invisible observer. She liked watching the people in a park, and the animals and insects. She loved the freedom to come and go as she wished with no responsibilities. Every place she saw she said she was only visiting, it was not really her "home." I knew she had eventually entered a physical body because that was what I was speaking to that was lying on the bed. At one time I thought we had succeeded, but she was again the observer watching people. "I don't know what the body feels like. It doesn't even feel like it's there. (Laugh) I have some kind of weight because I'm on the solid ground. I feel more at home with the grass." She felt more a part of everything, and focusing on herself only confused her.

I was getting ready to move her again when a being appeared next to her. She felt comfortable with it, so I thought we could get it to answer some questions and shed light on this.

Very often when an entity suddenly appears like this it could be the client's guide or guardian angel. They can appear any way they wish to, but are normally seen in an unthreatening way. So I thought I would pursue that line of thinking for now instead of calling in the SC. Sometimes these entities can supply some answers.

D: *Ask him: We were drifting through several lives where she was not in a physical body. Has Marie had other lives?*

Marie chose to answer instead of allowing it to, but she was supplying important answers.

28

M: I feel I've been more in space than a body most of my life. It's almost foreign to feel "myself" and not be combined with everything else. I am used to total freedom... free flowing. I don't understand how to go from nothing and feeling spacious and with the outside around me, to feeling alone and in a body and having to be somewhere.

D: *Was this her first time in a human body? What does he say?*

M: Whatever you want it to be. (We laughed.) He says I need to get out of the sky and feel solid and feel the ground beneath me and the earth. I don't really know what that feels like. More than being part of vapors and being part of something solid. Down to ground. Touch the ground and feel like I'm on something. Be still and touch the ground with hands and touch the trees.

D: *She can pick up things and feel them and know that she has a real body. Is that what you mean?*

M: Yes, I guess so. I have to sit down, lie down and feel grounded. And I don't want that to limit me to feeling I'm being encased because the other one felt like I was "one" with it and melded into it. Now that I feel solid I feel separate. I feel I'm not a part of it. Maybe that's why I want to be solid. It feels right to not always be floating like a helium balloon that's always going up and up and up. I want something like a string for somebody to hold me with and tie it to something, so I can always stay here on the ground instead of trying to find out "up there." And see it as a good thing, not a limited thing. Something that is opposite of floating so it's just as good as floating. It just feels so comfortable to float instead of standing there. Freedom... maybe that's a lot of it. Floating feels free.

I suggested that she could have both. She could float free at night when she was sleeping and then stay grounded during the day. That way she would never lose that part.

Marie had a severe physical problem that was one of the main reasons for having the session. She had developed exema over most of her body which made her miserable with the constant itching and burning. She would scratch it to the point that it would bleed. The doctors could do nothing except give temporary relief. I then decided to call in the SC. The guide had helped but I felt he was limited in whether or not he could answer these questions.

D: Is this true that she has had many lives as just forms and parts of things? (Yes) Is this her first time in the physical body?
M: Yes. Accept the body. Accept this body. It serves you well.

The cause of the exema was an attempt to prove to her that she was physical. It definitely called attention to the body so she could be assured that she was in a body, and that she had to accept that. We worked to remove the symptoms by having her realize she had to live here and this body was necessary. She was no longer the nonphysical observer, but an active participant.

M: I know I'm grounded. My own weight will hold me to the ground. I'm grounded. I want to experience how it feels to be on the ground instead of in the air all the time. (Laugh) To feel what it's like to be in a body... not always floating in some never, never ethers. I don't need anything to make me feel human. I *am* human. I'm not scattered.

This is one of the main problems that first-timers face. They have never been in a human body before and they feel very limited and confined. They will develop physical problems, and often unconsciously try to destroy the body (through various ailments) because they don't want to be here. The main thing for them to understand is that they volunteered to come at this important time in Earth's history and they must stay in order to accomplish their assignment, their mission. There are no shortcuts, unless they want to risk going back to the other side as a failure.

When Marie first went to the beautiful gaseous star I thought she had gone to another planet, but it had no form and neither did she. I think it was a different description of going back to the Source. It is usually described as being in a bright light or great sun, but it always has beautiful colors. It always gives the feeling of complete love and the person does not want to leave because they are so happy there. Eventually they do begin their journey, and it is common to experience it first as simpler forms of life, such as rocks, plants. They like this better because the life is short, and they can come and go much faster. Yet it is the beginning of knowing what it feels like, even if they don't like losing their feeling of freedom.

THE SHIMMERING

Another similar case came from Hope, who volunteered to be the demonstration for my class in Perth, Australia. It was not just out of curiosity, she had some physical issues. She wanted help with leukemia so desperately that she was willing to allow the roomful of students witness the regression. When we began the session she did not wait for me to complete the induction. She was already describing something unusual. It reminded her of the snow-covered mountains of Tibet. She described them as beautiful, isolated, still and peaceful, majestic and powerful. The air was crisp and absolutely unpolluted. Then she described something in the air that was totally unexpected. Of course, I am so used to the unexpected that I just keep asking questions. "The air is like living crystals that have been developed into little pieces. They are everywhere in the air, not in the ground. They're in the air. I'm breathing them."

My first thought was that it would be impossible to breathe crystals. "Oh, they are tiny, minute particles. It's a very beautiful place, like another dimension.—I am so high up you can see things and manifest them, and project them to Earth. It's easy. It's my job. I am linked to everything, but to manifest this, I can't talk to people. You know what I mean? Some things have to be learned. It's an intrusion really.— Well, there really aren't any people here where I am. In place of people... energy. You wouldn't believe this."

D: *So there are no other people around you?*

H: They're on Earth.—I don't think I'm a person. I'm this shimmer.—Actually, now that you mention it, there are many beings. I was thinking of people? These aren't people. They are my colleagues. They're made of little proton things.

D: *So you don't really have a form. You're just moving? Would that be correct?*

H: Yes, thinking actually, manifesting. I am manifesting situations to be on Earth. We all are. That's what we're doing.

D: *You said this was your job?*

H: Yes, but I have to go down. I have decided to go down and be one of those humans because we manifest. We all do... the shimmers. There are many of them. Then they come down because you create it, you deliver it, you anchor it. We anchor it on Earth.

D: *Are your colleagues going to come down also?*

H: It's your own discrimination. It is your choice. You have to have someone to hold the energy here, you know? Some shimmer down. And I'm one of them.

D: *Why did you decide to come down if you were so happy there?*

H: The word "duty" comes to me. Because we all play our roles. We know our role. We all do. I'm coming down. Is that okay?

D: *Whatever you want to do, but you seem as though you don't really want to. Is that correct?*

H: You read me well.

D: *You were showing emotion like you really didn't want to come down.*

H: It's not a matter of wanting. It is a matter of what will be done.

D: *Does anyone tell you what you have to do?*

H: It's not forced. It isn't like that. There's no school teacher here. We meet, we know, we decide. It just is or we'll come down.

D: *Tell me what happens when you decide to come down.*

H: Well, Earth is very, very different. Where's the love? (Upset) I don't get it. It's all so dense. We can't breathe crystals.

D: *No, there are no crystals there, are there?*

H: All of it is tucked away. It's harsh... and people are... I'll tell you something.—Do you want to hear this?— Down where I am here they do not believe in the shimmering. (We both laughed.) If you speak about the shimmering your body gets ripped like this... pulled from one end to the other. Do not speak of the shimmering. (She put her finger to her lips and made a shushing sound.) Do you know what they do to people here? (She started crying.) They pull them apart. They do not realize what went into creating a physical body. They just destroy it and they have no link to the shimmering. I must find a place where they link.

Apparently when she decided to come to Earth it was at a time when there was much prejudice against people that were different. As a pure innocent soul she did not realize the danger of telling people about where she came from.

H: I didn't know this would happen. We meet secretly in little groups. If they find us, all in here... it's just (Pulling noise) fast.

All during this session Hope was using many hand motions that were impossible for the woman doing the transcribing to describe because she could not see them. I wished I would have had a video camera. The motions seemed to be referring to some type of torture. She made slicing motions down the front of her body, and across her throat. Also a type of pulling apart of her body. During the session it was like she didn't want to really be explicit about what had happened to her while in the physical. But I could sense from the motions and the emotions that she had been tortured and killed for her beliefs. The SC apparently thought it was gentler for her to tell the story without going into details. This was much kinder on Hope. I can only imagine how this must have affected a gentle, pure soul coming to Earth for the first time, whose only desire was to help the people. This would have been totally unexpected for a soul coming directly from a place of divine and unselfish love. The place of the shimmering.

D: *When you come down, are you in a physical body?*

H: Oh, yes because you have to be. You have to have a body down here. And they do things to the body. And the body is dense, heavy like lead.

D: *It's not comfortable, but you chose to enter the body so you could do a job. Is that correct?*

H: Yes, I forgot for a minute. It's to tell people about the shimmering. I'll tell you what it is. It's the poor people on Earth that have been cut off from this. It's so dense here with fear. Our job is to dissipate the fear and really connect them to the shimmering. Where they came from. And the possibilities vary because the shimmering can be lowered to be manifest. But it is not as easy as I thought. Because I've had no limitations, no, I didn't. They whisper it in the wind. It is whispered off, but you don't know, do you? So the question arises, how do we do it? How do I finish what I've come to do? How? I'm searching for an answer.

Sometimes I feel, "What is the point?" There's no good.

D: *But you know they're not all like that. There are some who will listen.*

H: It's not them you have to deal with. They too, come from the shimmering. They work. It's those—so many—who have forgotten where they came from. Their link, and their power, and their beauty. It's so heavy that you forget.

D: *Is there a way to help them remember?*

H: This is what I'm here for. I'm searching—I think I failed—call down more shimmerings. Call down more shimmerings so the energy is building. It is happening now... more light. And more recording.

D: *What do you mean, recording?*

H: More were called in.

D: *What about the ones who were already here on Earth? Are they able to do these things?*

H: They are shimmering here as people.

D: *So you mean they've all forgotten?*

H: I think it's more me. I think *I've* forgotten. I would have hoped not, but yes, it's definitely me, because there are many others I can see now; many others doing their work. Many have forgotten. Many have not. I'm one of them and I feel I haven't come up to scratch. I haven't succeeded.

D: *But you know when you get into the physical body, things are different.*

H: Not for some people... for me.

D: *When you're in a physical body, you start living the life of any physical person.*

H: Apparently so, much to my sorrow.

D: *Do you think there's a way to bring the memories back to this body you're speaking through?*

H: That would be my dearest wish.

D: *You are aware you are speaking through a physical body?*

35

H: Yes, and it's in pain.

D: *Why is the body in pain?*

H: Sorrow... it's just complete sorrow from having forgotten the job it came to do. Complete sorrow.

The SC said the sorrow was because Hope was not doing what she came to do. She had forgotten, and this was causing the pain in her body. I talked to it about returning the body to complete balance and harmony so she could do her job. I said, "She doesn't know consciously that she has stopped the process."

H: Aw, she's pretty smart. She's got a fair idea. She's getting there.

There was also a lot of fear originating from the past lives when she had been brutally hurt.

H: There are layers and layers and layers of lifetimes of ridicule, pain, humiliation.

D: *Why did she choose to have lifetimes of pain and humiliation?*

H: For the cause. Forgot the use of the energy, which is lost upon the planet. —I think she's allowing others to stop her.

D: *Who are the others that she's allowing to stop her?*

H: I think the church and this God and this everything piled up on top of her. It's very high all on top of her stopping her. —They're books. They're only books of incorrect knowledge. They're only words.

D: *We can just throw them away. She doesn't need them anymore.*

I did a lot of work having her visualize removing the books and layers and throwing them away. Also many suggestions to get her confidence back because nothing would happen to her in this lifetime if she chose to speak her mind. It

36

all related to the past lives and had nothing to do with the present one. It was agreeing with me and I thought we were making headway

H: She is a little confused because when she worked in spirit alone, she had everything she needed and she was alone and was happy to be so as a shimmering. As a person, she stays alone. She does keep herself alone. She would be far better to be working in groups, so that she had the support. She is used to being a shimmering all alone in a glorious isolation. If you could tell her it is not the same on Earth. That one cannot isolate oneself and survive. We don't like to criticize but it is a failing, if that's the word one could use. She needs to be social, but she's become hidden away. In a group she would not be alone.

I then asked the "eternal" question: What was Hope's purpose? What did they want her to do?

H: If she would only give the credence to herself and her work and her alone time, and not worry so much about others. She's trying to be normal. Big, big mistake. She can never be normal. You want to work, and most of the people in this room are not normal.

D: *You are aware that others are in the room (my class)?* (Oh, yes.) *Many of us are not what you consider normal?*

H: No one here is normal in the humans. I don't mean that rudely at all. I mean that with the greatest honor. She needs the support. It's like the olden days. This is her problem. She has gone past the church, but the church did give a group. She has not a group.

Throughout when she kept referring to the "shimmering," I saw it as just another word for the spirit form and the way they looked in that other world.

We now focused on the physical problems she had: leukemia and tumors in her throat.

H: She didn't want to be here. "What's the point?" she said to herself in secret.

D: *Did she just decide that she didn't want to be here?*

H: No, no, no, no, no. She saw what was happening and she started to pain, but underneath it all, the shimmering was not shimmering. Do you get what I mean? (Yes) She is actually here. And when she remembers the shimmerings I think she will want to be here.

The physical problems had come from not wanting to be here anymore. She was disappointed about her work and her career choice. She wanted to help people, but she didn't think it was working. Also she had given so much over to her husband that she was not living her own life. "She's living someone else's life." She was supposed to live her own life. Her husband would be agreeable to that. When it had all been agreed upon the SC worked extremely fast on removing the physical problem, the leukemia. It just made a quick motion over the body as though throwing something away, and announced, "It is done!!"

H: It was poison of thinking.

D: *Why did she develop it in the lymph glands?*

H: Hatred for her situation.

D: *By creating the white blood count so high, it was destroying the body.*

H: Yes. Where is the joy? Where? Not fair.

I emphasized that she could now bring joy into her life. And the SC again said she was not to be alone so much. She wasn't meant to work in isolation. I have found that many people who are the second wave of volunteers do not want to be around people. They would rather work and live in isolation. But herein lies the paradox. They are supposed to be helping people by spreading their energy, but most of them don't like people. So they would rather be alone, thus defeating their purpose.

She began to cough and I asked about her throat. She had a growth there. They said that was because she was full of fear and it settled there. Afraid to speak because of the unconscious memories of what happened when she did speak out in other lifetimes. The SC said the growth was hard as bone. It had been there for a long time and had calcified. After it studied it, it cracked it in half, like a walnut.

H: The walnut is broken in half. It is vanishing. Now one can speak the truth easily. She won't be afraid. (The leukemia, the lymph glands had been taken care of. It was gone.)

D: *When she goes back to the doctor and has the blood test, will he notice the difference?*

H: Yes. And will she be able to tell him why? It will be hard for her initially to tell him.

D: *But he will notice that something is different.*

H: He will say, "Spontaneous remissions do occur."—One day she will offer him a treatment.

D: *Have you completed working on Hope's body?*

H: That is done. As she moves, and decides her direction, her body will move and decide with it. We give her the information. Free will. She has to believe. She will like the shimmering. Her voice will take on a beautiful timbre of rhythm that we will like to listen to.—She needs to want to be here. And she will now.

D: *You know normally I have to ask you to come forth, but you've been here the whole time, haven't you?* (Laugh)

H: Was I not supposed to be here?

D: *Oh, no, that was fine. You knew what the students here needed. Sometimes you can just come in instantly, when it's important.*

H: And it depends on who you're working on.

D: *So it wasn't necessary for her to relive all those painful past lives, was it? It didn't serve a purpose. Just enough to know that was what was causing the problems.*

H: Yes. You may find that there will be a quickening in these sessions because time as we know it, is changing.

D: *So the sessions will go faster, and get to the point quicker?*

H: You could. Some will, yes.

D: *It always depends on the person.* (Yes)

H: This work is so important.—And to have the intent of the shimmering to bring heaven to Earth. And how beautiful to know that when you get into bed at night, with your work, you have brought some of the shimmering... heaven to Earth. We ask you, "What better job satisfaction could there be?" For every person you heal, the Earth lightens. We thank you for your work. We send the shimmers to you. We thank you. We honor you.

So in this case I would think the shimmering referred to either the God Source or the spirit side, especially when she referred to breathing the crystals. Either way, it refers to the starting point for some souls who make their first journey to Earth. They come with the best intentions and find it is not as easy as they thought it would be once they get here.

CHAPTER THREE

AN ENERGY BEING

Louise's main reason for coming to have the session was to find the cause of the fear of loss that seemed to haunt her throughout her life. She seemed to be on a constant search to find *her people*. She wanted to know how she could locate them and connect with them (whoever they might be). She was actively involved in metaphysical groups and teaching, and she had learned a great deal. Yet there was this gaping hole in her life that she was searching to fill. The feeling of emptiness, unhappiness and loss that had no logical explanation. Of course, we expected to find the answers in something that happened in a past life. But the SC had other ideas. Remember, it has a logic completely foreign to us because it can see the bigger picture.

When Louise came off the cloud she saw a strange landscape. The terrain was just jagged peaks, some very tall and some small. The entire ground was covered with these, nothing else. "Their color is light brown with sparkles, like they're crystals. All jagged and sharp." I wondered how anyone would be able to move and walk on such a surface. She said she was not standing, she was flying, floating, looking down on this. "Peaks are too sharp. Everything is too sharp. It's like the crystals are peaks in the other peaks, and they are the same shapes as the jagged peaks. They are long and shiny and pointy. There are some little bitty ones and some bigger ones. And there are many reflections of light bouncing everywhere. Some of the peaks are so tall they are mostly in the clouds."

I asked her to become aware of her body, or how she perceived herself. "I guess I must have a body because I don't want to step on those sharp peaks. I can notice sensation. I

41

notice warm spots and cold spots, and I can notice breeze and I can notice seeing.—I'm paying attention now to look between the peaks and crystals. If I look closer to the surface it's not static... there are things that move. It's sort of like pieces of a cloud except that they're not white or gray, and they shine more. And when they move they sort of glide around, and change shapes, but they're not a cloud. When I first landed here I thought it was empty, but I'm seeing it's not. They're almost like blobs that shine. They're not definite and they can roll around between things, but they can also float. They're like blobs, but some of them are little bitty blobs and some are bigger blobs, and they are not a definite shape. They are sort of like a cloud, except that a cloud is more wispy."

D: *Are those the only forms of life that you can detect?*
L: No. There are actually little bitty, bitty things that crawl on the surfaces. There's movement everywhere.
D: *Do you think these blobs are sentient beings that would be able to know things?*
L: Yes, they know things.—There's like a memory of inner soap bubbles. Except that they are all different shapes and sizes... integrated.
D: *Well, what about yourself? Do you think you look like one of them?*
L: (Laugh) That's what I wonder. I can certainly float and I can certainly change positions. I don't have a sense of what I look like. I feel things like warm and cold.—I can change form... can change size easily like nothing. —These others are floating around, or crawling. Some of them are so close to the surface that they're on it. I don't know if I'm like them or not.
D: *You can find out. The information is there. Are you like the other ones?* (No) *How are you different?*
L: It's like a simpler life form... it's a transition. It's not like a body. It's not pure light either. And I just stopped here, and I'm not like that exactly. (A sudden revelation.) I'm on a mission! This is like a resting

place.—It's a place in-between. I am on my journey home... and this is just a resting place.

D: *You're more evolved and they are simpler?* (Yes) *And you think you're on your way home?* (Yes) *What do you mean?*

L: (Whispering) It's where I live.

D: *You've been somewhere else?* (Yes) *Tell me about it. Where were you?*

L: On Earth. I'm not going back there. That's why I'm at this resting place before going home to get purified. All done on Earth.

D: *Are you glad to get away from there?*

L: No, I miss the beauty, but I don't want to go back there. —I miss home. Home... there's nothing jagged. There's nothing harsh. We all know. We all love. I miss home, but this is okay to be in this place. This is just a place to stop. I don't know exactly why I stopped here except to take care of a curiosity. I didn't know about places like this. You know that on Earth they call them "amoeba." Except some of them are very tiny and some are huge and they are intelligent. They can merge with one another. They can change shapes. They can grow. They can shrink. It's kind of nice to be like that. Maybe that's why on Earth I like water so much.

D: *But it's good to just be nothing for a while, isn't it?*

L: Yes. It's definitely nice.

I decided to condense time and move her ahead to when she arrived back home. I asked her what it was like. "It's really beautiful and shiny, and many things are blue and green and gold."

D: *Objects or just colors?*

L: Well, the objects *are* colors. Anything can be touched and felt, so there's no difference. It's solid, but also you can go right through it, but it does have all kinds of spaces. It can make a ship that can travel very far that's made out of particular light. And we can make beautiful things if we have memories of where we've been, and we create.

D: *You have to have memories before you can create something?* (Yes)

She was marveling at and was in awe of the magnificent things she saw that were being created. She sighed deeply. "It's so safe and so beautiful here. I missed it." She began to cry.

D: *But you went to Earth for a reason, didn't you?*
L: We wanted that, and we all went to that beautiful, beautiful place. We would like for them to know what we know, and to feel what we feel.
D: *But you know when people come to Earth, they forget, don't they?*
L: Some of them forget. Some of them don't.
D: *Is it easier when they forget?*
L: No, it's harder because they get so sucked into everything. They suffer and get stuck. No, it's easier to remember. If they're brave enough to tell people... but some of them get scared. Some of them know they are not going to be believed, and some of them just forget. But it's so beautiful there, and you know we also go to Earth and enjoy those places, so that we can collect memories, so we can be more creative so we can do more for others.
D: *So you have to go and experience in the physical to have the memories?* (Yes) *Without that you couldn't create? Is that what you mean?*
L: We can create. That's what we are. We're creators of light, and yet we also can enrich as much of the planet as a whole. See, there's connection everywhere there. It's not like people think. On Earth people accept it, but there are different planets that are not the same. On

those everyone knows that it's easy to send the messages. It's easy to connect. It's easy to move on. It's easy to travel. It's easy.

D: *Because they haven't forgotten what they are supposed to do.* (Yes) *But isn't that part of the test, to forget when you come to Earth?*

L: No. Actually I think that when we raise their consciousness on Earth more and more and more, they're going to remember. That's what all of us want to do for them there. So they will treat each other better, so they will not have to suffer to learn their lessons. It's not necessary. That's what has been done, but it doesn't have to be.

D: *It's easier to simply remember without the suffering. Is that what you mean?* (Yes) *But humans don't listen, do they?*

L: No, not always.

D: *Do you know you're speaking through a body that's living now as Louise?*

L: Yes. But this is my home in this lifetime.

D: *I was wondering if this was before she entered the body of Louise.*

L: This is also before and also after.

D: *So after she finishes here she will go back to the same place?* (Yes) *But if she was so happy there and it is so beautiful there, why did she decide to come back as Louise?*

L: Before Louise it was a volunteering to go to Earth.

D: *So she's returned again and again.*

L: Yes, but Louise is the last one. I know this. Because it's over after Louise and she gets to go home again, just like I am home.

D: *So you think by that time she'll have finished all of her lessons?*

L: On Earth, yes... not all of the lessons.

45

D: *Did she know coming in that this would be her last time?* (Yes) *It's been difficult, hasn't it?* (Yes) *Did she create those difficulties for a reason?*

L: Wanting to be as complete as possible.

D: *What do you mean?*

L: When we go from this place of light and leave this galaxy, as we call it, and we go to other civilizations, as they could be called, then we take on some of their karma. And then we complete all our human karma from this journey.

D: *So Louise has also been to other places besides Earth, and you're saying that you take on karma from other places?*

L: The karma that Louise is completing is just from her human life.

D: *Then it's time to close that chapter?* (Yes) *She's learned everything that she can learn in those lives.*

L: Not only learn, but also contribute. For the reason of the trip was to contribute.

D: *What was she supposed to contribute?*

L: Teaching people how to think... teaching people how to love... teaching people how to care for one another... teaching people how to have faith... teaching people how to create peace... teaching people how to overcome disease... teaching people to be connected to nature... teaching people that the essence of despair is connection... teaching people that they can be with one another in harmony... teaching people that war is something that could end a life.

D: *Those are all wonderful things, but when we come to Earth it becomes hard, doesn't it?*

L: Right. But there are so many of the other ones. See, some of us forget, but the other ones were not us. Those are new. They are just learning. Different levels. Different things to contribute... different lessons to learn. And also some from different areas... some

46

have had more human lives. And actually there are also other ones from other galaxies that have come.

D: *Also there are ones who have been coming back again and again and again?* (Yes) *Are they the ones that are more stuck on the wheel of karma?*

L: Yes. And that's why "outsiders" come to help them. —Many people want to be helped but they put themselves into their own boxes. They know they want to be helped; it's just that they get so stuck in their point of view. They get so stuck in their limitations of that moment in time and their bodies, that they don't believe they have anything else. They want to get help without doing anything different. They think that is all there is, the body or that food or that place or that sight. Louise gets stuck at times. She had other lifetimes that she also remembered. This time she came to remember who she was and what she can do. She's doing a good job, but not as good a job as she would have liked.

It appeared that some of the volunteers were really old souls who decided to come here to help also. They also seemed to be new to the Earth's vibrations, and this caused them problems. One of the main things that would distinguish them from the first-timers would be that they have more experience. Yet Louise recognized that they all had to work together to help those on Earth who were "stuck."

CHAPTER FOUR

THE OBSERVER BECOMES PHYSICAL

P aula was the one chosen for the demonstration at one of my hypnosis classes in Arkansas. I never know how these sessions will go because the person is in a "gold fish bowl" situation, where everyone is watching. This could make them self-conscious and nervous, and it could affect the outcome. My job is always to make sure they are relaxed so they will go into trance without the feeling of being exposed. The demonstration is always done on the last day of the class, and by that time most of the students have become familiar with each other. So it is not the same as feeling they have to perform in front of a group of strangers. I admire them for taking the chance because I respect their feeling of vulnerability. It is always an adventure because no one knows what the outcome will be. Somehow it always seems to work out perfectly. I suppose because "they" are in charge.

Paula didn't wait until I completed the induction. She was already in another life when I asked her to find a place that was beautiful and peaceful. I knew it was not the typical beautiful place as soon as she began to describe it. She saw an ocean and a crystal dome on a beach. She called it her "home," and the dome opened up as she entered it, disclosing clear walls that could be seen through. I asked her what was inside the crystal dome. "It's all in the center. It circles into circles. From the center everything comes out, spiraling on the outside of the dome towards the center where I sit. Through the center of the dome is the center of everything. This is where the energy comes."

D: *The energy focuses there in the center of the room?*
       (Yes) *Where does the energy come from?*
P: Within! It just generates. It's alive.

She said she lived in this place by herself. When I asked her about her body, she said she didn't see a body. She perceived herself as light.

There was no need to consume anything in a light body, so she said she just existed in that place. There were no other beings around.

D: *When you're generating this energy, what do you do with it?*
P: I go everywhere. I can go around the planet.
D: *So you're not confined to that place.* (Right) *Do you go outside of that crystal dome?*
P: Yes, I do. I can. I go around it. I seem to just be there.
D: *Are you happy there?*
P: I'm lonely. No one else.

She could not remember how she first came to be in this place, but she knew she had been there for a long time. "I created it."

D: *How were you able to create it?*
P: I don't remember. I don't see anything.

It seemed like this was not going anywhere, so I decided to move her. Even though time would not exist in a place like that, I had her move forward to see if there ever came a time when she was not there alone. When I asked her to move she could not see anything. It was blank. So I had her move to when she no longer had to be in that place. When I asked her what she was seeing, she began to describe a chaotic scene. "Fights... war... horses and swords and lots of fighting." She was not a part of it, just observing the war. "Horses...

50

many people on horses... fights... war... spears and swords and awful fights. I am watching them."

D: *What do you feel about it?*
P: I can't stand it. I am watching. I would rather observe because I don't want to get hurt. I can't stop it. (She began to cry.) A lot of suffering!

She continued to cry as she felt helpless to do anything. I assured her it was all right to feel emotional. And I moved her forward to see what happened. When I did she found herself in a physical body for the first time in this session. "I'm walking... hot... it's hot... the desert."

D: *Why did you come into a physical body?*
P: To learn. I had to stop being the observer.
D: *Did anyone tell you to make that change?*
P: It was my choice. I had to learn.—So now I'm just walking on the desert. I'm just trying to find a place to rest.

She felt like she had been there in the desert for a long time. Again she felt like she didn't have a home. She was just looking for a place to rest, she was very tired. "I have been walking a long time... I think I'm going to die. I don't think I'm going to make it. I'm tired and weak."

I condensed time and asked, "Do you find a place to rest?" She saw herself walking through the streets in a city where there were many people. She saw that she was male, and as he was walking through the streets someone grabbed him and put him on their horse. He knew he was in trouble. "I'm rebellious.—They put me on a horse. They're taking me away. They're taking me in a hurry. It seems like I'm going into the desert again. We're going out of the city. We're going out... not again.... He's taking me to the dunes.—I'm unconscious. He hit me on the head."

D: *What happens next when he takes you out to the desert?*
       (Pause) You can look at it as an observer if you want to.
P: I don't seem to see anymore. I think I might be dead. I think he might have killed me when he hit me on the head. My body was already dead on the horse. I don't see anything.
D: *Why did he take you out there?*
P: He didn't want me there.

She couldn't find any more answers, but I knew that now that she was out of the body we would be able to understand everything. "We can find the answers to these things because now whatever happened has already happened. You're on the other side of it."

P: I'm happy to be out of the body.
D: *But you said you came into the body to learn. Do you think you learned anything?*
P: It's so short. Everything there was so short. When I was an observer it was longer. This is short.
D: *What do you want to do now?*
P: I do want to rest. That was traumatic.

Because this was a demonstration for a class I knew I would not have as much time to explore, so I had her leave that scene and I called forth the SC. I asked it why it chose those two lives for Paula to see. "The first one where she was the energy and the observer. The one where she was living in the crystal dome and generating energy."

P: It was simple.
D: *It wasn't human, was it? (No) Why did you want her to know about that life?*
P: To connect with oneness. That was her beginning.

D: *But she was lonely in that life.*

P: Yes. It was peaceful. We wanted her to remember she is one with everything. We wanted her to remember that you're never alone.

D: *Why is that important for her to know?*

P: Simple... simple. Because we're all the same. She thinks she's special. We're all the same. We're all special. Sometimes she forgets.

D: *She has gone through some bad times in this life, hasn't she?* (Ohhh, yes!) *But she survived.*

P: Yes, she did.

D: *Why did those things happen to her?*

P: She wanted to go there. Every life was chosen by her to learn. Every one.

D: *Even when the life is difficult?*

P: Yes, it's just illusions.

D: *Then you showed her the life where she was in the desert. She was in a human body then.* (Yes) *Why did you show her that lifetime?*

P: To show her how bad life can get. Hungry and alone and hot... everything. All the major extremes that the body can endure.

D: *Why did you want her to know about that?*

P: So she can see how good she has it now.

D: *But she was mistreated as a child, wasn't she?*

P: Yes... not as bad as she thinks.

D: *Then she went into a bad marriage.* (Yes) *What did she learn from that?*

P: Humbleness and patience.

We then focused on Paula's physical complaints. The SC went about healing and repairing. It said it was using liquid light. "It flows from the Source." She had been having problems with the small of her back and had had an operation there.

P: Yes. She's been fused.

D: *What caused that?*

P: Guilt. Guilt from other lifetimes. It's unimportant. Don't hold onto the past. It's gone.

They then separated the vertebras and repaired them using more liquid light. "It is beautiful!" This was also removing the guilt, "She's got to let it go. Let it go." They then made minor attunements in the kidneys, liver and pancreas. It said this was caused by worries. I asked, "What does she have to worry about?"

P: I don't know. She's silly.—The human body is a miracle. You don't want to harm it.

Parting message: Just trust and believe in herself.

So many of these volunteers have been observers through countless lifetimes throughout the universe. What could be more natural than that they continue to be observers now at this important time in Earth's history?

CHAPTER FIVE

THE PROTECTOR

Richard was an older man who had retired from a successful professional career. He was born in 1948, which could put him in the First Wave category. He considered himself a loner and had no family. He had no problems, and seemed content with his life. When I spend most of my work dealing with devastating problems and major illness, it is refreshing to find someone who is relatively happy. Of course, there was the "eternal question": What was his life purpose, and how to accomplish it?

When Richard came off the cloud he saw two images or scenes spliced together, and he was uncertain which one to focus on. He saw a greenish, long-necked dinosaur standing under a tree calmly eating leaves. And yet there was also a pyramid in the distance. "The dinosaur's on one half of the picture eating leaves, and the pyramid in the sand is on the other side. I'm just sitting here looking at them. It's as plain as day."

He decided to focus on the pyramid and walked toward it. It was very large and the top was very pointed. The thing that made it different and interesting was that there was a very bright orb in the top part of the pyramid. It was as bright as the sun and it shone in all directions. Similar to a lighthouse except that the light did not revolve, but stayed stationary emitting bright yellowish white light.

I then had him become aware of his body, and he saw that he was a young male wearing leather sandals and something similar to a short toga that only came to his knees. The unusual thing was that he saw he had very long gray hair, which didn't seem logical for one so young. He lived all alone in a very small stone house near the pyramid. I asked if he had anything to do with the pyramid.

R: It's like the pyramid's light is keeping me safe for some reason. It's coming off the top of the pyramid and it's watching everything. Wherever it shines everything is safe. That's what I feel. I'm happy doing my job. I'm singing and humming.

D: *Why did you say it's like the light is watching?*

R: I'm aware of it, I guess. I'm aware of it even when the sun is out. The light is still there. It's not the sun. There's a sun in the sky, but this pyramid is there and it watches over the whole land... not just me. The light just comes out in our direction. I'm safe. I'm definitely safe. Yes, I don't feel any troubles. I'm happy and my life is happy or elated there, yes.

I asked if he had ever been inside of the pyramid, and he looked to see if there was any entrance. "Yes, there are steps that go up the side. And I go up and there's a door just below that big ball of light." When he entered the dark room there was nothing there except a glowing pink crystal floating in the air in the middle of the room. He took it in his hand and held it. "The beams of light are shining all around in my hand... if I close my hand light shines out my fingers. I haven't seen it before, but I just know that it's safe to hold." I wondered if it had a purpose, and it came to him that if you held it and asked it a question, it would answer.

D: *That's interesting. Do you think it has any connection to the larger light that's on the top of the pyramid?*

R: They are definitely connected. Yes, they are in tune with each other in some way. It's like a silver thread or something connecting it that you can't see.

D: *Well, let's ask it questions about this pyramid. Maybe it has answers about this place.*

I then began asking questions for the stone to answer. Richard repeated each question after me, and said what he heard. Many times the answers didn't make any sense to him. I will condense the answers here.

R: The pyramid was built by the Ancient Ones from another world. The purpose of the glowing light on top of the pyramid: it is protection. It protects everything. There are things from space that can come in and harm the planet if it doesn't protect it. I don't know what type of things. We need to protect. It just says, "I protect this place from each other." The Ancient Ones put that light on top of the pyramid. They came here, built the pyramid and went away in some type of spacecrafts. The pyramid is just a solid block except for the little room that has the floating pink crystal that glows, and the big ball on top. The light just shines like a lighthouse, but yet it doesn't circle. It just shines light in all directions. It's not necessarily a light that you see. It's like an energy that goes in all directions. There is another pyramid that does the same thing, but it is far away, way away, and there appears to be rock and sand between the two pyramids. Nothing else.

D: *Is this located on Earth?*

R: At first I thought it was, but now I don't think so because the sky is kind of purplish. It's not like a sky I've seen. Now I see that I'm the keeper of this place. I'm part of this place. It looks like we're one together. I keep it running, whatever *it* is. I watch it to make sure it's running right, but I don't see any controls or anything. I guess I communicate with it mentally... yes.

D: *So you're happy there?*

R: Extremely happy, yes. My body feels young, but I feel like I've been here a long time... a contradiction, but that's what it seems like. I am happy being here alone.

I moved him ahead to an important day. "There's a cigar shaped spacecraft that's hovering over the pyramid and it's friendly and a part of it, not that it's important. I'm glad to see it because it's dropping off supplies, but nothing unusual. It's just that you don't see it very often. It is just hovering, dropping things. It doesn't need to land. It floats the supplies down and puts them in place. Whatever it is, I am glad to be alone here, and it comes by and gives me supplies and asks me what I'm doing, and that's it. It's not very dramatic.

D: *Then you don't need to go onboard and have contact with it?*
R: No, I don't see myself contacting anyone onboard.
D: *So it's an important day because it's a break in routine.*
R: True. But I'm not sad as I see it go. I see it come, and I'm happy, but when it goes, I'm still happy. I'm a happy person in this life! (Amazed) I'm healthy. I'm smiling and grinning and I am just having fun. I'm just enjoying it.

Every time I moved him to another scene, it was the same. Everything seemed to be pretty monotonous. "This is a very happy place. I don't need anybody at all. It sounds weird, but I don't need anybody."

It really sounded like every day was just like every other day, but I guess it didn't matter because he was happy in his solitude. I didn't think we would be able to learn anything more, so I moved him forward to the last day of his life, and asked what was happening.

R: All of a sudden this big beam of light comes out of the sky and zaps me up. And I'm taken somewhere and that's it. I'm gone. It just came out of the sky. It's not from a spaceship. It just came from out of the sky, but I'm ready for it. It's not like it's a surprise. Because I have my arms stretched out, and I see it and beams just

58

come out and pick me up. And I'm gone, and where I go I don't know. Let's see.

D: *So it took the physical body?*

R: You know what? It didn't. Now that you said that, what's left of the physical body is just laying there on the ground.

D: *Was there anything wrong with the body?*

R: Must have got old because it's very wrinkly. Must have lived a long time. Boy... that's interesting!

D: *Let's see where it's taking you.*

R: I'm in this room with this council of elders.

He had obviously gone to the spirit side, and was appearing before the board for a life evaluation. This is covered more fully in my other books about life after death.

R: I am standing in the front of these people who are sitting down. I really can't make out faces, and they are just asking me questions. "Well, did you enjoy that?" and I'm saying, "Yes, I did." "You did a good job." And "It's time for you to rest." And they are all smiling at me, and saying, "You will do it again... something like this next time."

D: *How do you feel about that?*

R: I have a big grin on my face. I'm happy as always. Boy, this is dull if I'm happy all the time. (Laugh) We're friends... we're old friends. I'm talking, and it's good to see them. And I'm in a dark red robe for some reason. It's interesting. I'm in a bright red robe and they're all in white robes, so I don't know what that means.

D: *Ask them what that means.*

R: The first thing I get is that, "You've finished that level and you're going to move to another level." Whatever that means.

D: *How long do you have to rest before you have to do it again?*

R: First thing that came is, twenty years; whatever *years* are.

D: *Ask them, when you do it again and come back, is this going to be the life known as Richard, or are there others in between?*

R: No, that's the one! It will be the life you're in now,

D: *Is this the first time Richard has been on the planet Earth?*

R: They said, yes... yes, it is.

D: *You've never been on Earth before?*

R: Definitely not... you have not.

D: *Won't that be kind of a shock to his system to come to this planet?*

R: They said, no because you know how to be alone and handle the energies. So why am I going there? "You are there to protect. They won't know it, but people around you are protected. Wherever you go they are going to be protected in some way."

D: *Like you did in the other life at the pyramid? Things were protected.*

R: Oh! (Recognition)... maybe so. "You have a healing presence. You'll just walk around and wherever you are people will get something good out of it. They won't know it consciously, but they will subconsciously. They'll feel something." —Richard will be safe. He will be protecting people, but not in the way he knows that you normally protect. It is the way that you don't know about. Come to protect people... just by being there. The presence will protect people in ways they don't understand. And he won't be aware that he's doing this.

D: *The energies of Earth are very different, aren't they?*

R: "Yes, but you're going to be building something out in the country that you don't know about yet. It will be made known to you later. It's not time for you to know. It's going to be something grand; not necessarily big, but for protection to help the planet. It's going to be some type of energy force that's going to help protect; higher energies of some type. Even though the planet energies are not necessarily good, you are fine with it. You can handle it. It's not anything you can't handle."

D: *So he can live on Earth in these energies without accumulating karma?*

R: Absolutely! "Yes, you will live on the planet without any karma." Wow! That's interesting.

D: *We don't want to tell him if it's not time, but is that his purpose?*

R: His first purpose is to experience the planet Earth living amongst its people, but the main purpose is to build something later on. That's the main purpose; something to direct and to help the planet. —"You are to be alone. Enjoy being alone. Enjoy the aloneness this time."

D: *Is this one of the reasons why Richard has lived alone most of his life?*

R: Yes, because in many lives he's been alone. He likes it that way. He's used to it.—There needs to be other people doing what he's doing. But the time is not right with the world yet for us all to do our thing. To just hang out... just enjoy hanging out. It's a lot like taking care of that other planet. Playing... enjoying yourself. —There will be some type of network for the good of mankind. He says many people are still just going to be stuck in their rut. He says, "You're way above that now. You know because you see that they don't get it, but you can't worry about them. You have a higher purpose, and it will be revealed at another time."

Richard had a question about repeating UFO dreams that he had had all his life. "They are to show him his roots. To always remind him that he came from above. He is not from Earth. We need people like him to help this planet. It is a tough place, but it's a testing ground for many things. It is lower vibrational, but it's what you make it. You know it. We don't have to tell you. You're above it. We needed you here at this time for a reason that you will know about later.— Within five years he'll know why he's here and what he's supposed to be doing. At that moment things change." (This session was conducted in December 2009.)

I asked about 2012. "2012... people spend too much time worrying about it. They need to work on their lives. They're telling me they need to get themselves 'cleaned up.' It will get worse because the vibrations are increasing, and the people that don't increase their vibrations... it'll be harder for them, so more and more people will be 'checking out.' They don't know how to handle the energy. It's not necessarily 2012. That's just a date, but it's coming soon. It's just that someone put that date out, and it just happens to be that things are kind of culminating around that date."

D: *Will people know anything has happened?*
R: Yes. We can't tell you at this time, but it will be made clear to everybody when this occurs.
D: *I've been told that some will be left behind. They can't adapt to the energy?*
R: Yes, many people will be left behind. But it's okay.
D: *Will Richard be working with the new Earth?*
R: Yes, yes he will.
D: *Will I still be around to work with the new Earth also?*
R: Yes, yes, you will.
D: *There is one question many people have asked me, "Will people just disappear?"*
R: No, they won't just disappear. Not in the way that you think of disappearing... again, you'll just have to wait and see.—Even though it's frustrating at times, you want things to happen, but things can't happen yet. There are other things that need to take place. I'm asking them, "Is there going to be any type of disasters?" All we can tell you is the oceans and water

at this time will be flooding more of the planet. It does not have to do with global warming.

D: *Nothing to do with the melting of the ice caps?*

R: No, possibly a big meteor splashing down or something. Right now problems with water, yes.

D: *Is that when many people will leave?*

R: Yes, definitely yes. The people will split into two kinds. Ones that want to stay here and deal with the change, and the others that want to check out and can't handle the vibrations. It will be tough at first for the people that want to stay, but they want the toughness. They can handle it. They will be ready for it.

D: *So it will be difficult in the beginning.*

R: It will be only because most people are not ready for it. It will catch people off guard.

D: *So our job is to try to help people understand what's happening.*

R: Yes. People can't help other people if they have too many of their own problems. They can't do what's right for the planet if they can't do what's right for themselves. They have to learn to let things go. They're holding on to too much that doesn't make sense to them. They're driving themselves crazy. They don't think. They don't allow. They need to allow things; not force things and listen. They need to meditate more. The quiet. People need to quiet themselves a lot more. They need to be alone and be in quiet. Too many people are afraid to be alone. There's so many that don't get it. That's what's bringing the Earth down. The vibes... it's a poignant effect. The higher vibration is one effect, and the people that don't want to move to the higher vibration is another effect, and it's going to cause a change. It's like magnets... the opposites.

After Richard awakened I turned the recorder back on to record a memory that he retained.

R: It was explained to me that the vibrations are getting faster. It's causing a force, a different force and you either go with the vibrations and make yours faster, or you get stuck. And most people on the Earth are refusing to raise their vibrations, so that means the two forces are becoming stronger, opposing if they are not together. They are further apart and eventually soon, it will cause something to happen to the planet.

D: *Like two magnets?*

R: Two magnets, instead of two opposites attracting... opposites in this case repel very badly; will repel and cause something negative to take place, or positive, depending on what side you are on.

So it seems as though the first and second wave of volunteers have other assignments besides just *being*. Their energies can be used for other purposes. In this case some of them are here to use their energies to protect anyone that comes in contact with them. Even though no one is consciously aware of what is happening, it is a good feeling to know that they are there.

CHAPTER SIX

A WEARY VOLUNTEER

Sally had a long list of problems that she wanted to address during the session. She was involved in a loveless marriage to a controlling husband, which she desperately wanted to get out of. This had been a pattern in her life because she had also had a controlling mother. Naturally I was not surprised that all of this had taken its toll on her body, and she had many physical problems that would need to be addressed. She really wanted to heal people (using sound), and had gone into debt to open a holistic healing center. However, it was not working and she was worrying about the lack of money.

When Sally came off the cloud she saw a strange sight: "A metropolis... a city within a city... it has a dome over it. Almost like a cake glass on top of the city. There are tall and short buildings. An enclosed city with a bubble over it. I'm looking from the outside of the bubble."

D: *Do you see any people or vehicles or just the buildings?*
S: Just the buildings... there's no one outside. Everyone is inside. No one travels outside the dome.
D: *What is on the outside of the dome? Can you see?*
S: It's almost like the atmosphere is around it. Like looking at the outside of a planet. Standing at the outside looking in... almost like night sky, the stars. It's like you're viewing the Milky Way standing on the outside of a glass city. It's almost like the Emerald City in Wizard of Oz.

D: *Is the city floating out there or what?*

S: Yes, it is. Just out there in space.

D: *That's interesting. Do you want to go inside the dome and see what the city is like?*

S: Absolutely. I'm looking... wondering how the people go in and out. It's like a dome that retracts and opens. You travel through this portal... It opens and closes. It opens when they choose to travel outside their world. —Now I'm inside a big room. There's laughter. There's a table. There are beings of energy around the table. I've arrived at a council. There are twelve chairs and it's the council, they say... the "council of lights."

D: *Is that what they look like, lights?*

S: They do. Each one has a different color of light.

D: *That sounds beautiful. Become aware of your body... what do you look like?*

S: There is no body. I'm a ball of energy.

D: *Are you a certain color?*

S: I'm lavender. With a red at the bottom and it moves to a lavender... almost a flame. They are taller. Their structure seems to be different. They are sitting around this table. They're using words, "The spark of creation where experiment began." Where the life plans are made and the journey to travel is conceived. This is where I came from. It has a spark... the God spark to create a plan for this lifetime. Of lessons... of contracts.

D: *This is where it's all decided?*

S: That is what they say.

D: *Does this mean when you started out on all of your lives or just the present one?*

S: It's where all the lives are created. All the journeys... all the legends. I'm looking for understanding there... clarity.

D: *So what are they saying to you?*

S: They're sending me off, releasing me. They're releasing me... letting me go. There's no... all of a sudden there's dark. It's back into the atmosphere. (Confused.)

D: *Did they give you any instructions?*

S: I did not hear any.

D: *They just told you it was time to go?* (Yes) *How did you feel about that?*

S: Not well... not sure... confused... not really wanting to accept the assignment... not wanting to go where they want me to go. I thought I was finished. I thought I was complete.

D: *Had you had other lifetimes and lessons before?*

S: Yes, many. I am weary. I was in retirement. (Laugh) Not wanting to go back to density... to the heaviness... through time.

D: *You thought you were finished, but they told you there was another assignment?*

S: It was my part in choosing to be in the excitement... the awakening... the experiments, but weary... so tired... not wanting to come back... not sure the energy would support my travel... had not recuperated enough... had not had time to regenerate.

D: *Is that usually what happens? You have time to recuperate?*

S: Yes, very much so. The density... the lessons. Hard... they were hard... had to struggle barely through... was ready to go home to recuperate... rejuvenate. Flow back into Source... to rest. I was beginning a rest journey. —And then awakening to the experiments that would happen. It would be able to come this time. I wanted to be here. I wanted to see and experience that shift, to help, but my being was so weary.

D: *So it was your choice then?*

S: It was a choice I was not happy to make, they say. (Both of us laughed.) They asked if I was up to the test of making this transition one last time. I could rest once the awakening, once the shift, the experiment was successful. Then it would be time to relax.

D: *If you had been resting, you would have missed everything, wouldn't you?*

S: Part of me aches for that rest. Part of me does not know how to move out of the density. The energy is so low in the physical being. It's struggling to move upward... the life force... is weakened.

D: *Yes, but you said, "Once the experiment was successful." What did you mean by that?*

S: That Earth was on her path to succeed into moving into her next dimension... into her next life.

D: *It is because Earth is alive too.*

S: Yes. She was going to do something that's not been done in many, many eons, or *ever* in the Source's path. It is a historical marker for all beings; for all entities to witness.

D: *So when they told you that, you agreed to come?*

S: I did. I wanted to be a part of this. To be a guide... be an assistant. I could choose where I would want to return to begin a new life... create a new world... to create in the Creator's image. Energy of lights... energy... new energy. —Or returning home.

D: *What do you think would be the best choice?*

S: The creativity. It's creativity my soul cries for. To create new things and new ways of doing things without the density... a lighter, quicker... portals... travel... portals again. I wanted to witness that new creation.

D: *So you chose to come into this life now?* (Yes) *Are we speaking about the life of Sally?* (Yes) *They have faith in you or they wouldn't have sent you.*

S: She does not have faith within herself anymore.

D: *Did she choose the family she was going into?* (The controlling mother.)

S: Yes. It was the lessons of the heart, freedom of choice, that she came to overcome. It was one last hurdle, the quickening.

D: *Did she have any karmic relationships with the family?*

S: She chose the name. The vibration was a must. It's something that she chose within her... the name to be chosen... (I changed her name for anonymity). It carries a numerical vibrational pattern, connects to her cellular structure. Then when that name is spoken, it feels this new life, this new energy.

D: *So names are important that people choose?*

S: Yes. You have a residence within the cellular structure. It's part of patterning. It's part of coding. It's part of awakening and the process. She chose that body, and insisted that name be given. The mother did not know that. It was not the mother's choice. It was a prerequisite of sorts for the soul to be named that incarnation.

D: *I've heard that the astrological effects have something to do with it too, don't they?*

S: Yes, very much so. She was born specifically in 12-1959 as a portal, an entryway with a walking activation of energy. Her birthday is a gateway.

D: *What do you mean by being a gateway?*

S: It's a travel way for souls and consciousness. An opening door that activates on a cellular structure our very being. Those who come in contact with her are offered this activation in order to guide them through the solstice, guide them through to eclipses. And awaken their light in their DNA, activated within her in recent weeks. She has felt that shift within her body, within the ability to focus light through her and to anchor into the core. It has begun within the last four months. And if she continues to anchor and pull into the core of light, it becomes stronger for those around her.

D: *So other people are being affected just by being around her?*

S: By the field she creates, it is the portal, the expansion. It's a healing portal for others. To support them on their journey.

D: *This way she is symbolically a portal? Is that what you mean? (Yes) And they should come to her for healing?*

S: They eventually will as the residence gets stronger. It will be like an attraction as she anchors it into the core.

D: *But you know Sally has many problems, doesn't she?*

S: Her physical being has not been well kept.—She fights herself. It is a fear that she has come to overcome, to help others overcome and that stops her. The fear, the expansion... the fear of not being loved.

D: *She said she has experienced fear as a small girl. Why did she come in with this feeling of fear?*

S: As she entered into the doorway the fear attached to her because before she left us, she was not sure she could accomplish. She was not sure she had the tools before she left us. The emotions, the family, the setting was too much. She came in as a clear and open empath. It was too overwhelming. The density hit her more than she thought it would.

D: *As an empath, that means she picks up other people's feelings?*

S: She did. It was overwhelming. It closed her; stopped her from moving forward for a very long time. She was afraid of the energy that was around her. She did not understand and she came with no understanding. She was closed to the Source and closed herself from Source.—She wanted to go home immediately. She asked us to go home.

D: *She forgot her contract, didn't she?*

S: She did.

D: *What did you tell her when she wanted to go home?*

S: That there was time. We were here. She was not alone. She was well-equipped and talented. She had the opportunity to grow and expand beyond what the mind could understand and accomplish. Her soul's path was to be the recorder to the Source, to be the eyes, to be the ears, to be the very beating heart. To relay the energy back to this council to be the witness.

D: *But she hasn't been living up to this assignment, has she?*

S: She is gridlocked with fear and uncertainty. It's her perception. The old tapes that she listens to. They play over and over in her mind. She has the fear of not getting it right. It is a hurdle and an obstacle that she must overcome.

D: *Do those fears come from another lifetime or from this present one?*

S: It is a patterning within her very soul, from the very beginning of the God spark. She has managed to somewhat conquer that fear. This was the opportunity to move forward quickly as things were moving and changing, evolving... spinning with one big leap.

D: *So when she first came in, when she first left the Source, she was afraid she wouldn't be able to do it?*

S: No. She returned to the whole soul again in this lifetime to merge all that is within her, to bring all aspects home, and complete the next three years to return to the one soul.

D: *What do you mean, in the next three years?*

S: She has a window of time left. She will and must accomplish bringing those aspects home. It's part of her contract. Part of what she came to do in this lifetime is to return to one, to the whole soul.

It was explained in the *Convoluted Universe* series that we are part of a larger soul, an Oversoul, or as they say a "whole soul." This is our true self, but it is too large to enter into a body. It has said that if all the energy of a person were to try to enter into a physical body the body would be destroyed. It would be too much. So the soul is like a diamond with many facets. In order to learn as much as it can in the least amount of time, the whole soul will send out splinters, shards or aspects of itself to experience as much as is totally possible. This goes back to the concept of simultaneous time because we are truly living all our past, present and future

71

lives at the same time. This is done so the soul will gain as much knowledge as possible through the experiences the different aspects are living through. When the New Earth is finally accomplished all of our individual aspects are called back and reunited with the whole soul.

D: *And she has three years to accomplish that?*
S: That is true. That is her truth.

This session was conducted in December 2009.

D: *What if she lets the fear win out?*
S: She will return back home to us. There will be no reason for her existence here.
D: *But if she listens and does what she is supposed to do?*
S: She will move to the bounty, will move to the essence and travel throughout time and space. She was meant to return to the eternal being and to create planets, new life, new systems.
D: *Will she be here whenever the new Earth takes its leap, like you said?*
S: Not if she does not complete her mission. If she does then she will witness and assist. Right now she is very much resistant.—Her husband will not travel to the new Earth until he chooses the lesson before him.
D: *I have been told that if people are still holding onto karma, they can't go.*
S: They will not travel. They will stay in the density to work out their lessons. They will not travel to the new light, to the new consciousness.—She needs to be the bridge duality to the new world to walk from one to the other. To have one foot in both worlds. She has not managed to move the other foot across the bridge. She stays in the density. The vibration is overwhelming of days and times.—There is one more shift in consciousness that must take place before the skills she has brought with her, the tools she has brought with

her, can manifest. Mankind must unravel one more time in order to bring forth the information, the changes, the vibration that is needed to advance the civilization to its next step. There are many pieces yet to go. There are many decisions yet to be made. Many have not made them. Many are in fear of stepping into their guideposts.

D: *So this is not the final one we're looking at when they talk about the new Earth?*

S: The experiment is behind. It is not traveling as quickly as predicted. There are guides coming to this Earth to support this process that has come to almost a screeching halt to this space in time we are speaking. There is re-evaluation going on in many dimensions of how to get the spiral to move forward as it had begun. It had stopped. It is stopped as we watch. It's in a place of holding. Many are in holding.

D: *What caused it to stop?*

S: It's the blanket of fear that resonates through. Energy just filters down into a core. Many, many choose to succumb to a vibration that has slowed events of what has been put in motion. It is temporary. We have sent many to put holes through the atmosphere of fear, so that mankind can be able to breathe again. To allow the energy to tumble forward as they move into the universe. There are entities and beings in human forms that have abilities to poke holes within this gridlock around the Earth, and they are beginning their jobs of removing the fear of opening the portal space to travel through once again.

D: *What is the one more shift that has to take place?*

S: The bubble of density of fear must be reduced. It must be pulled back in order for her to expand and bring knowledge through for these fear-based entities to understand and to incorporate within their beings. She must release fear within her own being. She is the first to move this energy.

I then decided to focus on her physical body. They said, "It's very dysfunctional for the job she has to do here." She had complaints of chemical sensitivities, problems with her liver, heart and a fibroid tumor.

D: *Why did it get into that shape?*

S: She has not listened to the messages that it has sent her. She has done what many have done, and take all the strain and worry and put it within her and made it a part of her. Instead of releasing, she was storing the fear and it began to build in all the cellular structures as stop signs for them as blockages. And then each one begins to build on each other, and then it all came to the slowest trickle we have seen within this physical being. She still has not learned to let go of what burdens her. It is stored within her. It must be released. —It can be done within a session of opening the flow, beginning to take the works away from the dam as we see it. We will allow the opening of the flow into the cellular structure. —She must claim her healing and claim that as what she chooses because her fear is: if she is healthy. If she is not in physical shape and good standing, then she cannot accomplish things. The fear holds her back. So she must release that fear of being healthy as much as she chooses and wants it to be. It is a fear of: What will life be like if it is healed? She must accomplish things then and move in her life if it is healed.

I then asked for a visualization that would help Sally release the fear and introduce healing.

S: The flow begins in celestial realms of watching as the crystalline river comes through the beginning of time and space and flows down through the crown chakra opening through the third eye down through the face...

74

down through into the third chakra... down into the center of the heart... through the torso into the hips and down as the river flows through each side of each leg... down into the core, into the heart of the mother, into the divine flow of opening.

D: *Is this a river of energy?*

S: It is.

D: *It is healing energy.*

S: It's crystalline charged.

D: *It is very, very powerful. Are you healing the parts that the energy moves through?*

S: It's allowing for the oxygen to move to the cells. Bringing life back into the lungs... she does not breathe. (Deep breath)

D: *What about her heart? She was worried about that?*

S: It's the energy she must move of heartache. There will be enough to support the work that she continues. The flow will begin to slowly open, but she must finish the healing in that area. That is hers to repair. She is the one that closed the door in the beginning. She must open it. We will offer the river of life through her being for her to work with her body to tap into this river, and to expand and to use freely, but she must choose the river. She must choose the light energy. She must offer through the organs and she must move it to the being of energy that calls her human. She must see the flow as all things are living. She must see it as a living elixir. She must see the motion as it comes from the high. It comes from the Source and through. She must feel the lightness, the healing energy that carries a gift with it. That is the only way the body will open and accept.

D: *When do you want her to visualize this?*

S: Just before she goes to sleep because all healing takes place in the body at night.

D: *Because then the conscious mind can't interfere.*

S: It cannot.

75

D: *So you want her to picture this river of energy... this crystalline energy flowing from the crown chakra moving down and through the other chakras?*

S: Into the core.

D: *And you want her to do this every night when she goes to sleep?*

S: Yes, not when she is in crisis, and not when it is in chaos. It must be done every night in quiet and peace. The body does not heal in chaos. The body only heals in peace.—Then she will have the ability to transfer this energy as it flows through her to others. Energy will flow through her hands into their crown chakra and they will begin the flow of energy within them.

This is a very valuable and effective healing technique that anyone can practice. I use it in some of my workshops because it is very easy to visualize. This crystalline river of energy is very powerful.

I asked about her liver, which she had been having problems with. "It is like a dirty sponge that needs to be cleaned. This elixir, this life force, will offer the energy to clean in slow increments as she begins to release the anger that is piled up in there. We have started the spark. We have started in each organ a light of healing. She must not let the light extinguish. The healing has begun and she must carry through.

D: *She has to do it herself.*

S: It is her choice.

D: *You said she was also holding anger as well as fear. Where does the anger come from?*

S: She knows she is to advance to a different place. She is angry she is not there yet. She knows her mission on a soul level, and becomes aware of that more frequently than she realizes. She knows that this is not the world she is to be living in at this moment. She gets angry and frustrated and becomes fearful. She knows this is not the world she came to step into. She has been in a world of heaven on Earth. She knows that this is not where she is meant to be and she gets very, very angry at herself. It sends her into the negative cycle and she is meant to crack the cycle's duality and show others and set the example.

D: *She needs to do a lot of work on herself.*

S: She does. She has been as we call "spiritual coasting." She understands the concept but has not incorporated it into her daily life. She is very good at telling others how to do this, but she has not done it yet herself.

D: *You're there to help, but she is going to have to do it herself.*

S: She must. It's her lesson.

I then asked about the fibroid tumor Sally had in her uterus. She had many things wrong with her physical body.

S: She has asked us to remove it on several occasions, and we have shown her how to go into the cellular structure into the mitochondria to change the cellular structure of the fibroid. She has done this several times, but does not believe that *she* is the impasse. She must believe that she can change the DNA of her body; that she can change the structure of this fibroid. We're there to assist and we have given her the tools. It is another thing that she must try to do each day. To go into that cellular structure... speak with it... understand it and release it.

D: *What was the cause of that?*

S: It is the pain and suffering she has carried in her womb of her betrayal of herself. The betrayal she feels of her family. It goes back to many lineages of her life. Her creativity as a soul has been extinguished. It is something that overshadows her creativity and is something that overgrows and has expanded and blocked her ability to be in the divine feminine.

This was another thing the SC wanted Sally to work on herself. I have seen it many times heal these things instantly, but in some cases it feels the client should work on themselves. Then they will understand the process involved, and be better able to use it on others.

S: She must begin to reduce the size of the fibroid in order to complete and open the flow into her creativity. We have begun the healing for her. We will not complete it. It is her journey. It is her lesson to complete. It will take three months to heal the body if she focuses daily. It has to come from the heart, from the truth.

D: *And to believe it is possible.*

S: And to know that she has the capability to make this change within her. It is the catalyst for her to see that these are the ways to make the changes in her life. If she does not see that this will be accomplished, she will not believe that she can make those other changes.— She has been in fear and this has kept her from stepping through the door. She goes quite frequently to the door, but she cannot step through now, and she must step over and does not have the energy or the strength to, but she tells herself that. As she gains confidence and using this healing technique, she will see that her body is gaining strength and light, and will have the trust in her knowing it is not necessary to take these medications as she has the light within to heal. Everyone has that. She knows that. She is meant to teach that. As she transitions, she will be able to support her body with light instead of medicine. It will be a transition of time. The light will be feeding her cells. Her body is switching from the herbal plant base to the light as a crystalline being and the light will feed the crystalline being.—We are always with her, but she does not open to us. She must begin to really feel us and know that the support will carry her, and we will

have opened all the doors she perceives as closed.—
These fears have also held back her healing center.

D: *She has a very important decision to make.*

S: She must decide. It is a decision that kills her each day
and her energy field is to stay or to go as she wanders
through this field of uncertainty. It is the density that
pulls and weighs on her physical being. It is as if her
physical being is being suffocated by not making the
choice.

D: *And if she decides the other way she won't be able to
stay on Earth. Is that right?*

S: That is correct. Her journey will come to an end. She
will no longer need to be here. She will not stay in the
density with the others. She will turn back to the
Source. She will have no meaning to move forward.
Her job will not be here. She has a three year window
to make this decision and to move within her field.
This is now a crucial time. She must get off the fence.
She will not move and we have told her and she hears
us and she knows, and we offer it with all our love and
with all our support in our very being within.

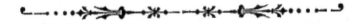

D: *What was that city with the dome on top that she saw?*

S: It is her home and they call it Atlantis. It is not in the
form of the Atlantis that you know. It is in a new
dimension. It has taken on a new life. Those souls have
carried on and were lifted and transferred into a new
dimension in time and space, and she has gone to that
dimension in space, not to the lifetime when she was
there.

D: *But it wasn't important for her to explore that life at
this time?*

S: It was important for her to return to the council because
it is only the truth of the council that will get through to
her, to remind her that we have sent her here for an

important mission and we know that she can and will accomplish this. And she must hear those words that she must and she can accomplish this. It is written and it has been said and it is so. She must hear it and feel it and be it, and the choice will be simple for her to move into the space that is created for her.

I think it is important for the first and second wave of volunteers to understand that their own fears and the feeling of not wanting to be here on Earth can create powerful blocks to hold back their advancement. Many say they just don't want to be here. It is too difficult, and they just want to leave. If they truly want to return "home" then they better begin to understand and work with these feelings. Otherwise, they will be stuck here and will not fulfill their noble contract.

CHAPTER SEVEN

CHECKING ON THE KIDS

I could fill many, many books with reports of "normal" pastlife regressions. Out of the thousands of therapy sessions I have conducted I have never found anyone who has not been able to go back and find another lifetime. For many years they were all reporting lifetimes on this planet Earth in every form imaginable in every environment imaginable. I just allow the SC to take them to the most *appropriate* time and place. I never know where that will be, so my job is just to ask questions and try to find the relevance to their present problems. There are still many coming for sessions who go to these type of lives, but I am now convinced that they are people who still have karma to work out and that is the reason for showing them these connections.

From the examples in this book it is now becoming obvious that many souls are coming to fulfill other roles. The majority have never lived on Earth before and find it a confusing, uncomfortable and alien place to be. They are the ones I call the "first-timers." But others have come on assignments unique to their talents they have perfected in other times and places. We have already seen some that are here to be teachers, protectors and those who are only to influence by their unaware presence and energy. In this chapter we find another unique being who had a specific talent that the powers that be thought would be helpful at this time.

Laura came down in front of a medium-sized pyramid and was perplexed at why she was there. She discovered she was a young, strong male wearing short skirt-type clothing with leather sandals that laced up his legs. Then she saw that he was wearing a big metal pendant around his neck. It had something similar to a sun carved into it, with rays coming out in all directions. "It seems like it's not jewelry. It's part of what I'm supposed to have or wear. It seems like it's there all the time. It has a purpose."

As I asked questions the purpose became clear. "It's a star gate. It helps me go places. I stare into this pendant, and it is a portal to take me places." He was now standing inside the pyramid and trying to remember how to activate it. "It's odd that there's no one else around. —I'm still trying to remember. The pendant seems to be connected to the pyramid. I used to know how to use it, but now I don't really totally remember."

I asked him to see himself doing it and it would come back to him.

L: I find that I hold my pendant up to face the center of the pyramid... I line it up to the center of the peak. I'm holding it flat. Up to the peak... that's going to be how I do it... the energy, yes. I see the light now coming down through the pyramid and hitting my thumb. And I know that's how I can go where I want to go. I don't know where to go, but I know that I can go there.

D: *Have you been taught how to do this?*

L: I just know it... but I'm confused right now. Because there's no one else around, and I'm used to having many people around. We were all learning together. We were a group. We were in a classroom. —I guess this is my journey... I'm supposed to be alone. I'm supposed to be learning about my powers and myself.

D: *What were you learning when you were all together?*

L: About the stars... about the vastness of the world... symbols... I feel like I'm supposed to teach others, but I don't feel like I know it enough yet to teach.

D: *Now that you're there at the pyramid, does that mean you have already completed your classes?*

L: It must be. I must be starting on my journey. I feel like I'm supposed to be testing my powers... my ability to do what we were taught.

D: *Where do you feel you should go if you're going to test it?*

L: I feel like I'd just let the pendant decide where I should go. The light comes down from the peak of the pyramid. And it activates the pendant, but I'm feeling that I have to have a destination for my mind to take me there.

D: *What do you decide?*

L: It would be nice to visit the entire galaxy. It would be.

D: *There's a lot to visit there, isn't there?*

L: Yes, it sure is.

D: *What is the purpose of doing that?*

L: It's like checking on the kids to make sure they're okay. In different places... like a teacher would check on the kids to see if they were being good.

D: *Do you think that's your job?*

L: I don't know. I feel very lucky to be able to do it, so it's not work.

D: *Do you think the most important thing is to check on the children rather than the adults?*

L: Yes, I guess I think of all of the humans as children. — You're right. It must be my job.

D: *If it feels right. Do you have to report back to anyone about what you find?*

L: I don't feel like it, but maybe I'm just on holiday. Maybe I'm just seeing what's out there.

D: *Where was the classroom? What does that look like?*

L: Outside... people sitting on the ground cross-legged, and it's funny... the classroom is all male and we all have skirts on. There are no females. There's a teacher. He's very radiant... very advanced. We have great respect for him.

D: *This is the one that was teaching you about the stars and everything?* (Yes) *Is he the one who taught you how to use the pendant?*

L: I think so. I'm not really sure who. The pendant has always been there. It's like we're born knowing.

D: *And one of the things you were learning was about the stars?*

L.   That's important. So that we can come and go at certain times. You have to make sure you know the times. There are rifts, and the rifts can be dangerous to travel unless you travel at the right time. They were teaching us how to travel. (He had a hard time explaining.)

D: *Ask somebody there why it would be dangerous to travel at certain times?*

L: I'm asking my teacher. He knows.—He's not getting through to me. He's too knowledgeable and I'm not knowledgeable enough.

D: *Ask him to tell it to you in simple language because this may be something important for you to know.*

L: (Whispering to teacher.) He's saying there are portals and the galaxies need to align themselves a certain way, a certain time, and then you can just slip through the dimension. If I don't, I can get lost. I can go to another dimension then I'll be lost and I won't have the same class or the same... I'll be out of my time slot, he's saying. That's what a rift is, he's saying.

D: *You wouldn't be able to get back?* (No) *That would not be a good thing. Can he tell you how to avoid that?*

L: We're supposed to learn the stars and the alignment and know when to go and when to get back. He says it's like crossing a river and you have to go with the rapids. Otherwise, you'll get whisked away and won't come back.

D: *That makes sense. But do you know where the portals are?*

L: I'm learning. I'm learning. That's why we're in this class. But no girls. Why no girls? Why are there no girls in our class? (Pause) Too risky... it's too risky. There are not enough women. They're not expendable. They need to make more babies. They're not expendable. We are. There are more men than women, and the women are needed to grow.

D: *So the men are the ones who need to learn to time travel.* (Yes) *Why do they want you to know how to time travel?*

L: Oh, we're supposed to check on the kids. To make sure that they're doing okay... how they are growing.

D: *The children are important, aren't they?*

L: Yes. But when they say, the "children," it doesn't matter what their age is. They're calling the children the ones learning... the humans... the learning ones.

D: *They are still just children.* (Yes) *You have to make sure they're okay because they are the future?*

L: Yes, you're right. That is my job. I report back to the teacher. I go back to him and tell him because he is the one that is getting us prepared to go.

D: *Do you know what he does with the information once it's reported to him?*

L: Not yet, no. He is very wise. Sometimes you look at him and just see white light.

D: *Can you ask him what he does with the information?*

L: He plots it on charts. He keeps charts; many, many charts and he plots the information. There are more than just me that go out. There are many people that go out and then they bring him the information and he plots it.

D: *Do you all have different jobs, or is it just to check on the children?*

L: That's *my* job to check on the children. I don't know what the others do, but they go too. They know how serious it is to go at the right time.

D: *Does that mean that you don't actually have a physical body when you go places?*

L: I don't feel physical when I travel. I feel all over the place. I can see. Scary.

D: *So you don't have to take on a physical body.* (No) *When you saw yourself by the pyramid, was that a physical body?* (Yes) *Why did you have to have one at that time?*

L: To learn.

D: *So there might be times when you'd have to have a body? Does that make sense?*

L: Yes. We all have bodies there.

D: *But when you're going out and finding information, you don't have a physical body.*

L: Maybe it's too much trouble to take it.

D: *That makes sense. And you travel with this pendant?* (Yes) *Do they tell you which place to go?*

L: They must, but I don't hear them telling me. You think and know... implanted maybe. The knowledge is there. —The knowledge wasn't there about the planets. They had to teach us. He taught us with a pointer showing us all the stars. They're very wise.

D: *Have you ever had to come to the planet Earth? Do you know which one that is?*

L: It's possible, but I don't think so.

D: *So your home planet is somewhere else?*

L: I don't know where it is. It's certainly ground, and very topography, but I don't know where it is.

I decided to move him ahead to an important day, and he went to the day of his graduation. They had all finished everything they had to learn, and now it was time to leave.

L: We're all standing in a hall and each one... he touched our forehead. And told us that we had a third eye, and that we now needed to go out.

D: *Go out and do what?*

L: I don't know. Maybe just more of our jobs. We're
       finished being together. That group is done.—I am to
       go out and try to share the knowledge.
D: *Who do you share it with?*
L: People, peasants, sheepherders....
D: *Can they understand what you're trying to teach them?*
L: A little bit... I stay on.—They seem so grounded. They
       think they have to stay there with their sheep. They
       don't have to. They can go anywhere. They don't
       believe they can do it.
D: *Do you feel your job is to teach them?*
L: I don't know what my job is. I'm confused that I don't
       make a family. I just wander.

It sounded like we had reached a dead-end. He was
probably going to be doing that the rest of his life. And that
was okay because he apparently had found his path. So I
moved him forward to the last day of his life. "What's
happening? What do you see?"

L: I'm in the meadow, a field, and I'm attacked by a huge
       cat. But I've lived a long life. I'm still alone, and I'm
       not upset that this cat... it was fine. I'm at peace.

I moved him to where it was all over with and he could
look at the entire lifetime from a different and much broader
perspective. I asked him what he had learned from that life.

L: It feels happy just to be thinking about that.
D: *Why does it make you happy?*
L: Hard to put into the words... just the energy. The
       energy is light. I learned just to believe. We can do
       anything that we put our minds to. Nothing is
       impossible.

I then called in the SC. "Why did you pick that life for
Laura to see?"

L: For her to know she has powers. She can learn to use them.

D: *Everything we have ever learned, we never lose, do we?*

L: No, but we bury them.

D: *But will she be able to use them now in this lifetime?*

L. Some of them, yes. She can use them to get places. To go places.

D: *With her mind, you mean?*

L: With her body. She needs to go and check on the children.

D: *How do you want her to do that?*

L: Collect them. Put them all together. Teach them.

D: *How do you want her to collect them?*

L: Call them. They'll know. Call them together. To gather the children.

D: *I'm thinking that most children have parents, families. You can't go out and gather them all together, can you?*

L: The children are big. They're not little. Adults.

D: *That's different.*

I asked the SC to give her advice about what she was to do.

L: I'm seeing a mountain coming apart in the middle. People need to prepare. Changes... their lives will change. They need time to prepare. Mother Earth is changing. They need to change with Mother Earth. They need to know. Children are growing old and dying without ever growing up. Their habitat is going to change. They need to change. I see many Earth changes flashing in front of my face, like a volcano and a mudslide and things that are going to change the face of the Earth.

D: *What do you want Laura to do? What's her job?*

L: Help them prepare to change, to adapt.—She doesn't know.

D: *Not on a conscious level.* (No) *Are you going to give her the knowledge she will need?* (Yes) *To remember the knowledge and abilities she had before?*

L: Yes. It will come back when it's needed. She has to share it. The children don't know.

One of Laura's questions dealt with a private plane crash she was involved in that changed her life. She wanted to know why it happened. She had been a very successful land developer and this had made her very wealthy. Her career was the main focus of her life, and she had decided not to have any children. All she thought about was money and success, until she was almost killed in the crash and spent a long time in the hospital recovering. "She was on the wrong path. She wouldn't listen. Hard headed." It changed her life in many ways. Immediately after she felt driven to have children, and became pregnant on the first try. She had two daughters a year apart.

L: The children were waiting to come in. The children were supposed to be there already.

D: *Yes, but she was so involved in her business that she didn't take the time to have them.*

L: The children were to be diverted to another family. But they said, "No, we'll wait." (She started crying.)

D: *But the plane crash turned her life around and she's on the right path now, isn't she?*

L: Not totally.

D: *What else do you want her to do now to get her on the right path?*

L: Just to be aware that the children are going to need help.

D: *So you'll give her messages on what she's supposed to do next?*

L: Yes, it's not written yet. Things are moving very fast.

D: *That's why you don't want to tell her yet?*

L: Yes, I don't think it's set.

D: *So you just want her to be patient and you'll tell her.*

L: Patience isn't in her. She has none. (Laugh) Just be ready.—Her teacher has always followed her. He is here to prepare her, so she won't be afraid.

D.   *Everyone has a job to do and as you said, time is moving very quickly. I've been told about the new Earth and the things that are going to be changing. Is this all connected?* (Yes) *To be prepared to go to the new Earth or what?*

L: Maybe go to a station. Some people will go to a holding station while things are recreated.

D: *Some of them won't go directly because it's not time yet?*

L: Yes, their preparations are not finished yet.

D: *I've been told their frequencies and vibrations have to be right, or they can't go. Is that what you mean?*

L: The preparations are different places... sort them out and go to the right location.

D: *So many of them will go to the holding stations? Is this after they leave the physical bodies or before?*

L: They're going to take their physical bodies with them.

D: *Then they will go to these places when the disasters are happening here on Earth.* (Yes) *To be ready to go on to where they're supposed to go?*

L: Yes, it will happen very quickly.

D: *So she has to help people get prepared.*

L: Yes, the children... to save the children.

Parting message: Just dream it and do it. Pay attention to the dreams.

D: *That's how you communicate, isn't it?*

L: Yes. Just love and be loving.

So this was another first-timer that did not consciously know her mission on Earth. It involved something she had done throughout the universe, checking in on the children, the kids, and see how they are doing. And helping them to see what they need to do in the coming times ahead. So she had a specific mission, but it had almost gotten sidetracked by her preoccupation with her corporate job. It took a plane crash that almost killed her to get her attention, and put her back on her path. As they have said, time is short and sometimes they have to take drastic measures to turn people around.

CHAPTER EIGHT

THE EXILE

Doris' main complaint was that she felt she was floundering and not knowing which direction her life should go. She had already been involved in several successful businesses, and was now thinking about starting a metaphysical center. She felt she had many talents and abilities, but wanted advice on how to use them.

When we began the session, Doris had a difficult time seeing anything or identifying where she was. All she could see was dark, and the feeling of lots of space around her. After much questioning she began to sense something, as though she was in a big, cold place. Then she sensed that her arms were hurting and she couldn't move them. "I think they're tied up. I'm not sure. I can't move." I gave suggestions for well-being so she wouldn't feel uncomfortable. The rest of her body felt numb from my waist down. "It feels like my body is confined. I can't move."

At least we had made a beginning, but she was still unable to supply much information. So I moved her backward to before she got into this restricted place, so we could find out what happened to cause this.

Do: I knew something. I knew too much. I had to be put away. I could tell things. It feels like a different time. Like the Middle Ages, but not the Middle Ages. I see people in long black robes, but they're not people.

D: *What are they?*

Do: I don't know. They are wearing black. They're hurting people. In the square. And people are not doing what they are supposed to be doing.—They're controlling them with something. They are making them do something. They are making them stay away. I help the people. I wasn't supposed to help the people. But the people don't know.

D: *Are you male or female?*

Do: I'm neither. I'm not I just um. I don't know what I am, but I'm not like the people. I'm like "them," but I don't want to be like them. I don't want to hurt people.

D: *Can you see what your body looks like?*

Do: It's very long... tall. It's like a pencil tall. I am wearing black like them.

D: *Why are they hurting people?*

Do: They're not doing what they're supposed to be doing. They want to control them. They want to put them to work.

D: *Have you been there very long with these people?*

Do: Yes, I've been there a very long time. They're my friends... the people. I've been helping them. I've been teaching them. (Laughing sarcastically.) I've been teaching them, but now they're being hurt because I taught them and now they know too much.

D: *What were you teaching them?*

Do: How to farm and how to live.

D: *I don't see anything wrong with that. Those are good things.*

Do: I thought they were. I thought I was supposed to go there and help teach them.

D: *Were those ones in black there the whole time?*

Do: No, they just came to see what was happening. I've been there a long time.

D: *Did somebody tell you to come and help?*

Do: I just had to come. I don't know why. That was my job, to help people.

D: *Were the people different when you first got there?*

Do: Yes. They were coarse... very coarse. They didn't know how to feed themselves well. They were eating berries and bark and bugs. They didn't know how to grow anything. I was supposed to help them evolve. I thought I was doing what I was supposed to be doing. But they came and told me I was teaching them too much. They were growing too fast. They shouldn't learn that fast. It wasn't good... but they were learning.

When he first came to this place he put on the black robe to hide his true appearance. He actually had a body similar to a large green grasshopper. On his original home planet everyone had the same appearance. He had to hide because he wasn't like the people, and he knew his body would frighten them. He said that no one told him to leave and go to this place. "That was my job to go. I've always done this. I help people."

D: *So you went other places before coming to this one?*

Do: Yes, but this one went wrong. They say because we worked too much too fast. But they learned, so I taught them and they seemed to understand. I taught them how to care for one another. I taught them about the land and the water and the trees and the plants. I taught them they could find nourishment, and I taught them how to keep records. I wasn't supposed to teach them how to keep records. It was all right to teach them about food, but I wasn't supposed to teach them about keeping records. But it's important to keep records to know how to track time and seasons and the way things were in the world. They needed to know how to keep seasons... to know when to plant. They needed to know how to do that. They couldn't just go on without knowing. How could they plant? How would they know? They needed to keep track of who they were.

D: *Did you teach them how to build houses and things like that?*

Do: Yes, they learned. They learned how to use wood and trees. They learned how to live inside. They learned to live together as a group instead of individually, and life was easier.—Then the other ones came, and said I was doing the wrong thing. They weren't supposed to know that much. It was too soon.

D: *But you didn't know that. You thought you were doing what was right?* (Yes) *Then you said they were hurting the people?*

Do: Yes. The ones in black started wars, and people started hurting each other. And they would forget. They wouldn't keep going.

D: *So the wars were to keep them from progressing?* (Yes) *Forget what you had taught them?*

Do: Yes. Life was too smooth. They were learning too much. They were growing. They were afraid if they kept going the way they were going, it would be too soon.

D: *Why was that a problem?*

Do: I don't know. I didn't understand why that was a problem. They just said it was wrong.

D: *What do you see now?*

Do: I'm seeing light and I'm seeing space and stars. I went to space and went back home.

D: *What was happening when you felt you were tied or confined?*

Do: They were putting me in something. They were taking me away. Out to space. I was inside something, and I couldn't move. They took me away from the people. I cared too much for the people.—Then they let me loose. I am in a vehicle in space, and I can see the stars. It's beautiful! —But I can't go back.

D: *Would you like to go back?*

Do: I don't know... afraid. The people got hurt so much, but I don't want to go back.

D: *What does your body feel like now?*

Do: Loose... it feels loose.

There was no one with her on this vehicle that was transporting her. She was all alone. "It's peaceful." All she could see was space and stars. She had no idea where she was going. So I moved her ahead till she stopped somewhere, and asked what she could see.

Do: I don't know. It feels very heavy wherever I am. I don't know where I am. It looks kind of barren. There's not much here. There are no trees. It's not beautiful. The air feels heavy.

D: *So this vehicle was programmed to take you there?* (Yes) *What is your body like now?*

Do: It's a very weird feeling. My feet, my legs, and my hands are very thin. Very, very thin. I don't have fingers or toes. It's just flat. My body feels round. It's bigger. It's tall and round. I don't have a robe on it anymore to hide it, so it's like a grasshopper's body, but I'm standing up.

D: *What is your face like?*

Do: I have big eyes... very big eyes.—Here, I don't need to wear the black robe because there's nobody here. It's just me. There are some holes in the rocks that I can go into and out of. There's nothing to do.

D: *Do you have to eat?*

Do: I think I get what I need from the air.—It's a very heavy place. I don't think I can stay here long.

D: *What are you going to do?*

Do: I just have to be there.

D: *There's no way for you to leave?*

Do: No. They sent me away. They sent me there, so I wouldn't interfere with them anymore. I can't leave. I have to stay here.

D: *When you think back, when you first went to those people ... how did you get there?*

Do: I just chose to come. I was watching them and they needed help, and I volunteered and said I'd go and help them. We'd been watching them a long time. We go around from place to place.

D: *The other ones were watching what you were doing, weren't they?*

Do: Yes, they must have been, I guess, but they didn't interfere with what I was doing. It was to see what I was doing. I volunteered.

D; *But now, they sent you to this barren place where there's nothing?*

Do: Yes. There's nothing. I liked that other world. It was so beautiful.—I'm going to stay here. I don't know what else to do.

This could have taken an extraordinary long time if the being did not require food, and might not even have a way to die, as we perceive it. So I decided to move her ahead to another scene to find out what happened. She suddenly let out a loud sigh of relief. "AH! I have no body. I'm gone. I don't have to be there anymore. I can go."

D: *What happened?*

Do: I felt something and then, I just left. I left.—I was there a long time.

D: *You never saw anybody else?*

Do: No. It was very heavy, but beautiful. The planets, I watched the planets. I watched the stars. It was beautiful like an orchestra. Oh! It was so pretty!

D: *It was like a punishment to be sent there, wasn't it?*

Do: But it wasn't. It was beautiful in the end.

D: *Then did you just decide to leave?*

Do: I don't know. It was like I opened up and I was gone. I just left.

D: *What are you like now?*

Do: I'm like the stars and the light. Like tiny stars.

D: *What do you think of that life?*

Do: It's like living two lives in one.

D: *Did you learn anything from that experience?*

Do: Things aren't always what they seem to be. Much good can be bad and much bad can be good. It doesn't matter. It's all the same in the end. (Laugh)

D: *It's hard to tell when you're in the middle of it.—Where are you going to go now?*

Do: I don't know. I'm fine. I feel very sparkly.

She didn't see anyone around that could tell her where she had to go next. So I moved her ahead to see where she ended up.

Do: I go to the light. We're all going to the light.

D: *You see others?*

Do: Yes. All of us are sparkly things. We're all going to the light.

D: *What is the light like?*

Do: It's great! It's beautiful! It's very warm.

D: *Do you know what the light is?*

Do: It's everything. Oh, this feels wonderful! Now I'm home. The light is everything. It's everything.

D: *So it's good to be back home now.*

Do: Wonderful. But they say no, I'm not going to stay there long. I have to go out again.—I just know it. I just sense, yes. I'm not going to be there long.

D: *But you're going to enjoy it while you can.*

Do: Yes. That's what I'm supposed to do. I have other things to do.—I don't know. I have to learn something.

D: *Is it something you can't accomplish in that place?*

Do: Everything is there. You can't learn when *everything* is there.

D: *So you have to learn something different?*

Do: Yes. There's always more to learn.

I moved her ahead to when she decided to leave again and go somewhere else. We did know that she left because she was now in the physical body of Doris.

D: *Does someone tell you what to do?*

Do: No. You just know. It's time. You can feel it. Something's happening. I'm moving.

D: *Away from the light?*

Do: Yes, I'm not at the light anymore. Like a comet shooting through the stars. That's what it's like! I'm going away very fast and the sparkles come off like the comets. It's very beautiful.—It's like being on a pulley and somebody pulling you, but you don't know who. And you go in a certain way but you don't know how. You're just going, but there's nobody there. It's like you're on a path and you can only go that way; you can't go any other way.

D: *But you know it's going to be all right, don't you?*

Do: Yes. It's always fine.

D: *So you're moving through space and the stars are very, very beautiful.*

Do: That's the best part.

I moved her ahead to where she would finally stop, and asked her what she could see.

Do: I don't know. I've never been here before. It's like being in fire. It's like standing in a flame but it's not hot. The sky is all different colors. It's like standing in a flame. You have the colors all around you. It feels okay. It's just different. It's not heavy. It's not hot.

D: *Are there any other beings around?*

Do: Yes, there are people, but they don't see me. They look different. They look old like they are wrinkly, but they are made out of rocks. —Not rocks. They look big and bulky. They don't see me.

D: *Let's move ahead and find out what you're supposed to do there.*

Do: They have cities there. They needed help. I'm going to help them. At first they couldn't see me. I had to change. I had to be more like them so they could see

me. It's a vibration. That's what it is. That was a
different vibration. I had to study them so I could
change my form because I was supposed to help them.
They have trouble there. Something with the planet is
not right. They're going to die if they don't change
something they're doing. They're doing something to
the planet.

D: *What are you going to do to help?*
Do: I have to teach them something. I have to find out what
they're doing and teach them something else. That's
part of my job to find out what they do, and what they
need.

I moved her ahead so we could find out what it was.

Do: Something about the middle of the planet; they are
getting too close to the middle of the planet, and it will
change the way the planet orbits.... They are mining or
digging. It's going to change something in the planet.
It will affect everything. They have to stop. They have
to learn that they don't need what they think they need.
I have to be careful and see if they will listen. I don't
want to lose another planet. I have to be careful.

I then moved her away from that scene, and I asked the
entity if it knew it was speaking through a physical body. It
said that it did know, "I feel it."

D: *A physical body known as Doris.* (Yes) *Why did you
decide to come into a physical body after you helped all
these people on other planets?*
Do: I always have to look like everybody else. Can't do
anything if you don't.
D: *So your job has always been to go from place to place?*
(Yes) *When you're finished with one place, you go
somewhere else?* (Yes) *Did someone tell you to come
to Earth?*

101

Do: Yes, they told me they needed my help. That's my job.

D: *So this time you had to enter a physical body?* (Yes) *Why did they feel you needed to become a human this time?*

Do: It didn't work last time.

D: *Do you think it will work now if you're a human?* (Yes) *How do you feel about it?*

Do: I do what I have to do. It's working better. There's a lot of people now. There's many more. A lot of the Watchers are here.

D: *You mean more of them are coming?*

Do: Yes, and there are many here. They're working together.

D: *Last time they weren't?*

Do: It was just one. Many of us came to *this* planet.

D: *Why did they all decide to come this time?*

Do: It's an important time. It's important for everyone... not just this planet. It's important for all the planets. It has to do with the vibration. It's the vibration from planet to planet. It goes throughout space and time and it changes.

D: *And you're here to help with the vibration?*

Do: Yes. I'm here to help the planet.

D: *Do you think you'll be able to help better by being in physical form?*

Do: It was the only way this time.

D: *But you know when you come here you forget, don't you?*

Do: Yes, it was hard. I didn't understand.

D: *Is this the first time you've come into a physical body?*

Do: I was a grasshopper.

D: *That's true. —What do you think about learning lessons on Earth?*

Do: It's hard.

D: *Are you under any kind of restrictions while you're in the physical body?*

Do: I don't want to interfere in human life.

D: *What do you consider interference?*
Do: Sometimes I try to tell people and they don't understand.

I then decided to call forth the SC so we could get more answers, especially those dealing with Doris's personal questions. First I wanted to know why it showed her that lifetime.

Do: She needs to know she is who she thinks she is.
D: *She's a very powerful spirit, isn't she?* (Yes) *This spirit has a great deal of abilities.* (Yes) *So she has not had any lives on Earth as a human?*
Do: A few, not many.
D: *I have heard of other spirits like this who have volunteered to come. They are doing great work, aren't they?* (Yes) *But do these type of spirits accumulate karma?*
Do: No... They can. They don't have to.
D: *Why did she choose such a difficult life this time?*
Do: To help. To know how to help and understand, so she wouldn't do what she did before.
D: *What do you mean?*
Do: To help more than she needed to.
D: *When she taught the people too much?*
Do: Yes... to go beyond.
D: *In this life, she had a lot of problems as a child growing up.*
Do: Yes... for her to know how to be human.
D: *To be a human with all of its faults, all its problems.* (Yes) *That way she doesn't judge, does she?*
Do: No, she doesn't judge.

Doris always had psychic abilities and she could do many things. She knew things other people didn't know. She could see things about other people. She wanted to know about that.

Do: We help her. To know why she's here. She was allowed to have these abilities so she wouldn't forget.

D: *Why* is *she here?*

Do: To change... to make a change... to save the planet.

D: *But she's just one person. Or is it a combined power of all the others who have come?*

Do: Like being part of a grid. She's one of them... and she holds the light, and people she talks to can feel it. They don't understand it, and they think she's different. She is. She talks to people. She plants a seed, then it's up to them for the seed to expand. She's always done this. She just didn't understand.

D: *Are every one of these special spirits part of the grid?*

Do: Yes. They are saving the planet. It's working.—She needs to teach. Other lives... other planets. Teach about the universe and the stars. There is other life.

CHAPTER NINE

A BEING FROM THE COUNCIL

I am constantly encountering clients who are in contact with councils or are a part of a council when we do the sessions. I have found that there are many types of councils. There are councils over the solar system, over the galaxy, over the universe, etc. There are definite rules and regulations that help keep everything running in proper order. Nothing is left to chance. There are also councils on the spirit side that have other types of jobs taking care of the records of those living on Earth. All of these councils seem to have a great interest in the accumulation of knowledge and information. I am glad there is someone taking care of all these things, otherwise I believe there would be total chaos.

When Susan came off the cloud she was standing in the warm water of the ocean. She was near the shore because she saw steps coming down into the water. The steps went up to a temple. She saw three women standing by the right side of the steps. Then three more appeared on the other side, welcoming her.

S: They are wearing simple light colored gowns. The ones that are deeper down the steps are getting wet up to their knees and thighs.—They're bringing me in. I think I have to tell them something in order to go through. Not just anyone is allowed to come here. There are words they're speaking.

D: *Do you know what to say so they will let you come up?*

S: I'm familiar with the order. They are expecting me in a way. They're not of my order.

D: *What do you mean by "order"?*

S: A group of individuals concerned with the same thing.

Susan began making intricate hand motions. I asked her what they were for. "It's a signal for an energy exchange."

D: *Is this part of what you had to do so they will recognize you?*

S: They accepted me for who I say I am. They were aware of my arrival.

D: *They knew you were coming?* (Yes) *Where did you come from?*

Susan continued to make hand motions, and pointed upward. "What are you pointing at?"

S: (Surprised) Wow! (Laugh) It's a star base.

D: *Are they familiar with that?* (Yes) *How did you arrive there?*

She was surprised at her answers, and responded to my questions with disbelief and humor. "I came through the portal into the water. It's awesome.—They knew I was coming."

D: *This order you belong to, is that on the star base?*

S: It's intergalactic.—I had to adapt to the surface requirements by accepting physical form to take part in the general culture of the time. I look like a female that is dressed as they are.

D: *What is your normal form, when you are at the other place?*

S: It's light. I'm a light body.

D: *Are the others on that place you came from the same?*

S: Correct. Absolutely. We are here to help.

D: *So when you come into a place like this, you have to resemble the people there?*

S: At this time I am. Otherwise, it would cause confusion.

D: *But now they accepted you and welcomed you?*

S: It was foretold by the stars and the astronomers. It was an appointed date.

D: *They knew someone was coming?*

S: They represent the delegation from time to time for information exchanged.

D: *They have done this in the past?*

S: Yes, many times. But I only come periodically.

D: *You said for an exchange. What kind of exchange?*

S: Information exchange... for the gathering support with great concern that we must use at this time.

D: *Why was there great concern? Is someone misusing the information?*

S: The tendencies are there and the seeds of greed are beginning to grow. We are aware of it. These people use their influence. We have hope that things can be shifted at this time before the seeds of greed have sprouted.

D: *Have you brought information before that you think has been misused?*

S: At different times.

D: *Did you just give it to everyone when you came before?* (No) *Who did you give it to at those times? This group or another group?*

S: Another group. This isn't the first time there's been disaster on this planet.

D: *What caused it the other times?*

S: The manipulation of matter. The manipulation of natural law and matter for human gain.

D: *By the beings who were living in those times?*

S: Yes. You know the story.—The Earth was covered in ice, was one of the times.

D: *That was to stop what they were doing?*

S: To start again.

D: *It always starts again, doesn't it?*

They have told me this many times, and it has been reported in my other books. There have been many civilizations in Earth's distant past that had reached the height of perfection, only to be brought down by man's inherent greed for power.

D: *How were they destroyed other times, besides the ice?*
S: Great explosions. There's a missing planet in this solar system. It exploded.

She was referring to the planet between Mars and Jupiter that exploded and created the asteroid belt. This has also been written about in my other books.

D: *I have heard of that one. It caused a great deal of chaos, didn't it?*
S: Natural Law is meant to not be tampered with.
D: *Somebody tampered with the Law at that time?* (Yes) *How did the explosion of that planet affect Earth?*
S: It caused great destruction and fire that rained from the sky.
D: *So these were times when civilizations were destroyed in the past?* (Yes) *But you have come now to meet with these people, and you mentioned that something else is going to happen?*
S: We're concerned with the seed thought forms of greed that are circulating in the minds of these people.
D: *But this group is not doing it?*
S: Not at this time. We're here to give advice and information.
D: *Do you think they will listen to you?*
S: We have great hope.

She said she was going up to the temple to meet with the ones there. So I took her ahead until she was at the temple. "Are you meeting with many people?"

S: Just the delegation sent forth. My father is the priest who presides over this temple. He has influence with the others.

D: *What is the advice you are giving this group?*

S: Cease experiments with Natural Law.

D: *What experiments are they doing that's against the Natural Law?*

S: Gene manipulation... genetic manipulation.

D: *Why are they doing that?*

S: Because they can. They are powerful.

D: *How are they doing gene manipulation?*

S: I'm not sure that can be shared.

D: *You don't think I should know about it?*

S: It's not you.

D: *What will happen if they continue what they're doing?*

S: Destruction.

D: *They're not aware of this?*

S: No. It's starting to be divided. They've been self-governing until this point, but politically there's some distress and different schools of thought that have been trying to hold to the way of the light.

D: *Are you allowed to stop it if they are not going to listen?*

S: They will be set on a course of self-destruction.

D: *I wondered if you could come in and keep them from doing what they are doing.*

S: That would go against the Natural Law. We can only advise.

D: *And if they don't listen, there's nothing you can do about it?*

S: Nothing we can do.

D: *You said you've seen this happen before?*

S: In many times in many worlds.

D: *Then if they don't listen, they have to rebuild again, don't they? They start this cycle over again?* (Yes) *But this time you're hoping they do listen.*

S: We have great hope.

She was to give the information to the priest and then he was to go and talk to the people who were doing the incorrect thing. She would not stay; she would return when she was needed.

D: *Will you be able to see what they are doing?*

S: Yes. We are all aware.

D: *By "we," do you mean the ones in the group you come from?*

S: The council. They are the ones who are watching.

D: *Are they on the other side of that portal?* (Yes) *But they are not allowed to interfere?* (No)

I moved her ahead to see what happened.

D: *Does the priest go and talk to the others?* (Yes) *Do they listen?*

S: For a time... over 962 years have passed, and it has been destroyed again by its own hand.

D: *What happened?*

S: It blew up. The seeds of greed had grown. Natural Law had been manipulated to the point where great destruction was brought down upon themselves again. (Crying.)

D: *What does it look like as it happens? You can see as an observer, even though it's hard.*

S: It is like waves of energy reverberate around the planet. It explodes... debris and fire, water.

D: *What caused the shock wave?*

S: The energy beams came back on themself.

D: *Did they know this might happen?* (Yes) *But they continued anyway?*

S: It's about control. We can only advise and counsel.

D: What do you see as you're looking at it?

S: Ruin... complete ruin. It's so sad... smoke, burnt flesh, fire.

D: Were there any survivors?

S: Yes... a few.

D: Can you see what's happening with them?

S: Regrouping and rebuilding. They're regrouping themselves.

D: Do you think they've learned anything from this?

S: I hope so. Wow! —There is nothing we can do. We're pulling back again. To the council. The great council.

D: Back past the portal?

S: Yes. It's a Star gate actually.

D: That you use to go back and forth?

S: Correct. 14932-11

D: What does that mean?

S: That's the name of the Star gate.

D: That sounds like a long number, so there must be several. Is that what you mean? (Yes) How is that number used?

S: For identification purposes.

D: So you can go back and forth? (Yes) So it's possible for human beings to go through this portal?

S: Yes. If they are in their light body, the capability would come forward.

D: They can't go in their physical body?

S: No. Not at this time.

Humans have to go out of their body to be able to find these places, so they are not easy to locate.

D: What is that place like where they have the great council?

S: It's beautiful. (Sighs) We are light people. I see many light bodies and energy, and it smells beautiful.

D: What's causing the smell?

111

S: The light. Earth stinks.

D: *What do you do while you're there at the great council?*

S: We plan to help wherever we're needed and we are here to advise and support.

D: *So you're mostly concerned with Earth?*

S: I've been assigned in this sector.

D: *Is that what you mostly do with your time?*

S: We teach. People need us on the astral plane. We are able to teach the humans things they should know that would bring goodness into their lives.

D: *Then you don't need to come down physically like you did before?*

S: Only in circumstances when intervention is needed.

D: *So you are teaching people when they are in the astral? Do you mean when they are traveling out of the body at night or what?*

S: Yes. The human soul is capable of being in many places at many times. That's when we can be of the greatest assistance. We can assist there, but again, not interfere with free will. That is the governing of Natural Law.

D: *It's not interfering with their free will if they seek you?*

S: Exactly.

D: *The body is rather restricted, isn't it?* (Yes) *I've heard much of this happens at night when people are sleeping.*

S: Or when they are in states *you* help them to obtain. We have been watching you and helping you for a very long time on your astral plane. You are a wonderful, willing student.

D: *I know I have been getting a lot of help. I couldn't do it by myself. There are many strange places that you want them to know about?*

S: Absolutely.

D: *But the physical is the least of all, isn't it?*

S: But necessary for learning.

They verified that they have contact with people while they are asleep at night or in these types of altered states, and they can give them much information. I decided it was time to move forward, so I asked them if they knew they were speaking through the physical body known as Susan. They said that they were aware.

D: *You know when I do this we think we are going to go to past lives, don't we?*

S: It's your recipe for healing. This is what you have contracted with your team members to facilitate the healing in the physical. We consider that a recipe. The ingredients are good.

D: *But she didn't go to a past life, at least not the typical type with a physical body.* (Laugh)

S: No. No need for that. Some people need that, but she does not. —You know she's not going to like this. (Laugh)

D: *Why not?*

S: She doesn't want to believe in stars.

D: *Why not? I know they're real.*

S: You're guilty. She's not going to like it. (Loud laughing) If you tell her it's an angel, she'll say, okay.

D: *So it's all right if it's an angel, but not a being of light.* (Laugh)

S: Exactly.

D: *She can consider you an angel in another form.*

S: That's fine.

D: *When we first began, it sounded like she was you. Are you an aspect of her or what?*

S: Yes. You know! (Joking)

D: *I know, but we're trying to help her now. Some of this takes a little bit of adjusting.*

S: We've been working on it for awhile. (Still amused.) She's ready or this wouldn't have happened.

D: *Did you tell her to come here to my office?*

S: Absolutely.

D: *She was surprised because she said she had never heard of me before.*

S: Aren't we clever! (Laughing)

D: *My daughter calls you my PR people.*

S: So happy to be of service.

D: *You do this quite often, I've found. But this session is going to be different from what she expected, with her way of thinking?*

S: Oh, absolutely. We feel she's ready at this point in time however; but she'll go through an adjustment period. We arranged enough support to be with her so she's able to hear and digest at her own rate.

D: *We don't want to give anybody anything they can't handle.*

S: You know very well. (Laughing again.) We've been watching you for a long time. She is ready to hear from you because she feels a kinship to you in a way and she will be able to understand and relay how she feels. And you'll be able to help her and nurture her along her journey. That's your part in this.—She wants to believe that she isn't as worthless as she was programmed to believe in her early years. And for her to find that she goes through the council, that it is her origin, she won't believe it. She won't believe it.

D: *How is she going to explain it now, that you are speaking to her?*

S: She'll hear it in the voice. We already manipulate her voice. She knows, but she'll hear the authority in the voice.

D: *So it's time for her to know she's bigger than she thinks she is. Is that what you mean?*

S: Absolutely. This plain smile is getting nobody anywhere, and you know we all need to facilitate the new Earth and help people adjust to the new Earth. This is our primary motive here. Things are changing. People are needing someone to help them adjust to the dimension of changes. And people like you and her are so necessary. Helping people adjust and facilitate the adjustment to the new Earth.

D: *That's what I've been told. Things are changing so fast, and you don't want everything destroyed again.*

S: It cannot happen. You know this. It cannot happen and will not happen.

D: *It just takes so long doing it over again and again. That's why you are creating the new Earth?*

S: You know you're safe. She knows she's safe.

D: *We also know everyone's not going to the new Earth. That's what I've been told.*

S: You've been told correctly. You see the split. You see the divide. You understand.

D: *I try to. It's complicated.*

S: It is very complicated. That's why we need easy recipes for people.

D: *You have to start out with little baby steps, the little crumbs.—Why did you show her that destruction in the beginning?*

S: She has cellular memory in her body from that time from a place... you would call them parallel existences. And no, she was not a direct part of the destruction. It's encoded in her cells from the witnessing of the destruction.

D: *Why did you want her to know this?*

S: She underestimates the power of the tools she had been given to share with the planet Earth at this time. A time of great awakening... a time of the new Earth... being integrated into the Earth. She underestimates this. We wanted her to see how valuable it is to share the light. She underestimates her power. The light is critical to be spread at this time.

D: *But she is doing a great deal of good, isn't she?*

S: Yes, she is and we are proud of her. But still on a smaller scale. Until she believes in herself, it's hard to take her to a larger scale.

D: *Do you want her to go to a greater scale?*

S: Not until she's comfortable with it in her physical body.

Susan had been hearing beings speaking to her for a long time, but she assumed it was her angels. Actually it was the council. They laughed, "She's not going to like it at all. Break it to her gently, will ya?"

S: Her contract is to connect people to Source light. She hears the connector part only. (Laugh) And that's okay.

Susan had also had many physical things happen to her. "Nudges. Pretty hard nudges. It's only necessary when everything else fails, and we regret that she felt punished in any way."

The SC went through her body quickly and fixed all the physical complaints that Susan had on her list.

**** "Fear is an illusion of this world and that's all it is."

CHAPTER TEN

THE DESTRUCTION OF A PLANET

In 2009 was my first time to go to South Africa, and Cathy was the person who invited us to come to Johannesburg and arranged the class. I decided to choose her for the demonstration on the last day of the class. The people there in Johannesburg have not been exposed to much in metaphysics, so they were extremely eager to learn. They have books, but not many speakers and teachers. Everything about the class was new to them because they were at the most basic level of understanding. This was the way my lectures were also. It was refreshing to find such wonder and awe and enthusiasm in people. Everything went smoothly during the class, and I had taught them the basics about using my method of hypnosis for simple past lives and healing. That was what we were expecting in the demonstration, the reliving of a normal past life. That would be the limit of their level of understanding at this beginning stage. So when we began the session it took a turn that left them totally stunned. It was normal for me, but it presented ideas they had never heard of. The looks of astonishment were evident on their faces. They kept looking at me to see how I was reacting, since it was a total departure from what I had just taught them. I was well aware that the sessions are no longer strictly exploring simple past lives, but venturing into the unknown (especially the three waves of volunteers). I think it surprised them that I didn't end the session, but continued as though nothing unusual was occurring. Of course, for me it was not unusual. I tried to give them looks of reassurance as I continued the session. I knew that I could explain it further afterwards. I had not had the opportunity to bring up this possibility before the demonstration. I suppose "they" think my students are now ready, no matter where in the world they are located.

As we began the session Cathy liked being on the cloud and was hesitant about floating off it. She became emotional and started crying. There was nothing to indicate why it was affecting her in this way because she had not even seen anything yet. Yet it is always an indication that we have found something important (or in her case, that something important would be coming) when the person shows emotion. Emotion cannot be faked, and later does not even seem rational to the client. "Why was I crying? It doesn't make sense. Why did that upset me?"

I knew I had to get her off the cloud, so I asked if she could go *anywhere,* where would she want the cloud to take her?

C: 　I want to go up! (Deep sigh) I want to go home.
D: 　*To experience it again for a while. You can do anything you want to do. Which way would you go?*
C: 　North.—I see stars. They're beautiful! They're bright and spinning.—Now I see a pink land. It's the color of roses. It's far away.—That's where I live. I'm coming closer. I see a lot of wind... a lot of clouds leaving. The clouds have a soft pink color. And there are lights... they come from the stars.
D: 　*Do you want to go toward the surface so you can come down?* (No) *Why not?*
C: 　Because it's not there anymore.—It's just dust. It's gone.

She began to sob loudly. The students were looking at me very confused.

D: 　*Did something happen to it?*

C: I don't know.—There isn't any life. There's just dust bowls and hot air.—I can't get close. It's not letting me.—It's too dangerous.

Cathy couldn't explain why it was dangerous, but as she floated she had to remain at a safe distance. All she could see was clouds and dust. There was no sign of life, buildings or vegetation. Just a barren planet. It made her incredibly sad. "I can't go back. We lost everything. It's gone. Everyone's gone. It's not there. Everything's lost." She said she was not there when whatever happened, but she knew it had once been a thriving place with people. And she knew that she had lived there for a short time. Since she was unable to get any more information, I decided to move her backwards to before the catastrophe happened, before the bad times and see what it was like. She was eager to try that, and went quickly there. "I see children. They're playing in water. There's lots of water.

D: *Is it still a pink color?*
C: No. It's a white. And the ground is green.—The children are playing. They're dancing.

She said the children looked human. When I asked her to look down at herself and tell me what her body looked like, she said she couldn't see her body. I asked her if she could feel her body. "Yes. It feels calm.—I see a city... a white city. It has tall, gray marble walls with corridors, and there's lots of laughter. It shines. There are always lights."

D: *Did you live there at one time?*
C: I think I visited there. It was not my home, but I lived there.
D: *Why did you go to visit?*
C: To teach.—To teach the children love and happiness.
D: *Were you told to go there?*
C: Yes. It was beautiful. Simple people, but good.

She had journeyed to many places where she felt drawn to in order to teach, where she was needed.

D: Is that what you like to do?
C: I don't know... (Sigh)... not anymore. (She began crying.) Because it hurts.
D: It hurts because the planet was destroyed or what?
C: Yes, because it happened. Then when I leave, I don't know what happens to them.

She would intuitively know when something was going to happen, but the people did not know. So she left long before the disaster happened. She still didn't know exactly what caused the destruction. "When I am needed I go and teach."

D: What do you do when you're not needed? We can look at that. (Pause) Is there something else you do then?
C: No. I just wait until I'm needed.
D: Where do you wait? You can see it.
C: It's hard to explain.
D: Do the best you can.
C: It's complete peace. It's softer.
D: Does it look physical?
C: No. It's almost like motion... like a song.
D: It sounds beautiful. Is anyone with you or are you all by yourself?
C: I'm not alone, but there's no one physical there. Yet I feel there are others around me always.
D: So you like that place?
C: Sometimes.—Sometimes you need to get away and see things. It's a place where I wait until I have to go and teach and help others. Then I return here.
D: Have you ever lived in a physical body?
C: I can't remember. This is all I remember, this place of pure peace and beauty.
D: That's very good. You're a very loving person. You have to be full of love to teach love. That's wonderful.

—Are you aware you're speaking through a physical body at the present time? (Yes) *Why did you decide to enter a physical body if it was so beautiful there?*

C: I don't know. (Laugh)

D: *Do you want to find out?* (She laughed.) *We can. It would help, wouldn't it?* (Yes)

I then took her to the point where it was decided. When she left that beautiful place. "What happened?"

C: It was time. They had to make arrangements.—My job wasn't finished. I had to teach more.

D: *Is anybody talking to you?*

C: We're all talking together. We're deciding what's best.

D: *What are you deciding?*

C: Who's going to do it.

D: *Do the others want to go too?* (No) (We both laughed.) *Why don't they want to go?*

C: Because it's big. It's a big challenge. They don't feel it's right for them to go.

D: *Is there a reason why?*

C: Because they weren't needed. (She started crying again.)

D: *But you think you were?*

C: Oh, yes!

D: *What do you feel you were needed to do?*

C: To change things... slowly... to shift it... to help people remember that it's okay.

D: *What did they forget?*

C: Themselves. They forget who they are... who they really are. When they come into the physical they forget.

D: *Who are they really?*

C: That's for them to learn. They believe they're something else and they're not.

D: *So you're going to help them to remember?*

C: That's part of it, yes.

121

D: *What's the other part?*

C: To help change things.—The flow. Like a current... change the flow.

D: *The flow of what?*

C: Everything. It's going the wrong way.

D: *What caused it to go the wrong direction?*

C: Forgetting... forgetting to love . forgetting to love and to play.

D: *So when the people started forgetting, it caused the flow to go in the wrong direction?* (Yes) *If the flow continued to go in the wrong direction, what would happen?*

C: They'd die. Their soul. (Sobbing.)

D: *So you took it on yourself to come and make a difference?*

C: A small... small difference.

D: *That's a big decision.* (Yes) *It takes a lot of courage to do that.*

C: It takes stupidity.

D: *Do you think you can make a difference?*

C: I don't know.—Coming into a physical body was not what I thought it would be.

D: *But these other beings you were with, they didn't want to take the chance?* (No) *So you feel like you're all alone doing this?*

C: No. I know I'm not.

D: *Are you aware there are others helping too?* (Yes) *Are they people that Cathy knows?* (No) *But maybe they don't know what they're doing either.*

C: They are learning.

D: *But you said you miss home?*

C: Yes. I was really happy there and that was part of it.

I decided to call forth the SC and get answers to her questions. I asked why it chose to show Cathy that scene. "We were looking for past lives, weren't we?" (Yes) "Is there a reason why she didn't go there?"

C: She can't remember them. She's not meant to.

D: *Sounds like she was just going from place to place like a spirit form?* (Yes) *Doing a lot of good?*

C: She tries.

D: *So she came to Earth to do another mission?* (Yes) *Was that what you wanted her to know?*

C: She knows.

D: *But she didn't know consciously.* (Yes) *Do you think that's important for her to know?*

C: It's important... yes.

D: *This will help explain a lot of things going on in her life?*

C: Yes. That's why we led her to you.

D: *Is she one of the volunteers I have spoken to before?*

C: They're different.

D: *How is that different?*

C: Because she doesn't usually do this. We had to ask.

I asked the eternal question: What was her purpose? What was she supposed to be doing in this life? "Do you want to tell her?"

C: Not really. (Laugh) Because it's bigger. She's on her path. She'll know when the time is ready.

D: *So right now she's not ready to know the whole picture?* (No) *Must be pretty big.*

C: I can't say. (Laugh)

Because the SC wouldn't reveal the bigger picture, I turned my focus on her physical purpose. She had been involved in the corporate world and became disillusioned, and got out. "She was trying to be human. She wanted to fit in. She wanted to do what's best for this planet and she thought she'd be able to do best there. More people there." When she was working in the corporate world she got very sick. That was one of the main reasons she had to get out. They said it happened because she was not happy. I asked them about her physical body, and to do a body scan, but they were ahead of me and were already working on it. The doctors thought there was something wrong with her blood. They diagnosed it as severe anemia which caused her to be weak and to pass out at unexpected times.

C: We're working on that. She can feel it. She can feel it.

D: *What was wrong with the blood?*

C: Nothing major. It was just the flow. She had stopped the flow.

D: *She was talking about the flow, but I thought she meant the flow of the world. But she hooked into that?*

C: It's all part. It's the same thing.

D: *The doctors were saying it was something very serious.*

C: It was.—But she listened. She got out of that company.

D: *What are you doing to the blood now?*

C: I'm energizing it.

D: *How do you energize the blood?*

C: I just do it.—It'll get better... a lot better. We have been doing it while we're talking. Keep 'em guessing... yes.

The doctors also said there was something wrong with the liver. "They" said it was part of the same problem, with the flow, and this caused the blood to go bad (to become poisoned).

D: *Have you corrected it?*

C: Give me a minute. We still need a minute.

Then they focused on her back. It had been causing her problems because she had a hard time letting go. She wanted to stay connected. "It's like one foot in and one foot out." They corrected the problem, "Just correcting the flow, and taking away from who she was to who she is now.—We're going to look into it some more, but we can correct it. We just want to do it in strides." All the other physical problems (neck, legs) were connected to the initial cause. They would continue to work on her after the session.

She had wanted to know about contracts or karma with people in her life, but if she had not been on Earth before, there would not have been any. "She has teachers that teach her how to live. Her parents were the ones to bring her in. Only to teach her." When she was growing up she felt a lot of anger and aggression. She wanted to know where that came from. "It was grief. That planet... that loss."

D: *What happened to that planet?*
C: They gave up on themselves.
D: *She said she wasn't there when it happened. Everything was destroyed.*
C: No, they took her away. She would have hated to see that. It was very sad.
D: *What caused the destruction?*
C: Themselves.—It's hard to explain because it's so different, but the intent was they gave up the fight to do better... to love. They forgot what they needed to do.
D: *So everything was destroyed.*
C: Yes. They chose that.
D: *Is that why she had to come to Earth now?*
C: Because the people were choosing to kill themselves, yes.
D: *And you don't want it to happen again?*
C: We'd like to give them a chance. We are trying.
D: *You don't want it to repeat itself?*
C: We don't like losing. (Laugh)
D: *She doesn't want to go through that again. She has a big job that she volunteered for.*
C: We asked her. She eventually agreed. She understood what it would take. We are very proud of her for taking the chance. But we knew that she would. She does a lot for us.

125

Another question she had was about visitations she had at night when she was a child that had frightened her.

C: Because she lives in both realities. One foot in; one foot out. She has a hard time letting go and she has that connection back to the Source.

D: *Why did she perceive that as being frightening?*

C: Because it was. It was very frightening. To encounter negativity and—how do I explain this—not evil, but not understanding. She perceived it as something physical. It was physical energy. She could feel the energy. It was a person, but not what she thought it was. It was from the spirit world.

D: *But sometimes she still has visitations.*

C: Because she can see through to the next reality.

D: *Through the veil?* (Yes) *But she shouldn't be afraid of it?*

C: No, but we understand why she is. The next time she will understand.

D: *If you understand things, you aren't afraid of it, are you?*

C: That's right. That's right.

D: *We have one more question. She felt she could fly as a child. Was that true or is that just her imagination?*

C: Well, everybody can fly. Everybody.

D: *Why don't we know it?*

C: Because we forget.

D: (Laugh) *We just feel tied to the Earth?*

C: We believe we are.—As a child she knew she could do it, so she did it.

D: *Do you mean if we started remembering, we could still do it?*

C: Yes... if we learn to play. We need to play. Just play... just feel joy and love and acceptance. You get too serious. You have to bring joy back into your life because your soul dies if you don't have it. It's not that bad. It just seems that way. Play, have fun. Then we can change the flow.—Remember what it was like to fly.

D: (Laugh) *I just see a picture of everybody flying.*

C: It happens.

D: *Maybe it's time.*

C: I hope so. I really do.

D: *Anyway, you want us to remember where we came from; what it was like and why we're here?*

C: That's for you to find out. That's not my job. Become aware.

D: *And we can make a difference?*

C: Oh, yes. Everyone has their path.

D: *Or the world would die like the other one?*

C: Maybe worse. We don't want that.

I was getting ready to close when the SC unexpectedly asked me, "Is there anything you wanted to know?" This always takes me by surprise because my main concern is the interest of my client. So I thought off the top of my head, "That I want to know? —Why did I have to come to South Africa? It's my first time. Why was I needed?"

C: Because of the balance.

They didn't expand on that statement, so I can only speculate. Maybe they meant my energy was needed to help balance that part of the world. They have told me many times that when we go someplace, we leave a part of our energy there and we influence more than we can ever imagine.

After lunch I spent a lot of time trying to explain the session to the best of their limited understanding. It was also difficult to explain to Cathy because she had no memory of what she had said.

This was another example of what I call the "second wave." She was here as an observer, but also as a teacher to help people remember. In this case "they" asked her to come instead of her volunteering, but she did so reluctantly.

Another unusual thing happened immediately after the session. It was hot this time of the year in South Africa, and rain was unusual. But unexpectedly a heavy thunderstorm suddenly erupted over the building we were in. There were strong winds, rain and loud thunder. They said this was extremely unusual and never happened during this time of the year. When we returned to the house where we were staying we asked Cathy's brother, James, about the rainstorm. He said there had been no storm in that part of the city. It seemed to have been localized only over the building and street where we were conducting the class. Did it have something to do with the energy generated from the entities involved, or the SC?

Unusual weather phenomena have occurred during some of my other classes. When I gave my class in the desert in Dubai a sudden strong dust storm erupted around the building where we were conducting the class. During one of my Transformation Conferences that we have in Arkansas we suddenly went under a tornado alert, and a tornado was sighted directly over the convention center. Perhaps one of the strangest unexplained phenomena happened while I was conducting my class in November 2010 in Sydney, Australia. This was a large class (over 60 students) and the room was packed. I was conducting the interview just prior to performing the demonstration on the last day of the class. Suddenly the room was thrown into chaos as a gusher (a true waterfall) of water burst through the ceiling directly over some students seated at their table. The water was pouring in from around the light fixtures. They screamed and jumped up, drenched, as someone grabbed a huge trashcan and sat it on the table trying to collect the water which would not stop. Disruption reigned as someone went to find the people in charge of the building.

At first I thought it was rain, but that did not make sense because we were on the third floor of a five story building, and the sun was shining outside. The most obvious solution was that a water pipe had burst in the ceiling. The downpour continued for at least five minutes slowing and then increasing again. I found it amusing and finally said, laughing, "Okay, guys, you have made your point! You can turn it off now!" I didn't know for sure, but I suspected it was just our friendly gremlins playing tricks again. When the people came in who were in charge of the building, they stood there dumbfounded with open mouths, staring at the waterfall and the trashcan half full of water. They kept saying, "This has never happened before. There are no water pipes in the ceiling. There is nothing that could cause this." Then as the water slowed to a trickle they asked if I wanted them to clean it up. I told them it would be all right, since it was the last day of the class and I didn't want any more delays. The students just moved to dry tables and chairs. It was months later when I asked "them" about it during another session. They said there were at least three people in the class who were skeptics, and they thought this would be a way of convincing them that I was truly working with something unusual during my sessions.

Many other unexplained phenomena have occurred in the room during my classes (as well as during my private sessions in my office). I do not think these things are by accident or coincidence. It may be the combined energy generated by the students, by "them," or by the SC. It only serves to show that we don't know our own power. Think of what we could do if we learn to harness this incredible energy. Save the world? Or maybe we could fly!!

CHAPTER ELEVEN

ANOTHER PLANET DESTROYED

Terry was another client who was trying to discover who they were. The planet had always felt very foreign to her and she was trying to stabilize her identity. Another case of someone who felt they didn't belong here, and had had difficulty adjusting.

This session was held at the guest house where I was staying outside of Santa Fe, NM. I had gone there to conduct my class at the Northwestern New Mexico College at the El Rito campus. I was seeing a few clients while staying there.

When Terry came off the cloud she found herself in an "empty place." There was uncertainty as she tried to describe. "I don't recognize it. It's open. It's a large space. It seems like there used to be something here, and it's not here now. It's like something was destroyed. It's a desolateness. And it doesn't feel like there's life here now. The terrain feels scorched. There's the feeling that there *was* vegetation, maybe trees of some kind. Maybe buildings. There's an impression of them, but I don't see anything *left* of them. Like nothing. It's strange. And it feels like... a loss. And I feel alone there. It feels like... everyone left."

I asked her to become aware of her body. She was wearing a smooth, seamless garment that reminded her of suede, but in layers. Her body seemed very light and thin, with not much substance. When she looked at her hands they were larger than she expected, and the fingers were unusually shaped. When I asked about her head and face, she said she was wearing a tight-fitting hood. Her face: "Smooth features.

An oval kind of feeling. A very small mouth and a tiny nose. My eyes are small, but wide. More horizontal shaped, almost like slits." She was surprised that she had no difficulty breathing the atmosphere in this desolate place.

T: I feel like I've been here before. This is a place I used to know. I feel like I heard that something happened,

D: *And when you knew it before, it wasn't like this?*

T: No. It was whole. Many people, and activity. It was a busy place. I hadn't seen it myself. And it's sad. There are many different stories. But I think it was some kind of... almost self-destruction. Some have said that it was destroyed by outer forces, but I don't think that's true. I think it was something that couldn't be helped. Well, probably could have been helped, but they didn't know what to do.

D: *Do you think this was your home?*

T: Yes, I do. I don't think I've been there for a really long time. It seems like I can feel the others, the people I knew, that didn't get to leave. That were also destroyed or lost.

D: *Then some did get to leave.*

T: Yes. I don't know why I did, but I did. And I happened not to be there when it happened.

She said she didn't have to come to this place *in* anything. She just thought about it, and she was instantly there.

D: *Where were you when you were thinking this? Let's move to that place. When you decided you wanted to see it, where were you?*

T: It's in space. No planet. Just out there. Part of everything.

D: *What do you mean?*

T: It's just... a space.

D: *No craft or anything physical?* (No) *Well, how can you exist out there?*

T: You don't need much.

D: *What do you mean? Because it seems like you have a physical body, don't you?*

T: I don't when I'm out here. When I'm out here in space, there's no physical. I feel like a point of light. As soon as I wanted to leave again, the body just disappeared. I no longer needed it.

When she spoke of feeling like a point of light she was seeing herself as she *really* was. When all of us were first created we were just sparks of light who were sent out to learn and have experiences. When you strip away the body and the physical trappings that we surround ourselves with in order to live a life, all we truly are is an eternal point of light.

D: *You said you left this planet before the disaster happened?* (Yes) *Can you see that time? Did you have a physical body then?*

T: It seems like I did. And I am in some kind of craft.

D: *Are there others with you?*

T: Many people. The craft is small.

D: *When you left, did you know something was going to happen?*

T: Not for sure. I didn't leave *because* something was going to happen. But it was felt that something *could* happen.

D: *Were there others that left at the same time?*

T: Yes. But again, not because they felt something was going to happen. People come and go.

D: *What was your job?*

T: It involved me flying in this craft. I flew away for a long time, but we would definitely go back and forth.

D: *Tell me what happened on this trip when you left. Where did you go?*

T: It seems like it was far away from the planet. It feels like we were watching other planets? Other beings? Maybe. And we were taken far out of... even that universe.

D: *And what was your job out there?*

T: Just looking. Just watching. Gathering information. To see what else is happening in other areas.

D: *Is that what your people do?*

T: It seems like *part* of what we do. It feels like exploring, and then bringing the information back. And then working with others with that information. And going out again.

D: *Do you like that kind of work?*

T: Yes. It's interesting.

D: *So you were onboard a small ship or a larger one, when you're out that far?*

T: It feels like a small one.

D: *Do you land on these other planets, or do you just observe?*

T: It feels like we just observe. I don't remember landing.

D: *You don't remember interacting with the people then.*

T: No. It feels like from a distance. But we can still tell a lot of what's going on, at a distance.

I was trying to move the story forward and find out more about all of this, so I had her move to an important day when something was happening.

T: (Confusion) We see an unusual planet of some kind that's.... It's like a liquid orange. And it keeps changing its shape.

D: *Is that what makes it unusual?*

T: Yes. We haven't come across that exactly before. It doesn't seem to be inhabited, but we're trying to figure out a function and purpose of it. Because it's not a fixed shape. And it actually seems like it could be causing a disturbance... (confusion) affecting its surroundings. And it looks like it's causing some trouble for other planets.—Even planets that don't have inhabitants seem to have some purpose. And it's like this one's run amok. The way it keeps changing its shape is causing the disturbance.

D: *Fluctuation.* (Yes) *Are you supposed to do anything?*

T: We're supposed to mostly just observe, but there's some sense of alarm. And we have to go back and give this information to those in charge. There's an urgency about it. And a different feeling. This somehow is what affected our planet.

D: *Even though it was so far away?*

T: Even though. I know. Yes. It's causing great distress.

D: *Throughout the whole universe or what?*

T: Yes. Sometimes in subtle ways and sometimes in big ways. I don't have the understanding of *how*, but it does feel urgent. It could pose a danger to our world, and others.—We're going back. There's nothing more we can do here, or more information to gather. It's time to go back, and relay the information.

D: *All right. Let's move time ahead to where you go to report the information. What is that place like?*

T: It has structures that are hard to describe. We *do* make them. They are not natural forms, but they look like natural forms. And inside... just lots of space. It *is* a building, but it looks like it comes out of the ground.

D: *Where is this place located?*

T: This is that planet, my planet. And I went there to relay the information. Those in charge are in this building.— They are concerned. And they're going to send out others, a more scientific team, to find out just what's going on with this planet. They have other ways of testing, or gathering information. We are the ones who do the exploration. And now people with other tools will be sent out.

D: *You don't go back with them?*

T: No. For a little while we stay where we are. We don't stay there long ever, or not for a long time. Then we are sent out on another assignment.

I moved her forward to another important day, and after a long pause she answered slowly and sadly.

T: I'm in a craft again. There's another team person in the craft. And we get word about our planet. And... it's sketchy. But we hear that there's been destruction. And... (had difficulty verbalizing) and... we don't know what to do.

D: *Do you think it was caused by the planet you saw?*

T: (Big sigh) We don't know at that moment. It does seem... that is the first thing we think about. And... we don't know what to do. We don't know where to go. We're kind of floating. It's like we're lost out there. Our mission is fruitless. Don't know where to go. We were never told what to do if something happens. And I know there are others out there, but we're not near them.

D: *No way to contact them.*

T: It doesn't seem like it. Although someone got hold of us.

D: *And sent a message to you.*

T: Yes. We don't seem to be able to get hold of anyone.

D: *Well, maybe they wouldn't know what to do any more than you do.*

T: No, probably not.

D: *How many are on your craft?*

T: Just two of us.

D: *Do you have to eat or consume food?*

T: It doesn't seem like it.

D: *Do you think you can live out there for a while?*

T: Yes. We're not concerned about that. It's... we don't know where to go. And what to do, exactly.

D: *Well, let's move time ahead. We can do this very easily. Move time ahead and see what happens. Where do you go?* (Pause) *What do you decide to do?*

T: We decide to explore, and see if there is any other place we can land. We'd like to find our kind, if possible.

Here a loud electronic buzz started on the tape, and partially obscured the words. It had not been evident during the session. It could only be heard on the recording during transcription. This phenomenon sometimes occurs and I think it is from energy being generated. The tape can also speed up and sound "chipmunky," or slow down so that the voices sound deep and dragging. It is never caused by the normal mechanics of the tape recorder.

D: *So what are you doing?*

T: We had the experience of this exploration, and we have maps. So we feel our pull in that respect, but we don't have a plan, exactly. We're going to continue exploring, but now... for us.

It appeared that during this time of exploring they returned to the planet they saw at the beginning of the session, and found it lifeless and demolished.

D: *Well, let's move time ahead. Do you ever find a place to go?* (Long pause) *So you can stop exploring, and be safe somewhere?*

T: (Pause) It doesn't seem like it. It seems that.... We change our form instead.

The electronic buzz stopped as suddenly as it started.

D: *Oh? What do you mean?*

T: (Confused) I don't know how, but we were able to... leave our form behind on the craft. And just be in space.

D: *Is that when you became the point of light?*
T: I guess so.
D: *Why did you decide to do that?*
T: We must have had the knowledge that we could. And without our planet, it just seemed that our bodies didn't make a whole lot of sense.
D: *You didn't think you'd be able to find another place?*
T: We never really wanted to. We wanted to see if we could, but it didn't seem that important at that point. Or necessary. We couldn't go back. And we would have felt—even though we were together—lonely, on another planet.
D: *So the two of you decided to do this together?* (Yes) *Is this a form of dying? Do you understand that concept?*
T: (Big sigh) I believe so. Yes. It was at will, but, yes.
D: *Because I wondered if your bodies* could *die.*
T: Well, we just didn't need them anymore. It wasn't that they gave out. It was that they weren't ever going to serve a purpose.
D: *You could have just kept traveling and traveling, but you don't think there would have been any sense in that?*
T: No. It seemed pointless. Even though the point was to find a new home, we didn't think any home would have been the same. And that was sort of sad.

The buzz returned just as I reached the end of the tape and turned it over.

D: *What are you going to do now?*
T: It feels good. It feels like some kind of continuation. There's a watching.
D: *Still exploring.*
T: Not so much exploring, as holding.... I want to say, something like a stabilizer.
D: *Is there anyone or anything that will tell you what you're supposed to do?*

T: Hmm. I kind of just know, but I do think I've been instructed, as well. (Pause) It's more the stationary point of light, in a way, than all the moving around I had been doing. And in this way there's some kind of assistance that this is providing on a bigger level. It's a tiny point of light, but it feels very big. And it feels very solid, in a way, and stabilizing. It's like a stabilizing point in the universe that helps things function in a way that they need to.

D: *Do you stay out there for a long time, just stabilizing things?*

T: Yes. Stabilizing, keeping things where they're supposed to be. So that things don't get thrown off course.

D: *You mean like planets... or things in the universe?*

T: Well, it's new.

D: *Do you ever have the desire to stop being that, and become a physical body?*

T: It doesn't seem like it. I like this.

D: *Do you still need instructions on what to do?*

T: I got the preliminary, the initial instructions. (Pause) And not so much right now. But I have a sense of what I need to do, if I need to do something different. It could change, but it will be whatever else is needed.

D: *But are you aware that you are speaking to me through a physical body?*

T: I think I know that. I do and I don't. (Laugh) I am aware of this body laying here.

D: *Yes, that you're speaking through.* (Yes.) *But you're also out there stabilizing things.* (Right) *Because I don't want to get you mixed up or confused.*

T: It could happen.

D: *Well, let's move ahead in time until you decide to enter this physical body for the first time.—What happened when you decided to enter a physical body?*

T: This one? (Yes.) Well... I'm not sure it was my idea.

D: *I wondered if you had instructions.*

T: Yes. It was necessary. There was something I was supposed to do, or needed to do, in a body. I was pretty comfortable doing what I was doing, and it's like that had to get shaken up a little bit. And there was some experience that I needed to have, that I couldn't have as this point of light.

D: *But you were given instructions to do this?*

T: Yes. It was not my idea because I was pretty happy.

D: *You had been in the physical.* (Yes.) *But had you ever been in the physical on the planet Earth? Because that's where we're speaking from.*

T: Right. (Pause) I don't know... it feels fine. I'm trying to look back.—They told me to come. They did.—Something to do... and it feels like something for me, too. Something about experiencing the density. And learning how to deal with the density. It feels very different.

D: *Is it different than the other planet?*

T: Yes. Even though we had form, everything was lighter. It worked differently.

D: *Do you think it's going to be easy to experience this body?*

T: It doesn't seem like it. I'm willing to go. And I know it is right, but I can't say I'm looking forward to it. It seems kind of odd.

D: *You had all that freedom out there.*

T: Yes. And all the exploring was fun.

D: *But there must be a reason, or they wouldn't have asked you to come.* (Yes.) *It must be important.*

T: That's what they say.

D: *Is there any preparation before you come into the body?*

T: It seems like I see a lot of pictures. I'm somewhere where I'm shown something like pictures of life on the planet, and it goes very fast. Lots of information, fast.

D: *Things you'll need to know?*

T: Yes. Kind of how things work here.

D: *It would be hard to come in with no knowledge,*
     wouldn't it?

T: Yes. It's in preparation. And almost like a class. And
     it's fun to learn, or what to learn.

She was obviously describing the imprinting process,
which is described in detail in my other books. This is usually
done with a spirit that has not been on Earth before, in order to
prepare them. So it was obvious that she was a first-timer.

D: *So you'll know what it's going to be like where you're*
     going.

T: And it seems different, but not... that bad. (Chuckle)
     Not as hard as it did initially.

D: *What did it feel like when you first entered the body?*

T: (Pause) Hmm. Not... hard. It's an uncomfortable
     feeling. It feels like... I'm not sure about this. It's very
     different. It's... hard to adjust.

D: *I can understand that. Well, this was why I was asking*
     those questions. Because I am speaking to the physical
     body, and she has questions. As to why she felt
     different being on Earth in this body.—Why do you
     think she was shown this past life, where she was the
     explorer, and the planet that was destroyed?

The buzzing had continued throughout this side of the
tape, and was becoming quite loud and disrupting.

T: (Big sigh) She needed to see her other existences off of
     this planet.

D: *Where she came from?* (Yes.) *Why is that important*
     for her to know?

T: She longs for it.

D: *But life on the other planet doesn't exist anymore, does*
     it?

T: No. But she had to know that it did. And it is where
     she is from. She would rather be there, if she could.

D: But, of course, it's impossible, isn't it? (Yes) *And she could have stayed in space, doing that also, couldn't she?*

T: She would have liked to. But she needed to have this lifetime. There are things she can bring to this place at this time.

D: *Do you know what she is supposed to be doing in her life right now?*

T: Yes. The healing work needs to expand in new ways. But she's on the right track.

D: *She had a question. She kept wondering about it all her life. She felt like she didn't know who she was. She was trying to discover herself. She spent a lot of time inventing characters because she didn't know who she was. (Yes.) Can you explain why she felt that way?*

T: Well, it's sort of amusing, but not very good for her. She does not know how to do this, live this Earth life. She's been sort of trying on hats, and none of them have fit. And she was getting lost. It was difficult, and she's now beginning to feel more of who she is. And that's the direction she does need to go in. But she almost got lost completely.

D: *Because she didn't know who she was.*

T: Right. It was debilitating her.

D: *But you were able to help her understand?*

T: Yes. We sent the right people to her to meet and work with to help her.

D: *So she can become more anchored in the physical body?*

T: More altered. More remembering who she is really, and finding the way to manifest that physically.

D: *That's why she almost became lost because she wasn't sure who she was, and what she was doing here?*

T: Right. She got confused. We will help her because she wants it. And it is good for her. We'll do what we can to move her along with that. She needs to be here. Whether she likes it or not!

D: *She'll be able to adjust, won't she?* (Yes.) *You'll help her to find her identity, and adapt.* (Yes.) *That's very important. But another thing that's been troubling her: ever since she came into this body, she's had physical problems.* (Yes.) *Why has that happened?*

T: Mainly it has been the adjustment. It was not an easy adjustment into the physical. And there were times when she wasn't sure if she was going to stay. And she was brought into an environment that was not very pure, polluted. In combination with the newness of the body, that made for a difficult beginning. And the lack of knowing herself was also a hard physical strain.

D: *Yes, I can understand that. I've been told by others like you, that sometimes the energy is so different, it has to be adjusted when it comes into a physical body for the first time.*

T: Yes. We did make some adjustments. The circumstances were very difficult, with the parents, and the birth. And we could only do so much.

D: *Why was it difficult?*

T: The parents were a different type of beings, and much, much denser energetically. They were the right beings, but not a very good energetic match. But it was what was needed. However, it made it difficult for her to adjust. And she tried.

D: *But she's had physical problems all her life. It's time for that to stop, isn't it?*

T: Yes, for her to do her work. And to move where she needs to go. She has also needed further adjustments some time in the past. This was what was causing the headaches and fatigue. It was also adjustments we were making, and also, through her spiritual development type work, she was involved with making adjustments on her own. But we can see that she needs to move beyond that now. She has taken on a lot. And also, with still not fully adjusted to being on this planet. But we are helping to adjust in what she is doing. The body reacts. And she can continue to make progress in another way without the physical hardship. It's time.

The SC proceeded to do a body scan, to look through the body to see what was needed to be worked on.

T: There's something going on in the brain that's—umm, it's hard to explain, but—a connection's not being made. We just have to reconnect. It needed an adjustment basically.

D: *Can you do that?*

T: Yes, we're doing it. That should help. And we're relieving some pressure from the head. And there's a lot of stress in the system that we're going to alleviate. All throughout her body.

D: *What else do you see that needs attention?*

T: The adrenals, kidneys, liver. Most of the organs are toxed. Not diseased, but toxed. They have been working overtime. So we'll help restore health there. We'll help her to have the stamina that she will need to be functioning all together, in order for her to do what she should do. She wakes up with headaches, and then has trouble going back to sleep. So this will help with that.—The organs are being rebuilt.—She can't have the fatigue any more.

D: *Maybe she was doing that because she didn't want to be in the body.*

T: Yes, that was part of it. It was a bit complicated. From time to time she was looking for a way out. It found itself overwhelming. But we've never really seen her have disease because she's stronger than she thinks. And she does have something to do here that's important. It's not time for her to leave. And she knows that. And she never would have taken herself out. Life will be a more pleasant experience for her now.—We're just circulating light through her whole system to regenerate.—It was getting almost impossible for her.

D: *Are you almost finished?*
T: Yes, we're done.

At this point the loud buzz suddenly stopped and did not return for the remainder of the session.

D: *The whole body? You've gone through it all?*
T: Yes. And it will continue. But we have it started. And there's a lot more light in her body now. And there's more strength.

Parting message: We are always here. We are here to help her. And she can call upon us at any time. And she has much assistance on many levels.

D: *When she calls upon you, how should she address you?*
T: Just think of us. Just think of the All.
D: *Think of the All and call it in when she wants to talk to you. That's wonderful. Is that all you want to tell her before we go?*
T: Yes. And to trust completely in what we have done here today.

CHAPTER TWELVE

MORE DESTRUCTION

Ellen hesitated for a while about coming off the cloud, then announced that she didn't want to come down, she wanted to go *UP*. I told her she could go anywhere she wanted to. She was giggling as she floated up away from Earth. After floating through space, she unexpectedly floated underground and came up out of a cave. The terrain was sandy red soil with a flat horizon.

E: It's reddish brown... mostly reddish. At first it reminded me of Sedona, but it's not. It's sort of that color though. Just rocks and the sand. No vegetation. I'm at the opening of the cave looking out. There's a drop off that goes straight down. I floated up out of the cave and came to the opening. It's much brighter out there so it's hard to adjust.

I wanted her to look at her body, and her conscious mind kept trying to interfere, telling her she couldn't be seeing what she was seeing. As I kept talking to her she responded, "Kind of stumpy... stumpy feet. (Laugh) I don't know how to describe them. I don't see any shoes. The ground out there is hot. I'm standing on the sand, and it doesn't make a whole lot of sense. I don't feel like I'm human. Sort of tan colored, but not like people who get a tan... like beige... I'm just kind of, I don't know... a weird little body. It feels like I'm making it up. Sort of a weird, beige, squishy, stumpy thing. (Laugh) It doesn't feel very tall. Short. My arms feel kind of long though, short legs and chubby, stumpy feet." I asked if she

147

was wearing anything. "It's like I don't need clothes, but I don't feel naked."

D: *Does the body feel male or female?*

E: Neither, or more male... it doesn't feel female.

D: *What does your face feel like?*

E: It's kind of a big head with larger eyes. (Laugh) Kind of like wearing big sunglasses. I don't see hair anywhere.

D: *Are you carrying anything?*

E: I have some kind of instruments, but I'm not really sure what they do.

D: *What does the instrument look like? Maybe we can figure it out if you describe it.*

E: Long and cylindrical, and it has some sort of grip to it... kind of like a gun, but it's not a gun.—I think it's to test the soil. As if I came up here to test the soil outside. I think it collects the soil samples. It might be two feet long.

D: *Oh, so it's not small?*

E: Maybe it's not that big. Maybe it just looks big because I'm so short.

D: *How do you test the soil with this instrument?*

E: Oh, just scoop a little bit of it up in there, and run some kind of test for something from the atmosphere to see if it's still contaminated.

D: *So you test the atmosphere as well as the soil?*

E: It's like something in the atmosphere affected the soil. I'm testing to see if it's clear and see how much it's still affected.—There's nothing here anymore. (She began to cry.)

D: *Why is that making you emotional?*

E: We didn't used to have to be in the cave. We used to be on the surface, but something happened.

D: *Are there others besides you?*

E: They're down there. I just came out to do the testing. We live way down. That's why I was floating up out of the cave.—It's all gone.

D: *What are you looking for in the soil?*

E: Radiation. To test the safety levels. And it's some better because we can come up. It's better than it was. We've been down there a long time.

D: *When you were living on the surface, what was that like?*

E: It was similar to Earth. There were plants and green and water and people and anything you have in civilization. It's weird because what seems like was there before... it's translating very much like a happy Earth. But that was a long time ago, and the body I have now doesn't seem like the body I had then.—I can't see that much of the place. It's more the feeling that what was there is gone.

D: *Were you there whenever that happened?*

E: It's like the being that was checking the soil isn't the being that was there when it was a city. It's confusing. I think it was a long time before he came out to take the samples. But it's like he found this place later. It seems the group underground lives down there because they can. But they came after the other ones that are gone from whatever happened. And they're learning about it. They knew it happened and they wanted to come and study the planet after the destruction. They came to see if it would support life there again.

D: *So you and other people came from somewhere else?* (Yes) *Did anyone tell you what caused the destruction?*

E: It seems like it was either a nuclear blast or some kind of big catastrophe, but I can't see exactly what happened. We were supposed to watch over them (getting upset) and we cared about them a lot, but they died. There was a war, but they were defenseless. They were attacked.

D: *But it makes you sad.* (Yes) *You said many people came with you?*

E: I'm not sure how many are down there, but there's enough to do the work that needs to be done.

D: *Let's see what it looks like where you came from. Where you were before you came to this place. What does that place look like?*

E: I came in a ship. There doesn't seem like that many in the ship. It looks kind of small. I'm only in one area. There are screens and panels and lights and that kind of stuff. We're in space.—I'm not sure where I came from before the ship.

D: *Did someone tell you to go to this place?*

E: It was like we weren't allowed to interfere.

D: *Anyway you landed on this place and it had already been destroyed?* (Yes.) *But you knew you couldn't live on the surface because of the radiation?*

E: Something about it is toxic, but it's also just a natural opening where we can live instead of building something out there.

D: *But you knew you couldn't stay on the surface?*

E: It's not very pleasant. It was nicer to go underground. It's very bright out there and hot. The cave was a natural formation that we could live in. It's like a laboratory set-up. We brought our instruments to do what we need to do.

D: *Are there many of you down there?*

E: It's not a high number. It's hard to tell... maybe six or twelve of us. I think some might be going off to other parts to do things.

D: *Do you have to eat food?*

E: I don't see anything around, so we must not. It doesn't look like we sleep either.

D: *So you could stay there a long time.—But your job is to go to the surface and check the soil?*

E: Yes, that's what I was doing. It's strange. It's like the bodies we have now are suited to our environment. It's just nicer to have shelter. I think it's also where we won't be noticed so much.

D: *But you said it made you sad to see what happened.*

E: It makes *me* sad. I don't know if it made *him* sad. It seems like it did, but I don't know what his emotions are like.

I moved him forward to an important day. "We're underground in our lab. We're preparing to leave. We collected our samples."

D: *Did the atmosphere change?*

E: It looks improved, but we're going away. It's like it was, and... that was it. It's still just rocky sand. It's not anything where life could be. The soil is somewhat less radioactive in comparison, but it's not what one would call someplace you could grow things.

D: *So you feel your job there is finished?*

E: Yes. We leave a lot of the equipment there. So if we needed to, we could go back later. It's highly unlikely that anyone would ever find it.

D: *Where are you going now?*

E: There's a meeting. We're on the ship, but we're also talking with others that are not on the ship.

D: *What's the meeting about?*

E: It's important to try to make sure that doesn't happen again. A lot of research was lost. Based on our analysis the planet could not be restocked or re-grown. Life couldn't be brought back in a timeframe that was acceptable, so this must be avoided in the future. Everything was destroyed.

D: *So it's just going to be abandoned?*

E: That particular one having been destroyed. And there are other places where we don't want this to happen.

D: *How do you feel about that?*

E: Like we failed.

I moved him again to another important day. "I've been offered the opportunity to go to Earth."

D: *How did you get the opportunity?*
E: I volunteered. I asked for it.
D: *Did they ask for volunteers?* (Yes.) *Where are you when this happens?*
E: I'm on a ship. My superior, my leader, said that in order to prevent this from happening on Earth they need people to go.
D: *Are they afraid the same thing could happen to Earth?* (Yes.) *And you want to go?*
E: I do. It seems like it will be very scary. Fear is not something I understand well, but after seeing the destruction first hand it was very scary.
D: *Are there others on the ship that want to go and volunteer?*
E: Yes, yes. We want to make a difference. Our crew is going. Some will stay on the ship. Some will go. The ones on the ship provide support for the ones on the surface. They'll help us remember because it's hard to remember when you're down there.
D: *What happens to the body when you leave the ship?*
E: I have to be like an Earth person.
D: *I was thinking of the body you were in... does it stay on the ship, or does it die or what?*
E: It's almost like it was a suit or a vehicle. It was utilitarian. There wasn't any pleasure or what humans would think of as normal life. It was to go and do a job. We change them a lot.
D: *Do you mean it's not a really solid body?*
E: It was solid, but it's almost like it's made of some synthetic. It's also biological.
D: *So when you leave the body, what happens to it?*
E: Well, it is not dead. It's not alive. It's a functioning bio suit.
D: *Does it deteriorate whenever you leave it?*

E: I don't think so. I'm not really sure. Perhaps others can use it for their jobs.

D: *If you're going to go to Earth to volunteer for this project, do they give you any instructions?*

E: To remember. That we would have many challenges and many things we do not understand and... to just remember to be happy. Being happy is very important.

D: *Do they think it will be easy to be happy once you go to Earth?*

E: No. There's a lot of unhappiness there. There are many sad beings there and we do not want them to be sad. They say the main thing is to be happy. That's sort of a vague concept for us because we're not really sure what that will mean.

D: *So there's not a job you have to do?*

E: Stay alive. Keep an eye on things.

D: *You said there would be many challenges.*

E: Things we haven't dealt with before.

D: *But you still want to do it?*

E: Well, it's very exciting. (Laugh) It's a lot more exciting than collecting soil samples.—The people there have forgotten certain things and they're teaching each other all wrong. And we want to help them so they won't destroy themselves. We have to help them remember.

D: *When you go to Earth to do this job, are you going to take on a body?*

E: Yes. I'm going to be a girl. (She laughed playfully.)

D: *Did you have a choice?*

E: Yes. I think so, but it's kind of weird.

D: *What's weird about it?*

E: I chose it because it's not the dominant on the planet. I wanted to see what it was like to not be of the superior—not superior, but not the dominant—not the more favored. We see that women have much trouble. Men too... but the women can have babies. And the women will help change things since they're the ones that carry the babies. They will be especially helpful in deterring the war and the destruction. If you create a life you do not want to destroy it.

D: *But when you enter the baby, do you remember why you came?*

E: At first, but when I get here nobody from my crew is around me. Or if they are, I don't remember, and I can't tell. It's very confusing.

D. *I think you are very brave to go and do it without anyone around to help you.*

E: There are some around to help us, but it's hard to... I don't know.

D: *But you don't have anybody around of your own kind, your own people.*

E: Well, we're all kind of the same everywhere, but we're all in different bodies. There are people back on the ships that can communicate with us. They can communicate with everybody, but not everybody listens.

D: *The other people don't listen?*

E: Not as well. They're not sure what it is. It scares them.

D: *If they are able to communicate with you when you're in the human body, that means you're not really alone, are you?*

E: No, but being in the physical reality you feel very separate. I don't like it... being separate.

D: *How are they going to communicate with you while you're in the body?*

E: They'll make changes to raise the vibrations. It's like getting an upgrade to the body. It's bringing in new programming. Somehow because we're doing it, it helps the others to do it.

D: *Upgrade programming?*

E: It's like if you change one part of it or even several parts of it, it starts to change even more of it without... it's hard to explain.

D: *Do they do this to the physical body before you enter it?*

E: Maybe some, but more will be done later.

D: *So it will be an ongoing process?*

E: Yes. They said we would forget for a while. Not everybody, but some people. Depending on the environment they entered into.

D: *This is important to do the upgrading and reprogramming, so you won't get lost?*

E: They say we never get lost. The human side of the mind though is sort of fighting with the nonhuman side of the mind. One wants to relax and let everything be, and the other one is just completely confused... too much going on. It makes me not want to understand everything all of the time. It makes me want to not feel stuff. I think the part that gets confused is the human part. That part isn't aware that it's something else. It's really strange. It's like being two people in one body.

D: *Did they say when you are going to remember these things when you're in the body?*

E: Eventually. Ellen knows some of it now. She worries about it a lot.

D: *Are you supposed to do anything when you get into the human body? You said you're there to help.*

E: By being here it helps... to live a life.

D: *Just by being alive?* (Yes) *You don't have to go out and do things?*

E: By living the life you have learned things and experienced things. And the information is transmitted back to the ship, and they analyze it and they make corrections.

D: *How do you transfer the information back to the ship?*

E: By being... by living... they can read it all.

D: *Well, do you know you're speaking through a physical body now?* (Yes) *And this physical body is confused.* (Yes) *She doesn't understand why she's here.*

E: She's making it more complicated than it is. She keeps thinking she has to physically go and do something.

D: *She thinks she has to change the world all by herself.*

E: That's because she thought she was alone for so long, so all that weight made her feel that way.

D: *She said she wanted to be of service to help people.*

E: She is. Deep down she knows she is, but she thinks it's not enough.

D: *She has tried to leave the planet, hasn't she?* (Tried to commit suicide.)

E: She thought she was alone, and she wasn't sure what this life was. She didn't understand the pain.

D: *She's had some negative things happen in this life, hasn't she?*

E: Yes. She wanted so much for there to be only love here. (Laugh) But she didn't understand that just by showing up she made a difference. I think she thought it was going to be much faster. She wanted to go back and not have to deal with that anymore. It seemed that things would not change, but now she knows it's different.

D: *If she had gotten out of it quickly, she wouldn't have done her job, would she?*

E: No, and she wouldn't have gotten to see the end of it from where she is now. She would have wanted to go right back to Earth. (Laugh.)

D: *Because she'd say, "I didn't fulfill my contract."* (Laugh)

E: That, yes. It is strange here.

D: *She said Earth is difficult.* (Yes) *It's not easy to be here.*

E: No, but it is not without its beauty.

D: *Do you think it will be easier for her now that she can understand what she is supposed to be doing?*

E: I think so. She has been trying to work it out for a long time. She was looking for some bigger project, but the thing is that she's already part of a bigger project. She doesn't need to go looking for something else.

D: *I've been told when the volunteers come in just to be, their energy affects many people.*

E: It does, and that's what scares her.   She didn't
      understand these emotions, especially the negative
      ones. She doesn't like the way they feel because she
      has found herself feeling badly toward other beings,
      and that scares her. She came here to help bring love,
      and when she feels bad, she feels she is spreading non-
      love.
D: *So she is supposed to love these people that have
      treated her badly?*
E: She does.
D: *That's important because we don't want her to
      accumulate karma.* (No) *We don't want her to be stuck
      here.*
E: No, and she was afraid that she already was.

One of Ellen's questions was about unusual geometric
symbols that she had been drawing. She wanted to know
where they were coming from. For many years I have been
dealing with the symbols and people's compulsion to draw
them, so I thought I had most of the answers to this, but I
always want to see what the SC has to say. Verification is
always good.

E: The symbols are part of the DNA upgrades.
D: *So it has nothing to do with what's happening on the
      ship?*
E: Kind of because that's one of the places where
      information is being transmitted from, particularly to
      her physical vessel. I'm not sure that they're
      translatable. I think some of what she is writing is a
      conflation of symbols that she has seen off world, and
      symbols ancient on this world. They cannot do any
      harm. They are powerful in some senses and they are
      positive, but she should not force it. When it is
      appropriate it will come. She has to learn more in this
      world about energies.

D: *But another part of her understands what these symbols mean?*

E: On some levels, yes. That's why she's interested in them. She used to be afraid that they were something negative, but now she's not afraid of them. She just didn't know where they were coming from. They are speaking to the smarter part of the mind which doesn't surface very much. (Laugh) She doesn't need to worry about interpreting them. She will meet others that will have the symbols too, and they will talk about them.

Ellen had some negative experiences with men in her life, and she wanted to know if there was anyone positive in her future. The SC said there was someone coming, but it didn't want to go into details because it didn't want to spoil the surprise. It found this amusing, so I knew it would be a positive experience awaiting her. She was also concerned about her son.

D: *I've been told that it is unusual for your type of being to have children once you enter the human body.*

E: She wanted to have that experience. She was afraid to have the experience. Even though she allowed it and wanted it to happen, it was decided that she was not ready. She had not adjusted. She's still working on it. She's getting better at it. He is also like us.

D: *That's why they're compatible?* (Yes) *But she wasn't to have the experience of raising him?*

E: It would be different. It would not be the full Earth experience for him, or rather so he could understand.

D: *That's why he had to be raised by the grandparents?*

E: Yes, for a while. Things will change.

D: *She wanted to know if she would be able to get custody of him. What do you think?*

E: It may not be an issue in the future. Things are changing. Custody may not be an issue. It all depends on the timeline and when we make the shift. In the new Earth it will not be an issue. He is okay for now.

D: *So it will not be an issue because some people are not going to move with the shift?*

E: Not all.

D: *But the son will because he's one of the volunteers also. (Yes) Probably the only reason she could have that baby with that type of soul.*

E: Yes. He was important because he kept her going when she did not want to.

Ellen had several questions about unusual things that happened to her as a child, but the SC said it didn't want to go there. It was best if she left that alone. She didn't need to explore it further. Things that would only upset her, that she doesn't need to worry about. She is aware, but it doesn't serve her. She needed to move forward. "That part of her life is almost like another life. It was a lot of training... a lot of Earth experience. Trying to understand the beings here. That part of her life she sort of slept through. When I say 'slept,' I mean not consciously aware of what she was doing here. They're her experiences in consciousness. She has helped many people that she has never met. Other people like her even helped her so that she could remember. It is not about physical contact. It is about the frequency and when souls move through difficult situations, it moves up different pathways for others. Mostly in their struggles, when they come through them, is like opening a door for other people. She chose to come and help work with the addictions. That's a big one. That is a big challenge to overcome it and doing that helps others to overcome it."

I asked about her physical body, "She is taking pretty good care of herself. She went through a time when she wasn't. She pushed it to the limit. It was almost 'kaput.'"

Parting message: We are trying to make her calm. She is sad that we are leaving, but we are not really leaving. (Laugh) We just want her not to worry. She is always taken care of.

I have similar cases that are sprinkled through my other books of people who had been present when a planet was destroyed. They were either a witness to it, on the surface or from a spacecraft, or returned to the planet to see nothing but destruction. This is always a very emotional experience for them. It had a lasting affect that carried forward into the present life, although on an unconscious level. Many have reported a deep feeling of sadness that was overwhelming, but had no logical basis. Some have told me that even from childhood they felt intense sadness. They said their family could not remember ever seeing them smile or appear happy.

Others talk of an irrational fear that has haunted them and held back their lives. Naturally these type of underlying emotions caused problems in their present life. It also explains their eagerness to volunteer to come to Earth at this critical time in history. They had seen terrible destruction first hand, and didn't want it to happen to another planet. So when their superiors said that Earth was in trouble, they were among the first to raise their hands and volunteer. Yet they did not realize the difficulties that would lie ahead with all memories being erased upon entering this world. It does help now to realize they have an important job to do, even though it is not dramatic. Their energy is incredibly important in order for the necessary changes to occur. All they are to do is simply *be!*

CHAPTER THIRTEEN

LIFE AS A TREE & LEMURIA

Marian raised horses on her ranch, married for several years with no children. She didn't talk about any problems, only wanted to know about her purpose. I always tell people if they come to see me merely out of curiosity that they are going to get more than they bargained for. This is a case in point. I must always expect the unexpected.

Instead of coming off the cloud, Marian went very far out in space. She could see the Earth as a beautiful, blue-green sphere with stars all around it. As she floated she became aware of some type of spaceship "parked" out there. When I asked her where she wanted to go, or what she wanted to do, she said, "I want to go live on the ship. I like the idea of being on the ship and not being earthbound. Being able to fly all around to different galaxies, and go to different planets. I don't really want to go back to Earth." I asked if she wanted to explore the ship closer. "I think I already know what the ship looks like. It seems I've already lived on the ship, and I have been on Earth for awhile, for some reason. And I'm wanting to go back home. The ship will take me back home." I told her she could do anything she wanted, and she said she wanted to go onboard.

D: *All right. How would you get on the ship?*
M: I think I can just beam myself over. I can just think myself on.—(Surprised laugh) I come into the holodeck where... I come into a redwood forest. The beautiful

trees and the ocean with the sunset, but it's really on the holodeck on the ship. I'm there, and I'm creating it within this hologram. It's beautiful. Those trees are my family.

D: *Why do you think that?*

M: Because I lived in one of these trees at one point, for a long, long, long time. I think I just decided I wanted to be a big tree, and to experience being a giant tree. But I grew up as a baby tree, so the big trees all around were my parents, and aunts and uncles, where we were all family. I started out as a little nut that grew into a seedling, and grew and grew and grew. And we would absorb the healing energy of the magnificent sun. And it would send out leaves, and it would feed the planet. And we were just *so* happy there. (Emotional.)

D: *As a big tree you would have lived a long time.*

M: I did—thousands and thousands of years. But then the tree didn't die, I just left the tree.

D: *You experienced all you could.* (Yes) *What was it like to be a tree?*

M: (Deep sigh) Ahh.... wonderful! I had all the squirrels and birds. It was like I was a consciousness, and they all lived within me. And I loved them and nurtured them, and they loved me.

D: *But then you got to the point that you couldn't learn any more from being a tree?*

M: It was like I was told that—I don't know who told me, but I was told to go back to the ship for my next assignment.

D: *That's where you get your assignments, on the ship?* (Yes) *So right now you're looking at this again on the holodeck just to remember or what?*

M: Yes. I need to be reminded of why I am still so connected to trees. Why I paint them, why they speak to me.

D: *So that's the way it works? You learn all you can from
      one experience, and then go on to the next?* (Yes) *So
      what are you going to do now?*

M: I get beamed back onto Earth into what looks like
      Lemuria, over by where Hawaii is now.

D: *You didn't get to go back home?*

M: No. I was sent back on another assignment. I was sent
      to Lemuria. I haven't been home in a long, long, long
      time. (Becoming emotional.)

D: *Where is home? Do you know?*

M: (Softly crying, then a whisper.) I think it's on the Sun.
      It's very bright. It's so full of love (Emotional).
      Nobody has bodies, we're all just light beings. There's
      so much love. (She began to cry.)

This is the way many of my clients have described
God, the Source that every one of us originally came from. It
is often compared to the bright light of the Sun and sometimes
called the "Great Central Sun." It is always described as a
place of incredible love.

D: *But you had to leave home at one time?*

M: I was supposed to. I was told to. I was told it was my
      job, and that I could come back. That I needed to go
      and spread some light. (Crying.)

D: *Did you go many places?*

M: Yes. (Sigh) I've been everywhere. (Still crying softly.)

D: *Just on Earth, or did you experience other things?*

M: I think mostly on Earth. I think the Earth was where I
      felt would be best.

D: *So now you long to go home, but I guess you can't go
      back until you've finished the job?*

M: I think I can go home soon. I think I'm going to be
      able to go home after this life, after Marian is done. I
      think I've *earned* it.

D: *Have you learned everything there is to learn?*

M: Yes. I think I'll go home in a vehicle, though, like a
      Merkaba, with lots of light and colors. It's like it's my
      own little ship.

In the Old Testament the Merkaba refers to the fiery
chariots seen by various prophets, especially Ezekiel. In
modern day it seems to refer to a UFO that was described in
the best terms they could find in that time period.
      I wanted to find out more about her mention of
Lemuria. Lemuria was supposed to be a lost continent that was
located in the Pacific Ocean. It is believed that it met the same
fate as Atlantis, which was located in the Atlantic Ocean.
Lemuria is believed to be older.

M: Hmm—The land of Mu. I was supposed to be a healer
      of some sort, but I was a man. It's kind of like what the
      kahunas are now, but I was some sort of village
      shaman. We put energy into rocks.

Kahunas are the women holy priestesses that are now
on the islands of Hawaii.—I asked her to see herself putting the
energy into rocks.

M: I was living in a village. It was beautiful, it was by the
      water, and we had these big rocks like monoliths. They
      were really giant rocks! We didn't put them there, the
      ships put them there. But I would go and put energy
      into the rocks. (Pause) I just put my hands on the
      rocks, and infuse the rocks. I touch the rocks. And I
      focus real strong on this energy, and it goes into the
      rocks. And it stays there. Then people that are sick can
      go to the rocks and extract the energy, and be all better.
D: *So the energy remains in the rocks so it can be used
      later.*
M: Yes. Still there. Even though now the rocks are
      underwater.

D: *You said the rocks were put there by others?* (Yes)
      How did that happen?
M: They moved them with their ships, in the air.
D: *From other places?*
M: Yes, from other places because they were too heavy.
      It's over land, so they would just bring them—they
      floated through the air. It was really something to
      watch.
D: *You were privileged to be able to see it. What did it
      look like?*
M: (Chuckle) Seemed normal because I was used to it.
      Not everybody was allowed to see it, though. They
      usually did it early in the morning before everybody got
      up. But it just looked like a big disk ship sort of going
      "jzhhhhhhhhhhh" with one of these big rocks that were
      like long, cigar-shaped rocks. And they would put
      them in the earth.
D: *They laid them on the earth?*
M: No. They would dig out a hole and stick them in there.
      And then sometimes they would carve the rock, like
      faces. But that wasn't my job. Mine was just to put the
      healing energy in the rocks.
D: *Why did these beings put them there?*
M: I think they wanted to show us what they were capable
      of, and they wanted to help us. It was a teaching
      mechanism, somehow, because we were also taught to
      move things with *our* minds. We were able to do that
      too because the rocks we moved were smaller. Some
      of us, not all of us. You had to really, really, really
      believe that they were just like us.
D: *You don't think you could have moved a big one with
      just your mind?*
M: No, but I could have with some others, like twenty or
      thirty more.
D: *They would all focus?* (Yes) *And they wanted to show
      you it was possible?* (Yes) *Of course, they did it with a
      ship, a craft, didn't they?*

M: No, they did it with their minds on the craft.

Somewhere in here the tape began to speed up, and got worse by the end. It sped up so bad that the voices sounded "chipmunky," and were difficult to transcribe. I wondered if it had anything to do with the subject matter: putting energy into objects?

D: *I thought maybe the craft was generating an energy.*
M: Well, the ship and the beings on the ship were all like one being. They did it all through magnetism. So they would focus the magnetics.
D: *So they were able to function as one mind?* (Yes) *And were then able to move these things.* (Yes!) *Did they tell you to put energy into the rocks?*
M: Not with words—because they didn't talk with words. They talked with blocks of thought, so they sent me these blocks of thought. And it felt very good that that's what I could do.
D: *Did you ever see these beings?* (Yes) *So they weren't always in the craft?*
M: Oh, no. Some of them would sometimes come out. They scared some people though. But they were mostly beings of light. They were like spheres. They could take a form, but mostly they were just spheres of light that emanated all these beautiful colors. And they were scary because they emanated so much love and wisdom. And they would take forms that would look sort of like a human form, but it was really light. Light beings. They didn't really have arms or legs. They were tall, and just luminescent, liquid diamond light.
D: *Sounds beautiful.*
M: They were from the Sun.
D: *Did they tell you that?*
M: I think I just knew because that's where I was from. And they were just coming to check on me because we were all from the same place.

D: *Did you have a memory of coming from the Sun?*

M: Kind of. I remember just rolling into a baby's body and thinking, oh no! And feeling really heavy, dense.

    I asked what he and the others in the village looked like. He was very tall, with long thick black hair and golden brown skin. He had feathers and stones and rocks around his neck and head. And was wearing something like a skirt. The women in the village were beautiful with long curlier hair. Looking rather like modern day Indians or Hawaiians.

D: *Were you trained to be a shaman?*

M: I think I was born to it. My parents, my mother was a medicine woman. They're gone now. They died, but I finished doing what they did. I was doing other things—hunting, and people would come and talk to me. And I would talk to them about things, and give them rocks to hold onto.

D: *Why did you give them rocks?*

M: Because that would change their vibrational frequency. It was physics. It would make them feel different, and better. And they believed it. So because they believed it, they would make it so.

D: *Were these just ordinary rocks?*

M: No, basically they're lightly colored stones that we would find—gemstones and pebbles—on the beach. I would put the healing energy into them.

D: *Just like you did with the giant rocks.* (Yes) *So you would give these to the people, and it would make them well.* (Yes) *But then you were told, through your mind, to also put the energy in the large rocks?*

M: Yes, because it would make the Earth feel better. It's for both the Earth and the people.

D: *Were the large stones put in any kind of a design or formation?*

M: Sort of an antenna. But it's in a formation that looks like a straight line.

D: *What do you mean by an "antenna"?*

M: It sends out frequencies into the solar system. To let all the beings in the solar system know how precious planet Earth is.

D: *Do these beings live with you, or do they stay on their craft?*

M: They go all over, They just come and check on me. They go everywhere. They go to other planets. They can do it really fast. They just sort of zip in and out. But I have to do this with them, or call them, and they will show up. They're family. I don't call them unless I really need something though.

D: *Why do you call them "family"?*

M: Because we're all from the Sun.

They were all connected, just like when she was the tree and was connected to all of nature because everything came from the Sun. He, at one time, had a real family, but they had gone away. But there were many little ones in the village, and everyone was happy living there together. They all took care of each other. There was very little sickness, mostly accidents because he could heal the people. There didn't seem like much more to explore at this point, so I moved him forward to an important day, and asked what he was seeing.

M: The whole island just wiped out. A big flood. We sink; the whole island sinks. And then I die. But we don't really die, we're just all covered with water.

D: *Was it sudden?*

M: Yes, all of a sudden. Just one morning, like a tsunami.

D: *You didn't have any warning it was coming?*

M: No. But it's okay.

I asked if the beings tried to warn them, but he said they weren't around. There probably wouldn't have been much that they could do anyway. It happened so suddenly that the entire island was covered.

M: Many people died. Of course, nobody really dies. They just floated off to another place. It was scary, though, of course. It was a huge island. So many thousands and thousands, hundreds of thousands died that we didn't even know of. It was like a continent sinking.

D: *A continent rather than an island?*

M: A big continent. We were just on the edge of what we thought was our island. But we didn't know how big it was because we only went so far. But when we got out of our bodies and looked down and saw how big Lemuria was, it was the size of a huge continent. We were just another group on the other side. We just stayed close by because it was safe. From here I can see that the whole continent sank, and just went underwater. It was like a big crack in the Earth, like an earthquake. That's what it was, a giant earthquake. And the ocean floor just opened up and sucked under the whole thing. Swallowed it up. And all the water from all over came rushing in. The Pacific Ocean is very big.

D: *I wonder if the beings could have done anything even if they were there.*

M: I think they were watching and maybe took some on their ships. That was all that was meant to be.

D: *There was nothing they could do to stop it, I guess.*

M: No, it was Mother Earth doing this. She was calibrating herself. There was some disturbance on the other side of the planet that was causing an adjustment.

D: *What are you seeing?*

M: I'm seeing these big waves of solar activity coming into the Earth. An adjustment. I don't know what it means, other than it was necessitated by some group that messed up the balance around the grid of the planet. And that made the earthquakes and the tidal wave.

169

D: *What was the adjustment on the other side of the world?*

M: I think it was another experiment. They did an experiment trying to adjust something, and it backfired.

D: *From your perspective you can know a lot. Who were the ones who were doing the experiment?*

M: They're not from Earth, they were from another system. I don't know who they were. I can't see them. They're like a group mind, somehow, but they're not from the Sun. Our group would have never... our group loved planet Earth because our group was from the Sun. So we help nurture planet Earth and her lifeforms. We helped—not just us—we all helped make her into the lush paradise that she is. Our group still loves this planet.

D: *Can you find out anything else about the experiment?*

M: I think they were just curious to see what would happen if they messed up the grids. Just kind of watching as an experiment. (Sigh) I can't pronounce where they're from.

D: *That's okay. But they were allowed to do this?*

M: They're in this dimension of free will, and no one stopped them. They had no regard for all the life forms that would be affected. They were just cold and observing, not malicious. Just like, okay, let's see what happens if we do this.

D: *Do you know what they thought after it happened and they saw all the destruction?*

M: They had no human remorse. They didn't have the genetic code to feel compassion or remorse. They just left to go and find another venue for experimenting. Back to their own dimension to report back.

D: *As you look down at the Earth, does it take it a while to return to normal?*

M: Oh, nearly hundreds of thousands of years. It's as if she just needs to rest and take a nap, and heal. And let the healing power of the Sun help.

D: *But all the humans weren't destroyed, were they?*

M: Some survived, and others were brought in. The beings came in to help change the DNA to allow for... it was all an experiment, too, but different from the seeding. The Council of Nine took it upon themselves to help repopulate the Earth.

D: *Why did they have to change the DNA?*

M: Because the DNA was only two strands, and the Lemurians had twelve.

D: *Does this make any difference?*

M: Yes. They're able to be one with nature, and they're all connected to the universal mind.

D: *That's why they were able to use the energy?*

M: Yes, because they have powers.

D: *This is because of the DNA?*

M: Partially. We came from the Sun.

D: *I was wondering what was so special about the twelve strand DNA?*

M: It had volume to it and it was so vast, interdimensional, the power of the Creator. They were very loving... only for the good.

D: *After everyone was destroyed and they decided to repopulate, why couldn't they just allow it to be the twelve strands like it was?*

M: The Council of Nine felt this would be better because they thought too much had been given to us too fast. We weren't ready, so it was a way of slowing down evolution.

D: *They thought it was better to go backwards?*

M: Yes. Weird because the cavemen and the Neanderthals and ancient men after Lemuria, only had two strands. And their brains were not like... they were like animals.—They came in and interspersed with their DNA. And it became very complex, and then we had gone back to the early stages, and they left.

D: *But they thought it was better to go backwards and have people start over again?* (Yes) *They lost all their powers, didn't they?* (Yes) *Do you think that was a good idea?*

M: It's not for me to judge. I was just observing.

D: *But do you know what the plan was, if it was returned to just two strands? Was it supposed to develop further after that?*

M: It's changing now.

D. *How is it changing?*

M: I don't know how to explain it, other than "it just is." It's part of the plan to allow it to morph into what it could be, should be, has been, to help take all of us to a new frequency. Not everybody can go. Not everybody will get their twelve strands.

D: *This will take a while, won't it?*

M: It's been going on for a long time.

D: *The DNA being restructured?*

M: Yes, it's coming. It's happening faster now.

D: *Why is it happening faster?*

M: Because of the quickening... because of the grid being aligned... the tears being repaired.

D: *So now the DNA is being allowed to change again?* (Yes) *How will people notice that in our world today?*

M: Well, some people won't notice, but those that are aware will feel well connected to "All" that is. Their senses will be heightened. They'll become lighter... more transparent.

D: *Will people around them notice this?*

M: Some will. Some will just keep sleepwalking.

D: *I was thinking if they were becoming more transparent it should be noticeable.*

M: They'll just become invisible.

D: (This was a surprise.) *Eventually?*

M: Yes. But they'll still be there. It's like changing channels on the TV.

D: *But if they become invisible, those around them won't see them anymore?* (Yes) *Where will they be?*

M: On a different channel.

D: *Another dimension?* (Yes) *Will they be aware of it?*
       (Yes) *They'll know something has happened?* (Oh,
       yes.) *But the other people won't?* (No) *Is this changing
       of DNA going to have an effect on psychic abilities?*

M: Yes. People will become much more telepathic. No
       need for words, communicating through the heart and
       through thought blocks. No way to lie or cheat. You
       won't need to.

D: *Everybody would know.*

M: Yes, that's a good thing.

D: *It is. But why is this happening now? It's being
       allowed to come back.*

M: It is time. It has to happen. Time flew for the Gaia
       (Mother Earth) to graduate and take her best students
       with her. And leave behind the destruction and
       corruption and negativity and darkness. It's like she's
       splitting off, morphing into two... a New Earth... a New
       Jerusalem, and there won't be a nuclear holocaust that
       was being created. This is all a part of the grand design
       of the great light in heaven, the Council of Nine.

D: *The ones who go are connected to the twelve strands of
       DNA or what?*

M: Yes, the ones that go—there will be some that stay
       behind to help the others that are left because they'll be
       so afraid. Some will stay out of sacrifice because there
       will be panic. It's very sad.

D: *The ones who are left behind... their DNA has not been
       changed?*

M: No, they won't allow it. I don't know how it works,
       other than the people have lead shoes on their feet and
       they don't want to lighten up.

D: *So it's a personal choice then?* (Yes) *Okay, you can
       see everything from there. You said Lemuria was
       where Hawaii is now?* (Yes) *That's all that's left of
       that whole continent?*

M: Yes, that and part of Japan and Singapore. It was a huge continent. The Baja peninsula, California was part of the coast. It was huge.

D: *Are there any other parts still left?*

M: Yes, but I don't know the names of the islands.

D: *The islands in the Pacific?*

M: Yes. It went as far as Japan. It was very big.

D: *So it sounds like it covered most of the Pacific Ocean, didn't it?*

M: I think so.

D: *We have heard a lot about Atlantis. Did that come after Lemuria? (Yes) Were there any survivors from the Lemurian disaster?*

M: Some of them went over in the beginning. They were the good ones. I think they were airlifted by some of the space brothers to where Atlantis would develop.

D: *So they started a new civilization in that part of the world? (Yes) These are things we don't know about today.*

M: Many people know about this.

D: *Well, they know about Atlantis, but they don't know much about Lemuria. (Yes) And they don't know about the DNA. But this is part of my job, to get all of this information. (Yes) But eventually you were told to live in the body of Marian? Is that right? (Yes) Why did you decide to come back into a human body in our time right now?*

M: I just came to be part of the shift.

This part was answering the questions so well I didn't think it would be necessary to call forth the SC. It agreed, so I switched to Marian's questions. Of course, the first is always what I call "the eternal question." What is her purpose? Why is she here? What is she supposed to be doing?

M: She's just a light being from the Sun that is here to raise the vibrations, to help purify the water and to help raise the vibrations so that everybody can feel better.

D: *It doesn't sound like she has had too many lives on the planet Earth. Is that right?*

M: She's had 500 or more.

D: *On Earth?* (Yes) *I didn't think it was that many.*

M: She's had a lot of experience and some were quick... just to experience the births and the deaths. That's really not many lives when you consider over millions of years.

D: *Yes. Why did she come to Earth to experience all of these things?*

M: (Laugh) Because she loves the rush and remembering where she really comes from. She loves the rush of love and giving and receiving. She loves this planet.— She just wants to have fun. She doesn't want things to get too heavy. She gets so sad when people are sad around her.—She can read minds.

One of her questions dealt with whether she had any karma to repay. If so, she wanted to get rid of it. They said, "She's done pretty much. It's taken her a long time." Marian was essentially living a perfect life, a resting life: doing what she wanted, no physical problems. She was sending out light to everything, the people, the animals and the earth. It sounded like she was one of the second wave: the observers who are just here to generate and spread positive energy to others. And she was doing her job well.

I asked about some problems she experienced in her early years when she was growing up. "She has always been protected. She was a catalyst for others working out their karma. And it helped her too, but mostly she's always been a catalyst. For people to learn love."

Before we came to the end of the session I thought of a few more questions, "Those rocks that were in Lemuria, the ones that were placed there that had the energy, do they still exist or did they go to the bottom of the ocean?"

M: Some are still on the Big Island of Hawaii. They're hidden. They're buried in the lava.

D: *There's a lot of lava there.* (Yes) *So that island still has a lot of energy from them?* (Yes, oh Yes.)

CHAPTER FOURTEEN

THE COUNCIL

Whas confused. "It
feels like it's the wrong place. It doesn't feel like
it's an Earth life I'm looking for. I feel I'm in
another dimension. I see the universe. Stars and galaxies. The
cloud feels like a vehicle of some sort. It's taking me through
a hole. I just zoomed out there and the cloud is more like a ball
of light. I see many things... galaxies and there's some place
I'm trying to go. I'm going to a certain system where I've
lived far longer than I have here. There are several stars and
several solar systems and I feel like I'm going home to my
friends. They missed me."

D: *Are you drawn to one certain place in this system?*
C: Yes. It just appeared there. I'm on one of the planets
     now.—There's a very large building. And many people
     walking around doing their thing. And the building is a
     headquarters of some sort. I'm walking in.
D: *Why do you think it's some sort of headquarters?*
C: My office is here.—There are some people that are
     aware that I just go there energetically. I spent a lot of
     time here.
D: *Do you want to go to your office?* (Yes) *Tell me what
     that looks like.*
C: It's on the top floor and it's all glass. I see mountains
     in the distance and water fountains everywhere in the
     city.

D: *What's in your office?*

C: Not much. It's very large and spacious. The computer is in my desktop. The whole desk is my data base. The screen is the top of my desk.

I asked her to become aware of her body and it seemed human, yet somehow different. She didn't feel male or female, "Neither. Both." She was wearing pants and a shirt and a jacket that flowed. When I asked if she felt young or old, she said, "I feel very old and young... ageless. I'm like a human that doesn't identify as male or female, or young or old. It's a very advanced human society."

Besides her entire desktop being a computer there were also other strange things in her office. "There is glass hanging in the room. These are windows and screens for data bases. I can point to them and they activate."

D: *So it's not the glass windows you look out of?*

C: Right. It's not the glass windows. More like glass panels. When I point at them they activate and things move as I look for data. Different ones do different things.

D: *What is your job in this office?*

C: I'm a director of some sort. I'm part of a council.

D: *Is that why you have to have a data base?*

C: Yes, we monitor systems.

D: *Other systems besides your own?*

C: Yes. There are other buildings on other planets that are part of this network. These are benevolent governments. It's the same building on many planets. (She began to cry.) I miss this place! My friends are here. My whole family is here in this system.—I've been stuck on this project on Earth.

D: *What do you mean, the project on Earth?*

C: We're part of the experimenters with the project on Earth. We're the ones who masterminded it. We're the part of a group of species... many... we aren't the only

178

ones. We're part of the human experiment on Earth, and gave it its challenges and watch its projects and process progress.

D: *Were you there at the beginning?* (Yes) *That would have been a long time, wouldn't it?* (Yes) *But you said you were monitoring several different systems.*

C: There are many different experiments on other planets in the universe. Earth is not the only one. There are more messed up ones.

D: *Earth is one of the more messed up ones?*

C: Not Earth. The human species has gone off track.

D: *Have they gone off track everywhere?*

C: No. Some have evolved quite nicely.

D: *What caused Earth to get messed up?*

C: It was interference.

D: *Can you tell what it was?*

C: I'm looking at it right now... the data base... I'm checking history. Some sort of biological bacteria introduction that messed up the DNA, but we decided to go with it and see what happens.

This sounded exactly like what Phil reported in *Keepers of the Garden* about a meteorite that crashed into Earth in the early developing times. It carried an unfamiliar bacteria that introduced disease. It ended up spoiling the grand experiment of creating the perfect human being on Earth. She was correct in that the council was very sad that their experiment had been ruined. They had to make a choice, either destroy everything and start over or allow it to continue, knowing it would never be the perfect species it was intended to be. It was decided that because so much time and effort had been invested in the experiment to allow it to continue. This is also an explanation for some of the experimentation still being conducted by extraterrestrials. They are attempting to bring the human race back to the original plan, of a species where the individuals would never get sick and only die when they were ready.

D: *You mean the meteorite spoiled the original plan?*

C: Yes, but we believe that nothing is an accident.

D: *I've been told that the human body shape is the most functional. Is that why it's used in many places?*

C: Yes, it's a combination of many species. There is Reptilian. There is Silicon. There are many species that contributed to the human vehicle for their consciousness.

D: *If you have been around since the very beginning, you are ageless then, aren't you?*

C: We're not in time. We're not in the same kind of time.

D: *On Earth we think of it as a great amount of time going by to develop from a cell to the human body it is now. But you don't recognize time?*

C: Things just manifest. As they're thought of they are born.

D: *But you were apparently happy there on the council, weren't you?* (Yes.) *Why did you decide to leave?*

C: I decided I wanted to experience it from the inside out instead of watching. I knew it would be hard, and I was greatly discouraged by others from doing it. They needed me there. And they didn't want me to not be available. But I decided to go because I thought I could fix things from the inside. I'm a Master.

D: *If you're a Master, you ought to be able to accomplish anything.*

C: Yes, but it didn't work out like that.

D: *Sounds like you're stubborn if you went against their advice.*

C: Yes, and that is one of my qualities. Because I'm an inventor, and in order to invent and create you must know creation from all angles. I'm a Creator.

D: *You said you helped create life on Earth from the very beginning?*

C: I just helped. There was a large team.

D: *But then you decided to go and experience it?*

C: Yes, to make myself small. To be in a microcosm.

D: *You had to start there? I'm trying to understand what you mean.*

C: Well, microcosm was at the smallest level of being, started at molecular with protocols. Before going into forms.

D: *So you have to start out at that level if you go to Earth?*

C: I didn't have to. I did what I wanted to. Other people see the need for that, but I didn't.

D: *So is that the first form you go into? The microcosm level?*

C: Particle... the consciousness of a particle. Smaller than an electrode... smaller than nuclei... smaller than... small. No word for it in this language.

D: *What were you going to experience at that level?*

C: Energy, just energy. It's a very huge thrill being this small.

D: *Are you going to have to go through a very long process before being allowed to go back?*

C: I can go back any time.

D: *If you wanted to start out by being pure energy, what kind of a form do you move into after that?*

C: I tried them all when I was tree, was electron, was particle, was wave of light, was nuclei, was star, was planet, was ocean, was water, was animal, was reptile, was human, was me, was rock, was pebble, was many things.

D: *Did you learn anything while being all those different forms?*

C: No, nothing to learn... just to be. It's not about lessons. It is about experience. Just to experience.

D: *But you didn't have to come. It was your own decision?*

C: Yes, and I had to push for it. They tried to block and I said, "Move."

D: *Then they didn't try to stop you?*

C: No. Free will is always honored.

D: *So you went through all those forms and then you decided to go into the human body?*

C: Yes, and I was human for a while, and stopped being human... was too crude at the time.

D: *When you were human did you experience many different kinds of lives?*

C: All of them have lives. Experience them all. Wanted to find out what was wrong. What is wrong in the wiring? How did the bacteria interfere and how to repair.

D: *How to repair the damage?*

C: Damage was redirection into a different type of evolution. Can only fix the damage from inside in this situation. Cannot fix as the observer.

D: *So this is why you experienced many different types of lives?*

C: Yes. Had to look at it all.

D: *And some of the lives were negative as well as positive, weren't they?*

C: Yes, but negative is an illusion. Negative and positive are both construction material. Negative is evolutionary catalyst.

D: *But you know humans consider something negative as being bad.*

C: They should reword it to *evolutionary catalyst*. We have been given on purpose these catalysts for evolution. These things that appear negative... these things are on purpose.

D: *But you've been doing this for a long time in Earth terms, I guess.*

C: I have gone back and forth. I have not been here all the time. Yes, and longer than human projects on Earth, we have had more before this. There were more human experiments before the Ice Ages of the Earth. There have been six... the sixth of many... of several.

D: *What do you mean? Explain what the six are.*

182

C: Earth has been hundreds of thousands of years with no life on it at all. And in between are small windows to have complex life forms and we have utilized those every time.

D: *That's what I was wondering, what the six phases are.*

C: These are not phases... only experiments. Six windows in time when human complex life form could be here in Earth. When human and plant and animal could exist. Was not human the first two times. First two times was only other species. Not necessarily ones you would recognize in this space and time. The humans are a more recent experiment with combinations after experimenting with many other life forms. Human was maybe the greatest idea.

D: *The way they are right now?* (No) *That was the sixth phase?*

C: No, there were no phases. It was just experiments. And this was the sixth experiment here, and the human life form was in the last four experiments here. But we have experimented with humans in many galaxies, and they are the more recent invention than the other species that are older. But have had flaws and we are finding more consciousness that can hold more consciousness. And to find a physical vehicle that can hold and guide consciousness. We have not perfected this idea of physical vehicle in any form yet, but we have eternity to discover this.

D: *To try to perfect it?*

C: No perfection... more experience. As soon as you reach perfection it is not perfect anymore because you want to try something different.

D: (Laugh.) *But some of the species, the humans, that were on Earth didn't survive and continue, did they?*

C: That is correct. It wipes the slate clean. Started over.

D: *It wasn't working out the way it was supposed to?*

C: There is no "supposed to" or "not supposed to." Sometimes we let it go until it looked like it was no longer constructive. Sometimes the devolution would endanger other experiments, and we would need to contain the experiment.

D: *It's a very large project, isn't it?*

C: It is universal. There are other universes too.

D: *And each one would affect the other, so you would have to monitor it all?*

C: Yes, and be careful that experiments do not bleed into each other. They will cause damage to the progress of another. The human experiment when humans have sometimes evolved technologically interfered with other experiments and needed to be contained.

D: *Are there other beings like yourself that have come to Earth?*

C: Many. Specifically now.

D: *They could have stayed over there too, couldn't they? (Yes.) They all volunteered to come?*

C: No one is forced.

D: *I have talked to many different types of volunteers who chose to come at this time in evolution. What is your job while you are here?*

C: Rewire from the inside out.

D: *All humans or just certain ones?*

C: Just certain ones that teach others to rewire themselves. We are here to teach. Each person can rewire themselves... rewire... their neurological system is damaged. And so neurological rewiring can only be done by each individual in every form, and cannot be rewired for them. And this is an experiment, and we are assisting in this experiment to nudge it in a certain direction at this time. We will leave after this time.

D: *Why does the human need to be rewired?*

C: To hold more consciousness.

D: *So it's not to hold more knowledge.*

C: No. Explain: the evolution of the heart and compassion is what is missing technically. Humans have proceeded to technological advances before without heart balance,

184

without heart evolution. And it has been disastrous. So we are here to evolve heart first until the heart is aligned with this knowledge.

D: *Why does the human have to have more consciousness?*

C: In order to wield power benevolently because misuse of power is human misfiring. This biological bacterial damage done to neurological system happened early in experiment before human was fully formed.

D: *So the idea is to stop negativity in this way?*

C: Or to redirect how negativity is used because each is required. Both positive and negative, cannot be one without the other. And dark and light are part of the tapestry that builds the picture. Both must be learned to be used wisely, for positive can be misused as well.

D: *I know there are many volunteers coming who want to be in the human form just to help. But it seems you have a different mission.*

C: We are not here to save human race. We are here to see where this can go.

D: *Is this why you chose to enter the body of Carol?*

C: Yes, and why I chose the hardest miswiring to rewire. For this way is the only way to show others how to rewire this deep biological damage.

D: *You came into her body as a baby?*

C: I was born into this body.

D: *You'd already had other lives as a human?*

C: They are all my lives. I am one self. It is all the same one living all lives.

D: *So the purpose of Carol is that you'll rewire her so she'll teach others.*

C: Yes, for those who will listen.

D: *You know she has a metaphysical school where she's trying to teach others.*

C: Yes, I am one of the creators of the school. There are one thousand involved in the creation of the school. I am the one who has the—shall we say—brains of the operation.

D: *So you put the idea into her mind to have the school?*

C: No, it was the group who put the idea in her mind. It is an idea she was born with... an idea that was put in her mind. It was her destiny.

D: *And it's a good idea. She is helping people.* (Yes) *But she is having problems right now with the school.*

C: She is identifying too much with human conditions.

D. *She feels it's kind of stumped, and it's not reaching as many as it should.*

C: This is correct. It's not reaching as many as it should. She needs to simply relax and let it flow. Too much human condition involved.

D: *Can you give her any ideas on how to attract new students?*

C: We are setting that up. We are what she calls "in one."

D: *She's doing it on the Internet. I guess you know what that is.*

C: Yes. Elementary version of what we have. Internet is the birth of the mass conscious information access to all. It is the first step, but we will stop this if heart is not balanced in this species.

D: *How will you stop the experiment?*

C: We have cosmos destruction ability. All we need to do is redirect cosmic forces. Their destruction will happen if technological advances continue without heart.

D: *But that would mean everyone would be destroyed.*

C: No, nothing is destroyed.

D: *That would destroy the whole experiment.*

C: It will continue, but it will start over. Nothing is ever destroyed. It is only turned into energy and energy can be reused and reassigned in a way that no one is killed. It isn't real.

D: *But wouldn't that be admitting defeat if you redid the experiment?*

C: No, it is admitting wrong direction... a different direction.—There is much confidence that it will go in the right direction for ones such as ourselves here. For we are nudging experiment from the inside instead of how we used to from the outside. We are nudging from inside instead of from outside. For this has to be an expansion from within the form.—We do see that direction is not fully completed. There are still many humans listening to... misdirection.

D: *Does this have anything to do with the new Earth that's being formed?*

C: There is only one Earth, but it will be transformed or not.

D: *I've heard so many different things. I've heard about it shifting vibrations.*

C: There will be other dimensions of Earth. There will be more than one... way more. There will be more than two. There will be many versions of Earth.

D: *But there will still be negativity on one version?*

C: Yes, and even darker reality than what you are imagining. There are hell versions of Earth, for we are testing human vehicle to see how much it can take.

D: *I've been told that the ones that are negative cannot go to the higher versions of Earth?*

C: They will settle into the version that they match. The ones who cannot match certain vibrations will die. We are cleansing the species of defective specimens. Anyone who makes choice from within gets to pass "go."

D: (Laugh) *So that is part of your job, to prepare people so they'll know something is happening?*

C: All know that something is happening. It is many offerings for many different styles. Hers is one of many different offerings for different styles. There are some who go with different styles.

D: *What do you mean by different styles?*

C: Of awakening. There is one goal but many pass.

D: *There's no "one way" that it has to be?*

C: There is only *the* way it has to be. Human heart must evolve to go any further, for we have let human experiment go on with technological advances in its present state without evolution of the heart. And we have let these go very, very far... have let these go extremely far to see what happens. And we have already seen what happens... no need to repeat. Now either new direction or not at all.

D: *So what did you see that was going to happen?*

C: Star Wars is true. It happened in a galaxy far away.

D: *So if they continue what they're doing, they can destroy the Earth themselves?*

C: They could destroy entire systems. And other experiments we do not want them to touch.

D: *So that's why you're watching so they don't go in that direction?*

C: To contain experiments run amuck.

D: *Humans don't know these things, and they do stupid things.*

C: She wanted to see what lifetime is connected to this present one, and I am the one.

D: *You're the one on the other planet who volunteered to come down and live in this crazy world.*

C: I did not come down. I came over. (I laughed.)

I then called forth the SC and asked it why it chose that lifetime for her to see.

C: So she can see that she's a group soul. This is not just one being. She saw one aspect on one planet, but there is a group on many planets that she's a part of.

D: *The other being on what it called the "council."* (Yes) *And she's a part of that?*

C: Yes, the council is all one being.

D: *Why did you want her to know about this?*

C: So she can see where the school really comes from. She has suspected that there is a group energy behind it. She knew that, but she didn't want to think it was so big because she didn't want to think of herself as "special." In a way she didn't want it to go to her head.

I then asked about her physical problems, especially the thyroid for which she was taking medicine. It was a very serious condition. The SC said it was caused by fear. "Anger, too caused it... incredible anger. There is more connected to anger than fear."

D: *Where did the anger come from?*
C: She's had a bumpy ride.
D: *She said she came to terms with all the things that happened in her life.*
C: In many ways she has. Her mind has let go of it. Her heart has forgiven. But the body hasn't let go. It's a cellular memory. It was a suicide wish, too. It was an unconscious suicide wish.

The doctors had told Carol she would die if she didn't take her medication. I had the SC work on the thyroid, and asked what it was doing. "Relaxing. Just relaxing and being at ease with being in a human form, and being here another forty or fifty years." It also said that her school would expand and go all over the world. "You haven't seen anything yet.—She has already been here forty years. That's a long time for a being not native to Earth."

Parting message: Don't be afraid of shining a light. Don't be afraid of being powerful. Don't be afraid of being more special. She is afraid of being more special than other people. She is not that. She is very afraid of ego, for ego is the downfall of the greatest and she is more afraid of ego than anything. She has seen so many egos destroy good work and she does not ever want her ego to destroy any work she has done. And so she keeps herself in an inferiority space in order to combat ego. She will be guided as to how to handle it as the accomplishments become greater; she will be guided on how to handle it.

So it seems that even master souls have volunteered to come, even though they were advised not to. It has been said that even an avatar can become lost and stuck in the muck and mire of Earth.

PART TWO

ETS AND LIGHT BEINGS

CHAPTER FIFTEEN

MORE VOLUNTEERS

It may seem a little strange to combine UFOs and ETs with the Three Waves of volunteers and the coming dimensional shift into the New Earth. But actually it fits quite comfortably. This is because the whole subject of aliens or extraterrestrials has been coated in fear and mistrust since the beginning. Most investigators look for and discover what they perceive to be evil and horror. This is all based on their belief systems; they create the very thing that they fear. They have never thought of the concept that I have discovered: *that we are them and they are us.* These beings created us, so they have no desire to harm their children. Because of free will and the law of noninterference they can only watch and shake their heads at the stupidity and juvenile behavior of these children. When the other investigators use hypnosis on their clients they normally keep the person in a light state instead of taking them into the deep state that I use. In the light trance state the person will be caught up in the emotions, and fear reigns. The ETs are well aware of the effect they have on humans, whether by their appearance or their actions, and they would rather the person not have any memory of the encounter. They are here for a definite purpose and it is one that the human, that has had their memories erased by rebirth into the physical body, would not comprehend. Many of the humans are not to remember their connection until it is time, until their mission has reached the proper stage that they will be able to understand. If the memories are brought forth too soon, then the experiment might be jeopardized. "They" have said that the ideal situation would be that the person never know what is happening, that they are having encounters. They do not want to disrupt the person's life. But because of the additives in our food, the pollutants in our atmosphere, if the person is on any drugs (recreational or medicinal) or alcohol, this changes the chemistry of their brain. This causes them to remember any encounter (whether an actual event or a dream) in a distorted fashion. It is colored by their emotions so they perceive that something awful happened to them because it is beyond the scope of their conscious mind to understand. This is why it is better if the memory is erased by the ETs. Fear is the strongest emotion that a human has. If it doesn't understand something, it brings in fear which will naturally distort the memory. In the method I use, I get the conscious mind out of the way so we can communicate with the SC, the part that has all knowledge. Then we can find the true story, or as much of the story that the SC thinks is appropriate. It knows where the person is on their journey and their assignment, and knows how much they can handle. They never give the person more than they can handle, and I must respect that when we do a session. If the SC says it cannot give any more information, or that it is not time for something to be revealed, then I have to respect that. The SC must always be treated with great respect, and I have set up a comfortable working relationship with that part of the client's mind. This is why I am able to obtain information that the other investigators would not even attempt to find.

The reason that the subject of extraterrestrials fits in with the Three Waves is because often these volunteers have come from other dimensions, planets or spaceships. As I have said before the volunteers are pure and untainted souls coming to Earth at this time to help us make the transition into the New Earth. The majority of them have not lived in a human body before and are not caught on the Wheel of Karma. In the *Convoluted Universe* series I found that many of them came directly from God, or the Source, and had never lived in *any* type of body. They had always been one with the Source and had not been sent out on the long journey of experimentation and lessons to expand the Source's knowledge. They were quite content to remain there in that total love environment, and only agreed to leave in order to help the Earth. In the *Convoluted Universe* series many of them speak of meetings being held on the spirit side and other various locations. At these meetings they were told that Earth was in trouble, and needed help from the outside. They asked for volunteers, and many took up the challenge. One said, "I stupidly raised my hand and said that I would go." When she said "stupidly," she meant that she did not fully comprehend the difficulties she was signing up for. These gentle souls only wanted to help, out of love. When they arrive here, they realize why it is called the most challenging planet in the universe. Also in this book we have discovered that some of them were spirits or energies that were traveling and exploring, and had never felt the urge to become physical. It is obvious why these souls have experienced problems adjusting to such a hostile and strange environment. They are considered brave and are greatly admired for agreeing to take on this daunting task.

Now we will explore the cases I have found where the person had lived on spaceships or other planets and dimensions and actually had no desire to explore Earth. In my book *The Custodians* I wrote about my twenty-five years of investigating normal UFO and abduction cases. In that book I thought I had found the answers to everything anyone could want to know about this phenomenon. But I was wrong, there is much more to discover. When I wrote that book, I had not yet been made aware of the connection to the volunteers and their difficult role on Earth. Seen from this perceptive, the ETs are not the invaders, but the protectors. They are only protecting and watching their own. Although these types of volunteers are not aware of it, they are never alone. The people they left behind are watching over them to make sure they are safe and adjusting well to this alien environment of Earth. I had already found some cases that were reported in the *Convoluted Universe* series, but at the time I did not have the whole picture. These will be referred to in this book as the continuing story unfolds.

MISSING TIME

*A*ll of my work was taking many twists and turns and proceeding in a different direction. So why should I have been surprised when my work with UFOs and ETs also took a different turn? In my past work I had investigated missing time episodes and condensed time incidents (reported in *The Custodians),* but I was always able to tie it in with physical beings on spaceships. To me this made it somewhat easier to understand if I could keep it within perimeters that our conscious minds could handle. But my work was now going in a direction that tied many events to beings and vehicles that were not physical. The subconscious mind recognized it as natural, even though the conscious mind of the person would not have considered such a strange concept. Our minds were indeed being opened, and *all* of my work was being affected. I was to have to change my way of looking at things *totally.*

Jackie was one of the twelve sessions that I conducted while in Laughlin, Nevada, directly after the attack on September 11, 2001. Naturally, because it was a UFO conference I met many people who wanted to see if they had had experiences of that type. Jackie was one of these. I had conducted the Experiencer's meetings every morning during the conference, with the assistance of Barbara Lamb. Jackie wanted to explore an incident of missing time that was troubling her. She and her friend, Elaine, had started out very early (3:00 AM) on a car trip to Sedona, Arizona. The trip normally took about four hours, and they should have arrived around 7AM. Instead they arrived hours later (about two hours missing time), and found themselves on a strange highway when they entered Sedona. I wanted to be sure they had not simply pulled off the highway and fallen asleep because it was so early in the morning, but she was certain they did not. That time of the morning there would have been very little traffic, and that was their main reason for traveling so early. There didn't seem to be any logical explanation for the delay. So this would be the main focus of the session. It helped that she knew the exact day and time of the incident. She had kept a record of this in her diary.

Another thing she wanted to explore was that she thought she had had an implant in her nasal cavity. She showed me a set of x-rays that her doctor had taken when she went for a checkup for a physical matter. On one of them there was a tiny white dot in the upper nasal cavity. Another set of x-rays that were taken a few months later did not show any such object. In the meantime she said something had come out of her nose. Because she didn't know what the object was, she threw it away. She wanted to find out if there had been anything in her nose, and whether or not she had any other implants in her body.

I would explore the missing time episode first. After she was in trance I returned her to her house in the early morning hours of July 1, 1993.

D: *It is very early in the morning, as you're preparing to go on a trip. You're drifting down into the house on that morning as you're getting ready to leave. It is now early, early in the morning on July the first, 1993. What are you doing? What do you see?*
J: My lights are out. I was just going out the door.
D: *Do you have all your things packed that you're going to take with you?* (Uh-huh) *Whose car are you going to go in?*
J: My Ford.
D: *Are you going to drive, or is Elaine?*
J: I'm driving. It's early, five after three. Still dark outside, and me and Elaine are in the car. I like my music. My music helps the time pass.
D: *How long is it going to take you to get to Sedona?*
J: About four hours. I've done this many times. We're talking about a new way to go, up seventeen and then straight over from Lynn's (?) Park to Sedona. Over a

mountain road. Less travel. We have never gone that way.

We had already found something she had not been conscious of. She was taking a different highway than the one she remembered.

D: *Was that way going to be shorter?*
J: No, longer.
D: *Why did you decide to take a new way?*
J: The appointment. I agreed to be there. To meet these people.
D: *Are they going to be on* that *highway?*
J: Yes. This way will make it easier to see them. *Sub*consciously I knew they would be there. Not consciously.
D: *What did you mean by an appointment? Is this something that's been arranged?*
J: My people. (Sadly) I miss them.

She was becoming emotional, and started to cry. I talked to her to gain her confidence, so she could talk about it. She was crying as she continued.

J: They are completely... light, They're made of light. (Sniffling) I've missed you so! (Emotional) It's a strange place here.
D: *Are these people you've known from somewhere else?*
J: (Big sigh) Yes!
D: *When did you make this appointment to meet with them?*
J: While I was asleep they told me where to come. (Sniffling) It will be somewhere on that road. I didn't know where exactly, but I had to hurry. Had to be there at a certain time frame.

D: *And that's why you wanted to leave at that certain time in the morning?* (Uh-huh) *But you said these are people you know. Where do you know them from?*

J: The light. (Still sniffling) (Emotional) They're of the light. They're light. The energy of it.

D: *How did you know them?*

J: (Emotional) I *am* them! (Emphatic) I *am* them!

I tried to find out what she is talking about, without leading.

D: *So have they been communicating with you while you've been on Earth?*

J: Always, but I don't always understand them. I forget sometimes who they are. (Emotional) A concentrated form of light. It's a max *blue* concentration of light. I *am* them!

D: *You are them. Well, let's move ahead in time, to where you're coming to the place where you're supposed to have the appointment. Does it take a while to get there?*

J: We need gas in the car. I need to stop for gas. I feel good! I feel alive, and awake. Full of energy and excited. But when we stopped for gas, I felt so sleepy. In a minute's time I was so groggy. By the time I walked around the car to let Elaine drive, I couldn't hold my eyes open.

D: *Well, it is early in the morning.*

J: This was different. It was not a sleep. She's driving. Seatbelts on. I look at the speedometer. And that's the last thing I saw, seventy-five miles an hour. I thought, we'll be there in twenty minutes.

D: *There's no other traffic?*

J: Well, I saw a car go by on the other side, divided highway.

D: *Then what happened? Because your subconscious knows. It doesn't sleep. It can tell you what happened.*

J: We stopped. We pull off to the right, a road. It was a dirt road. There are fences along it. A farm of some kind. Got the window down. It's very dark.

D: *So she pulls down the road? She didn't even question it?*

J: No. She was smiling. I was looking to the right. There was something.,, silver dome shaped, like a water tank. But it wasn't a water tank. Two "people" came to my door. One came to hers. And we walked.

D: *What do the people look like?*

J: Greys.

D: *And you got out of the car?*

J: Uh-huh. Elaine was okay. She was just walking quietly.

D: *Where are they taking you?*

J: We're on this ship... in this room.

Apparently the silver dome object was actually a ship.

D: *You're in the room. Then what happens?*

J: I'm being taught... by these robots... the greys. I feel the voices come from them, that I'm an emissary. (Almost crying) That I need to be left again. I don't want to go back. (Emotional) I'll go back, but I would rather stay with them. I really wanted to be with them. I'm a segment of the light. Segment light. Segment myself.—Go back.

D: *What do you mean, segment yourself?*

J: Divide myself from them again and go back to Earth. I have to go back down. I want to stay with them. (Emotional) They're so full of love. And every molecular space is light. (Sniffling) I don't know if I can do what they want me to do.

D: *What do they want you to do?*

J: Spread the light. Spread the light. Go back and augment the God source by spreading the light. (Sniffling)

D: *Do they tell you how you can do that?*
J: They say I know how.

The idea occurred to me that this was somewhat similar to the little light beings in the Bartholomew story in *The Convoluted Universe, Book One,* who came to Earth to spread light.

D: *Are they the ones that are telling you, or are there other beings in the room?*

She was correct when she called them "robots" because they are biologically created machines that only do what they are told or are programmed to do. So I knew they normally do not think for themselves. They just do the menial tasks. I wondered where they were getting the instructions they were giving her.

J: It's more like a telephone. They're talking to somebody very far away.
D: *And they're repeating it for you?*
J: They're a telephone. They're broadcasting. They contain the messages. And they are of the light, too. This is so wonderful... but I feel so fragmented when I go back. (Sniffling)
D: *Why did they bring you to that ship on this very early morning?*
J: I needed a... device. It's a device. They put a device in my brain. (Still sniffling)
D: *How did they do that?*
J: With a metal extension. It went into my right nostril.
D: *And this inserted it in the brain?*
J: Close to the brain. So that I can think with them still. As I live, I'll have concepts that they project to me. To help me to live. To help me to teach. The concepts will appear in my mind like pictures. Words, but like pictures.

D:	*So it will help you to know what to say and what to teach?*
J:	Yes, but sometimes I think it's not helping.
D:	*Why?*
J:	Trying to teach dummies. (Laugh)
D:	(Chuckle) *Well, does it bother you that they put that in your head?*
J:	Oh, no. I know I need it. It's my... telephone card
D:	*So you can communicate with them. So it's not like mind control or anything like that, is it?*
J:	Oh, no, because I *am* them. I am them.
D:	*And it's just their way to telephone you whenever they want to send any information?*
J:	To help me. To keep me from harm. To let me know. To alert me whenever there's harm.
D:	*Do they also take information?*
J:	Yes, oh, yes. Everyone I talk to. Every concept. Every idea. Every value. Every experience. It helps them to grow too. *Us* to grow.
D:	*What do they do with the information?*
J:	It builds like... crystals? It builds on the God source. Adds to. Completing the function. Adds to the God source. Adds to the knowledge and the light. Creating a function. God's function. He has to have a function.
D:	*Is that the only way they can get the information?*
J:	No, they have many, many segments like myself that they send. If I don't do my job, then somebody else will.

Maybe this is one of the reasons I am encountering so many people telling me the same things. Am I finding more of the many segments that are doing this job on Earth? If so, they seem to be scattered all over the world. Maybe this is the purpose, so they can gather information from many different places.

D:	*But is that the only way they can retrieve information, with these little things they put in your head?*
J:	No, there's another way, but it's not all connected. And if we think something, we all know something at the

202

same time. Knowledge of existence, telegraphed to one another and another and another. And the whole of the light knows the same thing at the same time. But this is a more physical way to relate to me when I'm on Earth.

D: *Have you had these in your body before?*

J: Yes, before this life. This time, no.

D: *I mean when you were younger.* (Yes) *Then why did they have to put in another one?*

J: Sometimes the body absorbs. And sometimes they just need to update, so they can gather all the knowledge that they need.

D: *So it can happen as a child also, and then occasionally they have to replace them?*

J: When I was seven. I was so lonely. And they made me not feel lonely. They let me know that I wasn't alone. (Sniffling) I still felt alone. This Earth is a strange place. Hard to talk to people. It *was* hard to talk to people. It's getting easier.

D: *Well, on that morning, is there anything else they do while you're there?*

J: (Still emotional) They tell me to quit stalling... but I'm going to do what I need to do. The other time was much more complete. When I was a blue light, a block of blue light on that other place. A whole block of blue light.

I tried to understand what she meant.

J: When I was with them. It was always complete when I was with them. Time doesn't exist. When I was a block, a solid block of blue light, that was my happiest time.

Apparently from my questions I didn't understand what she was saying.

D: *Was that when you were younger?*

203

J: If we were to talk of your imaginary time, in years it would probably be 500,000 years ago. I was happy then. (Chuckle) A comfortable solid blue light.

D: *And then what happened? Did you have to leave that light?*

J: To help the function. When we come here we augment with our deeds. We are in*deed,* If we do had deeds then we are not traveling in the light. And by our deeds we create energy, to help the God source, to augment the God source. It's a block of light that originally was to create newer and better universes each time. Neverending and neverbeginning. And sometimes on physical planets you get dim and cold. Heavy and dark. And lonely.

D: *What was that big block of blue light?*

J: God! It was the God source. We each are in our own way a concentrated energy. In that particular life I was the closest that I'd ever been to God since my first... leaving? (She was unsure how to word it.) Since my first spark off of that God source. It diminishes sometimes when you're in the darkness. I feel separated and lonely. Very much alone. But I know that I'm not. It's just sometimes I wish it were easier.

D: *Did you volunteer to separate and come down into the physical?*

J: Yes. Responsibility. The hardest thing that we have to learn is responsibility. We're responsible for our own spark, our own augmenting of this God source. And it's difficult to understand sometimes because I know that I need to do it, to help. I get so tired sometimes.

D: *In the present life as Jackie, you mean, or just in all the journeys?*

J: In all of them.

D: *Why do you get tired?*

J: It's not fast enough.

I had heard that before, that things were too slow in our Earthly dimension. In the other dimensions, especially on the spirit side, thoughts materialize instantly. Everything is so much faster. Our slow and dense dimension is frustrating to energy beings who are used to creating immediately.

J: There was a time when it was slow on other planets and other places too.

D: *They were different?*

J: It's never very dark.

D: *But it's all lessons? That's why you have to go to these places?*

J: Yes, we know it's always lessons. This particular planet is not working out like it should have because many of us allow ourselves to be tired, and to drag our feet about what we have to do. We need to stay on the vertical path. Material things don't matter. That's not the reality. Not the Reality with the big R. The Reality with the big R is what counts. Life with the big L is what counts. And this is not Life with the big L. So I feel resentful sometimes about being here, but it's necessary to augment the source, this energy, this crystal to create.

D: *That's what Jackie wanted to understand, why these things were happening to her. It will make her feel better if she understands her purpose.*

J: I understand the purpose. I just don't understand why I let myself down by getting tired.

D: *Well, as you're looking at that, does Jackie have any other implants in her body?*

J: Yes, there's one in my finger, left hand.

D: *What is that for?*

J: I want to say "health," but they are telling me it's for my blood. My blood doesn't have enough oxygen because Earth is a heavy place. And my body didn't make enough... there's not enough oxygen in my blood. It creates more white cells because the balance isn't right.   I picture shots of beams, like laser beams, brought into my body through this thing.   It's such a little guy.

D: *Is this balancing the oxygen in the blood?*

J: Yes, but I don't know how.   I don't understand. (A revelation.) The light is a... propellant?   It gives the little molecules a kick in the butt. (Laugh) I need it. For another twenty years I need to be strong. Very strong.

D: *Another twenty years? So this helps the body to be in balance and harmony. Are there any other implants that she needs to know about?*

J: Behind my left ear.

D: *What is the function of that one?*

J: Communication.   There have been several behind my ear.   One when I was seven that is higher up. And one recently.

D: *The one when you were seven, what was that put there for?*

J: To make me listen to what I was hearing... about faith. To help me to hear, to clarify to my brain patterns the truth of what I was hearing.   And to sift and to sort what was truth and what wasn't.

D: *Is the implant that was put into Jackie's nose area the one she saw on the x-ray?*

J: That was in my nostril.

D: *But what was the purpose of that one?*

J: Communication. When they want to know something, or to see something. They see all and hear everything I do. And when they want to tell me something, they put it into my brain. And I see it sometimes in pictures, and sometimes in words. The one that showed up on the x-ray is a communication device.

I have heard this same information from everyone that I have asked about implants while in trance. Some of these cases are reported in *The Custodians*.   The ETs said it was very important that we understand the function of the implants.

Implants have been given a very negative connotation, and are even being removed by some investigators. The purpose of the ones in the nasal area are always reported to be the same: communication devices that collect the information that the subject receives in their brain. This information is downloaded directly into computers that record the history of our civilization and our Earth. Some implants are monitors so the subject can be located, and protected if need be. Others are similar to time-release pills or devices that dispense medication into the body to help with any illnesses or malfunctions. I have found the implants to be very positive. I have never found any negative implication from them. The only negativity is reported by those who do not know the entire story.

D: *So it's different than the other one that was put into the brain?*

J: That's the one. It's close to my brain. The ones in my ear are also close to the brain. One when I was seven years old, and one that I know about in '95. The one in '93 is in my nostril.

D: *Is that the one that showed up on the x-ray?*

J: '93. That was put in at the time of the trip to Sedona.

D: *Why has it disappeared now off the x-ray?*

J: In '96 I had missing time, again early in the morning. And they came. It was loose. And I thought that they came either to take it out, or to adjust it. But the next day it came out. They came to loosen it, I think.

D: *Why did they loosen it so it would come out?*

J: Because I knew what they were doing, and it didn't work as well when I knew.

D: *Is this the one that Jackie found when it came out, that looked like a little green square?*

J: Yes. (Chuckle) When a child wants to ride a bicycle with training wheels, they become dependent on the training wheels, until somebody takes them away. The implant they took was those training wheels. God, I'm on my own! I didn't realize I was doing it on my own.

(This was a surprising and disturbing revelation.) I'm alone.

D: *But if they've taken that out, how do they communicate with Jackie now?*

J: Crystals. The crystals. The telegraph system that I mentioned that was most active. It is becoming more effective now. Who needs the training wheels? I have communication without it.

D: *This means that Jackie is not alone. She still is in connection. It's just not through a physical object.*

J: They should be teaching me to be more non-physical. Spiritual. To teach with the spirit. To teach the people to die with the spirit. (Emotional)

D: *That's very important, isn't it? And this is the job that Jackie is doing right now. A very valuable contribution. They're helping her to know what to say to these people.*

Jackie was working as a nurse's aide in a nursing home, and was in constant contact with the elderly and those who were bedridden.

J: I'm still not sure.

D: *Well, it's a beginning. Like they said, Jackie has twenty more years, at least. In that time many things can happen. But Jackie had some more questions. She was wanting to know about cleansing out the karma. The bad feelings she has about her family and people not understanding her.*

Jackie had been having problems with her family in this life. There was a misunderstanding of what she was doing in metaphysics. This often happens when a person changes their direction in life, especially if it is opposing their family's belief system. Many marriages break up when one partner begins to grow in another direction. It often takes much understanding and love to allow them to explore their newfound interest.

J: The family that I lost... it's a small family that I lost. It is symbolic of the big family that I lost. It's made me lonely being here. It's part of the experiment. Because I needed to know that I could run the training wheels without them, and still be close to them. As with my light family. The family from that place of light.

D: *That is the real family that she's been missing, the light family?*

J: And this family that I lost here was a small example. It was telling me that they were taking my training wheels away to teach me responsibility. That I'm responsible, and don't need to lean on anything or anybody. (Crying and sniffling)

D: *And she has the telephone system where she can connect with the larger family.*

J: It's more like a telegraph. (Laugh)

D: *But Jackie is doing a very important job with her work with people who are sick and dying. Is this what she's supposed to be doing with the rest of her life? Can they tell you?*

J: I know. I need to be responsible, and stop sniffling. Do it! Just do it! Explain function to people. Explain God's ability to give birth to newer and greater universes. I need to teach that to dummies.

D: *Will it be made clear to Jackie so she can teach it? Because you have to know what it is before you can teach it.*

J: Bad question. It *should* be positive. It will be made known. Clear. It needs to be positive. State everything positive from now on. But then I have trouble with that. Because when I state things positive, people that don't understand, resent me. They think it's a command.

D: *But there are always people that are going to resent because of whatever level they are.*

J: The information will come from the people from the light. The graduated souls. They are being divided from the lesser. They have the understanding already. Time is short. The alumni are the enlightened. They were traveling in the light; they are beginning to reach back and teach the others. Those are the alumni.

D: *It refers to the graduates. The ones who have already finished the course. Is that what you mean?*

J: Well, even the graduates are neophytes, but the lesser ones don't know that. If a kitten is born in a room with stripes, the stripes are the only thing they see their entire life. They cannot see anything horizontal. This is a *fact*! And the mind is like that. So I can't teach somebody what they cannot comprehend.

D: *She also was curious if she's had past lives where she was teaching.*

J: Yes. She has had many lives going back to ancient Egypt where she tried to teach the accelerated teachings. But she felt it was teaching fools.

D: (Laugh) *Yes, people don't understand.*

J: Not many of them. The fools.

D: *But she's supposed to be teaching the same principles now?*

J: Black against the light. Stars against the light. Negative to positive. I just need to do it. I need to do it.

It is amazing to me how many times I hear "them" tell the person that their purpose is to spread light and information and understanding. Many times this is foreign to their conscious thinking pattern. And although they agree it is a good idea, they have no idea how to get started. Maybe that is what she meant by the implants communicating with her. Maybe they tell her what to say, and what to do. And it would appear natural, like a natural instinct or impulse. (How many times have I heard that? People knowing exactly what to do when they are put into a desperate situation.)

Jackie wanted to know about a strange incident that happened when she looked at her hands and they were very red. "What was happening at that time?"

J: The gift to people is also healing. And my job was coming up to do this. And I do it with my hands, with my heart. My hands were the color of my heart. Deep red. No heat, but energy. Energy to help heal these dying people. (Chuckle) That sounds funny. Heal the dying people.

D: *That doesn't sound funny. You're helping them to cross over with love instead of fear.*

J: Oh, yes. They are so beautiful. Ninety-two and ninety-six years old, and beautiful. You can't believe how beautiful these people are.

D: *And the redness in the hands was to help?*

J: To help conduct the energy to them when I touched them. Touch their forehead, hold their hand. And to conduct it into them just like electricity into a machine. And turn the electricity into workable energy in their body. So at that time when I saw my hands turn red, it was to tell me this was the right path.

This was taken from a much longer transcript dealing with various past lives. Valerie is a registered nurse with many years spent working in hospitals. She was also at the expeniencer's group held every morning during the Laughlin UFO Conference in 2001. She had a suspicion that she might have had extraterrestrial contact, but there was no specific incident that she wanted to explore. This is the portion where I was asking the subconscious the questions the subject wanted to know.

D: *One of the things that Valerie is curious about, she thinks she has associations with what we call ETs, or extraterrestrials, in this lifetime. Is that true?*

V: She must realize that the web of life is very interwoven. There are many, many species of entities in the universe. And she has been incarnated among those species many times. It was part of her path of learning. And the different species learn from each other. There are, of course, many levels to what is happening with the extraterrestrials. It has many purposes on many levels, but this was an agreement. On one level, one purpose was to have these experiences happen to her from a very young age. And it would help her to *know* for certainty, help her to know beyond a doubt, that there is more to life than what was before her face. And it was to help her to ask bigger questions, like "Why am I here" and "How can I have a better life?" and "How can I teach others to have a better life?" And if it were not for these early visits, perhaps she would never have asked these questions. It helps her to remember who she is. It was like an early wake up call. Those who have these very, very early wake up calls, even as children, are the blessed ones. They are ones who have an advantage because it is often difficult to remember who you are, and what your purpose is. If you don't even have the stimulus to rise above those around you, who are only concerned with the here and now.

D: *She also wants to know about these babies that she has dreams about. Has she had these pregnancies?*

V: She has.

D: *She wants to understand that.*

V: This is something that many people have difficulty with. But it is essential at this stage in Earth's history that there be this continuation of the genes. Not just a continuation, but a modification of the DNA. You call it the "genes." There will be times in Earth's future when it will be necessary to have this material, and to have these beings who are part human and part—as you call "alien." To have these races to be combined because there will be future times when it will be necessary to have some of the qualities of both. And she has agreed to do this. And she is well aware, on a deeper level, of the implications of this. And has indeed willingly contributed to this project.

D: *She was wondering what happened to these children?*

V: They are safe. They are happy—in their own way. If she were to know all of the circumstances of their existence right now, her conscious mind would probably convince her that this is not the proper way to live. And they can't possibly be happy. So let's suffice it to say at this time that they are safe and they are happy. And she can rest assured in that. She does not need to know the details of their life because her conscious mind would convince her that this is no type of life for a child or a person to have.

D: *It is different than the life she knows.*

V: It is *very* different. It is very, very foreign to the one that she knows. But it is also with the choice of these children, these souls. It was their choice to do this work, and to come into that life, as it was her choice to come into her life. It is their choice, and it is their karma. They are doing what they choose to do. And they are doing it very well.

D: *She also wanted to know, does she ever get to see these children, or visit with them?*

V: No, she does not. It was their pact that she would give them the start in life. And when they need "mothering" as you call it, there are other women who have chosen to mother more than one child. And they can handle this, and they actually enjoy doing it. She felt that she did not have the capacity to go from one situation to the other, and come back here. So that is the way it is.

D: *So she doesn't have to worry about it. Everything is fine.*

V: All is well.

D: *All right. She had some more questions. Sometimes she has woken up with triangle shaped marks on her body. What is that from?*

V: There are many things that we are learning about, and we must learn how to integrate, how to *adapt* bodies to other environments. And we test people. We do take them onboard ships, and we test them to see how they are reacting to the different things in their life. Mostly things in their environment. We want to know how it is affecting them. Whether it is the food they eat, the drinks they drink, the medications, what they call their "supplements" they're involved in. The pollutants in the air and the food. We test these things. We have our instruments. And we gauge these things. And sometimes our instrumentation does leave marks on the body. These marks are of no consequence in the long run. It does not harm them in any way.   And many times we undo damage that we have seen in the bodies. And we learn by these tests. We can see also what is necessary to get rid of these "bad" things that are happening in the body, and to get rid of toxic substances. And it is a good thing.

D: *So she doesn't have to worry about it. It is just a curious thing when people find these marks on their body.*

I have heard from many people who have awakened to find these strange marks on their body, and we have always received the same explanation. That it was caused by various machines and instruments used on board the craft. I knew it was not negative, but I was glad to have this verification. People are most frightened by what they don't understand.

D uring another session with a different client another oddity was brought up. One of her questions dealt with her possible involvement with ETs. There is a theory that if a person has had contact with them something will sometimes show up on their skin that is only visible under fluorescent lights. Some investigators are using this as proof of extraterrestrial involvement. She wanted to know about that because she could see things on her body under these lights.

D: *What causes that? Where is that coming from?*
M: She was a busy girl. They had her very busy at night when she thought she was asleep. No, she wasn't! She was busy. She was working with others. That girl never rests.
D: *What makes the marks that are visible in the light?*
M: Whenever she is in contact with the other beings. When they touch her, it gets on her. And it's kind of oily, and it sticks around. And you know her, she was curious and she had that light. So she got it out and she could see the marks then. They were there because of her interaction with them, and her job with them. It's just something that happens during contact. When things are touched it just kind of rubs off.
D: *It doesn't harm the body in any way?*
M: No, no. It's okay.
D: *There are other investigators that say this is a bad thing.*
M: You know, there are many power trips.—And whenever she figured out she could see it, then she did. She thought she was sleeping—she wasn't sleeping.
D: *What is her job with them?*
M: She's helping people not be afraid. She's learning many things to be used later. And she has to learn it so she can teach it. The people really get afraid. And

215

because she's been there and done that, she knows they'll be okay. She's had a lot of that experience, and she knows it's okay. That's one of her jobs—she's good at it. So she's helping that way, and she's learning different things. And that's good. She wants to remember. There are many things going on at night, and there are many things in the sky.

D: *Is she still doing this, or did she finish that part of her work?*

M: No, that's still going on, and that's going to go on. Actually, there is going to be more happening. She's going to know about it, and she's not the only one that's going to know about it. But that's okay, it will be all right. She's a good worker.

So the investigators are correct, markings will show up under florescent lights. And this is proof that the person has had contact with extraterrestrial beings. So it is interesting for those who need proof, but the person has not been harmed in any way. There is still no negativity involved.

CHAPTER SIXTEEN

THE FAMILY

This session took place in early 2002 before I had discovered the theory of the three waves. It is obvious from my questions that I was thinking of ETs more than this concept. Victoria was a teacher in high school, and had contact with many young people. I took her through a very traumatic past life where she was killed (along with several others) for trying to spread information and metaphysical knowledge. When she died in that life, she ascended and combined with the others into one beautiful light. She wanted to remain there because the peace was so wonderful, but she had to come back in order to try and spread the knowledge again in this present time.

Victoria was not happy here on Earth. She missed her "other" family. She felt a separateness from the light, the spirit side, a sadness that she never could explain. But she tried to help by spreading love to the kids in the class and the halls of the high school where she taught. She tried to project love to them, and she thought it was helping. They could feel the love, and this helped her to know she was doing something positive, even if it was on a subliminal level. Of course, her conscious mind did not know any of this, except that she was very frustrated.

V: I see the kids that need it and I try and spread it. And they may not know, but I send it. It makes a difference in their lives, but they may not know how or where. And I see people everywhere and I send them love. And I have to keep sending this love and sharing this love. There are not very many of my kind around. And

I miss being with one of my kind. Someone we can meld spirits with and be at one. When I was there, we were all one spirit, but we had to separate. We had to come down here and spread the light around. Things are bad now. And we have to do what we can to make a difference *now*. We have to spread the love as quick as we can. And we have to try and get people to see they have to love. Love is all they have to do. If they would just learn to open their hearts, they would be able to change the world before it's too late.

D: *But there's always been negativity.*

V: Oh, I know, but now there are places where it's just overpowering. And we have to try and change those spots. That's why we're spread out because it has to start somewhere. And then there are other people who are spreading the light, too, but they don't know it. They're just doing it.

Victoria then indicated that the people who were involved in this special work were protected. When I asked who were doing the protecting, she answered, "They are. (Laughing) They're me. I'm them. They're always there with me. We were always there together before. And we came back down here. Together again."

D: *You're part of the same group, you mean?*

V: Yes. There are others that aren't with me, but the ones that are with me now, are with me always.

D: *It sounds like you're talking about extraterrestrials.*

V: I don't like name. I don't like it at all. I call them my *friends*. They themselves, us. And we are them from many, many years ago. They were here, but no longer, they left. But we come back and try and help and do what we can.

D: *Are they in a physical body?*

V: Some are here in a physical body. Like me and the ones around here or over there that are dispersed throughout the world.

I was asking about the helpers, the protectors. She apparently thought I was referring to those who were sent to do the work.

D: *Okay, but the ones that were just giving us information.*
V: That's my friends.
D: *Are they physical somewhere?*
V: Oh, yes, but not on Earth. There's just a few of us here on Earth that are physical.
D: *Where are they speaking to us from?*
V: I feel them right here, but I know you can't see them.
D: *No, I can't.*
V: Well, they're here. Right here.
D: *Here in the room then.*
V: Yes. They're here with me. I called them and I knew that they would be here.
D: *I was thinking of something like aliens or extraterrestrials onboard a craft or something.*
V: Well, they travel in their dimension. But, they're here with me in this dimension right now. They're my family. And we're here on a mission and we have a job to do. When the job requires it, like, this is important right now so they're here. And I called them.
D: *So they could give the information.*
V: I knew it was important that things come out. (The voice changed.) She doesn't know the truth yet, but there will come a day. And she knows deep down what her mission is, but she's not going to face it yet. She's still preparing herself.

Another thing that Victoria wanted to ask about was a strange experience she had that she thought might be connected with extraterrestrials. I used this opportunity to ask about it.

D: *She wanted to know about an incident that happened in the summer of 1995 when the sky lit up, and she saw three beings.*

V: She doesn't remember it all, but she knows it all. She knows the truths of it.

D: *Apparently she wants to know it consciously.*

V: Yes, I think maybe we ought to start letting her see these things consciously now. I think it's time.

D: *Will it be safe for her?*

V: Oh, yes. They're friends. They're loved ones, the family.

D: *Yes, but we don't want to do anything to disrupt her life.*

V: No. She's ready. She's been ready for a long time. She's fine. She's one of them so... no, I think it's time because we're running out of time. So I think it's time now.

D: *Then these things that happened to her were actually real? Were they contacts?*

V: Some were and some weren't, but it doesn't matter because it happens to her all the time. It's always all the time because there are so many things that have to be done. Back and forth, back and forth.

D: *I didn't want to open up anything that would cause her any harm.*

V: Yes. And they appreciate that because you look out for the people. They do appreciate that because they all have agendas. They all have things going on right now. They're trying to help and they appreciate what you're doing.

D: *Can you tell her what happened that night?*

V: Yes, I heard a humming noise, and I got up and looked out, and went to the bathroom and came back to bed. And then I got up out of bed and I reached out and grabbed him and I just went with them.

D: *The three beings?*

V: Well, let's see, were there three? (Pause) I think there were four that night.

D: *What did they look like?*

V: Well, that wasn't them. Those are just the helpers that came. They just came to escort me. I was so happy to see them, cause I knew where I was going then. They just help them because they have so many people that they have to get.

This is another common theme that I have found. The person is always escorted by smaller beings to the craft. It is as though they must have one of them on either side in order to make the journey up to the craft. Apparently they cannot do it on their own. They can break down the molecules of their body and go through the walls and ceiling on their own, but they need an escort to travel upward to the ship. They said in my book *The Custodians* that there were two separate processes occurring.

D: *You said you went with them. Where did you go?*

V: We went out that way, yes. (She pointed to the left.) That's where the light was. We went up. Up and up and up and up and up and up and up and up and then, this big area. Went in. Sat down and... it was a classroom or something. And there was something like a big screen. We were talking about what we have to get done. How much is left to get done? We have to get it done, yes. Yes, I know, we have to get this done. I agree, I agree. It has to be done, it has to be done now. Yes, I agree with you, yes. Yes, I do. Yes, my brother. Yes. I'm ready.

It was obvious she was conversing with someone in this classroom setting. I have described the classroom in *The Custodians*. It has been seen by several of my subjects, and appears to be located on one of the large mother ships.

D: *Do they give you more instructions or what?*
V: Yes, we talk about what's next. We plan. I do things
       too at night. I have places I have to go and things I
       have to do. And things I have to take care of. And this
       is like a stopping point to say this is what I have to get
       done tonight. And so I take off from here and then I go
       over there and... where did I go? I had something
       special I had to do that night, yes.

The majority of people don't realize that everyone goes
out of their body every night. The body becomes tired and has
to sleep, but the *real* you, your spirit never gets tired. It would
get awfully bored waiting around for the body to wake up so it
could continue with its life. So while you think you are asleep,
the real part of you is going anywhere it wants to go, having all
types of adventures. Flying all over the world, returning to the
spirit side for more instructions, and exploring other planets.
Many are doing important work at night when they think they
are asleep. You don't have to worry about becoming lost
because you are always connected by the "silver cord," which
does not sever until the death of the physical body. When it is
time to return to the body in the morning and wake up, the cord
is "reeled in" so you can return to your life, oblivious of the
adventures the *real* part has experienced.

D: *Is this your physical body or your spiritual body that
       does these things?*
V: No, this was not my physical body. Yes, this is my
       natural dimension. This is where I'm normally at. I left
       my body back here. But I'm here and I'm instructing
       someone else over there. I'm doing some kind of a job
       over there. And that was something special that night, I
       remember now. I had to do something special, and then
       I came back. The helper beings escorted me back from
       there. I don't know why. Why would they have to help
       me? Oh, I know why. Because they have to help me
       with the transition from out of my body. That's what it

is. They have to help me come out and help me go back in because I have become acclimated to this body, and it's hard to get in and out the way I need to.

D: *Yes. People say the body is heavy and restricting.*

V: Ugh, it's cumbersome. This, yech, meager body... It's a wonderful gift, now don't get me wrong, but it's restrictive. It's so different. So confining, but we'll take care of her because she's got a lot to do yet.

D: *But Victoria didn't remember anything about this because it's better that way?*

V: (Laugh) We let her remember just what she needed to remember at that time. We've been giving her just bits and pieces, and now she's ready. She's been picking up enough here and there. She's ready now and she already knows. She knew before she came to see you. She already knows the truth. I'm so sad to hear how humans are sometimes. But, you've got to love 'em. You got to love 'em. I think she might be a little intimidated by the helpers at first. I think she's ready. I think we're gonna let her see more of it now. This was just to break her into it.

D: *But, do it gently, we don't want to overwhelm her.*

V: We will. We will not shock the system. She will be fine. She has already seen quick little glimpses of us. And it has not registered all the way consciously, but it's been in the subconscious and of course, we all know what's going on here anyways.

D: *I know the little helpers are not negative, but they do frighten people at first glance.*

V: Yes, bless they're little hearts. I feel sorry for them, too once in a while. They get a bad rap.

D: *That's what I've always told people, they get a bad reputation.*

V: They're just programmed to do what they have to do, and sometimes people are not very friendly themselves, you know.

D: *In my work I try to let people know that they're not negative. There isn't any negativity in any of this.*

V: (Laugh) They're cute little guys really. If you look at them long enough, they kind of grow on you.

D: *I think they're really very cute. They're very sad looking. I don't have a problem with it.*

V: (Laugh) Poor little things.

D: *Do you have anything else that you want to tell her before we leave?*

V: (Low, soft, gruff voice.) No, must go now.

CHAPTER SEVENTEEN

ANOTHER ENCOUNTER

I have had countless number of clients who did not want to explore past lives, but wanted explanations for strange incidents in the present life that defied logic (at least to them). The memory and the feeling that *something* happened would not leave them alone, and they had not forgotten the incident. During my twenty-five years of working on these cases, many of them turned out to be typical UFO and ET abduction experiences. Some of these are in my book *The Custodians*. Yet over the years more and more of them leave the realm of "normal" alien encounters and reveal that something totally different occurred. I have touched on some of these cases in my *Convoluted Universe* series, and I thought they were isolated incidents. Yet now they are becoming the new norm, and I have been going away from the typical cases. Of course, this is happening in all of my work. It keeps growing, evolving and expanding. Just when I think I have it figured out and understood, I am thrown another new concept that steers my investigations down a new and untrodden path.

One of the things that Janet wanted to explore during this session had to do with a strange memory of a sighting, and missing time in 1974. I regressed her to the suspected date and time of the event. She entered into the scene driving her car on a highway late at night (11 PM). Her two children were in the back seat, and Janet was driving aimlessly with no destination in mind. She was very angry at her husband and just wanted to get out of the house. "I didn't want to see him. I needed to get away. He betrayed me. I trusted him." The highway was almost deserted, just an occasional car. It was too dark to see anything else. Then something caught her attention, "There's a glow. I don't know what it is. It feels really weird. Never seen anything like it before." Then she began to shiver, "I'm cold." Her facial expression told me she was watching something that was disturbing her. I encouraged her to talk to me about it.

J: It's lifting up now. It's lifting up in the sky.—Cold.—A disk. It's rotating. It's rotating. It's coming towards us. And I'm driving as fast as I can. I won't go any faster. It's this stupid car.—It's coming towards us, and it's really low. And I can't go fast enough.—I've got my babies.—It came from the right. It's coming towards us, and I'm going the other way. I'm going south, but I can't go fast enough. It's the only way I can go. It's coming towards us. (She was becoming emotional.) I'm scared! I don't know what's going to happen. My lights go out. And there's no more music.—It's over the car. The engine stops.—Rotating. Lights are rotating.— The motor has stopped. I can't move. The kids are asleep. *They* put them to sleep.

D: *Who are "they"?*

J: People in the ship.

D: *How do you know that?*

J: I just know it. They put them to sleep because they didn't want them to be scared.—I'm really cold. I don't know what's happening to me now. I'm floating up now. I'm in a light.

D: *Where's the light coming from?*

J: The ship. Not supposed to remember.

D: *Is it all right if you remember now?*

J: Not everything.

D: *Because I don't want to do anything they don't want us to do. I think they understand that, don't they?*

J: They do.

I was able to think and talk like this because I have worked with them so often that I think they recognize and trust me. I knew there was nothing to be frightened of. I just wanted information, as I'm sure Janet did also. So I would let "them" supply what they could.

D: *Why can't you remember everything?*
J: Too much.
D: *I can understand that. We just want to give Janet information that she can understand at this time. (Yes) All right. Did Janet get out of the car?*
J: No. She lifted out of the car.—Through the roof.
D: *How was that accomplished?*
J: The light body.
D: *Not the physical body?*
J: No. Time for her to know. The physical remains in the car. The light body's with them. Go with us.
D: *Where was it taken?*
J: On the ship.

They said this was not the first time this had happened. She had also been taken physically many times as a child, but they would not give any details. They said it was not really important.

D: *Why did you take the physical body at those times?*
J: To help monitor her. It's not easy for her to be here. There's too much trauma.—It's time to begin now. Time to begin her process. Time for her to remember now. For her to begin her true work.
D: *What happened during those times she was taken as a child?*
J: Adjustments. In her mind and her body. She was better able to understand. To accept.

227

Janet did not remember any of this consciously because it would have made it more difficult to be here on Earth. She had however agreed to come here. "She wanted to be here."

D: *Has Janet had many lives on Earth?*
J: No. No. No. No. No, she worked with consciousness at the beginning. Consciousness, and creation of consciousness. Seeding, and....
D: *Can you explain to her what you mean by consciousness?*
J: Seeding—original seeding of consciousness on this planet. In the beginning, and then at several different pivotal times on Earth. When major shifts occur. Major shifts.
D: *What do you mean by "major shifts"?*
J: Atlantis. Good long time in Atlantis. Egypt.
D: *Why did she have to be here at those times?*
J: She likes to come at those times. Changes in philosophy. Pivotal shifts are meant to take the planet in different directions.
D: *So she didn't have any reason to come and live the ordinary lives. Is that what you mean?*
J: Not really. No.
D: *Just when something major was happening? (Yes) So she can pick and choose when she wanted to come?*
J: Yes. There were times she wanted to come, but it was not good.
D: *Is there someone who advises her, or tells her when she should or shouldn't come?*
J: (Laughed) Headstrong. Very headstrong. (Laugh) Yes. Many. There is a group. (Laugh)
D: *A group of physical beings?*
J: Oh, no. She works for the federation. That's the consciousness. That's her specialty.
D: *Can you explain to her what you mean by the federation?*

J: Yes. Worlds. Many worlds. Creating new life. New worlds.

D: *This is what she's been involved with?* (Yes) *And occasionally she comes to Earth when the time is right?* (Yes) *Where is she the rest of the time?*

J: Doing other things. Looking for new places to create. Many places. Many places.

D: *So when she's not in a body, she's working with the rest of you?*

J: Your concepts are limited.

D: *That's why we're trying to learn.*

J: We'll learn. Your concepts are limited. All one now moment. You can be many places, doing many things all at the same time. So to ask questions that are linear.... Is she here, or is she there? She is everywhere. So, yes. She's just not here, but she's everywhere. She's not in your linear space.

D: *I am beginning to get many of these concepts from others, and it's still difficult for our human minds to understand this.* (Yes) *So she is on an assignment while she's also there. Is that what you mean?*

J: (Laughs) Yes. She watches on a screen. That's what she does with Earth.

D: *She can watch herself doing things on Earth?* (Yes) *What does she think of it when she watches it?*

J: She likes that. (Laugh)

D: *I don't know if "being" is the right word. But what kind of being is she when she is there?*

J: She looks human, smaller female. There are other manifestations, but that one, yes. There are many. There are more than you can imagine. As far as your human mind can go and go and go and go, and then more, and more. All of the ways that God can experience himself is all that is.

D: *But as humans, we're not conscious of all of this.*

J: Sometimes she is. Sometimes. Once in a while, she does connect. Not always.

D: *As a rule, we're not aware of the other parts of ourselves.*

J: No, none of you are. No. No. You're going to find that you're going to become more and more aware of other "yous." You're going to start integrating in more of who you really are. The other yous.

D: *But won't this be confusing for the human being?*

J: For the human being that you are today, yes. But the overall, you're all integrating more and more and more of who you are. You know your childhood, your adolescence, your other lifetimes, your other experiences, your other possibilities.

D: *But I'm thinking that the way the human mind works, this would be very confusing. To know of other parts of ourselves?*

J: That is what she is doing now. (Laugh) That's why she gets confused. Operating on multidimensional levels, aware of other *hers* she may not be consciously aware of. But she is aware. She can't remember anything (Laugh) because she is doing all these things on different levels. So she is in many different places connecting with different levels of her existence all at the same time.

D: *Does she have any physical sensations when these things are happening?*

J: Sometimes, yes.

D: *What does it feel like physically, so she will know how to identify this?*

J: Hold on. We will interpret for you.—You've already encountered this with others, where they cannot remember from one moment to the next. That which they just recorded to memory which no longer exists. (Laugh) From one moment to the next, that memory is gone. So you know this one.

D: *You mean what we call our short-term memory?* (Yes, yes.) *What is happening at those times?*

J: Operating on other dimensions and levels. Many of you are experiencing this. You can't hold a lot of things these days. Small things. You need to experience more balance.

This was also reported in *The Custodians,* as going into a room to get something, and then not remembering what you went in there for. Then after a few moments of confusion the memory will sometimes return quickly, with an, "Oh, yes!" They said at that time you have already gone to another dimension and returned, just that quickly.

D: *But returning to the night that her light body was taken up. Why did that happen?*

J: It was time for her to remember now. It was the first time she had broken away from her husband. The first time she had ever ventured away. The first time she had ever moved out of her obsession with him. She was afraid to ever leave. It was the perfect time. It was now time for her to remember that there was something more. So we had a meeting that night. And it was a beginning.

D: *And it was just for her and not the children.*

J: The children have their own experiences. Her son, definitely. Her daughter was afraid, but her daughter far more than she knows, as well, is very powerful. This was for Janet. This was a wake-up call. She thought her life was over. It wasn't. And periodically we've had to intervene with her because she becomes devastated. This is the problem with her not having many Earth lives.

D: *And you said other times she was taken for physical adjustments?*

J: Some physical, some emotional.

D: *Is there a reason for doing that?*

J: She's close to the edge with the physical experience.

D: *Even as a child?*

J: Yes. As a child, it was devastation. Tremendous loneliness and abuse. There had to be adjustments to keep her balanced enough to be able to function in the physical.

D: *Janet thinks she has been communicating with ETs, and I've found our understanding of ETs is very limited. Can you explain who she is communicating with when she's doing her work?*

J: She is working with many different races and many different levels. And they all work together. Some are nothing but a beam of light. Some are your prerequisite types with physical bodies of different types. And then there are others, some are just cognizance. Some are just light. Some are everything.

D: *And I've spoken to just about all of them.*

J: Exactly. You see?

D: *I think people are not used to thinking of multi-dimensional. We think of ETs and spaceships, and physical things.*

J: What is multi-dimensional? Multi-dimensional is a being who is aware of all of its lifetimes at the same time: past, present, and future. One being can be many beings all at the same time. That's what all of you are. You're just not aware of your multi-dimensionality. You're only aware of *you*.

D: *Because it would be too much for us to take, if we became aware of everything.*

J: At this time. You could in the future. Now, that means that one being can be many different things. So if you can imagine—let me say this to you. You could have many, many lifetimes out there, all interacting with the you that exists now. Couldn't you?

D: *But we're not aware of each other.*

J: No. No yet.

D: *During the sessions more and more people tell me, when they're in this state—or you tell me—that past lives are no longer important. It's no longer important to remember who they were.*

J: Well, the influence of the other lives is not as strong now. It's diminishing. People are coming out of the dream. Out of the illusion. Out of the influence, more into the cosmic family.

D: *What do you mean, "Coming out of the dream"?*

J: Out of the illusion of separation. Out of the illusion of living in a bubble of biology on your planet only, and nothing else. Those influences aren't as strong. Your DNA is opening. Your RNA is opening.

D: *We're so used to thinking of past lives influencing the present life.*

J: In a linear construct that's true, but you're no longer operating in the linear construct like you were. You're moving into another dimension, which would mean that the influence of that linear construct wouldn't be as strong.

D: *I still get some clients that I have to work with on that level.*

J: Yes. And if they're still operating within that linear function, then you would. They just haven't turned on yet. That's all right.

D: *They're all where they're supposed to be.*

J: Exactly. Not everybody needs to be all at the same place. Where would all the variety be? It wouldn't be as much fun.

D: *That's true. That's why I have to work with each one at the point they are.*

J: Exactly.

D: *I've also been told that karma is different now. Is that correct?*

J: Absolutely. At this point, this juncture, karma is a choice. Step in, step out. There are those that are still choosing to step into karma.

D: *Get bogged down?*

J: Absolutely. Look around your planet.

D: *That's what I've been told, it's like sticky flypaper.*
J: That's exactly right. And they are getting stuck if they choose it.

———————————————

D: *What happened to Janet in 1996 when she said she saw herself die. She had a massive infection. And she saw herself keel over on the floor. I guess she was out of the body. What happened at that time?*
J: She died.
D: (That was a surprise.) *Caused by the infection or what?*
J: Yes. She lost hope. She did not see her role on the Earth. She loves too deeply, and then it can be very damaging. So adjustments were made. Things were fixed. In doing so, though, it did impact her conscious memory. And she lost much of her conscious memory.
D: *Did she actually die that day?* (Yes) *Did she immediately go back into the body after the adjustments were made?*
J: No, she did not. The consciousness did not come fully back in for almost 36 months.
D: *I thought if the body died, she had to get back into it to keep it alive.*
J: She was taken care of. But she could not—all right.— We'll explain it to you this way. There was enough of her there to function on a very low level. However, over that period of time, the integration that took place, more of her came in, if you will, more of her higher self, more of the totality of who she is. Does that make sense to you? Now she was unaware of this, although at some level, she had some understanding, but not really. Hold on. Hold on. Yes. She was not allowed to experience the white light phenomena that humans experience. That memory was freed. She would not have come back otherwise.

234

I have had other cases where the person had a NDE (Near Death Experience), and came back with either no memory or partial memory of what happened. It has been described as so beautiful, peaceful and perfect on the spirit side, that if they had full memory of it, they would not want to return to this chaotic life.

D: *In other words, the body can remain alive without all of the soul, the spirit in it?*

J: There was a bonding with her soul that occurred. A stronger bonding with her soul that kept her warm there. The bonding with her soul was not strong enough because of the damage she had experienced. Not only the physical damage of the illness, but the emotional damage. Again, she's different in that she has difficulty being here. The soul damage is very deep. Now, there was an innervation process, based on that bonding with her soul that took place over those 36 months, that didn't bring back in more of who this person is. During that time, she was not able to function as the human that she had been before. Do you understand?

I really didn't, but I let them explain it the best they could.

J: And even in this last two-year period, again, in order for this all to take place, there is a process that occurs where she has conflicts from the conscious state with the other things that are going on in the multi-dimensional states. Where it is difficult for her to integrate, and therefore, she has the personality defects that she sees—and she calls them "defects."

In *Convoluted Universe, Book Two,* there were two other cases where the person essentially died, and the major part of the soul was not in the body for a long period of time. In both cases it was quite a while before all of the soul returned and the body functioned normally again. The person described it as the feeling of sleep-walking, or living inside a dream. They had difficulty relating to their physical surroundings. Others around them also definitely noticed that something was not normal.

J: We would say this to you. There are those of you that meet in the dream state that are far more involved with the orchestrations on this planet than you have any idea at this time. There are those of you that bring specific information to the form. We would also say to you that there are those of you that carry forward truth. That bring that truth forward without hidden agenda, without distortion. And therefore, those of you that come together that are of that ilk, that are of that nature, know one another more than you know.

Parting message: We would say to her, to have much faith and trust in everything she does. To move forward with that same level of commitment. That everything she needs will be there exactly as she needs it. We would say the same thing to you. Those of you who are acting as the bridge on this planet are greatly loved. This is not to say that others are not loved. We would say to you, you are performing a great service on the planet. And there are many that love and appreciate you. Stay clear with your intentions. Cannot fail.

ANOTHER CASE

I had another case that was an involvement with ETs, where a woman had been seeing bright lights and wanted to know about them. She loved to be around the ocean, and she especially loved swimming with dolphins. She lived in Hawaii for a while, and that's what she did there. Now she lives in California, still around the water.

"They" said the ETs are in communication with her, but she doesn't realize it because they appear to her as dolphins. When they are swimming, they are doing many things with her that she's not aware of. One of the things would be the removal of implants. I told them I have heard that the implants are not negative. They are in the body for a reason. And they said, yes, they do serve a purpose. And when their purpose is served, they have to be removed. You don't need them any more. But also the dolphins were transmitting information to her. So various things happen when she thinks she's just swimming with the dolphins. They appeared to her that way because she was also of the dolphin energy, and they felt comfortable with her. She had come from the water planet, and many of the soul group of the dolphins originated from the water planet. She had memories of that place, and that was why she was attracted to the water. It made her feel very good to have these memories again. Thus the ETs presented themselves to her as dolphins, so she wouldn't be frightened, and be very accepting, so they could do the work with her. Again, everything is not always what we think it is.

CHAPTER EIGHTEEN

ADJUSTMENTS

Janice was a social worker, happily married with three children. She came to my office with the main request of wanting to discover whether or not she had had a UFO experience. Her only memory was the strange sensation of going through the ceiling of her bedroom. Even though she could not remember anything else, she had the feeling that something physical had been done to her, and she perceived it as negative. She thought it might have something to do with implants. There has been so much negative information circulating in the UFO field that people think implants are something to be feared. I never tell the person what I have discovered in my work because I don't want to influence them. I would rather they find their own information.

When exploring things that have occurred in their present life, I never take the client directly into the suspected event. I always have the client go into this type of scene *before* it happened, so we can approach it from that direction, and then they will not resist. Otherwise, they are afraid they are going to experience something traumatic because they don't remember it fully and the mind has created fear. I call this the "backdoor approach." Then they can sneak into the actual experience without realizing what I am doing. Fear is the strongest emotion a human experiences. So if something happens that they don't fully understand, they bring in fear which distorts and colors the memory. I have found this occurring many times, that the story told under hypnosis is different from the one the person consciously remembers. Yet it makes more sense and can be handled without fear and distortion. My main objective is to not disrupt their lives.

Once Janice was in trance, I took her back to the date: August 24, 1995 (which she had recorded), and had her come down into her bedroom on that night. She described the room and said she was in bed reading (which was her normal habit). She could hear her children downstairs. After a while she laid the magazine on the floor next to the bed, turned off the light and went to sleep.

Then I asked if she slept all through the night. She answered, "There's a light or something. Something's different. What is that?—I think there's a light or something by the front window. It's not real clear. It's not something I've ever noticed before.—It's like a part of me knows this story, but it's not happening like I remember it.—Now I think the light is lifting me! Under me lifting me! I'm trying to figure out what's happening. I feel lighter.—I'm being lifted off the bed. I'm able to look down and see the floor next to the bed, but it seems like it's further away. Wait a minute! I'm going up or something's going up. I don't feel so much going up as I am looking down and things are not as close as they were.—I'm going up somewhere.—I'm up on the roof now. I don't know what's going on. I don't know where I'm going. I'm up higher... higher... going up higher. My house is getting further away. (Disbelief) I can't just be traveling by myself in space."

D: *Are you by yourself?*
J: I think I might be in a bubble or something. I'm not really feeling it. I just have the sense of something around me. I'm in this really small thing. It looks like a bubble or something. It's floating up at an angle, but it's going away from the house.
D: *Can you see where you're floating to?*
J: I'm going up into the light there. I don't feel my feet or anything. I just feel I am floating.
D: *Can you see where you're going?*

J: No. I'm not seeing. I think there's something that's merging with us; there's something that's opening up. It's like a ramp came down and I'm going up into where this ramp is. I think it's on a ship or something, but I can't see the whole ship. It's like something opened up and it came down.—I still feel like I'm in some kind of bubble. It keeps me safe or protecting me, transporting me. I'm floating in this thing.

D: *What's happening next?*

J: Seems it's getting brighter... something's brighter. An illumination inside this place I'm coming to. It's like from a darker space into a brighter space.

She was confused and had trouble describing what she was seeing. She saw a shadow or outline of a tall person-like thing. Then she realized she was no longer in the bubble because she was walking. "Where am I? Where am I going?— It's just a hallway. It's not very wide. I don't see anyone, but I heard them say I am going in a room with other people. I just saw a flash of something. It doesn't look human. I can't see them now. Where are they? There's activity going on and there are different kinds of shapes. I just feel I'm not anywhere. I had a flash of other shadows, other beings, but now... some kind of dark room and I think there are some stars outside. But it's night and there's some glass, dark windows on the sides. I think there's something driving whatever this thing is."

I asked if there was anyone around who could answer our questions and explain this to her. "Somebody's telling me I'm not supposed to be asking questions. I'm hearing, 'You do not need to know.'—Something is too vast. They say something or information is too vast... beyond comprehension.—What is this? I'm hearing this in my head but I don't know where it's coming from.—Something about being a small cog in the wheel. Like I'm more important than a small cog, but I must be part of something; part of a larger something." The information came slowly and haltingly in bits and pieces. "I see a female type being. I'm hearing 'protection.' She is protection. It's like a protection of sanity, like balance. Our family has a plan. It has something to do with universal consciousness. It's part of the universe.—I'm getting information that I don't understand. It is meant to trigger something."

D: *Something that Janice doesn't know consciously?*

J: I hear, "Yes, of course." It's an acronym. It's like anagrams or something. It's a way of organizing thought... of thinking. It's a mathematical formula. It's a way of training her mind for taking in information. It's an opening. It's like a passageway. It's clearing, a formula. It's like a pyramid.

I asked for a clearer explanation.

J: There's a vastness or a passage or a narrowing to bring the information through to collect the information, the vehicle. It's not clear.

D: *Is this the first time this has happened, on that night? Or had it happened before to Janice?*

Now the voice switched, and I knew we were in touch with something that could supply more information without Janice's conscious mind confusion.

J: Information's been coming all her life.

D: *Was it something about that night that triggered this?*

J: Her reading and curiosity, asking for information and a desire to know.

D: *That triggered a different kind of event that night?*

J: She was being taken to the Source as a gift.

D: *She remembered it as an actual physical experience, didn't she?*

J: It *was* a physical experience.

D: *Did she go in her physical body?*

242

J: Yes, she was taken in her physical. It was a jarri experience with an opening alerting her. It was breaking a shell protecting her. Forcing things to realization, breaking the old way of thinking. Like she was ready to be pushed out of the nest.

D: *Was this a real physical place that she went to?*

J: It was a ship. She has gone to ships.

D: *She thought something was physically done to her that night on the ship. Was it?*

J: Yes, that was part of it. She knows she is the mother of many. A necessary part of a bigger plan. Her physical material is being used for a bigger plan.

D: *The mother of many. What did you mean by that?*

J: Her physical parts were being used as a greater plan. She wants to help. She's providing a service. They can help other cultures, other civilizations. Her genes and DNA are being mixed chemically or enhanced or helped in some way... part of a larger project and something she had agreed to. She agreed to do this. We wouldn't do this if she hadn't agreed.

D: *That's what I have heard; you don't do it without permission, do you?*

J: No, it's something she had agreed to previously.

D: *When did she agree to it?*

J: In prior lives, this has been ongoing. This is not the first lifetime she's been involved in this.

D: *What happened in the other lifetimes?*

J: It was similar. What was needed was taken from her as agreed. She's contributing in this way. It's just like when she gives blood in this lifetime to help. She's giving parts that are needed to help others in the universe, her own culture, her own civilization.

D: *Why would these other cultures, civilizations and other universes need her genes?*

J: Some are dying. Some are ailing. Some are experimenting. Some are enhancing the many uses.

243

> a vastness to this project that is hard to
 n... larger.

*she did agree to this in other lifetimes. She just has
ntinued with that agreement?*

 es, and in other lifetimes she's been part of the
science that is doing these things She's been on both
sides of it. She's contributed, and taking and involved
in it on different levels.

D: *So in this lifetime, she's agreed to be on this side of it.*

J: Yes, that's true.

D: *Why did she suddenly have these memories begin to
surface now?*

J: She's been asking. She wants to know why she is here,
all of the questions. It was fine to awaken her to a
degree.

D: *Because when you are in the physical body, you can't
know it all, can you? It would be too complicated.*

J: Yes. And she doesn't know it all.

D: *She's better off that way, or she couldn't function in
this world, could she?*

J: Sometimes she doesn't *want* to function in this world.
She doesn't feel happy here at all.

D: *She has a good life; a husband and children. She has
her work.*

J: It doesn't seem like enough to her. It's not fulfilling to
her. She goes through the motions, but she is looking
for more meaning.

D: *So this is why this is allowed now, so she can have
some information, some explanation?*

J: It gives her a feeling of being more than she was; a
feeling of being part of something greater. She's
involved in doing something that part of her doesn't
understand, but it has given her some degree of more
importance.

D: *Many people are involved in these projects, aren't
they?* (Yes) *Many of them think that something
negative is happening.*

J: As she did in the beginning.

D: *They don't really know what's going on.*

J: Most don't know. Some do.

D: *She said she felt something had been put up into her nose. Can you tell her about that?*

J: Something for communication... something for balance. This tool was to help her as well as us. It was for communication and balance, and to draw in something... energy, too... like a processor. Like a microprocessor in a computer. That's what I'm hearing... microprocessor. I think they are studying feelings and emotions as it applies to her.

D: *Why do they want to study feelings and emotions?*

J: It has to do with human progression. There's a speeding up occurring. Some people don't have as much tolerance as others for this. Some are more sensitive to it and there's this need to understand better what's happening.

It sounded like they were referring to the coming shift, and the speeding up of vibrations and frequencies.

D: *How the human body is adjusting?*

J: It's more than the body. It's mental and emotional. Taking in the changes and becoming more sensitive.

D: *I've been told we are becoming more sensitive to the changing energies. Is that what you mean?*

J: Yes, likewise most are changing, accelerating, moving forward. Some are having more difficulty with this, so this communication and balance is a way of understanding from a different perspective how it's affecting humans. It's a monitor, but it's also an inventive and kind of enhancer, stabilizer. Balance for humans that are involved, so it's contributing and helping at the same time. Contributing to knowledge and it's also helping the person adjust as they watch the progression and balance it out.—There's much learning going on with this progress that involves many, many civilizations ahead of the humans, but progress is not a constant. It's not always the same for everyone. There are variables and issues that can come up so they are monitoring, assisting and balancing adjustments. Much help is needed in some cases.

D: *Because there would be variables even within civilizations. All the people would be different. That's what you mean?* (Yes) *Are you also checking to see that the mind is not harmed by this changing of the vibrations? Is that part of the monitoring process?*

J: The mind is grown... the expansion process, there might be blockages, tangles. So much of this is dealing with emotions. People's life experiences, if they have been abusive, negative, emotionally deprived, warped... I don't know the words.

This often happens that the SC or ETs cannot find the proper words. This is mainly because they work more on a mental communication level. I always tell it to do the best it can.

J: It's harder for some of these people with expansion when there's so much emotion wrapped up in everything. All their learning, fears, and there's just so much.

D: *Are there some people that are going to be unable to adjust to this because of their minds and emotions?*

J: Yes, you have been seeing this now for some time. There is so much anger and violence erupting and there is self-destruction, suicide; it's just self-destructive. Yes, some will not move on in the same way. They can't adjust or push through. There's just so much holding them down, blocking them that it's like a jumble of wires. It looks like it's not a clear mental thing when you have emotions twisting through everything, disrupting. Emotions are causing problems

246

for many.—All are receiving energy to their system. It's to the degree they can accept it and process it and expand with it. A clear tube or tunnel, the passageway is clear, more can flow through it and it can be better if there are no blockages in the energy system. It can't do what is intended. Our help is provided and assistance is available, but it's still up to the person.

D: *So it's an individual thing. Everybody's going to react differently.*

J: To some degree, yes.

Then after a pause, it appeared the connection was broken. No more information came through. I asked for a parting message: "What I'm hearing is to travel and experience. Strike out on my own and to not be afraid. Explore, be creative, listen to intuition.—She knows the rest."

CHAPTER NINETEEN

ET VOLUNTEER

Miriam thought she had had a UFO encounter, but was unsure if it was a memory or a dream. This was the only thing she wanted to explore during our session. I took her back to the suspected date and had her come down into her bedroom on that night. When I asked her what she saw, she hesitated and seemed confused. "I don't know where I am. I don't see anything. It doesn't feel like my house."

D: *What does it feel like?*
M: I feel like there's a lot of pressure on my body. The pressure is sort of from the diaphragm to my chin. It feels real heavy.

I gave suggestions that it wouldn't bother her, and she could talk about it.

M: It feels like the pressure is in the mid-section, but now it's going all over my body. The whole body is heavy. It's in my hands and it's in my chest area. It's almost burning. It's heavy. It's different and it's unusual, but I don't see anything.

I gave instructions that she could become more aware, and that as she talked about it, it would become clearer.

M: Feels like maybe I'm inside a container and it's putting pressure on my body. It's putting pressure from the

249

waist up, but not from my waist down. But I don't see anything or hear anything.

Whatever it was, it was solid because she couldn't see out of it. "I'm very heavy. I can't seem to figure out what this is." I tried moving her backwards to before she was in this container, but she still had the same sensations. Then I thought to move her forward to where she was no longer inside of whatever it was. She would no longer have the uncomfortable feelings and be able to see what it was.

D: *What were you inside of?*
M: It looks like a box made out of stainless steel. It's not stainless steel, but kind of stainless steel compression. Like a container, a metal box the size of an audiometric place that you'd just lay down in. It's sort of a cylinder, and I just lay in there and my body equalizes somehow. It's all metal.—I don't know how I got in there. (Confused) I feel like it equalized my chest. I feel like it had to do with energy that is of a healthy nature. It's a good energy... a healing energy. It wasn't very comfortable. I was aware of that because there was nothing else to see. It didn't hurt. And it equalized the energy in my body, balanced it. Just simply, it was out of balance. And I don't know why, but I was given this treatment.
D: *Well, you will know why. It will come to you.*
M: I wanted it. I remembered it. I was given that treatment by those little people with no interest. They really aren't very emotional. They just *do* it. And I don't know why I was doing it, but my body was out of balance.
D: *Can you see these little beings?*
M: I see them, but they don't really communicate. They just sort of do a job.

I thought she was referring to the typical "little greys," which are nothing more than biological robots doing their jobs without emotions or interest. But when she tried to describe them, it was difficult because it was not like anything she had ever seen before. It definitely did not sound like any typical ET from movies or literature. They were like a cross between a tall skinny figure with animal characteristics. "I don't see them clearly. Maybe I don't want to see them. They're strange looking. I've never seen anything like them in my life, in a book, in my dreams. They're not human chatty people. Let's put it that way. They just do their thing, their job. They just seem more to be there, to observe. But they are really curious looking. They look more animal to me. More like animal skin without fur, almost a mouse color. They don't look like they have any fear. Very strange."

Because it was disturbing her, I asked her to focus on the room. "The box is very clinical, and across from me are doors, like cabinets. And beyond the box... I don't know... looks like a big machine. I have no idea. It seems very complex.—The room... I'm not good at yards and feet, but maybe... forty by forty feet."

D: *How did you get into that container? If you don't remember, you can ask them and they can tell you. Just tell them we're curious.*

M: Apparently my body is still in my bed, and what I know as the etheric body that keeps the physical body good, was put in the container. They didn't need to take the physical. If I take this back and put this part into the physical, it will heal the physical. That's what they did to me.

D: *What is this place where you are? Can they tell you?*

M: It seems like it was right near my house. (Confused) What they said is that they keep track of people to maintain a good physical body, and they just bring people here. This is like a little scout clinic or something, a mobile clinic. Some of the people they are watching, if they see problems, they will correct with this little scout mobile. And they put that energized balance into the physical and they do that for certain people. It's just sort of a routine thing. People they know or they keep track of, but we don't look like they do. I don't look like they do.

D: *Is this place in the air or on the ground or what?*

M: It's in the air.

D: *So they're able to take your etheric body up there. Is this the first time they've done this?*

M: They've done it before. They did it when I was sick. I had rheumatic fever and they took me. I was little. I was six. I was sick... really sick.

D: *What did they do at that time?*

M: They did the same. They put me in a box. They put me in that cylinder and balanced—didn't balance—eradicated the problem. And then they put that energy back into my body. They didn't take the physical body.

D: *They can fix it without taking it. They kept you from getting sicker. That's very good. They take care of you.*

M: I guess so.

D: *Why do they keep track of you?*

M: (Astonished) Oh, boy! They said I was—oh, my! They said that I was one of them! (Disbelieving) I don't know about being one of them. Oh, my! They're really strange. They can't be seen here on Earth now. They are very strange. They couldn't be seen.

D: *They are afraid they'd scare people?*

M: Well, they would! (Matter-of-factly) And I used to know them, but since they can't come, then how did I ever get involved with this? I'm not "them," but I was. I was for a while, so they still keep track of me. Help me because they want to help here on this planet, and they cannot and so they help me.

D: *If they tried to help directly, it would scare people?*

M: Oh, it would!

D: *So they have to have humans to do the work?* (Yes) *But you said you were one of them. Did you mean in another lifetime?*

M: Yes. I was there for many lifetimes. I was where they live... their planet... their home base. They're showing me. What I'm seeing is... it's not very colorful. It's kind of gray like them. But they're very, very benevolent. They're very kind. They're very intelligent. They're very efficient, very organized. But they're not emotional and they don't have color. They don't have much color on their planet either, in their houses, in their architectural stuff. They have buildings that look almost metallic. It is a civilization, and the buildings are at angles instead of circles or rectangles or squares. It's sort of on a slant... tall and things on a slant. We don't build like that. I had many lifetimes there.

D: *Were you happy there?*

M: Happy? I wasn't sad. Was I happy? I was very safe and protected.

This made sense because she said they did not seem to have much emotion. I wanted to know more about the beings themselves. I will paraphrase her answers: They may have been sexual creatures because she saw male and female. She did not see children, but they could have been somewhere else. They had a digestive system, and ate something like a paste that was prepared from the light and the sun, but, "It was not a delightful encounter to eat. It's just that they eat to eat, to maintain because food was not important."

D: *It sounds like a good place. Why did you decide to leave there?*

M: I wanted adventure. It was too much the same. I needed to go.

D: *Did the body have to die so you could go?*

M: The word I want to use is "discorporate."
      Discorporate. It just is no more.

D: *Then how did you know where to go?*

M: From there I had seen visuals of this planet Earth.
      There were many options, but the Earth is so colorful
      and so interesting and so vibrant. I chose Earth because
      it has everything: adventure, color, variety, emotions.

D: *Did you have to get permission to do that?*

M: I did, but it was totally agreed on. It was just totally
      acceptable.

D: *How do you come to Earth? Tell me what happens, the
      process.*

M: The body is gone. The body dissolved at the other
      place, and this... it sort of reminds me of a "holding
      station." It's like you're an actor in a movie or on a
      stage. You have to prepare your lines. You have to
      prepare what that character is going to be like. I want
      to make sure this is the character, what you want to do.
      There's an appropriate period, and if you still want to
      do that, you advance to the next level. If that is what
      you really want to do, then you fine tune it. Where do
      you want to live? What do you want to experience?
      What do you want to gain? And then you keep fine
      tuning it until the people in the "holding area" decide,
      with your agreement, that this is where you go. And
      then you go through being born.

D: *What was that like?*

M: I don't know. I decided to not go into that body until
      the body was ready... until the birthing had been done.

D: *That's a good idea.*

M: I thought so.

D: *Then what?*

M: I'm seeing a couple of flashes of lives... recent lives...
      interesting.

D: *Besides the lives of Miriam?*

M: Yes. Recent ones like in Vienna where I was very
      rich... very famous... very high society. I'm on

something like a terrace, where you eat outside of a restaurant. I'm female. I have everything I could possibly want, and I hate my life.

D: *Oh? Why do you hate it?*

M: I want adventure. I have color. I have style. I want adventure, and I have to be prim and proper. And wear hats and ten layers of clothes and strut around like the most glorious... and I hate it.

D: (Laugh) *You didn't come here for that, did you?*

M: Well, it was emotions and it was glamour and it was style. I didn't have adventure. I had to be so protocol oriented. I also saw flashes of another life. From there I went from Boston to take adventure across the country to a new life in the west. I am female again, and there's no glamour and there's no color and there's no music and no fame and fortune and money. It's all adventure!

D: *It's the opposite of the other life?*

M: Totally opposite. Full of adventure, and I hate it! I have two children... two babies born en route. We started out on the trip and my two babies died (Crying). It was a wagon caravan. It was very hard. It seemed like forever. It took years! We never got to the destination. We were going all the way to Oregon... ridiculous! We stopped with some other people and stayed there to live. It's Wyoming. And I said, "There's no God!" I will come one more time. I decided to come one more time to know if there's a God... to know a God. I don't know if this is the time, but the time I am here now is to know that God.

D: *So each time has been for a different reason, hasn't it?*

M: Yes, but I like this planet more than the gray one. I like Earth.

D: *Are you here for any specific reason?*

M: I've come enough times to Earth that I don't know anything else that attracts me to explore. So now I want to know God as much as we can know God in the human body. This is more important. This is not where I'm originally from or that gray planet. The place that I'm really, really from is where I feel like I knew God. And I want the people from Earth to know about that place.

D: *What does that place look like?*

M: I see colors. I see the emotion Joy in colors. I see there is a sunrise. It's not really quite a sunrise in every morning. There are songs that are sung. All creation honors the morning. There is such joy... oh, my, my, my! That's my home! That's my home!

D: *Is it a physical place?*

M: It is a physical place, not a dense physical, but it's very physical. There are buildings, amphitheaters... crystal is used. The physical place is a planet, but there is no negativity. We don't know it. Negativity doesn't exist.

D: *It sounds like a perfect place.*

M: It's as perfect as I've known.

D: *But you said you came into the body of Miriam. Do you know what your purpose was? What you came to do?*

M: I came to find God. When I came to Earth and when I became free, then the only thing I wanted to do was to help everybody become free. (Crying.) To know what it's like being free. Wow! And I don't know how you help people be free.

D: *What is your definition of free?*

M: Free of guilt... free of shame... free of self-power... just free. That's it.

D: *You mean the people are not free?*

M: People aren't. No, they're not free. They learn from day one, you're guilty. "Shame on you for breaking that! Shame on you for not getting an 'A'! Shame on you, you're not a good enough pious person! Shame on you, you're guilty, you'll go to hell!" No one's free.

D: *That's why you came? To try to make a difference?*

M: I came to be free and if I can help anyone else be free. Oh, yes, there was a time in Egypt, in that school, when I was free. I don't know what happened, but I was free... black male... so free. I knew what it was like. (Deep sigh) So here we are again... free.

I didn't know where all of this was going, but I thought I should bring it back to the original purpose for the session. To find out more about that experience on the craft.

D: *So occasionally your body was taken to this craft to be worked on?*

M: It was. I don't know about now or in the future, but it was.

D: *To keep it energized and in balance.*

M: Apparently so.

D: *They keep track of those from their own place that take this journey. Does that make sense?*

M: They do because my spirit in the gray place—I don't know what it's called, the gray metallic place—was always wanting more. And there's still an attachment there. Weird, weird looking people.

D: *But they feel obligated to keep track of you.*

M: There's a bond.

D: *They take care of you.*

M: That's good.

D: *All right. Can you ask them more questions?*

M: The weird looking ones? *(Yes)* Okay.

D: *Miriam was wondering if she had any implants in her body. Can you tell her anything about that? (Pause) Do they know what we mean?*

M: They do... they're discussing it. They say that—I don't know who's talking—they're just telling me that I do have implants.

D: *What parts of the body does Miriam have implants?*

M: Oh, my! It sounds like there's a lot. I don't know if that's possible! There are some in the ears. I don't

257

know what those are. Oh! Those are so they hear through my ear. Hear what I hear. They have an implant in that knee area that I've always been curious about. (Pause) Much of my life I've had a very sensitive GI tract. I'll have to investigate this. They said that implant is to help with my weak predisposition to digestive problems, And I'll have to look and see if that's on the spleen (?) meridian of acupuncture.

D: *Does an implant in the knee have something to do with the digestive tract?*

M: Very possibly.

D: *Miriam thinks she has one in her forehead. Is there anything there?*

M: Yes. That idea is she cannot yet see, so it's blocked. If she could see what she cannot see now, she would not want to stay. This would show her a connection to the incredible vastness of the universe. Oh, I want to see it!

D: *Is that the third eye area?* (Yes) *Will she be allowed to see this in time?* (Yes) *So eventually it will be unblocked?*

M: Gradually, it will dissolve.

D: *She thought she had something in her right arm. Is there anything there?*

M: Not everything was removed, and what was removed is okay. There's a transistor. To keep activity... she has a tendency to be very introverted and to think within. This was a transistor to keep movement in the body, the energy activated in the body, but she now doesn't need it. It caused her discomfort many times, severe pain many times. We don't want that, but now she has finished her obligations to be free from guilt; free from shame and she has her own energy. This one did not interfere with her body functioning. She is finished with it.

D: *Are there any others in the body that she needs to know about?*

M: No. She should not be concerned about any implants. They're all beneficial.

D: *I have heard that some are like tracking devices. Is that correct?*

M: Yes, we can keep track of her. She does not need to come on the ship any more. We can do the balancing now without the need to come to the ship.

D: *She had a physical question. She wanted to know about her blood pressure.*

M: She should observe when her blood pressure is high, if she is taking on somebody else's responsibility. She wants to fix the world, fix everybody and everybody's problems. And she assumes that temporary karma. She should not carry this burden. That's not for her. Have her observe when her blood pressure goes high, whose burden she is carrying.

D: *Do you think it's her clients?*

M: Not the clients as much because there's a balance. She does her service. She is paid for the service. (Miriam was a nurse in a doctor's office, but she also did acupuncture.) It's a balance. But friends come to her because of her freedom, her wisdom, her caring. She feels that responsibility and that obligation, and it is not for her to do. It does not help the person who comes and dumps on her. She needs to realize that it is not her responsibility. It's very simple really. It's not her responsibility and when she begins to assume and fix it for other people, she needs to be objective and realize that she can listen, but she doesn't need to solve everybody's problems if she starts to take them on. So just observation would help her immensely. What she needs to do is let the people speak to her about their problems, but her benefit is to learn the razor's edge of listening without participating. And if she can do that, this will enhance the journey. As she desires her innate desire to know God, as this develops just with that desire alone, it will also advance her in the direction in which she wants to go, so it's not a thing to learn from a book or a class. Just her desire to know God will expand and deepen her work.

D: *But the doctors have put her on medication.*

M: Just observe, and as she realizes her blood pressure becomes more stabilized and more and more within keeping of a healthy blood pressure, she will be able to gradually eliminate the toxic medications.

D: *I know you don't approve of medications.*

M: No. We prefer not. Natural substances are fine, and are already beginning to help her.

Miriam had listed several unusual events that had occurred in her life, and she wanted answers to these. One was an incident when Miriam and her brother were driving at night and they saw three UFOs. It scared her, and she wanted to know if it was real or a dream.

M: That was a real event that occurred as you would say "out-of-body." It was not third dimensional. It was an agreed upon "out-of-body."

D: *But her brother was also present.*

M: That was the agreed upon meeting. They agreed to meet.

D: *They thought they were driving, didn't they?*

M: They were driving. That's the way it was remembered. (Laugh) They remembered it as a vehicle. The vehicle remembrance was a car. They actually had no car. They astrally met to observe UFOs. And they did not want to stay in that area, and they both immediately returned to their bodies.

D: *She said it frightened them.*

M: Yes. There were other events in the area.

D: *She thought that the UFOs were negative.*

M: It was not a UFO negative. She had to leave and return to her body, and she left quickly. That was not a UFO correlation. In her mind she connected the two. But it was not a negative experience.

This is one of the so-called "screen memories" or overlays. When you think you saw something one way and it was really a totally different thing. Now I see that it even extends to thinking you are *doing* one thing and it is really something else. Thinking she was driving a car, when she was really out-of-body. The screen memories are manufactured by the ETs with the help of the person's subconscious mind to present a memory that is safe and nonfrightening. So in these cases, "Seeing is not necessarily believing."

Another event she wanted to clarify occurred when she was living at her farm in the mountains. There was some kind of energy that settled all over the house and made the house shake. It happened several times.

M: On both occurrences these were real happenings witnessed by another person. This was to stretch her mind from thinking she has to see a third dimensional vehicle to accept that there are a myriad of ways.... (She paused and smiled.) The UFOs are not flying saucers only. Some vehicles are biological. They look five feet tall and you step in and they extend for five miles. There are frequencies that could house the planet.

D: *It's more of a frequency? It's not solid?*

M: It's not a solid third dimensional. It's a frequency vehicle.

D: *This was what made the house vibrate and shake?*

M: Yes. She will recall seeing third dimensional vehicles behind the house in the mountains. She went inside the house because she was very uncomfortable. And then came back out realizing that if somebody wanted to contact her, what good would the house be? They would come anyway. And then it was gone. But there are other vehicles and twice she encountered the force and the power of vehicles that are not visible or third dimensional. You can't see them, but you can feel them.

It was becoming more obvious in my work that many encounters and physical interaction with ETs were merely the beings keeping track of their own people. Those brave souls who chose to come to Earth. They were not abandoned here, but are being carefully and lovingly cared for.

CHAPTER TWENTY

TAKING CARE OF THEIR OWN

Judy was a therapist with many health problems which would be our main focus. She also had a history of problems from childhood stemming from her parents, which caused her to be very fear based and focused on negativity. I suspected all of this was the probable cause of her physical problems. Yet this session took an unexpected turn. When Judy came into the scene it was dark. I thought maybe she had come into a past life at night (which sometimes happens). But she said, "I'm at a dark place. It's not night, it's dark. I don't want the light on. I don't want to see it. I don't want to see what's there." I assured her she didn't have to see anything she didn't want to. But I continued to ask questions to start the flow of information. "It's a room. There's a light over there. They're doing something, but I don't want to go over there. I don't want to see it. I see movement. It's like a beam. There's one place in the room where there's a light. Bright. This beam... I don't want to open my eyes."

D: *You don't have to see it if you don't want to. You can perceive it another way. Where are you in the room?*
J: In the middle of the light. The room is dark, and there's a light in the middle, and I'm lying down in the middle of the light. It feels cold. Like steel cold.
D: *But you said you had the feeling there were others in the room?*
J: They're in the dark around the light. I don't want to see them. They scare me.

D: *That's all right. You know you're not alone. I'm here with you. We'll only see what you think you're ready to see. How old are you?*

J: Four.

D: *So you're little then. I don't blame you for not wanting to watch. How did you get there?*

J: Don't know. I was sleeping and woke up. They frighten me. They've got funny hands. They've got funny faces and I don't want to look at them.

D: *So they look different. You don't have to look. But what's funny about their hands?*

J: Long, curled fingers. Curled. They're touching me. I don't want them touching me. One keeps putting their hand on my hand. Touching my hand. I don't know what she wants or if she wants something.

D: *What does it feel like when she touches your hand?*

J: Clammy. Touches funny. Big head. Long fingers.

D: *Have you tried communicating with them, and asking them any questions?*

J: No. She wants me to. She does. The one touching me wants me to, but I'm afraid of her. She wants me to talk to her, but I don't want to talk to her.

D: *Why do you call her "she"?*

J: Don't know. She's a she. It feels like she's a she.

When this has happened before I often get results by having the subject ask questions and allowing the being to answer.

D: *Well, you know it might be interesting to talk to her. Maybe we can find out what's happening. That's a good idea, isn't it? Then we can understand. Because we're always afraid of things we don't understand, that we don't know. But you think she wants to talk to you?*

J: I think so. She knows I'm scared. I think she's trying to tell me not to be scared. Trying to make me feel comforted or something, but I don't trust her. Maybe they just want to trick me. (Whisper) I'm confused.

D: *Let's ask her some questions. That might help. Ask her why you're there. See what she says to you.*

J: She says I'm sick. They're trying to help me. Something inside of me, broken.

D: *Did you know you were sick?* (No) *Ask her what's broken inside of you.*

J: She puts her hands on my stomach, but I don't know. She doesn't really talk. I don't know how to explain it. She points, and I just know what she means. She's pointing at my tummy area.

D: *Do you want her to fix whatever it is?*

J: If it won't hurt.

D: *Tell her she can do it if it won't hurt. What does she say?*

J: It won't hurt. Others are coming. She won't leave, but others are coming to fix it.

D: *What are they doing?*

J: Something coming down. I don't know what it is. Something's coming down. Metal. It's on my tummy. I don't feel anything.

D: *Then she told you the truth, didn't she?*

J: Yes. It doesn't hurt.

D: *What does it feel like?*

J: Hot liquid.

D: *Can you ask one of the other ones some questions? Maybe one of the other ones knows more?*

J: I feel like I can't get them to talk to me. She's the only one that talks to me.

D: *Maybe they're too busy?*

J: Maybe. I don't know. But she's okay. She's not mean.

D: *Are they going to do anything else?*

J: Feels like they're opening me up, but I don't know. A line on my tummy all the way down, but I don't understand. I don't feel anything, but there's an opening, a line. It's like they're opening something.

D: *Ask her what they're doing, so you can understand.*

J: I just hear "repairing malfunction." I don't know what that means. "Repairing malfunction."

D: *Why are they doing it?*

J: Too much abuse, too much pain. I don't know, it's what I hear. I don't know what that means. "Too much abuse, too much pain," I don't know.

D.   *Why are they doing it to you? Do they know you?*

J: Assigned. Assigned? I hear, "assigned." Monitor. Assigned, monitor.

D: *It sounds like they are good people if they're taking care of you. Are they going to take you home after they get it all fixed? (Yes) So they watch you. They monitor you and know when something's wrong?*

J: Not the first time.

D: *Have you needed repairs before this?*

J: I don't know if it's the first time repair, but it's not the first time I've been there. They monitor, watch.

D: *But that's good if you have someone watching you and taking care of you. What's your name?*

J: Eleanore.

I was thinking we were looking at a scene from Judy's childhood, even though she had not mentioned child abuse in her interview. (I always conduct an interview with each client that may last as long as two hours or more, so I can get to know them before the session.) But now it took on a different light. This young four year old was not Judy, but a girl named Eleanore. There was definitely a reason Judy was being shown this, so I had to pursue it. Eleanore said she lived in a big house with her mother and father. When I asked if they were good to her, she replied, "Sometimes." I felt I couldn't come right out and ask about something so awful as child abuse, especially if it had caused damage severe enough to require repair. So I had her move ahead in time until they had finished and asked what happened. "How do they take you back?"

J: White. I see light. Beam. She came with me in the light and helped me back in bed. It hurts a little, but it's okay.

I had her leave that scene and move forward to an important day, and asked her what she was seeing.

J: I'm saying goodbye to my people. These are my people.
D: *Do you mean your family?*
J: No, they're my people. I'm their queen, or princess. I'm waving at them. There's hundreds, thousands of them. I'm standing somewhere high, and I'm looking out over them. I have to leave for a while.
D: *Where do you have to go?*
J: A mission? Something to help my people. It will help more than them. I'm waving at them. They're all so loving. I don't want to leave, but I know I must. I'm choosing to leave. (She became emotional.) I have so much love for them.
D: *Do you know what the mission is?*
J: To return to the place of origin and complete the cycle.
D: *The place of origin? What do you mean?*
J: That which we come from.
D: *Do you know what that place is like?*
J: Difficult, compared to the life I have here. This life is joyous, the life is beautiful. Difficult to go back to origin.
D: *Why is it difficult?*
J: Lack. Limitation. Poor comprehension. Difficult assignment, but necessary to complete.
D: *You said you had to complete the cycle? What do you mean?*
J: Yes, cycles. Everything cycles. Completion is needed to finish the cycle. Need to return to origin. Origin is old. Old. Old energy. Old lessons. Reversal of consciousness necessary for completion. Pieces are missing in the cycle. Need to go back and fill in pieces

so the cycle can complete. Origin is missing cycles. Cannot complete, someone must go back. To understand, to comprehend Source information, required to go back to origin and complete cycle.

D: *But you said there were some pieces missing?*

J: From the cycle that began there are missing components. Components that are required for the completion of the journey. Missing elements to the whole.

D: *You have to get another assignment in order to find these missing elements?*

J: Assignment has been made. I am leaving on assignment now.

D: *What is the assignment?*

J: Returning to Source. Malfunction. Returning to origin.

D: *What is the Origin like? What does that place look like?*

J: Dense. Difficult energy. Very old. Requires reassimilation to old energy. Patterns old. Thinking old. Consciousness lower vibration. There is a room with choices available for assimilation to lower energies. Make a choice. Choices available to complete the cycle. Group decisions, group involved. My primary purpose choice, primary me but primary group involved choosing.

D: *So they're helping you? Consulting with you?*

J: Consulting, yes. Consulting many, many choices; many, many options. Putting together a plan. Timelines are important. Looking through the timelines is important. Putting them together. Particular issues are being sought out, particular issues are being looked at. Various timelines offer opportunity for those to complete the cycle, once available. Ultimate choice is mine.

D: *And you're looking at all the possibilities?*

J: At once, yes. Requires time in those dimensions to complete cycle.

D: *Do you know which pieces are missing?*

J: Affirmative. Pieces are aware. We are aware. We know where I will go.

D: *What do you think of the possibilities? Do they look easy or hard?*

J: Irrelevant to assignment. Difficulty is irrelevant. It is necessary.

D: *So it's not always easy?*

J: Affirmative. The choice to depart one's home, one's people, is only difficult to leave their companionship. The choice to afford opportunity for completion of cycle is necessary and required of me. There are many choices in order to complete the cycle. Multitude, we're narrowing down to that which will seem as one experienced on many levels.

D: *Let's go to see which was the final choice. You've narrowed down all the possibilities. Which one do you finally decide on?*

J: Human.

D: *Have you been in human form before?*

J: Much time has passed for humans since I was human before.

D: *So it's been a long time between?* (Correct) *Do you think it's advisable to be a human again?*

J: The simplest route to achieve purpose. Human experiences all options for this particular journey. Important to choose correctly as options are many. Humans experience it for this purpose. Most direct route.

Now that she had made the decision, I moved her ahead to when she was in a human body, and asked her what it felt like. She was frowning.

J: Tight. Constrictive. Adjustments difficult.

D: *What do you mean by the adjustment?*

269

J: Difficult form. Compartmentalized. More difficult than realized to adjust circumstances.

D: *Are you in the body of a baby?*

J: Infant. Very sick infant.

D: *What's wrong with it?*

J: Emotional issues, emotional discomfort. The joining is uncomfortable. Infant is crying.

D: *So you're having problems adjusting to the physical. But this is a necessary thing to do, isn't it?*

J: Correct.

D: *You have decided to do this, but now you have to stay with it, don't you? (Correct) You can't return until you have found the missing pieces?*

J: Complete the cycle. Must complete the cycle.

D: *Do you think it will be an easy life, or a difficult one?*

J: For human, difficult.

Here her answers became more sluggish until she wasn't answering. I knew she was identifying more with the physical body she had entered, and the other more knowledgeable part was fading into the background. I knew it was time to call forth the subconscious to get some answers.

D: *We thought she would go to a past life. What was that about when she saw the little girl, and they were working on her?*

J: Correlating material for her to understand. Her digestive disorders in her present life emanate from within that timeframe.

D: *The life of Eleanore? (Yes) But they repaired the damage, didn't they?*

J: To a degree. There were additional injuries created through that lifetime. The repairs were attempted, they did not hold completely. Eleanore received much trauma, and it effected the present lifetime. She only lived into her teens. Much damage. She also suffered abuse in this lifetime, and was unable to handle it appropriately. Interventions were not all successful.

D: *But if Judy experienced it once before, why does she have to experience it again in this lifetime?*

J: Unable to complete her cycle without full integration of understanding root source of the issue.

D: *The first time she didn't complete all that she had to learn?* (Correct) *So it had to start all over again from the beginning?*

J: Not totally from the beginning. Just of that cycle. Partially complete. Not all lessons needed to be re-submitted. The area that was worked on was the most vulnerable in that area of that particular life.

D: *And then the second part you showed where she was leaving her people, and had to go to make a decision. Is that the soul that entered into the present Judy?*

J: Correct. That was her true origin.

D: *And she saw there was a part that hadn't been completed?*

J: Eleanore was not completed. So the soul decided to come back and finish the process.

D: *But it has been a very difficult life for Judy. Many challenges.*

J: Correct. She required many interventions to complete this assignment.

D: *But now she is concerned because she has these physical problems that you said are a result of the other life?*

J: Part of it is a result of Eleanore's life. Interventions not all successful. The assimilation of this soul group to this human has been difficult. The assignment is difficult. There is much damage to the body.

D: *Was this done by the abuse as a child?*

J: Correct. This is part of the assignment. It brings
        completion to the cycle. Brings awareness,
        consciousness to many to overcome such conditions.
        Choices are made to interact on many levels at once.

D: *Then did she have karma to repay with the other people*
        involved, her parents?

J: Some karma, but not as much as one might think. She
        (Judy) assumes a great deal more has occurred than has
        actually transpired in karmic terminology. She has
        become aware of the multiple levels, but this is causing
        disturbance to her energy in this form.

I knew it was time to address the physical problems
Judy was experiencing. This was the main reason for coming
to have the session. I wanted her to release it to the past where
it belonged. The subconscious agreed it was time to let it go.
Judy had problems with her kidneys and bladder.

J: A release inside her kidneys to assimilate old energy is
        presenting problems. She has to get rid of the old
        energy. Old energy is holding back, so to speak, the
        ability to move forward. She has feet in the present, so
        to speak, and body in the past. Lack of integration of
        the two.

D: *What about the problems with her lungs?*

J: Sadness at leaving family. Grief. Taking too long to
        integrate and to complete, longer than she had
        expected. Sad. Misses her people, her family.
        Misunderstood a great deal. Compensates overwhelmed
        the body. She has completed a great deal, but she is
        aware of lack. There is an incomplete portion she
        wishes to finish.

Then the SC set about making repairs on the damaged
parts of Judy's body. I always find this part fascinating, and I
like it to tell me what it is doing. "Energies are being removed.
Assimilating." I know the power of the SC and what it can

accomplish, but it suddenly ran into problems. "Opportunities limited for removal. Blockages. Damage. Working." I asked if it was all right if I continued to ask questions while it worked, and it said I could.

D: *Has she been having repairs done all her life?* (Yes) *Because she was wondering about whether she had connections with what we call ETs.*

J: Her assignments, they are part of the assignment. Interaction with these species is a requirement of this assignment for her.

D: *Like they were with Eleanore.*

J: Correct. Interactions part of this assignment. In her truest sense she benefitted from the interaction. Fear of Eleanore created some problems, but species were not harming her.

I knew this was true because I had worked on this for twenty-five years. I have never found a case where the person was being harmed. It was only their misperception and their reaction to something they did not understand.

J: Damage corrected at that moment, damaged again and again. Unable to repair every time.

D: *What about now? She's willing to let it go, to release the blockages, get rid of the old energy. Can you fix it now?*

J: Releasing. Abdominal still holding fears of unknown species.

D: *Then it will help when she realizes they were actually helping her.*

J: Yes. Confusion comes from poor consciousness. All assignment to this location required interactions. Species are benevolent. It is utilizing humans for their purposes. It is a joint contract. Unable to process this information. They are learning from the human species. They are in agreement. Appearances are often

273

misunderstood. Great misunderstanding. Completion between species is part of her assignment.

The subconscious continued to work on Judy's body and kept encountering difficulty. "There is a lesion in the stomach area which we are addressing. Attempting to work on this. This is an old energy, old tissue. There is a connection. There is more than one area in this body. This body is having difficulties supporting itself."

D: *That's why we want to have it repaired, so she can do the work she has to do.*

J: It is not her time. She has not finished her task. She will not leave. Her will is strong.

D: *She was afraid maybe she was dying.*

J: She has much work to do. She will choose her death. There are multiple lesions throughout the physical. Some are from this lifetime, some are not. They are intertwined.

D: *They've gotten all mixed up together.*

J: Correct. Confusion, old emotional. Attempting to clear. There is confusion. She is confused of who she is. She sees herself human, and she sees herself as another species. She was at one time one of the species she works with. She's rejecting her species. She has bridged the gap between these species. Part of her assignment to complete the cycle. Bridge. She needs a bridge between the two species. An energetic bridge is being formed. We are reviewing. There is a lesion in her fifth chakra, her energy field. Removing.

D: *We've given you a lot to work on.*

J: Correct. We are assimilating, adjusting. Removing blockages on multiple levels. Bridging identities. Confusion, dimensional confusion. Unable to assimilate vast amounts of understanding on her own. She is elevating consciousness as best she can. More is required. The body is not as elevated as consciousness, creating pain, discomfort, disintegration. Consciousness and physical need to integrate. Integration is attempted at night. Not assimilating correctly. Too much information. The body cannot keep up. The body is not assimilating correctly. The body is malfunctioning. We are adjusting now. No drugs, no surgery. This is ultimate desire on her part. It is in agreement. We agree she can assimilate, and request is being made to higher levels to create path for completion for assimilation. Still correcting. This is missing matrix. Realigning. Upon completion of realignment all matrix patterns will be completed. All will be integrated. This will require no effort. Lesions are removed. She must choose to live.

D: *I think she will choose to live once she doesn't have any discomfort anymore.*

J: Correct. Agreements are completed. Assignments are completed. Interspecies relationship has been completed. Repairs to matrix are in progress. Seeking higher level authority to complete.

D: *Are you being granted that authority?*

J: Awaiting. (Pause) Assignment complete. We have completed all the work on the body. She will be allowed to sleep now. Lower levels of awareness will be allowed to allow the physical form to fully heal.

D: *Because she needs to sleep so the body can rejuvenate itself at night.*

J: Understood. It was required to elevate consciousness, to integrate. Integration complete. She will be allowed lower level awareness to be able to sleep and regenerate this body to complete the task. Everything will be complete, in human terms, three months. She will not need any drugs. She will sense no pain. She will sense some discomfort. Three months to complete. It will diminish. It will subside. She will have awareness. She will feel no pain, it will subside. Balance will come. Discomfort in her spine is from genetic. We are

275

adjusting, correcting. This will correct other areas of the physical body and allow the body to realign, and all organ systems to function optimally. Blockages within the spinal column have created malfunctions in each organ that has been affecting her. This is being adjusted. She will find her hips are balancing. She will be able to carry her frame.

Then the SC announced that it had finished. Normally when I work with a subject there is only one or two areas of the body to focus on. In Judy's case there were multiple things that the SC had to focus on. It took it longer and required more dedication and concentration. Then it announced, "It is time for her to be alive." I then asked it, as I always do, if it had a parting message for Judy. "We welcome you, be at peace. You are one, you are awaited. Do not be in a hurry. She is honored among many for her achievements in completing what her task has been. She has done so with great courage. She is honored. Check in more often. There is another level of consciousness. She is aware of this. We are happy for you to be of assistance to her.

D: *I help many people with your assistance. I can't do it without you.*

The alien being that was so caring and compassionate to little Eleanore has been encountered by many of my clients who have experienced UFO encounters. It is always described in the same way: compassionate, caring, and as having a feminine energy. I call them the "nurse" type because they always seem to be reassuring the person the ETs are working on. The little greys or whoever is doing the actual work are usually described as being busy and very concentrated on what they are doing. The "nurse" seems to have an assignment of tending the person and making them feel comfortable and safe.

Even though they are described as ugly and often extremely wrinkled, they exude a beautiful and calming energy.

This case also shows the difficulty a new and pure soul has when coming into a physical body. As a human child she had great fear of the beings who were working on her, totally unaware that she was one of them. The memory had to be erased in order to live in this world and retain her sanity. So she viewed them as alien and frightening (as do most humans), and did not understand they were only taking care of and monitoring their own. They would never abandon one of their volunteers on this strange and hostile planet without support. But this deep fear had carried over into her present lifetime as Judy and had caused severe physical problems. The problems were also caused by the abuse in the prior lifetime that left cellular residue, so it was compounded and more difficult to alleviate. She had experienced child abuse in this life, even though she had not mentioned it to me during the interview. I always know that the SC will bring it up if it is appropriate. It knows everything about the person. There are no secrets.

CHAPTER TWENTY-ONE

A CHILDHOOD ENCOUNTER

I did this session in Charlotte, North Carolina in September, 2002, while I was on a driving lecture tour across North Carolina through Raleigh, Charlotte and Greensboro. I came to Charlotte to speak at a local UFO meeting. Patricia was a beautiful blond who looked like a model because she knew how to arrange hair and apply makeup. This was what she did for a living, and she was a very good example of her handiwork.

She had been interested in UFOs for a very long time, although she did not think she had ever had any experience. There was only one memory of a very close sighting in the 1970s. She remembered coming out of her apartment early in the morning to drive to work. When she closed her door she happened to look up. Directly overhead was a huge craft with swirling red and blue lights. It was very beautiful. She watched it for several minutes before it flew away. She was surprised that no one else was around to see it. It was so clear, large and distinct. The memory had fascinated her ever since, although she was positive nothing else had happened. This is what she wanted to explore during this session. She wanted to go back to that day and get more details about the craft. I warned her, as I always do, that sometimes if you want to have this type of session purely out of curiosity, you might open a can of worms that would be impossible to put back where it came from. The protection of my clients is always my first priority. I always tell them, "If it's not broke, don't fix it." I normally only explore UFO and paranormal experiences if it is causing problems in the person's daily life. If it is not, and they just want to do it out of curiosity, I tell them they might get more than they bargained for. This type of thing is better left alone. She understood, but thought it would be okay because she knew that nothing else happened that morning. It was just a close observation of a large spacecraft (or whatever). She had not been able to forget it, and it had kindled her interest in UFOs.

When she had entered the deep trance state I regressed her to the morning of the sighting. Normally I have to sneak up on the event from the backdoor, so to speak. By going to just before the event, and leading the subject up to it gently. This time was different. She immediately jumped into it with no hesitation. I had just instructed her to come off the cloud into her apartment on that morning in the 1970s, when she was getting ready to go to work. I had just said, "You're leaving the apartment now."

She suddenly blurted out, "They're watching me!" She became emotional with a touch of fear in her voice, "They're watching me!" I wanted to know who she was talking about.

P: Them beings, they're watching me.
D: *What beings?*
P: They've been watching me. They're telling me there are two of 'em and they're in a craft and they're above my apartment.
D: *Are you outside looking at it now?*
P: Yes, yes. When I first remembered, I thought that I had seen red and blue lights, but it's not. It's a craft. It looks like a glass ball. It looks like a Christmas ball on a Christmas tree, but you can see through it.
D: *How big is this glass ball, compared to the house?*
P: Maybe five feet. It's barely big enough; I don't know if a human could get in there or not. But it's transparent, it looks like it has a little top on it like one of those glass ornaments that you put on a Christmas tree. It's kind of shimmery, but you can see through it. I thought

it had color, but I don't see any color. Just a transparent ball.

So her subconscious apparently had put up a protective screen memory or an overlay so she would remember it appearing differently than it really did. I have investigated many other cases where we discovered the actual event was not like the conscious memory. This is often done to protect the person and not traumatize them. Thus they remember the event differently than what actually occurred. Of course, sometimes this causes problems not anticipated by the subconscious because often the event is remembered with fear as a negative experience. Apparently the subconscious thought it was time for Patricia to remember because it was allowing the memory to come through now with no blocks. Also I have found other cases where the object looked smaller than anticipated, as though it would not be large enough to hold very many people. But when they went inside the object, they found this to be deceiving. The inside was much larger compared to the size from the outside. As though the aliens can manipulate size and space as well as time. These other cases are explored in *The Custodians*. Another interesting aspect was that now Patricia was experiencing a sense of fear when seeing the object, although her conscious memory was one of only curiosity. This also occurs while under hypnosis that a different emotion will surface.

D: *You said there's someone inside of it?*
P: Yes. The only thing I can see are eyes. It's like beings with eyes. They're up in the sky and they've been watching me. And they're not gonna hurt me, they're just watching.
D: *How do you know they're watching you?*
P: I can feel it. They told me they were watching me, too.
D: *Is this the first time you've seen them?* (No.)

This was definitely not a conscious memory. Patricia had said she had never had any encounter experience.

P: I was three years old (very emotional) and they came through the window. (Crying in horror.) They came through the window. They came through the window (Sniffle). I've gotta wake up!

She was trying to force her eyes open. She was going to try to break the trance. I knew the experience would prove to be positive, instead of negative, so I prevented her from opening her eyes. If she had broken the trance at this point, she would have worried about the experience and perceived it as something negative. If she had been experiencing a great deal of trauma I would have handled it differently, but I knew she would be left with the feeling of incompletion. So I forcibly instructed her to close her eyes. She was still resisting and insisted that she had to wake up. I had decided to move her from the scene and explore it another way, when she saw something that caused her to stop me. Her curiosity was overriding her fear, and she was trying to keep me from moving her.

P: Wait a minute. Oh, my goodness, wait a minute!

I gave her instructions that she was safe and protected, and that she could watch the scene as an observer if she wanted to.

D: *You're never allowed to remember anything unless you're ready for it. You're perfectly safe. And if it's time you can remember. Your subconscious will only allow you to remember what you need to know at this time. Close your eyes.*
P: (Whisper) I didn't think they were open.
D: *Now you can watch it as an objective observer if you want to. What happened when you were three?*

P: They came in my room through the window. They crawled in the window. I'm lying there on my bed. And they came in the window.

D: *Is it dark in the room?*

P: It's bright enough to see them. They don't look like I thought they would look. They can't look like that! They don't look right. They don't... that *can't* be what I'm seeing.

D: *Tell me what you're seeing.*

P: It looks like kind of reddish eyes. A wrinkled looking face. And like no neck. Kind of hunched over. And... they don't look right.

D: *Are they very big?*

P: No, maybe five and a half feet.

D: *What color are they?*

P: I can't detect a color. It's just that they have a strange look. Between the mouth and the nose, it's all scrunched up together. And they've got these big open looking eyes, not slanted, these are big and open. And they're going through the room. It's like they're just checking me out. One comes over to the bed. He's doing something to my little night clothes, unbuttoning my night clothes. It's like a doctor. Just checking me out. He wants to make sure that the functions of my body are operating properly. I had Scarlet Fever and he wants to make sure that I'm okay.

D: *You've been sick.* (Yes.) *Scarlet Fever can make you feel bad, can't it?* (Yes.)

When Patricia awakened she said that her mother had told her she had Scarlet Fever when she was very young, but she did not remember anything about it.

D: *So he's just checking out your body. How does he do it?*

P: It's like he puts pressure on my chest. And maybe the vibrations or something go up and he knows if I'm okay or not. That's all I can see. He puts his hand on my chest.

D: *How many fingers does he have? Can you see?*

P: They're thick looking, and it looks like maybe three major fingers and maybe a thumb or something. Looks big and ugly, not like our hands. He's big and ugly anyway.

D: *Well, what we consider ugly.*

P: He's ugly. Surely, I've never seen anybody look like that.

D: *But he puts his hand on your chest, and sends vibrations through your chest.* (Yes.) *Does it feel good?*

P: It does. It's like warmth. He knows I'm okay.

D: *So he's being very kind, isn't he?*

P: Uh-huh. He scared me at first. It seems like he's telling me he's gonna come back and check on me some more. Then he sort of turns around and just goes out the window.

D: *How do you feel about him coming back and checking on you?*

P: He didn't hurt me. He looks ugly. (I laughed.) He looks like an old goblin. My mom reads fairy books to me, and he looks like one of the goblins.

D: *That's an interesting way to describe him.*

It was obvious that Patricia was not familiar with the different types of aliens, even though she is interested in UFO phenomenon. I have encountered this type many times through my work, and I have come to call them the "nurse" type. Although she described it as male, many others say it has a feminine feel to it, although there are never any description of sex organs. I call them the "nurse" because they seem to have more compassion than the typical greys. They seem to be more of a physical creature than the robotic little greys, and they seem to think for themselves rather than automatically performing the tasks. They are always described as wrinkled and ugly, yet they are very kind. Although this could be another type because the nurse seldom performs the actual healing procedure.

Often when the subject is onboard the spacecraft and on the table having an examination or procedure, they have much fear because they don't understand what is going on. At that time the nurse appears next to the table and soothes them. They always have the feeling that she is assuring them that everything will be all right. The little greys always go about their work very mechanically and methodically with no display of emotion. The nurse seems to be a different type. Even though her appearance is startling, her manner is gentle.

D: *But now he's gone?*
P: Yes, but they still watch me. I think they put something in my body.
D: *When did they do that?*
P: When I was younger. When I was a real child.
D: *Well, three years old is a child.*
P: Well, when I was younger. I'm big now.
D: *Three years old is big?* (Yes.) *When do you think they did that?*
P: I think when I was born. They put something in my body when I was born.
D: *What part of the body is it in?*
P: Let me see. (Pause) It seems to be something up around my pituitary gland. Something up around my forehead. They put in there, like a chip or something. It's like glass, but I don't think it's glass. I don't know what it is. I don't know if the man did it; maybe one of his friends did. I watched them put it in. They did it before I jumped into my body.
D.   *They put it in while your body was still in your momma?*
P: It was before I jumped in it, before I came in my body. They put something in there.
D: *They can do that even though it's inside your mother?*

285

P: Yes, they did it to me. (Laugh) Yes, they did! Something I was born with. It's something they said I'll have for the rest of my life, so they'll know where I am at all times. A tracking device.

D: *How do you feel about that?*

P: They didn't hurt me. I feel they're good. They've been kind to me. They play with me when momma's gone. We go out in the yard and nobody would be there. My sister's older and she was gone and dad was gone and they used to play with me. They always used to tell me not to tell anybody.

D: *Why not?*

P: Because it might scare them. It scared me at first because they looked ugly. Some people might be scared... well, they look ugly to me still, but they played with me. They were good though.

This is similar to a case I wrote about in *The Custodians* of a woman who had experiences when she was a child with an extraterrestrial who said he was her real father. He would come into her room and talk with her, and showed her how to levitate her toys. He even took her onboard his ship to show her some of the animals he had collected from other planets on his journeys. He stopped coming and erased the memories when it began to cause problems in her young life. She had no knowledge of the interaction until it came forth under hypnosis. I have had other cases where the adult remembers under hypnosis having pleasant childhood interactions with little greys. Usually these were lonely children and they greatly enjoyed the attention. There have never been any negative incidents reported to me from childhood erased memories. The aliens seem to understand that they are dealing with children, and are very kind and protective. Even though the conscious memories were erased or covered over, I suspect the person senses there was something unusual that happened as a child, but they cannot remember. Often it is replaced by a strange longing that they cannot explain.

D: *What kind of things did you play?*
P: They would show me things. They would take me out in the yard and show me plants and explain to me about plants. And they would pick up the earth and they'd tell me things about the earth. And the trees, and they'd explain why things grew here the way that they grow. And they explained the planet to me so that I would understand it.
D: *Did you find it interesting?*
P: Yes, they took me to a cave one time.
D: *Outside of your yard.*
P: Yes, they took me to a cave. We had a good time. They took me to various places within the cave. And each one was to be a milestone or certain event in my life.
D: *What do you mean by different milestones?*
P: Different events that might happen in my life. They would take me down this path in the cave. And they showed me little stones, big stones. And each time we got to a stone in a cave that would mean that when I got to that point in my life, that they would show me more. I guess about myself and what I'm doing here and their job here. And also it's like they're giving me in this cave events that will happen at that time in my life.
D: *So it's just different parts in one cave.*
P: Different parts and each stone, or crystal, that we come to—I don't know what it is, it's a shiny stone, but it's smooth. And things move inside the stone and it tells you different things about the planet, and about yourself at that time period. And they took me through there and explained the process to me so that when I get there, it won't be so much of a shock. Because Earth is a different place, it's a shock for me. And they want me to understand things. The cave was just to explain my

life to me before I get there so that I understand more of what's going on.

D: *Can they show you anything you'd be doing in the future?* (Yes.) *Can they take you to see what you'll be doing in the year 2002? That's a long time ahead, isn't it?*

P: Yes, it is. I'm only three.

D: *Ask them if they can show you that time in your life. You'll be all grown up, won't you?*

P: Yes. I see me walking down... it's a big stone. It looks like it has facets on it. And each facet has to do with my work and things that I'm doing. It's like I'm working with many people, but the people don't know that I'm really affecting them in a way they don't understand. And it was just my energies or my presence. And the things that they've done to my body affect these people. I can do peoples' hair, I can do my demonstrations. I can just walk among people in a mall and I can affect them in a very positive way. Because they've done things to my body, and these energies come out and they go into people.

D: *What have they done to your body to make that happen?*

P: Let me ask. (Pause) They're telling me it has to do something with the soul and on a molecular level as well. They have gone in there on a molecular level and changed my body. You know everybody has an energy in their body, like an aura. And when people walk into my aura, they are changed. And this is done on a molecular level. And it's also done on a soul level. So people are affected, not only mentally, but physically, spiritually and emotionally. And I have not been aware of that.

D: *Were these changes in the molecular structure done over a period of time?*

P: I came in to do this. I came in with the facets in my body to do this. The facets on the crystal that I'm looking at are like the facets in my body. And it's like they are different energy points in my body. And they run up and down my spine. And these energies, they can use a computer on the ship, and they can make things happen in my body to affect things on the planet and the people around me. It's all controlled by a little thing that they have on the ship.

D: *So you came in like this.*

P: Yes! They make adjustments to make sure that it's tuned properly, and they take this device and run it. I'm feeling they run it up through my spine or in my head somehow. And that's how they align it. And it's gotten out of alignment, and I've been very tired. Yes, I've been working a lot, but it's gotten out of alignment in the year 2002. 2003 it'll get better. I've gotten too tired, and it's thrown it out of alignment. And they know I can't do anything about it. I can see these little different facets on the crystal. They are like the facets on my body, the energy points on my body. And they tune in with what's on the ship. And they manifest energy through them like the psychic points of a body. But it's done on a molecular structure that affects me molecularly, therefore, it affects others molecularly. They come into contact with my energy aura and it changes them. I can be sitting in a mall, people can come within a hundred feet and they also are affected by the energy. And that's why it was put in that way.

D: *When they make these adjustments, do they have to physically take you anywhere?*

P: Yes, but I'm not aware of it. They take me onboard the ship. There are all kinds of beings there. I see some tall, skinny ones now. They're not ugly like the first ones. These are thin and look different. They have things like suits over them or something.

D: *How do you get on board the ship?*

P: They just take me. They change the molecular structure of my body and it dematerializes and they take me onboard the ship. I can't go physically because I wouldn't fit through the walls (Laugh).

This has also been reported to me several times and is in my book *The Custodians*. The aliens are able to break down the molecular structure of the body so it can pass through solid objects. It is common for the person to pass through the walls or ceiling of their room.

P: Yes, they have to change me so I go through the walls.

D: *Does it happen when you're asleep?*

P: Yes, sometimes they've taken me out of my car. Because when I'm in my car, I'm in a different state of consciousness. And sometimes I'm thinking about other things and they can come in and get me. I can still be driving the car, and yet they can work on my body.

D: *Without any danger of having a wreck or anything like that.*

P: No, no, no. It's my conscious mind that is doing something else, and they can come in and affect my body because I'm hooked up to the computer.

D: *When they take you out of your bed, is the physical body taken on board the craft?*

P: I need to ask them. (Long pause) The only thing that I'm getting is that they're taking me physically. I look back in my bed and it looks like I see something there, but I'm not there. It's like I see a shell, but I'm not there. It's like a piece of energy there, but I'm not in the bed.

D: *But they do this and you don't remember anything about it.*

P: No, no, they've never told me.

D: *Is it all right if you know now?*

P: They want me to know. I've never known about any of this. They've never told me. I've never had any marks on my body.

D: *But now it's time for you to know? (Yes.) Patricia was*
        wanting to know about her purpose. What will Patricia
        be doing at this time in her life? 2002. From there on,
        what should she be doing? Can they tell you?

P: Yes. They want me to be more understanding of other
        people. And to know that earthlings have limitations. I
        expect Earth people to be more caring and loving with
        one another and not have wars. And they're not doing
        that. And I'm frustrated because I can't change it
        myself, right now. They have spiritual laws of the
        universe or something. I don't know what it is, let me
        ask them. (Pause) They said they have a book of
        symbols and they want the symbols to come to the
        planet because when people look at the symbols, that
        changes their consciousness. And the symbols are only
        of peace and light and love. There are no bad things in
        the symbols. And it changes people's minds. Instead of
        thinking about murder and hate and greed and tearing
        up the planet. They think only of light and peace and
        harmony. They want this planet to be a planet of light
        and love and caring. And they want me to write down
        some symbols. They want me to write some words in
        some books. To tell people about the good things that
        they can do to one another. But my vocabulary is not
        such right now that I could tell you exactly. I'm young now.

Patricia was still seeing things from the child's
viewpoint. I had forgotten about that. I would have to have
her view this information from the adult Patricia's perspective.

D: *Ask them, is this what is happening in the year 2002?*
        Many people say they are drawing symbols? Is this
        what's happening?

I am working with other investigators all over the world
on this project. We are all being sent drawings of symbols and
strange writings that we are hoping can be deciphered by a

computer. The similarity of these is amazing, and it is becoming more widespread. I have also been told that this is the purpose of the Crop Circles. An entire block of information can be conveyed to the conscious mind by the observation of a single symbol in the circle. The person does not have to be physically in the circle. They only have to see the symbol for the information to be transferred to their subconscious mind. The circles are a language that is understood on the subconscious level. It is not intended to be understood by the conscious mind. More on this subject is covered in *The Custodians*. They have given me examples of the way our minds receive entire blocks of information from a single symbol, even in our everyday life. They have told me that the information is inserted into the brain at a cellular level, and it will be there to access when we need it. It will be spontaneous and we will never even know where the information came from.

P: The symbols are an attempt at our communication with mankind. The symbols, as I have stated before, are of pure divine light and peace and harmony. And when Earth people can look upon these symbols, and take them into their subconscious minds, they will understand the beauty and peace that we are all about. We are the beauty, the peace and the light and we wish this for everyone on the planet. We have great love for those on the planet.

D: *This is why these symbols are being communicated to the people?*

P: Yes, yes, yes! There are those on the planet that know their meaning and they will come forth and make the knowledge known to everyone on the planet because it's so important at this time. This is 2002.

D: *But you mean that people don't have to understand the symbols? They just have to see them.*

P: They go into the subconscious mind. The subconscious mind is all knowing. The subconscious mind came from the source of the One. The One has the knowledge. When they come upon this planet and they see the symbols again, they remember. It's a communication form that they know on a soul level. They don't know it on a conscious level. So when they read these symbols, they know the meaning of them, and there are those on the planet that can interpret them for the others. And that's why we're doing this. It's not to harm, it's not to scare; just to communicate on a soul level.

D: *That's what I've been told, so I believe that.*

P: I'm working with them. They sent me here. I didn't want to come, because I knew it would be hard for me. Physically, and the atmosphere is different here, and it's hard for me to breathe. I have sinus problems. It makes my stomach hurt sometimes.

D: *Where did you come from that was different?*

P: I came from a planet where it was more gaseous. I don't see a physical planet, it seems to be a gaseous planet. Lots of gases, but we have cities there. If you were to look, you wouldn't see them because where we exist is another dimension or another level. If you could see our planet, you would see gases. You wouldn't see our beautiful cities. We have palaces, we have magnificent cities and we live in perfect harmony.

D: *What kind of bodies do you have there?*

P: These are light bodies. Matter of fact, you can see us because we have an outward shell that can be visible. It's like a form. It's like the man that came in my window. He's not one of them; he just works for my people. That's why he looks ugly. My people have a body, and you can see the body, but inside, there's nothing but energy. We don't have organs, we don't have blood and we don't eat. We exist on a *high* spiritual level, a high spiritual plane. And we have bodies of light. And that's why we can move through time and space and people not see us.

D: *Why were you told to come to Earth if you didn't want to come?*

P: No, I didn't want to come because I knew I would have to go into a *thick* place. It feels thick and heavy here. And when I move around in my body, it feels heavy. Our atmosphere's not like this. And I don't like it, and people are mean sometimes. People aren't mean where I come from.

D: *Then why did you have to come here?*

P: They wanted me to come here to help change the planet. And they put these things in my body so that I could. They wanted someone to come and affect the lives of everyday people. If we're in a special position, if I were the President of the United States, I wouldn't have affected the amount of people as I'm doing now. I'm reaching everyday people. The President of the United States is just affecting and being around a certain few people on the planet.

D: *He's isolated from the normal people?*

P: That's right. They wanted me to affect the everyday people. And that's why they put these things in my body. So that when I'm around everyday people, I'm reaching masses. Although, I never thought I was reaching masses. That's what I wanted, I felt frustrated because I felt like I was only doing the hair of a couple of people. Or just going to the grocery store, just silly things we have to do here. I never felt like I was really out there doing what I really wanted to do. But they said, no, that's not true. That is because of this energy within my aura, the people that I even *walk* past are changed. People that I talk to are changed. If I talk on a telephone, the energies can go through the lines. It's just that way. They're all changed. They never told me this. They never told me a thing. (Laugh) They didn't want me to know. I'm so happy they told me now. Because I really didn't want to come here because it feels so bad. A body feels heavy. I hate being in this body, cause it's thick.

D: *But there are many others that are serving the same purpose, aren't there?*

P: Yes, there are *thousands* here. They're not all from my planet; they can be from other realms, other dimensions. This is hard to explain... it's like an elevator. If you go up in an elevator, there are many levels and there are many different floors on the elevator. And that's the way the beings are on this planet. It's like an elevator. There are beings here from many different levels and they're all here working within their own level affecting the planet. Like someone on floor ten is doing his or her work, but it's not greater or better than the person on floor one. It's just different. These thousands of souls have been sent from all around the cosmos to aid the planet because they were concerned that the planet was dying. The genetic structure had changed and the whole experiment would have to be blown up, through a cataclysm. And we decided that we wouldn't do that, that we'd change it. And that's what we're doing here.

D: *But it's very hard on these people because they're not used to Earth.*

P: No, I didn't want to come. For people like me, it's especially hard because we didn't even have mouths and we didn't have organs to consider. We didn't have to eat. And we could go anywhere that we wanted, and now I have to go in a car. Isn't that stupid? I have to go in a car.

D: *But Patricia feels beings have been communicating with her in her mind.*

P: The beings that have been communicating with her since childhood, that's us. We're her family from the gassy planet with the beautiful cities. We're tall, thin and we have the big eyes. That's us. She's one of us.

D: *But you said she was like glowing energy on the inside.*

P: Yes, that's right, inside we are all light. If another being was to look at us, we would manifest these shimmery thin, tall bodies with big eyes, so that this is a focal point. Through evolution we have evolved. We didn't originally look like this. Originally, we had a very small mouth. Originally we had organs, but through millions and millions of years, our bodies changed, our planet changed. It's no longer physical. It's gone from the physical to the gaseous. So it's gone through millions of years of spiritual evolution. And now, we're just beings of light. Our planet is of light, too.

D: *So you've been communicating with Patricia all of her life so she wouldn't feel lonely?* (Yes.) *She was wondering about you. And she wanted to know if you belonged to some organization or council?*

P: We belong to a council. I'm seeing... let me look... do you want me to be three years old?

D: *We can move forward in your age now as an adult.*

P: Okay, so I can get a little better understanding of what they want.

D: *Let's move up to the year 2002. In the year 2002, Patricia has more vocabulary and more understanding. Let's look at it from that perspective.*

P: The council that we belong to is a spiritual council. It's not a governmental body, it's a spiritual council. We follow the laws of One. These laws come to us directly from the Source. And we are keepers of the Light, and of the knowledge of the One. And that's why Patricia is here. She receives her information directly from the Source. From the knowledge of One. And we allow it to come through. These are spiritual teachings. These are more than just teachings. This is an existence. This is not only being good with one another, but being a light being yourself, being God. That's why she's here to teach people how to be God.

I returned to referring to Patricia's questions:

D: *She also wanted to know, are there any other types of beings communicating with her, or is it only you?*

P: We have others. They are here under our direction. And they are doing experiments with her to determine how humans react to us. Not necessarily to *us*, but the other beings who are helping us with the experiments. We have the little greys, we have some reptilian. We have some beings that in your mind would be very strange, like balls upon balls upon balls. Like three walking balls together, but really it's a being. We have some very unusual beings with us, but they are working with her to determine the reaction of humans to us, or to the different types of beings. She sees different types of beings, but she doesn't remember because they might scare her. We tried before and we scared her. We allowed this particular species to come in, to manifest physically and she was afraid. Therefore, we know that if they land in a big city or something like that, the people will react in fear and they might use nuclear weapons or retaliation of some kind.

D: *Which wouldn't be good for anyone.*

P: No, no. So we're just using her for this. She is aware of it on another level.

D: *Fear, that's the human side of people.*

P: Yes, but they have to learn to grow to realize that physical appearance does not have anything to do with the spirituality of the soul. We are very spiritual beings. Very loving, very caring, and they look at us and they feel fearful. And we're trying to work with different people on the planet to rise above this fear. We are coming to people like Patricia and we're manifesting ourselves. Sometimes they remember, sometimes they don't. To get them used to looking at us so that when we come in person, there will be no fear.

D: *People, humans just see the outer part.*

P: That's right, and they need to realize—and they will—
        that there is a spiritual side and people should be judged
        by their spiritual essence. She has to learn to get used
        to communicating with us in a physical realm.
        Heretofore, we have only communicated mostly by
        thought. That's why she has never seen us, she was not
        ready. We have to get her used to hearing physical
        noises. That's why we wake her up in the middle of the
        night. She has to get used to spiritual manifestations
        that make noise because we will communicate with her
        in the future. We are going to visit her physically. And
        she has to be able to accept this. We're going to be
        giving her some teachings, and we're going to have
        different types of beings coming in and giving her
        information, and they're going to come down
        physically. And she's going to be really scared. She's
        going to be very, very afraid. She's not going to be able
        to handle it. And that's why we're doing these
        experiments with her to prepare her in the future so that
        she can communicate directly with our beings. And we
        have many different organizations. Many different
        types of beings. I wouldn't call this an organization.
        These are groups of beings that are formed together for
        a purpose. That's why we call it an organization in your
        language. But in our language, it is a divine purpose.
        Each group of beings has a divine purpose. The people
        that she communicates with now, her own people, we
        have divine purpose that we receive directly from the
        Source. There are also other beings who receive
        directly from the Source, but they have different
        missions. And she will be communicating with all of
        these beings. Just as you yourself have your own set of
        beings that work with you through hypnotherapy. It
        causes a certain energy vibration that attracts these
        souls that work in that particular energy level or
        vibration.

D: *But she was concerned whether she was attracting other types that might be negative.*

P: None of them are negative.

D: *That's what I've been told.*

P: No, she doesn't understand because she wasn't ready. And we didn't want to tell her too much before she was ready. She's had many Earth things to deal with, but this was necessary to go through these Earth things to make her stronger. So that when she eventually does our work, she will be not only spiritually strong, but also physically and mentally, and she can handle Earth things much easier. Once she becomes more adept at handling Earth things, it will not affect her spiritual work. And that's why we have not come to her sooner than this.

D: *Some people have the mistaken idea that there are many negative beings out there. But I've been told that these are not allowed to interfere with people on Earth because of the council. Is that correct?*

P: There are beings that we consider *not* very spiritually evolved. That does not mean they are negative. We have no negativity within the universe. There is no positive and no negative. There is only the beauty of the One. What we have are beings who have not evolved spiritually as we would wish, but we would not call them negative. I wanted to bring out, for example, the extraterrestrial beings that are working with your government. Those beings are here for their own purposes to get metals from the Earth and different chemicals, elements and things that they can use. Sometimes they take out more of this than they tell the government. We don't approve of this, but we have allowed them to come down because the vibration of the planet is lower and they can come into this vibration and communicate with the governments. This does not mean that they are negative. They are growing spiritually. And we allow them to come in. They are not

299

harming the planet because they have learned that they must give. And they are giving technology to the government. So it's a give and take. We disagree, but they are not negative. I don't know any negative beings that are operating on this planet.

This was covered in my book *The Custodians,* that there are some beings that have only been coming in the last 1000 years, who are allowed to collect metals and minerals that they need. These are common materials on Earth, so they are not harming this planet by taking them. They're under strict observation by the council to make sure they do not do anything they shouldn't.

P: Some beings here think in terms of good or evil, and that's really not the way to look at it. It should be looked at in terms of spiritual advancement. Some of these beings just aren't as spiritually advanced as others. It does not mean that they are negative.

D: *Some of the other investigators think some of the things people are reporting that have been done to them are negative. And I see it in a different way because I get information as to what is really occurring. But, I don't find it negative.*

P: No, you are seeing in the way that we want you to see it. You are seeing it in the way that it really is. But trying to explain to people upon this planet, that some of us are not negative or some of these actions are not negative, their consciousness cannot accept at this time. Maybe in the future. You must pursue and keep on with your positive thoughts of us because this is what they need to know of us because this is the truth.

D: *This is what I've been trying to do in my lectures and my books, is to present it in the way it is supposed to be. One question I've asked many times, and I've been told part of it has to do with the cattle mutilations.*

Many people perceive that as negative. Can you tell us anything about that?

P: Yes. There are different species working with cattle mutilations. Here in the United States they have used many... hormones—I think that's what you call them— chemicals in the cattle. And some species are examining the effects of these hormones on the cattle. So therefore, they take the organs and the pieces of the cow that may be affected by this and they're determining the results. The adverse results of these hormones to the cows. There's another type of species, they are using the blood from these animals. Not only cows, but also sheep, dogs and cats. And they are determining the molecular structure of the blood. And there again people think these things are bad that these beings are doing. But it's not bad; they're examining the blood to determine the negative effects of the pollutants of this planet on these plants and animals. You don't notice it on the plants because—what's a plant? But when their best cow gets mutilated, then they will check it out.

D: *That makes sense to me. Because I know you are examining many things. I had some information, but I did not have the full answer. Thank you for giving that to me.*

Finally an answer that made sense. I had been told that they were very concerned about the pollutants in our air, and the preservatives etc. that we have been adding to our food. They are concerned with the effects on the health of our bodies, and also that these additives are causing an increase in cancer. This is the reason for many of the experiments so-called "abductees" talk about. The ETs are checking the effects of these additives and pollutants on the human body. And also seeing if it is affecting the genetic structure. What could be more natural, to also check the food that we eat for pollutants that affect our bodies? Somebody has to do it. Our government certainly isn't.

D: *I've also been told by your people that the diets of most humans are changing. I know mine has changed.*

P: That is because the energies of the planet are changing. If you didn't change your diet you would become very ill and you might die. The food upon the planet is changing. Everything on the planet is gradually changing. This is before we initiate this great explosion of light that we plan to do in the future. (See New Earth Section.) It's changing. We have to change it because if we didn't, you would die because of all the pollutants. You have to change your diet because your body has become more sensitive to the pollutants over the years and it's deteriorating. The divine forces have instigated this change through genetics to make people's bodies last. We want them to hold up. And they're not holding up, they're deteriorating. And this will help reverse that.

D: *This is what I was told; we're moving away from heavy foods into lighter type foods.*

P: Right, because as the bodies of the planet change, they're becoming less dense. And of course less dense bodies require lighter food. You know the cows are very dense. Chickens are better. They're lighter. Seafoods are better. Plants are the ultimate because your bodies are becoming less dense. You're going to be eating less dense food. That's axiomatic. Your diets will change, and that's to protect your body. So the genetic makeup does not become completely destroyed.

D: *That's why it's happening to me also.*

P: Absolutely! You're living here, aren't you?

D: *Yes, that's true. (Laugh) I was told that it is happening all over the world.*

They told me as we change our diets we will be switching over to more liquids, like soup and smoothies, and away from heavy foods.

As we were coming to the end of the session, the beings had a message for Patricia:

I want to tell her that we love her very much, and we are at her side constantly. She need not fear. We will always be here to protect her. We cannot appear physically because our bodies are such that it would be almost impossible for us to appear physically because we are light beings. And if we come down and appear physically, it would upset the spiritual energies contained within our being. And it takes us awhile to get over something like that. So we just don't make physical trips here. We do have beings that want to visit with her physically, and she will be happy to know that because that's what she's asked us about in the past. She's not ready at the present time. You must make sure that she knows she is not ready now. But she will be ready within Earth years in about ten years.

CHAPTER TWENTY-TWO

ANOTHER OBSERVER

This session was done as a demonstration for my hypnosis class in Hawaii. Teresa was already practicing hypnosis and working as a healer, yet she wanted to know if she was on the right path. She was plagued by many doubts and uncertainties. She went to a life where she was a type of drifter, a man who went from place to place working for a while and then moving on. Not having a real home, but it didn't seem to bother him, although he admitted he was lonely sometimes.

T: I like being by myself, but you don't get to know those people that well because you work for them. I stay maybe two months, then I move on when my job is done. I just know when my job is done, or someone tells me we're done, then it's time to go. I'm seeing this star right now. I keep seeing this star when you're asking me these questions. Sometimes the star tells me. Sometimes I know. When it's time to go, I just walk. Or someone comes and gets me, and I go to the next job.

D: *What do you mean, the star tells you?*

T: That's the funny thing. I just keep seeing this star and I know that it tells me things, and I listen.

D: *How is it telling you things?*

T: It's this golden beam of light that comes down and I know things.

D: *Where does the beam of light come from?*

T: Way out in the sky on a dark night. I don't know if it's a planet or a star, but it's something out there. When it comes down, I just know things in my head. That's why I have to be outdoors. I just feel like I'm closer to it... closer to everything when I'm outside.

This could have gone on for quite a while, so I moved him ahead to an important day. When we got there he said he was dizzy. "Everything is starting to spin right now. That's what I'm feeling in my body right now. Totally like I'm going round and around." I gave suggestions for well-being so she would not experience any physical sensations. "My whole body is spinning like I'm in this centrifuge. That's totally what it feels like. I'm not seeing anything. It's like everything's orange and my whole body is spinning and I can't stop the spinning. It's all dark... an orangey dark, an orange color. It's like I'm inside of something and it's spinning. I'm definitely inside of something."

D: *Do you want to find out what it is?* (Yes) *You can do that.*
T: I know I can. I'm pulling back, and I'm in some kind of a ship. I'm looking at the ship from the outside. It's flat on the bottom and it has a dome top and edges that come out like a bowl that's turned upside down on its top, and there's something underneath. Lights. I'm seeing it's not very big. And... I'm spinning.
D: *Is the whole ship spinning, or is it something you are in?*
T: I think it's the room I'm in. It's starting to slow down now. The room is inside the ship. There is a being. I'm not alone, but they're not in the room that I'm in.
D: *What do they look like?*
T: I can't really see. I just get a sense of this. It's a big being... tall. I want to say "creature," but it's not a creature. It's a being. I am seeing that from outside. I am in two places at once. I'm in the room, and I'm

306

seeing the outside of the room. I'm seeing the top of what it is. It's like a glass material. You can see in, but it's not glass.

D: *Is that the dome part that you're talking about?*

T: Yes. I can see controls or something. I would think it was controls. (She was smiling.) I know there are other beings... smaller ones. It's funny because they just look so different. (Big laugh.) They're not like I would imagine. They're little and kind of bluish, and not like I've seen in pictures. They're blue, and the other one is a different color, like orange.

D: *Can you see what their faces look like?*

T: No, I see them from the back. (Laugh) And actually I'm one of them. I don't see myself yet, but I know I'm one of them. I don't know which one yet. I'd just like to take off the mask. Take off the mask to be who I am... not the person that came in there. That's not who I am.

D: *So when you came in there you looked different?* (Yes) *Why do you think you were in that spinning chamber?*

T: To shift back to who I am. The spinning does something to your molecular structure. It changes your molecules. I don't know if it's my true form, but into another form. And I'm one of the big beings.

D: *Have you finished your job? Is that why you're there now?*

T: No, I don't think I'm finished. I just think that I needed to come back and be in the ship for a little while. They have to tell me things, and things have shifted and they couldn't connect with me for some reason. They couldn't tell me things and so I needed to come there and learn more. Something changed.

D: *So they wanted to re-establish the connection?*

T: Yes. I think I needed to be with them again. *I* needed it. It's lonely down there. It's not lonely here.

D: *What is your job when you're there?*

T: I'm some kind of a captain or something like that.

D: *What do you see yourself doing?*

T: I'm not doing anything because I'm not in the same mold anymore. But I can run the ship and travel and do things that I've been told to do. And I like it.

D: *Who tells you what to do?*

T: The person that I work with and work for. It's another planet. I was on Earth, but I'm not from Earth.

D: *Is that the only place that you go?*

T: No, I've been to other places, but right now it's Earth. I have a job on Earth. I just forgot what that was.

D: *What was the purpose for coming to Earth and doing these things?*

T: Exploring first and seeing what the people were like, seeing how evolved they were, and what their fears were.

D: *That's why you really didn't mix with them that much?* (Yes) *Just observing?* (Yes) *What do you do with the information once you accumulate it?*

T: Give it to someone else, and they figure it out. And then we go on another journey. I've been many other places besides Earth. I think it's very interesting.

D: *What do you think about the people of Earth as you were observing them?*

T: Well, where I was, there weren't that many people, and they're surviving. They're living, but not in a big way, yet.

D: *What are you going to do next? Do you know?*

T: No, they haven't told me yet. Maybe back to Earth. Whatever they want is okay with me. I hope they move to a different time.

D: *A different time period or a different place.*

T: Both. They choose.

I moved time ahead until the decision was made to return to Earth. "Have they told you where they want you to go and what they want you to do?"

T: No, they just put me there.

D: *I think you would want something to say about it, wouldn't you?* (We both laughed.)

T: No, it's okay. They put me there. Then they tell me everything I need to know.

D: *Where have they put you?*

She saw herself standing by the edge of a forest. "Did they tell you what you're supposed to do?"

T: No. I just know. I'll know when I see him, but still I'm an observer. I'm just an observer.

D: *You're not supposed to get too involved?*

T: No, I'm not. I'm just an observer. I watch. I don't look like a human. I don't know what I am. I'm tall and thin... I don't know if I'm a human. I feel like I'm on some other planet. The forest... there are structures that are domes that are familiar to me. They're metal with big domed roofs. And I look different. I'm very, very pale and thin and different. Maybe I'm a creature of this place, but it's not human now. I'm an observer. It's an interesting job. I'm just watching and seeing. It's kind of like the other job, but it's nicer. It's warmer.

This could have gone on for a while, and I could have explored this alien lifetime also. But at this point in the session it was time to call forth the SC so we could get answers and therapy. Besides, it was a demonstration for the class, and I didn't have as much time as I have in a private session. I asked the reason for showing Teresa that lifetime.

T: For her to understand more about what she had seen and go deeper. She needs to understand her past.

D: *Has she always been an observer?*

T: Not always.

D: *But in those lifetimes she was?*

T: Yes. She also needed to know how to help people. To see all facets of people... to go deeper.

D: *People are many faceted, aren't they?* (Yes) *Complicated.*

T: Very. She sees beneath the surface, but she doesn't always understand. She doubts herself.

D: *Why did she decide to become human if she had these lives as other beings?*

T: To go faster in her evolution. Then she was just a watcher, an observer. She can go much faster in a human body. She decided to do this, but most forget.

D: *Is that why you wanted to remind her of why she is here?*

T: Yes, she has much work to do. She is a traveler. She goes from place to place, but she has stayed at one place for a long time... too long. This time they picked a far place (Hawaii). Just to move around... she forgot she liked it. She needs to do her work now, as soon as she can. But she keeps making up responsibilities because she forgot.

D: *What is she supposed to do when she travels?*

T: Talk to people, listen to people, help them, and do her work. Helping to make people feel good again... be happy again, heal their pain. People will recognize her and they will come. She'll be able to help them. Question and then listen. Questions are part of listening. Other things are just doorways. They just got her to here. New things will be coming. She will be sharing.

❧ ──···◈►━◑━✖━━✦━◑◄◈◄···─◑

D: *She picked up that she was going to be around for three hundred years.* (We both laughed.) *What do you think?*

T: She could be if she really wants to be.

D: *We have control over the human body, don't we?*

T: Yes, but she didn't know that is true.

D: *I've heard you can live as long as you want because you can control the body, can't you?*

T: Yes, we can.

"We are shifting things inside of her... her DNA... it is changing."

D: *It's happening to many people, isn't it?*

T: Yes, it is.

D: *Why is the DNA changing?*

T: Because everything is changing. The planet is changing. *Your* DNA is changing. It has to change... to hold the energy, to hold the frequency.

D: *Some people can't handle it, can they?*

T: No, and they have to leave. And they are happy to leave. They know that's what they have to do. It is a good thing.

D: *The ones that are staying are adjusting their frequencies, and DNA is changing to adjust.*

T: Yes. You can feel it sometimes. You feel things in your spine.

D: *In what way?*

T: Just swirlings. This body is feeling it now.

D: *Some people would say that's just the Kundalini.*

T: No. This is not Kundalini. This is DNA.

D: *This means when things are changing we'll feel vibrations in the body?*

T: Yes, and sometimes headaches as we adjust. Backaches... headaches. But they will go away. They're not chronic.

D: *And as we become more and more adjusted to the frequencies, they stop?*

T: Yes, they do. We are giving her much more energy. She has been shut down to change. That is why she was feeling low energy. Many things inside her were changing, and now it will shift with this shift, with the DNA.

— — · · ·✦➤➤—◗—✳—— ✳—◖➤➤◖✦· · · — —

T: She argued with us to come here in the class. She wanted to come, but not come.

D: *What do you mean? Explain it.*

T: I will, but she needed to connect with you, not just with one of your students. She needed to be here with you, to hear you and to feel you because it shifted her energy. Your energy shifts other people just by being in your presence. It's not just what you teach. That's what you do.

D: *You said she didn't want to come?*

T: No. She wanted to come, but she didn't know how important it was to come. This was very important today to be in this time and this space with you and these people.

D: *Do you think this group is going to be able to do what I've taught them?*

T: Oh, yes... not all of them, but most of them. Some don't want to do it. Some came just to experience, but some will do it.

D: *We need to reach as many people as we can.*

T: Yes, we do.

Message: She is always being taken care of. She is loved and we are here always. We're always here for *all*. Never alone.

CHAPTER TWENTY-THREE

THE BEST AGENDA FOR EARTH

Randy worked at home with his computer. He was highly involved with metaphysics and was using that to search for meaning in his life. He was married with children, yet was frustrated because he felt there was something he was supposed to be doing to help the Earth. This was the main reason for the session, to help discover why he was here.

When Randy came off the cloud, he was observing a strange scene. He was somewhere in snow covered terrain in an isolated location, and was observing two spaceships that had landed on the snow. "They're on a really remote spot on the Earth. It looks like one of the poles... the North Pole." One of the craft had a diamond shaped insignia on it. They each appeared to be big enough to hold about ten people. He felt they represented two different factions, although he didn't know what that meant. There were people around the craft. "They're wearing light gear. I don't know if it's a uniform, but it's more a protective layer. More like a space suit than clothing. Their entire body is covered, even a helmet. They are well protected from the cold." He appeared to be only observing this, and was not participating. Thus the people were not aware of him.

R: They are like two different factions. They're talking about some sort of negotiation.

D: *Do you mean like two different countries?*

R: No, they're two opposing views or ideas. It has something to do with the Earth. They both want the evolution of the Earth to happen. They have input on ideas on the best way for that to come about. One group wants a direct influence, and the other group wants a less direct influence. It's the two different perspectives. The two different ideas; whether it's a direct influence or an indirect influence.

D: *Each one could have different results, couldn't they? (Yes) You said they both agree on the evolution of the Earth?*

R: Right. That's their common goal.

D: *What do they see as evolution of the Earth?*

R: The evolution of human consciousness. Snap them out of the cycle they're in. So one group would like a radical—I don't mean radical in a negative sense. A more direct approach, and the other group would be like a more subtle approach.

D: *But they both agree that it's time for the Earth consciousness to evolve?*

R: Yes. And also they're in agreement that they want to work together. They don't want to have the separate factions. They don't want to have two opposing models. That's part of what they're talking about. Just trying to see each other's perspectives so they can come up with a united goal.

D: *Do you know if anybody has told them to do this?*

R: No, it seems that they are at a higher level of consciousness where they can see each other's thoughts.

I then asked him how he perceived his body. I wondered if he was one of them. "Well, at this point in time I am just pure consciousness. Just observing."

D: *As pure consciousness, you can pick up on their thoughts?*

R: Exactly.

D: *Have they been involved with helping the people of Earth before?*

R: Yes, they've always been here.

D: *So this is not a new faction that has come in?* (No) *If they have always been here, what part have they been involved in?*

R: Subtle influences. They're held on multiple different planes, so in one sense, just their presence, their frequency.

D: *What has that presence and frequency accomplished?*

R: I guess you could say it's brought light. I already see the correlation.

As he started to explain, he suddenly became very emotional. He was trying to cry, but was attempting to hold back.

D: *Why does it make you emotional?* (Randy was still trying to gain control of himself.)

R: Sort of like being a parent... trying to provide a healthy, happy environment. It becomes a sense of responsibility.

D: *So what does that have to do with why you're here?*

R: So I can go back and I look at these beings that are here. They operate on multi dimensions. On one dimension they have ships. They have physical forms manifested. They have the ability to influence other beings and their intentions. And operate on that dimension as they can have an influence with just their mere presence. This will limit the amount of other beings that can come here and influence. So although they don't engage in anything, their presence is known, and on a higher dimension or a different dimension, the frequency of their consciousness, their intent, also helps create the protection around the Earth. It's not an encasement. There's still absolute free will, free flow, but there is an energy that is additive.

D: *It would be going against their free will if they influenced the consciousness. Is that right?*

R: Yes, but they're not. They are simply providing a frequency and an energy, so that's why I am saying it's like a light... a holy light.

D: *So they have the best intentions?*

R: Absolutely.

D: *But you said there are other beings that wouldn't have the highest intentions?*

R: Yes, on multiple different levels. That's where the friction is... the two different perspectives. There is a faction that wants to more directly influence, so in a broad sense that could mean they are here by interfering with the other group. That's one level, and they might influence by making material changes in this dimensional reality... observable changes. One faction thinks it would be more beneficial and the other group is more passive. They're still not sure.

D: *So it's still in the open on which way the Earth should go?*

R: It's not how the Earth should go. It's just a matter of intervention or maybe not intervention. It's the matter of getting back to the parenting thing. When do you guide, or how do you guide, and not interfere or intervene? So that's the fine line between interfering and intervention or something like that. They just aren't sure if the intervention, their interfering or whatever other direct action the other group is considering, is without consequence.

D: *Is there anyone that advises them?*

R: There appears to be a collective.

D: *It sounds like they do want the Earth to evolve; like it's something that is supposed to happen.*

R: Oh, yes. Yes, that's clear.

D: *Does this mean they want them to evolve positively, and away from negativity?*

316

R: I'm not sure they see it that way. I think they see it as evolving to be aware of their free will and free choice. So I guess the one group that wants direct action is a little impatient. (Laugh) That's my interpretation. They think it's taking too long, and that a few of their actions can be quickened. But again, the group that is more of the observer or the less direct influence, respect the level of consciousness here. And there's a bit of a Catch 22, and it's as if both consciousness isn't aware of free will, and it doesn't know that it has a choice, and it's difficult for it to move forward. So how do we introduce that there's the possibility of free will without affecting their free will? In other words, if they do not naturally evolve to the state of awareness where they recognize free will, then that could be potentially like it never happened. So it has to happen within their collective consciousness through evolution, or as the one group suggests, it could be more rapid by influence. And influence could simply be by introduction to new ideas and new concepts and belief systems. It doesn't have to be by physical contact or interaction necessarily.

D: *Then they can introduce new ideas into the collective consciousness of the human race?*

R: Yes, but it's already there. It's how to get people to look at it. How to get people to be aware of it. Right now people are just looking at their feet. They can't see anything but their toes, yet all of the universes' knowledge and gifts are right there. They don't seem to know. They don't have any of the tools at a conscious level of how to get that information.

D: *They probably don't even know it exists.*

R: Right. There's another aspect of intervention or whatever, and that is how to use that ability. It's a skill. Well, it in itself is just an idea. How do you get them to stretch their awareness?

D: *Do they have any idea how this can be accomplished?*

317

R: There are also different ideas within that group. The boldest one would be for them to make their presence known, but that seems like it would create a huge positive and negative event. The people that are ready would easily recognize it, and the people that are not ready would be easily susceptible to their fear and uncertainty and doubt, and would run in the opposite direction. So it would be extremely beneficial to some, but it could be potentially disastrous. Not disastrous in a global sense, but not helpful. That's one of the items that are on the table.

D: *What are some of the others?*

R: To contact a select few people that are ready and to work with them to come up with an idea.

D: *Should this be physical contact?* (Yes) *In a way that wouldn't frighten the person.*

R: Right. That's the crux of the matter. That is one of the things that is on the table. It's a really sticky situation. You introduce yourself to them, then suggest potentials, and then they get a few people to solidify the potential. Let it become very intense. Then you know you would not be infringing upon free will, and then the plan would be to make that a larger intent to introduce more people to the idea. So maybe that's the healing person that creates the ideas that spread it around, so that it instills a human consciousness based evolution.

D: *That way it's not going against free will.* (Correct) *The trick is to get other people to listen.*

R: That would be the human beings' responsibility or task. So the thing would be to get momentum inertia. To get critical mass and the critical mass can adjust the seeds of collective consciousness.

D: *Is it on their agenda to contact governments?*

R: No. There are many other ideas there. That doesn't seem to be a predominant one. It would be individuals that are ready.

D: *Are there any other ideas on the table?*

R: The last one we talked about seems to be the most possible, probable idea or solution, if it goes in that direction. So the other direction is the most passive direction, where they see that it would unfold naturally at some point in time, which would take longer.

D: *Well, if they contact these people, what type of information are they going to give them or share with them?*

R: I think it's based on the individual. There is no ability to share minds, so they know what the people they are going to contact are interested in or—interested seems to be the best word—know what their inclination is. And they would work with that person, based on what that individual's niche or individual interests are. To start with there would be an individual message to each person.

D: *Would the person be able to accept having contact with something that is definitely not human?*

R: The people that they contact wouldn't have a problem. Because they can see the mind of the people.

D: *Over the last many years, people have been seeing the craft, the ships in the air; and more and more people are talking about having contact.*

R: I think this is a different group. This is a group that has never been seen. This is a different group altogether. This is a group that has not intervened... has not interfered. They've always been the observers. They have always simply been present here. They are going to be more direct in the future. Right now they are not doing anything.

D: *I was thinking how difficult their mission has been to be an observer all this time and suddenly change.* (Right) *But they think this could be the best idea?*

R: A faction does, yes.

D: *How would they appear to people?*

R: However that person would best accept them. The beings that I'm looking at have multiple simultaneous potentials. They can be in whatever dimension they require, so they can be in a physical form shape, or they can be ether, so they could influence multiple levels of reality concurrently. So they would appear in the most acceptable form.

D: *What is their normal appearance?*

R: That's the interesting thing. It's parallel. They can be etheric or they can simply be physical, and they can be both at the same time.

D: *So they do not have a normal physical form?*

R: Yes... no. I guess you could say the lower frequency form is a projection of their higher consciousness, but somehow it's totally symbiotic.

D: *You are seeing these beings wearing suits to adapt to the environment, so I thought they had some kind of physical form inside of that.*

R: That was the interesting thing. Maybe that was just for the contacts because, yes, they do have physical form. I'm not exactly sure of what the frequency the form is, but that seems to be flexible as well. They were on Earth to have this meeting, which may be only for my benefit.

D: *Does this explain why you're here on Earth?*

R: So why am I here? I saw the parallel between their intention and my intention. (Laugh) I appear to be a little more "in it." It's to be here, to be alive, to hold frequency, to hold the good and to allow it to be accessible. Whether the people know it's there or not. (Becoming emotional again.) And it goes back to my frustrations about whether to intervene or interfere or... whether to have a more direct influence.

D: *And what do you think your job is?*

R: My job in this state of awareness or my job in human form?

D: *Whichever. You can talk about both.*

R: It looks like it's to individually observe. I feel it's as above as below... it would be to observe. It's difficult

320

to be a dispassionate observer. I think part of the challenge is to be the observer and only the observer with a particular perspective. At some level whatever transpires is appropriate. And I feel like there is a right and a wrong, or a good and a bad, or a light and a dark, or a better influence or a negative influence. And I choose to act there or make a difference or intervene or interfere. When I'm operating at that level, then am I the cure or part of the problem? And again that would take another level of looking at it, so I guess I'm not sure how to play.

D: *What part are you supposed to play in the game?*

R: I see if I influence, then I'm only influencing from the state of awareness that I'm holding in that particular place. But if I do nothing and only observe, that seems like a more natural state for me. That's why I feel alone there.

This was certainly a puzzle, and although we had received some information, I knew there was more that we would not be able to find out this way. So I had him drift away from the scene, and I called forth the SC. I asked why Randy was shown that scene when he could have been shown anything (especially when we were intending to find past lives.).

R: It was the most logical analogy.

D: *Why did you want Randy to see it?*

R: To put it into perspective. The reason for being in physical form.

D: *Explain it to him. That's one of the things he wanted to know.*

R: There are multiple levels of infolded and folded reality experiencing this broader creation. And I don't see a task per se in a physical form for him at this time. He has free will and doesn't know what to do with it. That's part of the way forward aspect because what is

321

the next level once you recognize you have free will? What do you do with it? And he's on the leading edge of that. When he figures that out (Laugh) then it will be additive to the evolution of consciousness.

D: *Can you give him any hints to figure it out?*

R: That's why we were laughing because that's the toil of us ever trying the intervention versus interference versus evolution.

Randy had taken many metaphysical classes and had explored many different avenues and modalities. The SC did not think that was important. "The simplest is just to express his free will. All he has to do is express it. That's the only thing left. There is no more knowledge, no more insight that is required. There is simply to get to a point of self-awareness. So I guess that is the self-exploration, trying to figure out what to do with the free will. Now that he understands free will and believes in free will and sees free will, now he needs to set his intention of how to express that free will. This is going to happen on the planet, and everybody, once they understand free will, are going to run into the same situation. So we have free will, we recognize it now. We can choose this, we can choose that, but again, they need to set intention in order to manifest reality. So simply knowing that they have the ability to choose free will or to choose right or wrong, left to right, up and down, has to be manifested in order to have the experience... to have the knowledge... to have the wisdom to make the evolution. If we are to see the concept of an idea, it wouldn't be evolution at its freest form."

D: *So he has to find it out for himself?*

R: That's part of the discovery process, yes.

D: *Is he concluding his cycles?*

R: Yes, correct.

D: *So if he has completed all his studies, this should be the last one on Earth?*

R: There are really no studies. There were no requirements. There was no traditional process there.

D: *I was thinking of similar to a school.*

R: Well, certainly, there is something to be learned anywhere and everywhere you have an opportunity to have an experience. The reason for this experience is to know, experience free will from multiple levels. The beings that traditionally incarnate here are moving up higher in awareness as well, and their reincarnation process is going to be shifting quite dramatically. And part of our incarnation manifestation at multiple levels in parallel is to assist in these levels in the parallel.

D: *How is the reincarnation patterning going to change?*

R: There are belief systems that exist on the dimension of reality that are also fabricated by levels of consciousness within that reality, which are self-limiting. And just like on Earth, the evolution of consciousness to become aware of something broader is also transpiring at the next level of consciousness.

D: *But there are still some people that have to keep coming back, reincarnating, aren't there?*

R: Yes and no and possibly. The people that believe they have to reincarnate, that are not willing to open themselves up to opportunities, can continue to perpetuate this reality indefinitely. The beings that allow themselves to be more receptive to other ideas and beliefs will have an opportunity to explore other options and move into different realities. Then there are the beings that have been waiting for this to happen for a very long time. So the people, the beings, that have been waiting for this to happen, you can say they are some of the masters that still exist around this planet and have stayed here to assist, to offer their support, their skills, their knowledge, their wisdom, their influences. They know there is something more, and they can move on.

D: *So everything is changing?*

R: Absolutely everything is changing.

D: *He's says he's looking for the truth. And what is truth anyway?*

R: The truth, from the broadest perspective, is everything and it is incomprehensible. You either see the broadest picture or you're looking at the very smallest details. So the truth—to answer the question—there is nothing that is incongruity, but his thoughts and his beliefs and his ideas. That there are no untruths, in other words. He's done all of the work. He has the knowledge. He has the experience. He has the wisdom. He just needs to choose what to do with it. If he structures his intentions, there are no limitations. He has unlimited potential. This is what is going to happen on the Earth plane. Its consciousness is going to awaken to its potential, and it will still not manifest its academic worth... its intellect. There has to be intention and inertia and motivation and direction and a solidification of that knowledge before it becomes real in that reality. And very few have been able to do that, and that's part of his job.

D: *Sounds complicated.*

R: (Laugh) It is as simple as flipping the switch.

D: *Does he flip the switch or do you?*

R: He does. We've never interfered. Let's rephrase the statement. Let's hold it in its context as a reference point. Here he is with the ability to create anything. He has the belief system that will enable him to manifest his intentions and desires... to support his intentions and desires. There is no conflict between his belief systems and the ability to manifest. The crux of the matter is, although he believes he has the ability, which he does, he has not put into motion that ability. So we say it's a switch, but it is a switch of intention. It's not a switch in any other term or way. But it's simply accepting yourself as who you perceive yourself to be. And it's not any intention of whether in a broader human collective consciousness term, you could say, "Who do you want to be today?" And defining that, then manifesting will follow. I'm having a very difficult time describing it, but when he gets to a point of merging oneself... a point of integrating oneself... the point where he no longer sees himself as a separate aspect. When he gets to that point, he will simply "Be." And when he becomes that point, then he will make an impact here, and so he does have free will. And it's not predetermined or predestined, but when he does reach that point, he will demonstrate himself. We're at a point where he has to make a decision to move forward. He has to make a decision to set his intention and to define his intention, and to create his own reality.

CHAPTER TWENTY- FOUR

AN ALIEN IS ABDUCTED BY AN ALIEN

Michael was a young businessman who had migrated from Russia to the United States. Although he was married with children and reasonably happy with his work, he had great insecurity and fears. He felt he was blocked and had a constant feeling of loneliness, of not belonging. These were the things he wanted to explore during the session. I knew the SC would find the answers, but it certainly took a strange route this time. Always expect the unexpected!

The first thing that Michael saw when he entered the scene was red soil and a sky that did not appear to be the correct color. Then as he looked around he became aware of some buildings in the distance, but as he looked closer they appeared to be the *remains* of buildings, similar to debris or ruins. No trees or vegetation, just the bare reddish brown soil and ruins. No sign of creatures. "There is a feeling that there was destruction. I don't feel any fear. I don't feel any terror or anything like that. I'm standing alone on this place and not understanding why I'm there. It looks like some kind of debris on the horizon." As he approached the ruins there was a burnt smell in the air, although he did not see any fire. There were the remains of several stone buildings that had been leveled in some type of destruction. I asked if he felt any connection with this place. "I feel that maybe it's not a place that I lived in, but I belonged to this place and I came and saw that it was gone. I feel sadness inside. I don't see myself being there when it happened." He perceived himself in a female type body that was basically humanoid, and wearing a type of loose flowing garment.

I was assuming that if she did have a connection with this place, she was probably somewhere else when it occurred. Knowing that we can move in any direction we want during these sessions, I had her move backwards to see where she was before coming here. "Right now I'm in open space, and I'm seeing the curve of the planet in front of me. I see the stars. Looks like a galaxy somewhere, but the color of the planet is a dark color. Like the dark side of morning, but the edge is bright. I am on the dark side of this planet."

D: *Is this the one you were just on, or do you know?*
M: I don't know, but I'm in space.
D: *Are you traveling in anything?*
M: I don't know how to explain it. There's a window, but the window is... suspended. It's not like a flying saucer, but the window is a semi-spherical in front of me, rounded with a curve on the top and straight on the bottom. I look through this. And it looks like I'm flying inside this vehicle or something.
D: *Is anyone else on the vehicle with you?*
M: I turn around. Looks like somebody. I cannot see the shape, but it looks like there are some beings. I'm not by myself. It looks like a silver type uniform and I have long arms. It's hot. I feel hot.
D: *What is your job on that ship? What do you see yourself doing?*
M: In front of me is some kind of aviation system... some lights. And it looks like I am doing some navigation because the system light is in front of this window. And I look like I'm maneuvering this vehicle.
D: *Do you have a home place that you started out from?*
M: It came to me: Mars. (Laugh) That's what first came to me.

I asked her to move back to that place that she called her home, and describe what it looked like. She said she was still feeling hot, and I gave suggestions that she would feel cooler and comfortable. "It looks like I'm inside a building that has a reddish color. I don't see a window, but the floor is stone. I'm trying to get out of this dwelling, and the sky is not a blue color, it's more like a gray. I don't see any sun. I don't know if this is where I stay when I am not traveling, but I saw this place on this planet." When I asked if she ate, she said she didn't see food being involved. I moved her forward to an important day and asked what she saw now. "I see myself looking at a much lighter environment in front of what looks like a space ship that is vertical. This vehicle is a silver color and it's standing on the ground. When I look around, there is green vegetation in the distance."

D: *So you're standing in front of what looks like a ship. Is that your ship you live on?*
M: No. I'm looking at this ship in surprise.
D: *What are you surprised about?*
M: Seeing the ship and looking at it in curiosity.
D: *So it's not one that's familiar to you?* (No.) *Tell me what happens.*
M: I see an opening on the ship under the door where it comes down, and it looks like somebody is coming down from the ship. His color is kind of greenish but with a large head and large eyes... thin arms... and it's coming towards me.
D: *It's different than your people?*
M: Yes, different... smaller height, and it feels alien to me. I'm feeling something different... some fear inside because I don't understand what it is.

He then saw a beam of light coming out of the tip of the tall ship and going at a perpendicular angle to his left.

D: *What is the purpose of the light? Do you know?*
M: I do not know the purpose, but I have a fear that this is something I do not understand. And I have a fear that it might have some—how do you say—negative motives

or something that I don't understand.—I'm having a feeling to run, and suddenly I am lifted off the ground and I feel like I am floating horizontally with my legs facing the ship. It looks like something is pulling me in. I feel the energies sucking me in from the ship, because I'm moving into it. Now I'm inside and it doesn't look very huge inside, but what I see are sort of compartments, sort of a room... it's like a holodeck or something. I see another being, which is different from the first one. Very thin legs, very thin arms, smaller head, a silver collar.

D: *But they are different from your people?*

M: They are different, yes, and I now feel I have nothing to fear. It's like they are trying to calm me down. It's a different feeling.

D: *Can you ask them why they brought you in there?*

M: I feel experimentation. I ask the question, why? "The DNA. It has to do with your patterns. Patterns. We have to realign them." I'm trying to get more information. I am hearing that .... It's an alignment restructuring. They are trying to do restructuring of the DNA patterns. Why? To improve the functionality. What kind of functionality? Better abilities. To open more sources. (He was talking to them.) Sources to what? To manipulate energy. To progress in a new direction... new dimension is what comes to mind.

D: *What do they want you to do with that energy, once they realign everything, or change the DNA?*

M: Bring peace to Earth is what came to mind. Peace to Earth.

D: *Do they want you to go to Earth?* (Yes) *With these abilities they are adjusting?* (Yes) *Why did they pick you?*

M: Destruction. I was there? I'm trying to find out. I am to use the energy in a more productive way. It is not good that I was there during the destruction, but what was the reason?

D: *But they want you to go to Earth with these abilities?* (Yes) *How are you going to do this?*

M: How? Reincarnate.

D: *Does that mean you have to die in that body? I am just trying to understand.*

M: So far, I'm getting hot. I'm getting different words, but not complete sentences. I'm trying to figure out flashes of information.

D: *So these new abilities have to do with manipulating energy?*

M: Structuring energy in a more productive way. To connect to other people... to transcend just words and I hear "graphic imaging." It's a little difficult to connect the dots. (Laugh) I just hear in my mind how they are going to do this. I wonder if I'm alone, or are there other beings they are sending to Earth? I am hearing... as a group.

D: *Why would they choose you?*

M: Because of the abilities to bridge energy. More focusing and concentrate.

D: *So these are natural abilities you already have?*

M: Yes, and they wanted to make them more focused. I have to use them when I come to Earth.

D: *So is this their job to go and find beings to change, so they can come to Earth?*

M: Yes. They know where you are and who you are. I am referring to a group of people, and they will know who they are and where to find them.

D: *And they find them and change the DNA so they can do this work?*

M: Yes. I am trying to ask them about the data banks. It is a huge storage in the galaxy of people with different abilities.

D: *Does that go against the people's free will?*

M: It's just where their group is. It's very confusing.

D: *That's all right because it's something you're not familiar with. But they want you to take these abilities to Earth and use them?*

M: It looks like.

I then thought we would be able to get more information by contacting Michael's SC. So I moved him out of the life, and called the SC forth. I asked why it chose this strange circumstance for Michael to see.

M: It was important.

D: *What do you want him to know about that?*

M: About his abilities. How to use them.

D: *In that life, he was a different type of being, wasn't he?*

M: Yes. He had the ability of manipulating energy.

D: *The other being changed the DNA to heighten these abilities. Isn't that true?*

M: Yes, but he misused his energy. This time it is to learn to use it correctly for the benefit of people. The misuse of energy was generic and had severe consequences.

D: *So now that has to be repaid, you mean?*

M: It had to change the way of using the energy in a more creative way.

D: *Is this what you want Michael to do? Is that why you showed him that life?*

M: It was an example.

D: *Is he supposed to use these abilities now?*

M: In a certain way to decode... decode what? Energy patterns... coming back to energy patterns. Some kind of energy patterns. Practicing focus. Focus on energy. System of energy manipulation. Restoration of peace. The universe and balance.

There was a loud thunderstorm going on during the session, and it made the transcribing of the tape difficult.

M:　To organize other people and promoting healthy lives. He can use his organizing abilities to organize people and create more impact on Earth on the lives of many people. It's more powerful. It's more amazing. An organization where people can collectively transform energy in a positive way so there is no negativity, no fear, no sorrow. It is a tremendous job. He is to prepare, and it gradually will come to him. A dimensional body and organizing people and they are going to a new Earth. To spread awareness about this, changing the shift. To help people understand this. A greater use of energy... about greater use of some magnetic field. Sound is very powerful, a structural component. He will help when he focuses and asks for support. I will provide all the sources he needs to proceed with this purpose. Anytime he chooses, we are there. He knows this.

This was a rather confusing session, and I hoped to have more information from the SC, but it appears that an alien can also be abducted and have experimentation performed on him. All for the same purpose. It does not appear to be a strictly human Earthling phenomenon. The extraterrestrials are also being included in the groups of people who were brought in to help the Earth at this time.

CHAPTER TWENTY-FIVE

AN UNUSUAL ALIEN BEING

Dorothy came all the way from Australia to have this session. She was a nurse working in a cosmetic surgery office, and had never married. She had many personal questions about the direction of her life, especially about finding someone to share her life. Also advice about her career. Under normal circumstances this should have been a routine, normal past life regression. But the SC had other plans, and it was definitely not routine.

Dorothy came down through blue light into a white patch of light. She felt surrounded by it.

"All I see now is white. I can feel myself wanting to touch it. You can feel it. It doesn't pull apart but I can walk through it. It flows. It's not solid. Now I'm walking through it and I can see different lights on the walls, like a tunnel. The walls are made of this light. The walls *are* the lights." As she examined it she saw that the lights were actually crystals that had their own lights. "I'm going through this tunnel and I feel my hands touching these, and they become solid and cold to the touch. I'm touching crystals and they are shimmering light, and now it's just a white light. I'm actually walking on crystals because there are crystals underneath me and they have lights. The color comes from the crystals... natural light. I can feel it on my feet and I can touch it with my hands." The crystals were everywhere so that she was surrounded by them and their changing colored light. Even though she was walking on them they were not uncomfortable.

Then as she kept walking, the tunnel walls became clear glass and she could see through them. She saw that she was in space in some type of craft, and was looking down at a planet partially covered with clouds. She was amazed at the extreme beauty as she floated around the planet in this craft. Then she became aware of her body, and it definitely did not sound human. "My hands... you couldn't call it hands, but it feels like hands because I was touching. I see some long little things, but they're not quite fingers. There's like jelly around them. Not like the tentacles of the octopus, but it has the little sucking things of the octopus underneath it. They are dark blue and a bit of orange on the top. I thought I had feet but it's something different. Is it tentacles? Weird... it's really weird. It keeps changing."

I then asked about the rest of her body. It seemed to be composed of the same material. "It looks like a sort of plasma... a jelly formed thing? It's different. It's not a human body. I'm trying to touch my face. It feels like a flower, the texture of a petal. Soft and silky like that, but I cannot distinguish eyes or mouth. Yet I'm able to breathe. I'm able to see. It's very hard to describe. It's like a piece of... how a fried egg texture looks. And as it moves it can change and it creates these tentacle things, and I can change very silky. Maybe more like a plasma thing. Very different... like a jellyfish."

This sounded similar to the creature on the Terminator movie series that could change the shape of its body. Normally such a description would be startling, to say the least, but after all these years of exploring these cases nothing sounds out of the ordinary because our costume that we wear during these life adventures is just that: a costume. It is the soul inside that is important.

DO: I'm still inside this glass thing that I can touch and it allows me to see outside in space, but this glass crystal thing also allows me to see everywhere.

D: *Are you by yourself in this place, or are there others with you?*

DO: I thought I was by myself, but there are two or three others there with me. We are looking at the planet. They are taking notes.

D: *Do they look like you?*

DO: No, they look different from me... different species... different ones.

D: *Are you taking notes also?*

DO: Yes. Not like I would do if I were human. It's all done from the mind, and I go into this chamber and it taps its brain. When you touch the glass and look out, the information goes through you and to this object, and this object will keep the record of what you are seeing.

D: *Like it is absorbing it?* (Yes) *What does the object look like that you transfer the information into?*

DO: It's solid black and yet it's tiny. It has little lights coming through it. It feels not cold, not warm, and I am extending myself to it. One hand against the glass and the other—what you could call a hand—goes to the other side and touches the object. And everything that I've seen just goes through me right into these machines.

D: *So it's like a little machine that's inside this chamber.*

DO: Yes. It's weird, it's a chamber because it's around. And I can see other beings... funny beings. They are taller and different, and they are touching things in front of them. Very weird beings, but they are all very busy. They don't pay attention to me. They are doing their own work, and I am supposed to be doing my own work with this crystal thing that I have with the different lights. I am just looking at them, but they keep on doing their note taking.

D: *But you're just observing this planet?*

DO: Observing, yes, observing the shape of this planet. The clouds are forming out of some sort of gas, that creates the clouds. We stay very close to the planet, and the

craft absorbs some of the gas and it goes through it.
And you can see where it goes through because it is
clear. We want to see what the planet is all about.
What it's made of and we take notes and we take
samples of the gas. And you can see it's coming
through the wall because it is so clear. It goes through
little chambers against these crystals, and it keeps it in
there, and then it becomes solid and we don't see it.
Our craft is floating in the gas of the planet, and
somehow something absorbs it in. And then it gets into
this chamber and you can see it going through, through,
through, and it goes into something, and you can't see it
anymore. It gets in there, but I'm not doing this.
Somebody else is doing that. Mine is by touching with
these sort of hands, these sort of tentacles. The
information goes into many, many little lights in my
body and it goes into this instrument that we touch.

D: *Is that your job to go to different planets and observe,
and absorb information?*

DO: Yes, but the information is to see what we can do with
the planet.

D: *Do you think there's something you're supposed to do
with this planet you're looking at?*

DO: Yes, it has to do with another planet we saw. It is to do
with the lights. This other planet I could see, we had
information that was full of different, different lights.
People, beings, are already there. And the gas is very
important for the resources of their planet. So we are
sent out to see if we can use it. And this is a very small
planet, and this other planet is a huge, huge, huge,
humongous thing... very big. We have been there, and
we have been to this little planet where we are going to
be using the resources. But we are not going to deplete
the planet. We are going to use the natural resources
that will help this big planet, but we are not going to
damage this little planet. The one that is home is so
huge, and this one is like a pea.

D: *Are you sent out to check other places as well?*

DO: Yes. Because these planets, their resources... we'd like to see how we could use it on these big planets. This tiny planet is fine. It's healthy, but it has no life on it. It has many resources that are used on our planet. This little planet is like a little pea size and our planet is like an orange size.

D: *Did you have to come a long way to find this planet?*

DO: No, no. That's the beauty of it. You get this peace and you attach to these films of light, and they will take you where you want to go.

D: *So you don't have to go in a ship or a craft?*

DO: Where we are is a sort of bubble—if you could call it that—made of this glass that you can feel, but then you can touch this light.

D: *So it is like a vehicle.* (Yes, yes, yes.) *And you don't have a fuel?*

DO: Not that I could see, but we need to touch this plate of light. And this plate of light moves, and when it moved we stopped where we have to be. It is the light, the plate of lights that we get attached to and then we go.

D: *Does someone tell you where to go?*

DO: It's already in the little capsule we have. It's already been put in there and we have to connect with the different colored lights. We all knew it was going to be very good. We're just taking samples and we'll come back later.

D: *You said you weren't going to deplete it?*

DO: No, no, no, it never happens that way. We make sure it's not going to hurt the planet or any inhabitants there at all. The gases are going to be very good for us. There are certain compositions that we require that we can use to create all things on our planet.

D: *Do you know what those compositions are?*

DO: I could only see them in colors, and we are after these gases with a sort of yellow color to it. And we see that this planet has this, but we need to clean it to get it to that color.

D: *What are you going to do now? Are you going to take the information back to your home planet?*

DO: Yes. We knew where we were going to get it. We just want to make sure that it is safe, it is right and it is what we needed. We take a sample and the information, and then we go and everybody has what they need to do.

D: *Can you go back and forth quickly?*

DO: Yes. We don't go back the same way we came in. We only get through one way, and then we go back in a different way, like wormholes, I think. When we are ready to go we just go through these wormholes that have streams of things or shreds of blue light. And we go through it and then it takes you home. Somebody knows how to do that.

D: *What does it look like when you go back?*

DO: I'm hovering above this. We're just about to come in. We hover. I'm amazed, and I always see this planet made of light... long streams of blue lights and white lights. You can see the sky against it. It's almost navy blue and you have little stars so far away. And if you look down at the planet it's just made of streams of light going in. When you go through this stream of light, it innately takes us to this. We just pinpoint where we want to go and we go. We have landed somewhere. I look up and there's the space and the sky has no stars, or hardly any. I see many little tubes that take you many different ways, but there are not many people around. It's because this is where we work. This is not where everybody lives, so only the ones that are meant to be there are there. There are many tubes, and you see other tubes with windows that crisscross, and they go everywhere.

D: *So that's where you work and not where you live.*

DO: Now it's taking me past somewhere like I'm on a roller coaster. I'm in this type of plasma jelly-like body, and

D: *Whatever it needs it makes?*

DO: Yes. This is a white platform where I stopped. And it's home. And there is this humanoid, but it's different than me. It's not like me. I feel like it's a wife. This is home.

it's fun to take this ride. I have stopped and I come down, and my plasma can stretch itself to form arms or legs if I want to, or it just floats.

D: *What does that place look like?*

DO: It's made of this crystal and white metallic. And you have windows that you look out. And when you look out you can see this space and there's hardly any stars. We use glass like windows. You can see outside and the walls are a mixture of metals and crystals and you have this whitish material, and you have different sizes. It goes in. It goes out. It goes around and it's white. And when you touch it lights will appear, and you know which one you want to press to which way you want to go. You don't walk. You float, and I'm talking to this being. And it's excited over what we have discovered. And it just looks at me and we're floating.

D: *Do you have to consume food in this place?*

DO: Not really. If I wanted to eat something I know that I could extend myself by a hand touch or light. And I press my hands to it and I get what I need.

D: *So you do have to consume something?*

DO: It's not solid. It's mainly little balls of energy that float. You have little tentacles. I know these little white lights are there, and when I press my hand to it, it comes into me and I feel lots of energy.

He explained that his wife was a different type of being. I asked if they had procreation, duplication, on that planet, and he did his best to explain it. "You can, but it's done from other places. How do we do this? Oh, yes. It's like you press your hands against this thing, and it takes a bit of you and it can take a bit of her. And they can mix it together and something else comes up. I'm asking her to explain to me how we can procreate, and I'm hearing her say, 'Aw, we just do this.' And then we can see in front of ourselves how the new being is created, and it goes into something else until it matures. But we don't keep them. They are not with us. It goes somewhere else and it needs to be grown. And after it gets to be grown it develops. Now we can see them when they are older. They need to go to a special place to grow." It sounded like some type of laboratory genetic manipulation that was done outside of the body. Probably done with cells and genes.

They had to live in these enclosures because of the work they were involved in. "We get into these allocated stations. When you are born you sort of know this. That's why you can do this. You're born with this." The *normal* people lived outside of these enclosures on the surface. "There are many different ones, different life forms. The planet has that. And they live in peace."

D: *And this is one of the main jobs is to go and find things that the planet can use?*

DO: Yes. This is my job. It is eventful. Hers is different, but she doesn't go out as I do. She stays in there and I will say that she does research.

If she appeared different, I asked him to describe her. "She has more humanoid form. A long neck with a little head, and sort of little arms. But I don't see any feet, maybe because she doesn't walk."

I thought it was time to move ahead to an important day, and something chaotic was happening. "Something went very wrong. There's a lot of very, very bad energy and everybody is panicking. It's in the station that I'm working on, that is inside the planet. An explosion! Something happened. Something leaked. I can see the explosion. Nothing I can do about it. I'm in the middle of it and all I can see is the explosion. It blinds my eyes. It is so bright. It just comes out of nowhere." He seemed to be in a daze as he repeated, "An explosion. It exploded. The place that I am. It exploded and everything went to space. It was big... something made the explosion, and it broke through this station we are in, and the explosion went way up into space. No one... no one survived! It was bad."

D: *You said it was so bright it blinded you?*
DO: Yes. I looked at it. It was in the middle of the day, and it exploded and exploded and became big and destroyed everything, and broke through the glass and went all the way out. I could see the explosion. I could see myself trying not to look at it, but... nothing is left. We lost it all. There was nothing left of the explosion of the station. Everyone died in there. Somebody didn't notice what they were doing. Something leaked and created this combustion thing and it went out and nobody had any time to get away.

So even with their great knowledge and expertise, accidents could still happen. He was now out of his body, but was still being affected by the reverberation of the blast. It was pushing him out and further away. "I feel tired. I'm still looking at the mass of explosion. But I feel like I need to rest. I need to drift away. It was quick. I'm seeing what happened, but it's not affecting me now."

D: *Normally on that planet did people get sick and die?*
DO: Yes. Like here now with the explosion I hear different cries. There's nothing they can do. They have to seal the areas and see if there are any more damages. I died, but I can feel my wife looking at what is happening. And there is nothing that she can do because they sealed off that area. She knows I have died in the explosion.
D: *But on that planet did people ever get sick?*

DO: Not really. They live for a long time.

D: *But it is possible to die?*

DO: Yes, yes. You could decide when to die. But it was not my choice this time. That was an accident. But on this planet you could restore yourself back to being young and healthy, or to just let yourself go peacefully... no diseases. You just decide to let yourself go.

D: *So it all has to do with the mind?*

DO: It's not in the mind. It feels like the essence. (Big yawn.) I saw the explosion and now I'm looking at it, and I felt sleepy. I'm drifting somewhere. I'm just floating. I'm part of the yellow creamy clouds. All I see is this yellow mass of light that I need to go into. (She kept yawning.) Someplace to rest.

She then went into the resting place, which would be natural after experiencing such a violent and unexpected death, so it was difficult to get any more information. Normally when the spirit enters the resting place, they can remain there for a long time if it is needed before they decide (or are told) to return to the karmic wheel. So I had Dorothy drift away from that scene, and called forth the SC. The first question I always ask is why the SC chose that particular lifetime. It always has its reasons.

DO: To show her that everything she thought was possible is possible.

D: *From a human standpoint that was a very strange life, wasn't it?*

DO: Not to her, no. She seems accustomed to this. To know about other worlds. She can handle it.

D: *Why did you want her to know that?*

DO: So she's assured that there is life and she had lived like she always wondered. And it is possible and it is true, and she does come from—as she says, "from the stars." We just wanted to tell her, "Yes, you were right." You've been up there all this time.

D: *She said she has always been interested in other worlds.* (Yes) *Is this why?* (Yes) *Has she had many lives on other worlds?*

DO: Lots of them... many.

D: *That one had a very strange body.*

DO: No, it's normal.

D: *As Dorothy, is this her first time to live in a human body?*

DO: No, no, not her first time.

D: *But you didn't go to any of those lives.*

DO: No need to. No need. This is more important. She has had lives in a human body, but not as many as other planets. She didn't need to know about the human bodies. She needed to know about her life on that planet.

D: *One of her questions was, does she have any karma to repay?*

DO: Done... done. Every day is a new day for her. She needs to learn a little bit more about love. Much.

I then brought up the eternal question that everyone wants to know: her purpose. She was unsure about staying in her present career as a nurse, and wanted advice. "She needs to learn to trust and manifest. That's why we showed her this, to wake her up. She has the knowledge of being something else. The vibrations will help her in this time. Tell her to focus on vibrations. She's on the right track. Vibrations, sounds... she needs the sounds... important. When she listens to sounds, the vibrations get better. She is not doing enough with her music. She forgot about being happy. Listening to her music. She used to have music in her life, needs more of it now. Lots and lots of it. The kind of music that moves her body is good. It makes it good for her vibrations. She is not doing that."

D: *She also says that smells, perfumes, are very important to her.*

DO: Her senses will get tuned in to the smell of perfume. That's what she needs, the perfumes. That's why we put the perfumes for her to be used. It's good for her. It clears her senses. That's what she needs. She needs to surround herself with more perfume plants. It clears the sinuses. She needs to focus on the training of her mind. We showed her how to manifest and she freaked out. No need to freak out. It's in her nature to do this. It will be an explosion of knowledge and awareness and she will be so intuned. It will be good for her. She thinks she does not deserve, and she deserves that and more. We can give her more. She just needs to allow. She needs to concentrate everyday... everyday until it becomes second nature to her. Then she can go to the next levels of her study, but her mind is so powerful for her to expand. We need her to let it resonate more. We need her vibrations. It is important to us. She needs to listen louder to us and her vibrations to go higher. The higher the vibration the easier she will listen to love. We need her to wear perfume for that, happiness for that and music for that.

CHAPTER TWENTY-SIX

THE BEACON

Alice came into the scene standing on a beach looking out at the ocean. She was focused on a beautiful rainbow on the horizon that was touching the water. She then dove into the water and swam out towards the rainbow. "Swimming with the colors, going toward the colors. I'm in them now. Yellows, orange, pinks, white. Beautiful. I swam into it. I'm in the rainbow." She sighed deeply, "It's beautiful! Surrounded by the colors. And then turning in them, or they're turning around me. I'm merging into the color. It's wonderful! It's warm, and so peaceful. I'm in a new vibration. I'm in crystal energy."

D: *Tell me about it. What do you mean?*

A: Crystal energy. It's an all-knowing. Why am I crying?

D: *Because it's beautiful. Why do you call it the crystal energy?*

A: (Deep sigh) It's a frequency. It encompasses. It's very comforting. It's very white with... I can't explain it. It doesn't really have a form. It just has some color. It's not a form.

D: *You also said it's all-knowing.*

A: It's just... a place. I do feel surrounded by the light. But I'm also picking up the vibration. So that's a difference. It's hard to explain it.

D: *That's all right. I've heard of this place before.*

It sounded like going back to the Source, which is often described as a beautiful, comfortable white light. It is also described as multiple pastel colors.

D: *It's a good place. How do you perceive yourself?*

A: I'm melting. Not melting, but I don't have a body. When I went into the color I dissipated into the color.

D: *So you don't need a body in this place?*

A: No. I wouldn't want one. Being earthbound you have to have the body, and that's very frustrating. I'm physical in this other vibration. I'm taking on the form of the vibration.

D: *So it has a physical sense, you mean?*

A: Yes. Because I still am there.

D: *Are you by yourself, or is there a feeling of others with you?*

A: There's no one here.

D: *Just you and the vibration?*

A: *You're* here. Or I can hear you.

D: *Is this a place that's familiar to you?*

A: It's not new. I'm leaving it now.

D: *Where are you going?*

A: I don't know. I left there and I'm going to another spot. I'm floating. I'm passing through, and it's nothing. Nothing. Just passing through. There's nothing there. Just the energy in this room now. Purple. It goes inside. It's a strong energy in your room—in this room. It's very strong.

D: *Where are you going?*

A: Don't ask me. (Laugh) I'm not sure. Going through the energy now. There's nothing there. Nothing.

I decided to move her to her house in Las Vegas so she could visualize *something,* and then I could move her to an appropriate past life. She found herself in her bed. But the next thing she saw was a bright light coming through her bedroom window. This was unexpected because she had not mentioned the possibility of an ET encounter.

"There's a very bright light. Oh boy! It's flashing. It's enormous. It's outside the house. That's too bright! It's pulling me outside! It's hurting my eyes now. We're going up—going up! It's pulling me up into this light now. Now that's all that's there. It's flashing as though it's in my third eye. They're putting something into my third eye. Getting information through my forehead. I'm in the light and it's pouring into my head. I can feel it now. (A whisper) Man! Let me concentrate on this. (Pause) Getting wisdom. Sounds ridiculous. (Pause) Whoa! Getting this crystal wisdom. It's coming into my head. It's pouring in. That's what's happening. I don't know where I am. It's very bright. I can hardly stand it, it's so bright! I can't open my eyes."

D: *But you feel like wisdom is coming into your head.* (Yes, yes, yes.) *Do you know what kind of wisdom?*

A: Yes. Tracking. I have to stay in touch. It's how I communicate. Oh, gawd! I'm going to cry again! (Emotional) I miss where I come from. They came to the house because they were trying to communicate, because—I swear this is ridiculous.—I'm from that ship! I want to get back. (Crying) I miss that ship! I'm connected to it. I'm communicating through my third eye. (Then a deep sigh and a sudden revelation.) Oh, gosh! I'm a vibration! I'm a vibration of something that's so huge—so huge. I see it. I see it. It's amazing—it's like a big strobe light. I'm connected to that. Oh, gosh! It's so far! I miss it.

D: *How did you get* here *if you came from there? Can you see how it happened?*

A: Yes, I can. I'm blasting through on a... it's a million little pieces... I see it. Oh, gawd, it's a million... shooting out—shooting out. Very small, but very bright.

This sounded like the separation from the Source in the very beginning when it exploded and all the little sparks flew out. The sparks that eventually became our individual souls.

D: *Did someone tell you to shoot out from that?*

A: Yes, it was a plan.

D: *Do you know the plan?*

A: Yes, I do. I'm not comfortable with that plan. I had to come here. Seeding... It's ridiculous. Seeding Earth. (Pause) Wisdom from beyond. Sharing wisdom from beyond, over centuries. And I mean *over* centuries. (Pause) I see the old man, the old sage. I was blind. I was an old man and I was poor. I came from beyond, I came from space, and they put me in a horrible body. I had so much wisdom, but I was poor. But my brain, I could see everything even though I was blind. So I had a decrepit body, but I knew everything. I was very remote. I was poor. People thought I was blind and pathetic. And I saw everything that I'm seeing now, and felt everything. They didn't give me a good body when they sent me down here, but they gave me the wisdom.

D: *Were you able to share it with anyone at that time?*

A: No. They didn't listen. They were afraid because of the way my legs were, and because of my blindness. It was part of the plan, and I didn't like it. And I don't like it now, either. (Laugh)

D: *You're still part of the plan?*

A: I'm part of the plan. I don't think it's a very good plan, to tell you the truth.

D: *But you're not the one that made the plan.*

A: No. Not the one.

D: *What happened after that, did you go to other bodies?* (Yes) *Were you ever able to share the wisdom?*

A: Yes. I shared it from constant communication with space. I'm always attached. And they visit and they bring me back.

D: *When they visit, where do you go?*

350

A: I go with them. I go on the ship. I do. I love it.

D: *Is that when they were downloading more wisdom?*

A: Yes. That is. I got on the ship. I go up and I go in, and I see the beings now. I love them and they're my people.

D: *In the beginning you said it was just from this light.*

A: I see it now. I'm in the ship. Or I might be in a planet. They come and get me. They can shoot you back down in a light. I understand it now. They shoot you in through light and vibration.

D: *And they come and get you every once in a while?* (Yes) *What do they do during those times?*

A: They regenerate me. It's wonderful. I have healing now. I have more energy. I have more telepathy. They put... it's like a charge of energy.

D: *And have they been doing this....*

A: Yes, forever. Forever.

D: *All through your life as Alice also?*

A: Forever. I had to get more. It's started to impact me more. They've had to come back and do more adjustments.

D: *What has started to impact you?*

A: New dimensions. I'm more multidimensional, and I have to be able to get out of the body quicker. I have to be able to leave quicker. And I have to be able to change into light faster, and they had to do something in order to—this sounds really nuts... this is crazy.— But I had to be able to transfer into a new kind of light energy.

D: *In order to do the things you have to do now, you mean?*

A: Yes. I have to be able to act back because they have new technology as well.

D: *They're growing also?*

A: They're growing, they're growing big time. I think I have a message for you. I know the message.

This is always a surprise, but not unprecedented.

D: *You have something for me?*

A: They want you to know that they're shifting, and they're shifting you. And that your energies are like our energy. That you're going to be able—you're flipping as well—I call it flipping. You're able to flip in and out faster now, and they're working on you. And their ships are growing in number, and they're all over this planet. And they want you to know that you're going to be quicker. And that they are taking you as well. And that... (A deep sigh) It's amazing. You probably already know this, but it's getting faster. It's getting so much brighter, and whatever they do here on Earth, they're never going to catch up. And they're circling the planet with so much light, and so much electric— it's not really electric as our physics on Earth know. But they're circling it because that thing that the Earth is doing is going to be able to penetrate because they're so much more advanced and so much faster. Have no fear.

This sounded like the blasts of light that the ETs were sending toward the Earth to offset the damage humans are doing to the planet. This was explained in *Convoluted Universe, Book Two.*

D: *Is there a reason why this is happening?*

A: Yes. Space technology and space on Earth. There's a big shift. Different stars. It's a protection, it's a layer. (Firmly) The government will never touch them.

D: *That's good, but what do you mean by a layer around the Earth?*

A: They're putting a layer around their ships. It's a new technology. They won't be able to get to them anymore. All because they had to do it in a light. It's a spinning frequency. They have to do it in order to

352

survive. They will still be able to watch here. They have to come and go because they left so many of us here, and they still aren't finished with us being here. And so they have to protect us, and they have to protect themselves.

D: *And this is the reason they're still in contact with those they've left here?*

A: Yes. I'm just a channel. All I do is submit information about what's going on around me. I pick up a lot. I send it back. (Pause) There's a big plan. They're empowering people. It's not just me, it's many people. They're doing it by vibrations. You have to be in a clear area though. There's lots of interference. That's why it's good where you're at. (I live in an isolated place in the country on top of a mountain.) For instance, I have to leave Las Vegas—there's too much interference.

D: *Yes, it's a very chaotic energy there.*

A: Yes, it's interference. So they're trying to move us out to places where it's clearer, cleaner—not polluted. No pollution, no interference. They have to have us because we're, for some reason, giving them feedback. I can't see how they do it.

D: *Let them show you.*

A: (Pause) What do they want me to do? (Pause) Nothing. I think I am like a beacon. I don't understand it either.

I have explained before about some people who are simply channels, antennas, or in this case, beacons. They don't have to do anything in order to help with the coming changes. They just have to simply *be.* In that way they are helping by unconsciously transmitting information.

D: *What do they mean by giving them feedback?*

A: (Whisper) What do you tell me? (Pause) It's so ridiculous. Should I tell you? It doesn't make any sense.

D: *Yes, tell me. It may make sense to me.*

A: (Deep sigh) Okay. I'm a beacon. If the wires are too crossed in a certain area, I can send them back fields of energy. (She was making hand motions.) I send them back when it's safe to come in. I can feel them now. It's so strange because they can't come in if there's too much chaos. They're monitoring the Earth, and some of it is going to be destroyed. A lot of it is going to be destroyed. And they're following us because we're connected, in order to get us to the safest places (Softly to herself: *"This is so bizarre."*) because some places are all tangled. The wiring is all tangled. So they're moving us to be able to have groups together. They want us together. It's a crystal energy. They're going to move people together. They need crystal energy. It's the way they stay in contact with the Earth without landing on Earth. They don't have to land here if they have us. We're not Earthbound. We're connected to them. It's safer for everybody. It's safer. It's clearer.

D: *So they don't want everyone in the same place, but they want everyone to be connected?*

A: Yes, they want us all connected. I feel these intense crystal vibrations coming down, and we're connected straight up so far, so far. It's beautiful! And we have something in us. Why do they want us all over? They want us scattered around because there's going to be places hit. And they want a nice pattern of scattered energies that they can transmit through. They want transmitters that they can keep connected to when there's a lot of destruction going on. Because certain places are going to blow themselves right up. Right up!

D: *Do you mean literally, or natural?*

A: There's natural, there's not natural. There's overwhelming destruction in certain areas. There's a war, of course, coming. Of course, we know that there's a war. But it gives them a little bit of extra first-hand knowledge about what's happening on Earth if they scatter us around. There are many of us, too. There are a lot.

D: *So we can be in communication without even knowing we are? When Alice came into this life did she come in with this plan? That she was to be part of this?*

A: I didn't want to be part of the plan. (Laugh) I saw the picture before coming in. I knew that I felt this was not a good plan for me to do because I saw it and I'd seen it before. I'd really like to retire. I'm very mundane. I'd just like to stay in the one vibration. And I don't care for chaos. I don't like drama and chaos.

D: *You said these other beings are accumulating the information we're sending out?*

A: They are.

D: *What are they going to do with it?*

A: I want to give you the correct information. They're compiling it. It's like a radio show. They're studying it for future generations. It's keeping a history. Planets. They're logging it. I see them now. (Laugh) Funny creatures. Yes. They're funny creatures. They're told to do it.

D: *Where do they get their instructions from?*

A: Let me look. (Pause) They're programmed. We're all programmed, it seems like. They're getting their instructions from the mother ship, the mother source. There's a big source, that's like the mother of invention. So funny, the mother of invention. (Laugh) It's like they're always testing. Okay. I won't make it up. Do you really want me to tell you what I'm seeing? *(Yes)* There are little blue crickets on this ship. There's a little office. It's so cute. They're putting little things away and they're really working hard. They're constantly working. They have long arms, like little worker bees, but they're not bees. And they're working hard. They're very mechanical when they're putting this stuff away, once you get up there...Is that me? Maybe. I don't know. I'm filing—putting things away. Putting things in their place. Everything's going in a place. I like putting things away. I liked that job, that was a good job. Ohhh, it's being accumulated! And it's like a Bible of sorts, so they can refer to it. They want to be able to refer. It's a reference guide for the future, in case they get people from Earth. Then they want to know, "Okay, is it agreeable to talk to this person? We want to be able to have a reference." They'll know exactly where to go. We're integrating our societies now, and they want to be able to have a record just like a hospital record. They want to know how to associate. And that's why they're putting beacons up in different locations. So they can have the record, read back in history so they can trace it. Seven hundred years from now they'll be able to look back. That's how long they live, seven hundred years. That's what they do for their life. They have to be able to come and do a job, and for us it's seven centuries, but for them that's just a lifetime. They have to look at this stuff, record it. They don't have an opinion. They are just watching. Recording.

D: *You said there was also an integration?*

A: It's an integration of societies. We have to integrate. We're becoming advanced souls. They want to advance us. I'm an advanced soul, you're an advanced soul. They're wanting to see how far they can go with a human body in order to advance us to their level. I'm multidimensional while I'm here. Yes, I'm supposed to accumulate this stupid rotten energy. (Laugh) Yes, I'm like the research rat.

D: *Is Alice supposed to use this in any way? Or just accumulate it and pass it on?*

A: That's a big question. I have the ability to share this with others by using my hands. I have the ability to put my energy onto someone's forehead. I can pass it on. I don't know if I'm supposed to do that.

D: *What do they say?*

A: I'm supposed to be transmitting wisdom, and yes, I'm supposed to do that. I can pass on this wisdom. It's in me. I can feel it right now.

D: *And you wouldn't even know where it was coming from.*

A: No, I wouldn't. Well, I know now. Work with the third eye. It's all about the third eye.

D: *But you said they want me to continue with what I'm doing?*

A: You are a beacon. That's why you have to go everywhere. (Laugh) They're sending you everywhere because it's imperative.

D: *They did say they were regenerating Alice's body.*

A: They're regenerating you too. They're regenerating you because you have to keep going to these different places. And every time you leave a place you leave some of you with it, and they can find it. They love you. You have to go.

D: *I'm trying to pass on the information.*

A: Yes, you leave it there and they'll find it. People that you're teaching, they'll find it because you leave something there.

D: *Are they regenerating my body?*

A: Yes. They're regenerating, and you know it. They don't want you to stay Earth-bound. They want you more with them. They want you lighter. They want you in clear light.

D: *So they will take care of my body so I can continue to do these things?*

A: That's what they want, you lighter. You're going to become like a crystal yourself. They're redoing your whole body. They're redoing everything about you. They're doing your brain.

I was told this same thing in the very beginning of my work. Before I had ever begun to travel, they told me that I would be going to many countries, and that everywhere I went I would leave a part of my energy. It would not deplete me, and I would not even notice it, but it would be left in that place and would be felt by others. They also said that my books would carry an energy that would be felt by others. So it appears many things are happening without our conscious knowledge.

CHAPTER TWENTY-SEVEN

ENTRYWAY

During the session Pamela wanted to explore something that she thought was a UFO experience. She remembered seeing what she thought was a UFO, but didn't know if anything else happened. I took her back to that night. She came into the scene while she was driving her car home. She saw something in the sky, but she had difficulty describing it. At first she thought it was a light up in the hills. But then, "No, it wasn't a light. It was a ship that looked like a huge moon. And I knew it really wasn't the moon. It just had the shape of a moon, and that was how it appeared to me. It seemed like I stayed in my car, and I remember parking in the driveway. But I knew that I'd gone up there, too. I saw myself driving. I saw myself continuing going home, but I also knew that I was up there. That I had been taken up to that ship. I can't even explain what I'm seeing."

D: *Like being in two places at once?*
P: Yes, because I was aware of being in the car and going home, but I was also aware of not being in my body. Yet I knew that the body had gone home. Now I'm seeing long... I have to call them "shafts" because I don't know what they are. It's just energy with points on it. (Hand motions of something going across horizontally.) They're flat, but it's energy. I don't think it's metal. I think it's a whole energy. There's a nucleus, and there's a center to this, and the center looks dark. And around the center is brilliant yellow light, but you can also see shafts of light coming out. It

must be coming from over here somewhere, on my left. Everything is just energy. There's no structure. Everything seems to be working together, but also going in different directions. And I see a wheel up here. (Over her.) Up over the top, a huge big wheel. And there's something over here (on the left) that has brilliant light coming out of it. It's *brilliant* light. It's almost like you can't look at it because it's so brilliant. It appears to be—I want to say the "Sun," but I'm not sure that's what it is.

D: *Does it have anything to do with that wheel?*

P: No, the wheel's gone now. It's just the brilliant light. I was thinking about the ship, and that's where it took me, back to this place. This place is where I belong.

D: *Why do you feel that?*

P: Because it's comfortable. That's who I am, that light. Wherever this place is, wherever it exists, that's my home. That's who I am is this light. And it's projecting—it's almost like spears, or big projections that are coming out. I really don't know what it's doing, but it's very bright and very comfortable, and there's a lot of energy there. There are many beings there and they're all energy. They're all one.

D: *And you feel you've been to this place before?*

P: Oh, yes. It's very familiar. And it glistens. I can't even think of an analogy to explain it. But it's just there.

D: *Is this inside this ship, or craft?*

P: No. I don't even know how the craft is related to that. But once I got on the craft I saw those shafts—there seemed to be shafts coming down at an angle—and then there were shafts leading away from this brilliant light, this home. It's just home, and everything is peaceful and incredible there. It just brightens up everything. There's a lot of energy there, and it's all one. You only become separate when you leave that space. But, in this body that's *here,* I can feel everything is molecular. Like you can feel every molecule that *this* is made up of. And I can feel that there's a connection between the two. I don't know how it's connected.

D: *Between the body and the place?*

P: And the light. It's an aspect of it. I guess you'd call the body a piece of it.

D: *But you said this is no longer a craft or a ship?*

P: It's another place. The ship was a portal to get through there, like a starting point. Once you got *there,* then you were taken here. So it was almost like a triangle, being here, and then there, and then over here. So that's how it's connected.

D: *First you had to go to the one that looked like a moon.*

P: Yes, and that was like an entryway. That's what it was. It (the ship, craft) was just an entryway, a passage to this place. This place is all one. It's an entire body of energy. It's a space where all the energy is intermingling. And we leave that place to go and experience the bodies. That brilliant, beautiful light that spheres are coming out from. And it's brilliant and sparkling.

D: *But you are living in a body on Earth. Why did you go back there on this night when you were driving?*

P: Just to visit. (Her voice broke as she became emotional.) I need to go back there just to remember a home. Just to remind me. Just to know that I belong there. And it's nothing but energy. There's no structure. *It's just home.* You would think I'd be able to tell you the name, but there's no physical name for that. Other than I can just tell you what they would say on Earth is "home." But *that's home.* It is just a loving reminder.

D: *Is that why you were allowed to go back on that night?*

P: I go back there often. I just don't remember it.

D: *Why did you remember it that night?*

P: I guess because I get frustrated with what goes on, on this planet. Because of all the sadness and all the things that go on here. And I feel helpless that I can't make it right.

D: *It is a challenging place, isn't it?*

P: Sometimes it's an ugly place.

D: *You said there were others there. Can you talk to them?*

P: You don't need to talk to them because once you're there and you're embodied in the Whole, everybody knows and understands, and it's like a renewal. You don't talk. You just *be*. And you know that it's all right. And that you need to be *here* to help. But once in a while you have to go back just to feel. Because when you get down here on the Earth you get involved with earthly things, and you get pulled in different directions. And you need to feel that whole again. You need to feel that love and the comfort in the light. You just need to feel that.

So it appears that these pure, innocent beings that have never been to Earth, and have been called to come here during the Earth's time of need, do feel isolated. I have had many cases when the beings on the UFOs interact with someone, and the person cries because they want to go with them. They do not want to be left here. They feel so close to these beings, closer than to their Earth family. But the beings usually remind them, "You can't go yet. Remember you are on a mission. You can't go until it is finished. But mostly, remember you are never alone." So it would make sense that they are allowed to return and visit "home" at times (and yet not consciously remember because the memory might interfere with the "plan") in order to make living on Earth bearable. Also if they remembered too much, they wouldn't want to stay here.

This *home* also sounded very much like the way the Source or God is described by people who return there. So are the ETs also able to help the person return there? If, during their monitoring of the person, they pick up that they really need to have a glimpse of where they came from, they can help take them there for a brief visit. There seems to be many different reasons for people experiencing what they consider to be an abduction. When they understand the real reasons, it is not negative, and can be extremely rewarding. To know that they are cared for so beautifully and lovingly.

D: *If that place was so beautiful, and you were so happy there, why did you come into a physical body?*
P: Because I really thought I could make a difference.
D: *Did anyone tell you to come?*
P: No. You choose to come. It's not that you get tired of being in the Whole because you are the Whole. But you go and do other things. I'm seeing a whole bunch of different things now. I don't know what these other things are. But you go to different places, and I came to Earth because I wanted to help.
D: *From that place could you see Earth and what was going on?*
P: No, I didn't see what was going on.
D: *Then how would you know that it needed help?*
P: You just know. It's part of who you are. It's part of knowing because you're part of the Whole. You're part of everything that is. You're that light. You just know. But Earth is not a bad place to be. It's just that you need to go home every now and then just to know that things can be tranquil and beautiful and peaceful.
D: *How did you think you could make a difference?*
P: I don't know. I'm seeing that portal again. It's that moon, and now it's in the upside down position. Just by being here. Just by breaking up the frequency that's going on here. I thought my frequency would make a difference. There are many of us that think that. And seeing it now, right now it does make a difference. It's just that the frequency, the energy, the mass energy, the whole, the tier on this planet Earth was... stuck? Is that the right word? It was stuck. It was not changing.

And so by different *shards* coming in at different places piercing this energy that's going on on this planet, that it would make a difference.

D: *Almost as though the planet's energy becomes stagnant? Would that be a good word?*

P: Yes, it's stuck. That's what I saw. Those shafts of light were those shards coming in. And the shafts going in the other direction were energies that were leaving. Those long shards that had pointed ends that were coming out before I saw "home." And once they left the light they didn't look like light anymore. They started looking brownish, or like they had more substance to them. Those were energies leaving to go other places, and I don't know where they all went. Some came to Earth and they would penetrate down into the Whole, the mass. And they would make holes and separate the energy. Yes, that's what it is. That's what makes the difference. There were bunches of them leaving at a time, but I don't know where the rest of them went. Some of us came here, but they all go to different places.

D: *What about the energy of the beings that are already here on Earth? Couldn't they do anything to make changes?*

P: They're stuck. They've done the same thing for so long that they're stuck.

Especially if they have lived countless lives on Earth and are enmeshed in karma. As I say, "They are carrying around so much baggage and garbage." They need to release all of that before they can begin to make a difference. And many, many of my clients are unable to release the karma, the very thing that binds them here. They say, "How can I forgive him (or her)? You don't know what they did to me." So apparently as long as these attitudes remain, they are stuck and unable to create or participate in the much-needed changes.

P: So we needed to pierce what was going on so the energy could be dispersed. And that's the only way they could make changes. It would be like if you had a large clump of something—and that's what it is, a clump. And if you sent shards down into it, that would break it up. And then the energy would start to be different.

D: *And that was what you decided to do.*

P: When I left the light, this is just where I came. Other ones did, too.

D: *Is this the first time you've ever been in a physical body?*

P: No, but I don't see myself ever looking like this before. I see myself as a substance. As thicker than energy, but I don't see myself looking like the body that I'm living in now. I don't see me as that, ever. I'm looking. (Pause) I'm not seeing physical. I'm seeing substance. I'm seeing filmy, etheric energy, but I'm not seeing solid substance. It's different from the Earth body.

D: *But it's different from the one you came from.*

P: Oh, yes. The one I came from is... I can't even explain the feeling and the euphoria because it's just wonderful. It's light and it's clear and it's high. Everybody is *one*, or everything is one. All energy is one, and everything is symbiotic. I guess that would be the way to explain it. And then when you start to leave you feel it's not as comfortable, but we all go. We can go into other realms and take on forms. And I can see forms, but they're not thick like this is thick. They're not that dense.

D: *Can you see what kind of forms those were?*

P: I can see a parade of forms, actually, where some are skinny and tall, and some are just filmy, and some are wispy. It looks like things are starting to go into a nucleus again, into a ball. That always looks dark whenever it starts to do that. It gets real thick and you can't see through it anymore.

D: *Do you think you were, more or less, experimenting with different forms and substances?*

P: We all do that. We go and experiment to see where we can live. Where we can do the most good. Where it's most comfortable.

D: *And some of them you didn't like?*

P: Actually, when I look at them they all look good. I think the best one is where you don't have a solid form, but yet you have enough form so you can move about and fly, and float. It seems like all the places that I've been, though, the planet Earth is the densest. It's just the place that has many experiences.

D: *Many lessons. Many things to learn?*

P: Yes. I just don't see how learning all this is necessary. Maybe when I get back it will make more sense.

D: *Then the body of Pamela is the first you've had as a physical body?*

P: I'm feeling that this is the first physical body I've had like this. It feels different. It doesn't feel really good. There were no limitations with the others. You could move around freely, and this body, you're stuck. Stuck is not good. You know you can do more.

D: *Pamela said when she was a child she could levitate things and move them around.*

P: Yes, that was fun times, when you're little. She could also pass right through things that you think are solid. But she can't do that anymore. (Emotional) I don't know what happened. That's why it's not fun to be here because you can't be who you are. You have to do what everybody else does. You can't do the things you know you can do. As a child she knew she could do those things. And she still knows she can, but it doesn't work anymore. It all has to do with belief. When she goes up there it's not stuck because the energy is different. And you can move about, and you can see, and you can feel. And you can do all the things that you can't do when you're stuck in a body. You get down here and

366

you start thinking you can do this, and you can do that. And then you start trying to make a difference, and that's where the problem's been. That's why I got to go back to the light, so I could remember this and be reminded of this.

D: *So she has to realize that she can't try to change everybody.*

P: No, that's not what she's all about. That's not her energy. Her energy is just being who she is. Everything is just perfect there. Deep down she knows these things. It's just that she doesn't practice what she knows. That's really tearing you apart whenever you know something, and then you keep trying to do something else. That's where all the physical problems come from. We keep trying to deny what we're here for. There are many of us down here. And there are people from many other places that are here, too, that are helping. There are many people.

D: *Did they all come for the same purpose?*

P: No. Many people—they're not people—many *energies* came here to feel how it feels. Some came down to learn. I guess all of them have their own reason. I don't know their energies. It feels like now that they came to help in their own way. I'd say, yes, that would be true.

D: *Did they all come from the same place?*

P: Oh, no. There are many places.

D: *So they didn't all come from the energy place.*

P: Oh, no. No, I'm seeing a place that looks like a reflective substance. And there's a bluish green light coming off it. Sometimes it looks like it has a pointed ceiling. And at other times it looks like it goes on for infinity. Many of the energies came from this reflective substance place. I don't know where that place is. It's far away. I feel these energies. I'm seeing another place, too. Ohhh, this place doesn't look really good because it has dark around it. It's a dark place, and those

367

energies aren't really good. But the energies that are coming from that reflective substance are coming to help.

D: *Are many of these coming into a physical body for the first time?*

P: Let me check. (Pause) Some. What I'm getting is that when we're in our energy state, we all feel that we can help, regardless of where we go. And we all choose to separate, at various times, to go to different places because we feel our energy would be an asset to where we're going. And most of the time, I would say it is. So I'm getting that we—I say "we" because it's all of energy—that we go to many different places where we think we can be uplifting, or experience something we haven't experienced before.

D: *But, of course, when you get down here, it's different, isn't it?*

P: Oh, it's very different. It's very different.

D: *Mostly because people don't remember once they get into the physical body.*

P: It's almost like you're cutoff from who you are. I go back often. I just realized that I get to go back often. And I remember wanting to go back and stay there. And I don't know who *they* are that tell me, or maybe it's me that tells me that I need to stay here. It *is* me. There are no *they.* I need to stay, and do what I came here to do. If I could cut it short I would have been out of here a long time ago. I'd have been gone, but that's not what the energy's all about. And I know that's not what it's all about. It's just that whenever you go to Earth and you get involved down there you feel like, "I don't want to be there. That place is ugly. I want to leave." But it's not that easy. And that's what I'm seeing now, is the energy that we've left behind is not letting us come back yet because it needs to experience that, feel it.

D: *It needs to experience?*

P: What I'm getting now is that I wanted to experience this. Imagine that. But that's what I'm getting.

D: *And you can't go back until you've done your job. (No) But many of the things that Pamela remembered, or felt, she thought had to do with ETs and spacecraft. This doesn't sound like that.*

P: Let me get the picture here. (Pause) Now I'm seeing many craft. Oh. you know what it is? That's how we travel sometimes. That's the craft that we travel in. I didn't. I say "we" because I'm thinking of the ones that came—*we* didn't have any craft when we came to the Earth. We just came down in our energy form. I'm seeing a little, teeny baby now. Isn't that funny? There's this huge energy that we are, and we come down into this little, tiny baby. It seems incredible because where would the rest of the energy go?

D: *Did you have to have permission to go into a baby?*

P: Somehow that was all worked out, and I'm not seeing that now.

D: *I was thinking there has to be rules and regulations.*

P: There's guidance. Everything is guidance. I'm not seeing that now.

D: *Well, what is the purpose of traveling in the craft?*

P: That's going to other places where you need to travel with your own kind of energy. Because where we are, even when I say that I can see the beautiful, brilliant, huge ball of light—that's a specific energy. That's a home energy. So when you travel outside of your realm, you need to travel in a craft that is of that energy that you live in, that you are.

I was also told this unique energy has to be contained, or it would merge with other energies that it was passing through. This was a form of protection. So many of the beings that travel on these UFOs are light beings. Many of them also have the capability to change their shape to conform with the surroundings they find themselves in.

D: *Does she do this in her physical body?*
P: No, no. That's just another part of her that's traveling. (A realization.) That's what it is because she's closely connected with these other parts. So she's feeling these other parts as they're doing these things, but she's not getting the whole picture. I'm seeing a part of her now traveling in a craft to a place that has very, very high pillars. There are crystals, and energy beings. And it's not where she is from, so she has to travel in her own energy to get there. I don't know what she's doing there. Actually, it's not a "she."
D: *But it's another part of her?* (Yes) *As though when she separated from the home light, the home place, it went into different pieces?*
P: Yes, there are many different pieces.
D: *And one of those pieces is Pamela?*
P: They're all the same piece, like when the shafts separate from the whole. That shaft can then go into many different places in different realms to have different experiences. Somehow I can't connect with all of those. I just know that's what happens. There has been a band placed around her head. It feels like a tightness that's around the head. (Hand motions showing it is across the forehead.) It seals that connection. It's a connection so that she's not getting the other parts. I guess she's not supposed to. Just to know that there are other working parts, other working energies. It's supposed to be a comfort to know that it's all right. That everything is in perfect order. That all the parts are working together and doing what they're supposed to do, and they'll be back together soon. That's what the message is, it's supposed to be a comfort.
D: *You know how humans are. If they don't understand something they either fear it or blow it out of proportion.*

P: You know what it is? It's because of the limitations that are here. I think once you're out of the body, you are who you are, and you're all connected. It's like a big pot of soup. You might be a carrot or a potato, but you're still soup and you're all connected. Then when you're taken out of the soup and placed on different parts or locations, then you're separated from the whole. You're not getting it and it's confusing. It's not making sense then. But once you're back home, or back together again, then you know it's all right and everything is just the way it's supposed to be.

D: *Then when she is having these ideas about spaceships and ETs, she's just getting the memories or the experiences of these other parts of herself.*

P: Yes, that's what's happening.

D: *She was wondering about implants. Do you know if there are any in her body?*

P: Yes, there are implants. There is one in the temple; on the right shoulder.

D: *Who put them in there? Or how did they get there, let's put it that way.*

P: Actually when she came in she had those, and they're energetic from where she's from. They have always been there. In recent years she's wondered about it, but she knows that they're okay.

D: *In my work I know that other beings will put implants in people for various reasons.*

P: No, I don't get that it is other beings, they're from where she's from.

D: *What is the purpose of them?*

P: It's information that she can call on. That helps her to locate portals so she knows how to get home.

D: *It was almost like they were put in when she came here, so that she wouldn't get lost. Would that be a good way to say it?*

P: Yes, that would be the right way to put it.

D: *So she wouldn't get lost in the physical, and to allow her to find the portals to go home.*

P: Right. It really is good. And it's also a reminder of who she is. I am being told that whenever they itch and cause her to notice them, that is when she has more contact with home. I don't think she realizes that.

D: *I see different kinds of people. Is she a different type from the ones I've worked with?*

P: No, I think you've worked with many of us before.

D: *Of course, I was told not to put these people together.*

P: That's true. They're more effective on their own. They get together and that just reinforces the need to go back. And they need to stay here.

D: *I was told the energy would be diluted if they were put in contact with each other.*

P: It would be diluted.

D: *I was told I would meet several, but I never know for sure. This is that type of energy then.*

P: It's a different type of energy. There were all different types of energies. We come from different places; we hold different things that make the parts of the whole. And the part that I'm from, I've not met before. I feel that you have. But I don't think on this planet Earth that these energies need to come in contact with one another because they're stronger alone.

D: *I was given the analogy that they're like two waves in an ocean.*

P: That's true. They go different ways.

D: *But whenever the waves are put together then it dilutes their power.*

P: Then they start going one way.

D: *So that's why it's alright for me to know about them, but I'm not supposed to put them in touch with each other.* (No) *Even though they do get lonely.*

P: I haven't found that I'm lonely in the body of Pamela. I feel very strong being alone. I have more strength alone than I do when I mix with the humans because they seem to be so scattered. They're so involved with what's going on on their planet that they forget who they are. And the body of Pamela, when she's alone, she remembers and she feels very strong. But when she gets with other humans and starts doing things that humans do, it pulls her in directions that she's not comfortable with. And that's why she likes being alone.

D: *But when she first saw the light, she wanted to go back. So I thought she was lonely.*

P: It was a feeling of desperation like you can't hardly wait to get home. There are many from different parts of the cosmos that come to help out and disperse the energy that's here. And it's much needed.

CHAPTER TWENTY-EIGHT

ANOTHER ASPECT (A HIGHER?) SPEAKS

T his session was done as a demonstration at my class at the Northwest New Mexico College in Santa Fe, New Mexico. This college is unique because it offers a four year course in all phases of alternative medicine and natural healing.

Jane was a beautiful young woman who was becoming well known for her work as a psychic healer. She was born with many abilities that she had been able to retain and utilize. They had not been pushed back and forgotten, as so often happens with these type of children. She mostly wanted information about her beginnings. This is another common question, "Where am I from?" Of course, the answer is always the same. People think they came from a certain home planet, but that is only one step on their long journey. We all came from the same place when we were created by God (or the Source) and sent out to experience our journeys. She also wanted information about her life path.

When Jane came off the cloud she was going up instead of down to the Earth. She moved out into the stars, and became very emotional as she did so. She said it felt like a homecoming, "Because of where I come from." She said she had missed that place, and it would be good to find it again. She wanted to go north and as she did so, she saw she was surrounded by crystals in the sky. Then as she moved very quickly through space, she was coming to the place she was looking for. In the distance she saw ships coming. "They're small and round, black and silver. And they're coming to welcome me. They're not really from where I'm from...

they're just greeters." Then she felt she was suddenly sucked into one of the ships. Next a strange phenomenon happened that I have had happen before. I am always prepared for the unusual because, for me, it is not uncommon. However, for a class it can be startling. A different voice came through, and it appeared as though I was in communication with some type of entity that was onboard the ship, rather than Jane. When this happens, I just go along with it.

D: *What do you see after you're inside?*
J: (Confused) I don't understand your language.

I gave instructions that it would be able to understand me and communicate with me. "Can you access that part of Jane's brain that can understand what I'm saying? I really would like to speak to you. Will that be acceptable?" It agreed. I explained that I knew it did not use language, but usually communicated mentally. However, *we* have to use words to communicate. "I want you to be comfortable and we can communicate. Will you be able to do that?" It agreed, so I began to ask questions.

D: *We're looking for information. Is it okay if you tell us about this place? (Yes) Is it a small ship?*
J: Yes. It's very small because I don't spend much time here. It is only used to go back and forth. It looks like a small airplane inside, except it doesn't have seats. It has a small metal kind of kitchen. I'm not sure how to explain it. I kind of make food there, but I don't really understand the kitchen.
D: *If it's a kitchen, do you have to eat anything?*
J: I don't have to eat.... I don't know how to explain that. Humans call it food, but we create minerals... no, that's not the right word. We just create things that our structure uses for energy. I can't explain it. I just feel it, but I'm being asked to let... there are people that

need to know this information because they need to work with this energy.

I asked for a description of his body. "I don't look like anything. I can't see myself. I feel like an energy... humans call it an orb. However, we are able to morph into different shapes depending on where we travel to."

D: *Do you do it just when you want to, or when the circumstances are....*

J: Only when it's necessary. We don't abuse our abilities.

D: *Did you at one time have a physical body?*

J: Yes, I'm very familiar with a physical body. I don't understand, but I know this feeling from when I was a child and my body would become energy and I would just disappear.

D: *So you did have a physical body at one time?*

J: Yes. I've had many shapes.

D: *Is that the ability of your people?* (Yes) *They can start out as the physical, then change?* (Yes) *Oh, that's very wonderful. So you don't need the body anymore. You just become energy?* (Yes) *Well, what do you do as energy?*

J: We teach people. We do many things. There's a lot of work to do in the universe because human beings mess a lot of things up.

D: *(Laugh) Oh, I believe that.*

J: So when they project their energy out, we have to realign the stars and we have to take out their gases. I don't understand what this energy is that they project. There are foreign energies that go into the universe and pollute the whole universe. It's very disturbing.

D: *Does it come from humans?* (Yes) *Are you near Earth?* (No) *So it extends out a long way?* (Yes) *What are they projecting out that's so negative?* (Jane began to cry.) *It's hard to deal with, isn't it? You have to clean up the mess. You have an important job. Why does it make you emotional?*

J: Oh, I just don't understand why all the humans don't understand what they're doing to us. They're misusing their alchemy on the planet. They are creating chemicals that spread to different universes, and they don't understand that,

D.   *They don't realize that it's not just contained in their own world?*

J: That's right.

D: *That is goes out and affects your world?*

J: I don't have a world. I just belong to the universe.

D: *You did at one time, didn't you?*

J: Yes... (Crying) before it was destroyed.

D: *Tell me what happened.*

J: I lived on the planet of crystals. And the gases were so strong it dissolved the planet, so we had to create a ship so we'd have some place to go.

D: *Why did it dissolve?*

J: It was the gases from the human world. They were too strong and melted it.

D: *The gases built up after a period of time?*

J: Yes. The gases destroy many planets, so we have to rescue many people, too. Many different beings on other planets. We collect different beings.

D: *So it destroyed many planets?*

J: Yes, it keeps destroying planets and we keep trying to....

D: *You mean the energy is still going out?*

J: Yes, and we keep filtering it and trying to patch it up, but they keep doing things to open up their ozone layer and it comes out and... (Deep breath) it's very disturbing. So much stuff needs to happen.

D: *So at the time that your planet was destroyed, you said you left?*

J: We had built a ship so we could leave and still do our work. And then we realized we didn't have a planet anymore.

D: *Did you have a physical body at that time when you were on the ship?*

J: It had a structure to it.

D: *Then what happened that you decided not to be physical anymore?*

J: We didn't need to. It was a blessing in a way to lose the planet because we were already evolving to the place where we didn't need a home anymore. And we didn't need any physical structure to contain our energy form.

D: *You had evolved beyond that.* (Yes) *So when did you become this energy being, the orb, that you are now?*

J: It was after.

D: *Did someone tell you that you had to do this job?*

J: It was decided by the council. Well, not just my job. There are several of us that do this.

D: *Did you meet with the council?*

J: I feel like they delivered instructions. We don't see them. We just communicate with them energetically, and they're all around us.

D: *And you agreed to go out throughout the universe and try to correct these things that are happening?* (Yes) *What is it like when you find the energy that comes from Earth? How do you identify that?*

J: It has a very dense, lower frequency, and I don't even understand how it gets out into these dimensions. It's almost like a black, smoky, snake that slithers through, but it hasn't overpowered us. It's easy enough to clean it up. It's just unnecessary that we have to spend our time that way when there are other functions that need to be performed.

D: *I was wondering how it could get so far from Earth to those other dimensions.*

J: Yes, it goes beyond our galaxy. It goes beyond and into other universes. It's very pervasive, and we know that humans don't mean to. It is very disturbing to watch it.

D: *They think it just remains on Earth and they are only hurting each other.*

J: Yes. We have closed many of these doorways, unfortunately the human beings feel they still need certain teachers. Human beings feel they need to learn things the hard way, so they invite in energies that teach them lessons in a hard way.

D: *Well, it is a planet of lessons.*

J: Yes, that's correct.

D: *You said these negative energies were easy to clean up? How do you do that?*

J: I don't understand the word for that... we surround them with a very powerful liquid crystal kind of an energy. We contain it and then we create different calculations. We have to test the frequency of it and figure out a frequency that is strong enough to dissolve it. And then it dissolves back into energy, but as I mentioned, it is very time consuming. There are other tasks in the universe that are much more beneficial to the collective.

D: *What is the collective?*

J: The totality of the universe and inhabitants in the universe. There are many other species, and humans don't understand that. But we like the humans. They are a part of us, and they discover that when they leave their body. If they knew this they would behave differently. They're very lovely. They mean well, and they all have this love in their heart, and we just want them to love from their heart. And if they love from their heart, they won't create these things that occur.

D: *Love is what it's all about anyway, isn't it?*

J: Correct. The Creator is very loving. They only have a glimpse of how much love the Creator has for them.

D: But I think that's part of why they're on Earth, to discover these things.

J: That's correct. They don't see the trees waving at them, and winking at them and saying hello. They just chop them down.

D: They don't see that everything is alive. They think everything is here for their benefit.

J: That is correct.

D: If you weren't spending so much time cleaning up the mess, what would you like to do?

J: Oh, there are many projects. There are many planets waiting to be born, but they know it's not safe enough to be born. And there are many other species that wish to become part of the process of evolving into the collective.

D: So this is part of what you could do?

J: Yes. It's very easy to create planets, just as it's very easy to destroy planets. Or shift them into other galaxies and formations that serve the collective.

D: I've talked to other people like you, who do create planets. It's part of the co-Creator group, isn't it? (Yes) Do you do it with energy?

J: Yes. It's more than energy. If humans were to understand it... we think it, then it happens.

D: That's why thoughts are so powerful, aren't they? (Yes) Maybe that's why the humans are not at that point.

J: The human beings are very resourceful in their brain. And if they used their thinking and their intention differently, they would create a much more peaceful existence. When we created the planet, it was created as an oasis. They are not meant to suffer. Someone taught them to suffer... not us. But they all know in their deep wisdom their brains are very powerful. They only use a little peanut size shape of their brain, but their brain is very large. And if they access all that energy in their brain, it will be a very different place on the planet. And actually they know what's happening. They feel it. They're transitioning it. And this planet Earth is not being destroyed. I really would like them to not focus on that because they are focusing on destruction energy and therefore are creating it.

D: *Anything they focus on they create.*

J: That is correct.

D: *Are you happy with what you are doing?*

J: Yes, I really love my job. When I say "job," that's what humans would say.

D: *Yes, that's what we would say. And you just travel from place to place and do what you're supposed to do. (Yes) That's wonderful and you're very happy with it? (Yes)*

It was now time to make the connection to Jane. "Are you aware that you're speaking through a human being?"

J: What I feel is funny, strange. There is some obstruction here.

D: *That's why you had to use a language. (Yes) Does that bother you?*

J: To use a human body?

D: *To communicate with me.*

J: No. It's necessary.

D: *I would like to clear something up. I want to know if you are her, or are you a part of her or what? How do you perceive that?*

J: She is a part of us.

D: *Is she a part of your group? (Yes) Tell her about it. She's looking for answers.*

J: She already knows the answers.

D: *Yes, but she doesn't know them consciously. Can you tell her so she'll understand?*

J: Yes. She's here to teach people how to create. How to use their energies from where she's from.

D: *Energies from where you come from?* (Yes) *She is really you, isn't she?* (Yes) *That's what gets complicated when we try to put it in our language.*

J: Yes. It often puts her in situations that are very powerful. And often, in her human existence she has had many of what you would call "high profile" situations. And people don't understand that she just wants to teach them how to create.

D: *If you were happy with your job there, why did you decide to become a human?*

J: It's necessary.

D: *It's restrictive, isn't it?*

J: Yes, and she does not like that.

D: *What happened the first time you had to become a human? Were you told to do it?*

J: Yes. It's difficult to explain because she has never signed up to be a human. But she has always accepted her assignments.

D: *You mean she didn't volunteer?*

J: That's correct.

D: *There are volunteers, aren't there?*

J: Yes. There are many that humans would call on a "waiting list" to get into the planet right now.

D: *But she didn't volunteer.*

J: No, she does not like a body.

D: *(Laugh) Then was she just handed an assignment or what?*

J: There are very many of us—many parts of the whole of who you're speaking with—existing in other dimensions currently, and she chose to be on planet Earth. But there are many other divisions of us elsewhere right now.

D: *I think I understand this more than most people because I understand we have many parts.* (Yes) *We're not just one part.* (Yes) *So she can be existing as a human, and also existing as you.*

J: That's correct. But she has a lot of duty, and she understands that there's a larger picture. And she needs to bring through the frequencies and the teachings that are necessary for humans to focus their energy. And to refocus their brain activity to be more serving to their Creator and their universe. And once they leave their body they understand that.

D.   *Oh, yes, it's very plain then.* (Yes) *But anyway, she decided to accept these assignments and become human?*

J: Yes. She never argues about that. That's why we give her the hard assignments. She likes that. She likes to be challenged.

D: *It's not easy when you're human and you have these different abilities (her psychic abilities). Isn't that true?*

J: Yes. She has done the best she could to make people feel comfortable around her before she shows them what's really going on.

D: *Well, this one you're speaking through, her name is Jane.* (Yes) *Has she had other lives on Earth?* (Yes) *Are there any that she needs to know about?*

J: No, it's not necessary to know at this time.

D: *So the one she's focused on at the present time is the most important.*

J: That's correct.

D: *What is her assignment this time?*

J: She has to teach many people, and there are many healers that need to remember who they are, and what their frequencies are that they bring here, and their energies, so they can do their work to the fullest potential.

D: *It sounds like a big assignment.* (Yes) *She said she remembers even when she was a baby being able to do very strange things.*

J: Yes. She used to communicate with us from her crib. Because of her assignment, she needed to not have the same level of forgetfulness as other humans.

D: *Because most people don't remember when they were babies.*

J: That's correct. Most people wouldn't want to remember that. But those souls are very beautiful, and humans don't recognize them as that, but they need to come in without a memory so they may be of service to people who may be serving the planet.

D: *Yet she could remember even as a baby being able to do those things.* (Yes) *But her family was very understanding.*

J: Yes, they were complicated.

D: *Yet she had to put these abilities on the back burner, if you understand what I'm saying.* (Yes) *Because in order to live as a human, you have to adapt.* (Yes) *She wants to know if it's possible to bring back these abilities now?*

J: Yes, it's time for that. She knows how to use them, but she needed to contain them because there were many—what humans call "gray" energies—in the school system she was working in. And she knew that they could see what she could do. So in order to protect the information, she needed to put the abilities on hold. She was protecting herself, but she was also protecting the information.

D: *So she had to blend in at that time and become human.* (Yes)

I knew the part that I was speaking to would be able to answer the questions that Jane wanted to know, so I knew I wouldn't have to call forth the SC. It agreed with me, that I was already speaking to it. This is sometimes difficult to know, to be able to distinguish the difference between a guide or another entity and the SC. The guide or another entity might not have access to the type of information needed, and often is the first to acknowledge that. Sometimes it will tell me that I should call forth the SC because it cannot answer the questions. It all goes back to the fact that we are all one anyway. All the other parts of ourselves plus the SC are all part of the Source. At first this one sounded like a typical ET or alien assigned to that small spaceship. Then it sounded like a Creator Being, and then it identified itself as another part of Jane. So it was many things, as we all are. Thus I knew I would be able to get information for Jane without calling forth the SC.

D: *We can just talk and have information, can't we?*

J: Yes, and you are a very wonderful conduit for this information to come through, and we thank you for everything you do.

D: *I work with you all the time.*

J: Yes, you do.

D: *I know your power and I respect it. But if she is allowed to bring these abilities back, will it be good? Will it be safe?*

J: Yes, we will create the protective mechanisms around her to bring that in. There are many humans on the planet right now that are waiting for this information to come through her. It is very much time.

D: *I am very protective, and we don't want to do anything that will hurt her, or disrupt her life. She has to live here after all.*

J: That is correct. That is why we restructured her atoms.

D: *Tell me about it.*

J: They hold more carbon and are able to hold more hydrogen, so the expansiveness of the energy and the strength of the energy is allowable into her energy field.

D: *Why did the cells have to be restructured?*

J: You can imagine the amount of frequency that will be coming through her. (Yes) So we don't want her physical body to be destroyed.

D: *I have been told this before. Some energies are so strong they could destroy their physical bodies.*

J: That is correct, and that has happened to many humans.

D: *Many times when your type of beings try to come in, the baby's body can't hold the energy.* (Yes) *It aborts or is born dead. That's what I've heard.* (Yes) *So you have to try again by making adjustments.*

J: The fetus is fine. It's the mother that's not caring for the energy that surrounds the fetus.

D: *It's too much for the mother.* (Yes) *Did you have to do something to Jane before she was born?*

J: Oh, yes. Jane did not enter the womb until about six months because they were working on her host. The mother's body. So she couldn't enter until six months in uterus.

D: *So the baby was developed six months before she was allowed to test the waters, so to speak?*

J: Yes. But she was busy doing other things. I don't know how to explain it, but basically the higher self of the human activates their own wisdom of how to create their body. And how to structure the fetus on a cellular level, so that the energy can come in.

D: *Many times you're so busy that you don't want to come in until the last minute anyway.*

J: Yes. That is what Jane was doing.

D: *You mean the soul, the spirit, that's going to come in?*

J: That's correct. They don't come in.

D: *They structure the fetus to what they want it to be?*

J: Yes. The fetus always structures the same, and then when the fetus is ready, it's prepared for the soul to come in, and it arrives.

D: *So they don't manipulate or change the fetus then?*

J: Well, they will, yes, but the mother needs to create the... the souls need to form. Sometimes energies or souls tell the mother that they're coming, then they are busy doing other things and they forget sometimes to come into the body.

D: *That happens?*

J: Yes, so then the baby is born without a soul in the body, and that's because other things take priority... that's all.

D: *How can a baby exist without a soul in the body?*

J: Well, the mother's human body is designed to send all the blood and all the oxygen to the cells to create it. And so the wisdom of the human body takes over in forming the actual fetus or the physical structure for the soul to arrive.

D: *The body is a separate entity, isn't it?*

J: Yes. So it's almost like a factory production. Time and time again the body knows how to create the fetus. That's why the soul can trust that it can arrive later because the work's already being done.

D: *That's why I've told people that the fetus is living off the mother, and her life force keeps it alive. So the soul does not have to be in the baby until it separates from the mother.*

J: No. Sometimes the soul comes and checks in, and that's when they feel kicking and things like that. And it leaves again, and that's why the mother cannot predict the kicks because the soul comes in and announces itself, and does some of its own imprinting, and then leaves again. Of course, the soul can be in many places at one time.

D: *That's what I tell people. It doesn't have to remain in the body until it separates from the mother.* (Yes) *Then it has to be there or the baby won't live.* (Yes) *But you said everything had to be restructured so that Jane could handle this energy.* (Yes) *And she has the memories of her abilities as a child.* (Yes) *And now she will be able to use these?* (Yes) *How are you going to reactivate it?*

J: We'll come to her in her sleep tonight and remind her. Remind her of how to work with it safely and how to be around other humans while using it. How to teach it safely; how to use it safely. It's very powerful, you know. She is ready.

D: *Which abilities are you going to bring back first?*

J: Well, she really needs to be in many places at one time. And so she will master that and then teach it.

D: *The bi-location she was talking about?*

This was another one of the abilities she remembered she had as a child. She could instantly move her physical body from one place to another by just thinking about it.

J: Yes. It's more than that. She travels a lot into the future and prepares her future already. There will be more of that and there will be travel to more countries simultaneously preparing the conditions when she arrives to teach them the information that they need.

D: *Will people see her as a solid human being?*

J: Yes, yes, she will take on different forms.

D: *You mean, she won't be traveling bi-location as a spirit?*

J: No, she will pick a form and enter it.

D: *Will it look like the form she has now?*

J: No... well, sometimes. It depends on where she's going and how she needs to blend in.

D: *So other people will see her as a physical human being?* (Yes) *In her body as Jane, will she be aware that she is doing these things?*

J: Yes. She's already doing it. She's just not aware of it.

D: *So it's okay if she knows now?*

J: Yes. She's always helping people.

One of Jane's questions was about a feeling that something was coming to her at night. They seemed to be different kinds of beings.

J: Oh, it's her many assignments. Based on what she does in the universe, people check in with her and let her know how they are doing with their assignments, and ask her to participate and assist in other areas.

D: *She said sometimes it bothers her.*

J: Yes, well, she likes to be busy.

D: *She said sometimes she felt there were adjustments being made.*

J: Yes. It's very challenging for her to continually leave the body, and so we have to keep adjusting her so that every time she returns to the body, she remembers she's in a body. So we do this at night.

D: *If she understands this it will make it easier.* (Yes) *What other ability do you want to bring back? You want her to master them one at a time?*

J: She will do it simultaneously. She has a lot of movement around her and she needs to learn how to move things more easily, and she spends less energy in trying to move things around. She can just move them before she arrives.

D: *The power of levitation she had as a child?* (Yes) *Explain what you mean.*

J: I am being shown a picture of her in her vehicle, and sometimes there are obstacles on the road, or there are other vehicles in the way. Or other situations occurring on the path that she's driving that slow her down from being where she needs to be. And so those will be moved.

D: *She'll just know this and be able to move them?* (Yes) *That's a very interesting talent to have.*

J: Yes, it is. Sometimes she forgets that her car is not a spaceship. (I laughed.) She drives fast. There are some larger projects there. There are some volcanoes in what the humans call the "Hawaii area," that are getting ready to erupt, and it's not time. So she will need to work with those to slow them down. Those kinds of movements.

D: *Oh? These are assignments you are giving her at night?* (Yes) *Will she be doing these in her sleep state?* (Yes) *So she won't have a conscious memory?*

J: She'll remember. We have to allow her to rest up at some point.

D: *Definitely. We don't want to wear her out.*

J: That's correct.

D: *So when she does these assignments she will have the memory?* (Yes) *She doesn't need to tell everybody, does she?*

J: She wouldn't find the right words to describe it.

I asked some more of her questions. One was whether she should move from Canada.

J: She does need to move. It's not quite time. There's a lot of very strong energy where she lives that needs to be dissolved. There's a lot of toxic energy and the city environment. There's a lot of pollution. I will remind her on how to dissolve that and how to filter the air, but she knows... she sees the dawn of that chemical that forms over the city. And she sees the large angels around it when she drives in.

D: *This is one of her assignments?*

J: Yes. There's a lot of pollution there... a lot of pollution in the water.

D: *So she has to do this before she leaves Canada.* (Yes) *She wanted to know the best place for her to go... the ideal place for her to be.*

J: She should go to Seattle. People would understand her there. And there is repair work that needs to be done on the land. There are parts that are preparing to sink. They are becoming overwhelmed with energy. She will move there in about a year, in human time. We will send her to the coastal areas. There's a lot of work to be done there. She's wanting to connect consciously with us. We're preparing to have meetings with her in her living room. What she wants is to see us because she misses us. And her human brain doesn't understand that our form is formless. But she would like to see us, and so we will arrive from time to time. We will select a form that she will be comfortable with.

Physical: We did a body scan. "The chemicals are not balanced. The hormones. The endocrine system is restoring that now. It was overworked. We need her to slow down. Her spine has been manipulated by so many uninformed practitioners that we will also need to realign her spine. They were working with a different body type than they are used to. We are adjusting, but it will take a few days. She shouldn't let anybody else work on her. Other healers don't understand this body. Also she doesn't realize she's taking on other people's energies. She needs to protect her stomach. She feels these things there. (They took care of it.) We created an energetic shield in her stomach area to protect her from the energies of the people she works with."

Parting message: We're very proud of her and we know she works very hard. She has an important job to do, and she loves everyone. We are pleased with the work that she's doing.

D: *We were looking to go into past lives, but you said those were not important?*
J: No. She's integrated all her multi-dimensional reality. This life is the most important.
D: *So we were shown the orb because that was one of her main energies?* (Yes) *And I didn't have to ask you to come forward.* (No) *You knew what we were going to do, didn't you?*
J: That is correct.

CHAPTER TWENTY-NINE

A TEACHER IS KILLED

Loretta was a massage therapist whose main concern were many memories of extraterrestrial experiences. She wanted to know if they were just dreams or real. Always expect the unexpected because the session took some interesting twists and turns. Loretta didn't waste any time. As soon as she was in trance she went immediately to a large pyramid in Egypt. She saw a large door opening into the pyramid and with no hesitation she went inside and down a dark tunnel. She walked past rooms she knew she was not allowed to enter, and continued on. In answer to my questions she said she was a young female with long black hair. Her voice cracked as if she was upset and scared. "There's a whole lot of emotion. I'm not afraid. It's energy. I can feel it in my solar plexus. I think I feel the energy of the pyramid.—There's a ladder. I'm supposed to go up the ladder, and into this room. So I'm in this room and over here in front of me are two big statues of black cats. They're guarding a doorway. It looks like there's a light back in there, but it's black in the doorway. I want to know what's in there. There's a torch over here. I'm going to take that torch and I'm going to look.—Well, there's another door. I take a key and I open the door. I don't see a room. I just see purple light everywhere.—I want to ask if it has a message. It's saying, 'Wisdom of the ages.' He said that's all... wisdom of the ages. This is a purple light that I've seen before. I see it often and when this purple light comes, it's imparting wisdom of the ages."

D: *How is it imparting it?*

L: Just in the knowing... sometimes I know answers. I know things and I don't know how I know it.

D: *Do you ask it for more information?*

L: I don't ask. It just comes. I never know what it's going to tell me.

D: *What is it wanting you to know today?*

L: It comes from the temple. (Amazed) Comes from a temple... that's the words that come through, but I'm in a pyramid. Oh! It's a temple built inside the pyramid.

D: *Are you connected to the temple in some way?*

She was getting information that the doorway protected by the black cats was the opening to the temple. The purple light was inside. She saw that her job was to work with the dead.

L: There's a slab there with a body on it, and I'm going to prepare the body.

D: *What do you do when you prepare the body?*

L: It's beetles... beetles and wrapping them like a mummy.

D: *What do you mean by beetles?*

L: Beetles... something with beetles. I put beetles on the body. There are jars, and the jars hold different dried plants. I put that on the body when I wrap the body.

D: *Why do you do all of this?*

L: It's to honor to prepare the body for the tombs.

D: *Are the tombs in the same place?*

L: No. (She was becoming emotional.) It's like I prepare the bodies, then they come and take them.

D: *Why is this making you emotional?*

L: It seems awfully sad. I don't want to do this.

D: *Why is it sad?*

L: Something to do with the beetles.

D: *I thought you were sad because the person had died.*

L: No. That is not bad.—I think the beetles are crawling all over the body so that they might eat the body.

D: *Are they underneath the wrappings?*

L: Yes. That must be part of the process. I can see right now... they're crawling on top of the body. I don't know if they're in the body.

D: *But why does that make you sad if it's part of the process?*

L: It brings tears. I wonder if the body isn't dead. Would they bring me somebody that wasn't dead? Maybe they're bringing me people to wrap up, to entomb that aren't really dead. Hmm.

D: *Can you tell by looking at them if they are dead or not?*

L: No. I think there's like a coma. They can be in a state like that and I don't know.

D: *They wouldn't be breathing?* (No)

Loretta had a sudden insight that was very unpleasant. "So what if that's... maybe it's not me fixing them. Maybe it's somebody fixing *me*, and *I'm* on the table?—I think that's it." She became very upset and scared. I immediately gave suggestions for wellbeing. That she would be able to watch objectively if she wanted to, and be able to talk about it. "They wrapped me up when I was still alive... (Tormented.)... and put beetles on me. They put me in a tomb. I wasn't dead! (Crying.)...Did they think I was dead?" She began to breathe heavily.

This tug-of-war back and forth about whether she was the observer or the participant was typical of the protection the SC does to make sure the person will not be given more than they can handle. I decided to move her backwards to before this happened. It would be a way to get her out of this unpleasant situation, and to find out what led up to this. She began describing herself, "I can see the back of my head and I have long, black hair, and I'm that young girl that I saw earlier. I have gold stuff in my hair. And I'm being told, 'For the good of the people.' Hmm... doesn't make sense. 'For the good of the people you will be entombed.'"

D: *Why? How would that help the people?*

L: It seems as though I'm a very outspoken young woman, and this will teach women they cannot be that way. By example. I was very outspoken. I was showing them by example the way I lived my life, so they made an example out of me. I see the purple light. I can see me standing before a man and him telling me they were making an example of me. And now I can't see me. I see the purple light.

D: *But you said you were teaching them by example?*

L: Yes, I was a good example. This man didn't want me to teach it. (Defiantly) But if I were teaching something bad, why would I see the purple light? I see them drag me away. Two men... one on each of my arms with my feet dragging. They hit me on the side of the head. That's what they did to me. They must have just knocked me out. Then they took me to... put the beetles on me and dried stuff, wrapped me up and put me in a *box*! They thought I was dead. They buried me alive!

This was all very emotional for her, and I had to keep reminding myself that the SC would never show the person more than they could handle. In many cases the SC has refused to tell the client about violent or horrible past lives because it didn't want to upset them. In this case it must have thought it was important for her to have this upsetting information. I moved her away from that scene, so she wouldn't have to experience the emotion. I still wanted to find out what she was being punished for. What had she done to deserve such a drastic death? "Were you a teacher?"

L: I was teaching magic. Magic is good. It had to do with the big, black cats.—I see what happened in that place. There was a circle of women in the temple with the two cats. I taught them in a circle and I think I was possibly teaching them what the purple light was teaching me.

D: *You said, the Wisdom of the Ages?*

L: Yes. The men didn't like it.

D: *They didn't want the women to know these things?* (Yes) *That's why they decided to kill you?*

L: Yes. When you do these things... look what happens to you.

D: *They wanted to frighten the rest of them.* (Yes) *Well, now you're out of that body and you can look at the whole entire lifetime from a different perspective. Every life has a purpose. Is there anything you learned from that life?*

L: I taught what I thought was right and I got sealed up in a box.

D: *So what do you think you learned?*

L: To fight harder maybe, for what I believe in.

D: *Even though you were killed for it?*

L: It's either fight harder for what I believed in, or say I died needlessly. I don't like to die needlessly. I don't know why it has to be a fight.

D: *Do you think that was what it was trying to teach you? You can fight for what you believe in?*

L: Yes, they had already done the worst. One of my favorite sayings is, "What do I have to lose?"

When I moved her away from that scene to try and find another lifetime, she just saw herself floating in space without a body. There was just the very good feeling of being energy. It was a peaceful place where she felt removed from everything. I tried to move her to something else, but, "I'm not seeing anything but energy going by. It goes by in blobs. Blobs of purple... darker purple and gray and orange. I seem to be in a world of light. Lots of energy. I am still in this energy world of these colors coming at me."

D: *Are you supposed to use that energy in any way?*

L: I'm being told, yes. To use this energy... colored lights. How am I supposed to use this energy... with my eyes? How do I do that... by just looking and being? It's that easy? It's that easy. I project the energy with my eyes. They are teaching me to focus.

D: *Where does it go when you focus it?*

L: To the person I am working with. I work with old people. I work with young people. I work with people on the street.

D: *Just by looking at them?*

Loretta was obviously one of the Second Wave.

L: Yes. People come to me to talk and they don't know why. It's for me to look at them.

D: *That doesn't require any effort, does it?* (No) *Did you know you were doing this?*

L: I thought recently, maybe. I know I'm doing more with my eyes; especially the old people because my eyes catch their attention and then they listen to me.

D: *Is this Loretta we're talking about?* (Yes) *So you came into Loretta's body?* (Yes)

Then the voice changed and it identified itself as someone or something from a ship, which it said was *her* ship. They began directing energy into her body to heal and make it easier for her to focus the energy she would be working with.

L: She looks at people and they get better. Whether it be physical stuff, mental stuff. She works with people and they don't even know it, but they get better. She has been doing this, but she didn't know it. It is all right for her to know now, because this is her work. She will be traveling, meeting people. Just kind of like the wind. The wind touches many people. And it's so easy. It doesn't have to be hard. Go wherever spirit sends her. Oh, there's something broader. She will work with another light. This other light is gold and bright. Open up wider experience... broader.

I asked for more information about the ship. "Why is it interested in Loretta?"

L: It says, "You are my daughter. You will work with your eyes. You are a child of the light."

The information stalled when I asked for more information about the ship. She seemed to be afraid, and that overrode the communication. So I called in the SC and I asked why it chose the lifetime we had gone through.

L: They don't all have to be that way. It was wrong to do that, and she doesn't have to do that again. She thinks she always gets punished for telling the truth. (She switched to first person, which meant that Loretta was trying to interject.) I think in many, many, many lifetimes I was punished and maybe now I don't know how to accept in this lifetime.

I used positive suggestions to release the things that happened in that life so they would no longer have any hold on her. This took a while of repeating suggestions, until she exclaimed, "I saw it. I saw the energy release!" I then returned to the questions and emphasized that she was to allow the SC to answer.

D: *She had an incident happen years ago when she was living in Edmond, Oklahoma, where she saw some beings in her room. She wanted to know what happened to her that night. Can you tell her about that? Was it a real event?*
L: Yes. It was a friend that came back for her. "I came back to take you home for a while."
D: *Where did it take her?*
L: To a blue planet. There were trees and grass, but looking at the planet from outer space, it looks blue. There's a city there too. She calls it the Golden City.

Happy people. They had a celebration to celebrate her coming home. She had been gone for a while.

D: *If she was happy, why did she leave that place?*

L: Supposed to go help... volunteered to help the universe. She volunteered to be a human.

D: *How was she going to volunteer to help?*

L: By being a human. By her energy to help.

D: *When the experience began that night, she saw something that looked like triangles.*

L: Yes. Bright white triangles! It goes back to the space ship. Right back to the space ship in a beam of light. The triangles were on the ceiling. They're energy. That's the energy that was needed to get her to go through the tunnel... through the worm hole.

D: *To take her back for a visit?*

L: Yes, and they were made out of white light. The triangles were the energy source. And the triangles were light beings also. They were energy beings. It took me back to the ship that had the beam of light on me overhead. (Loretta began interjecting again.) I don't think all those ships are good. They want to work on me. I remember laying on a really cold table with no clothes on. They're all around the table.

D: *Ask them why you're there.*

L: We are trying to help you. Help me what? (Asking them.) You guys need to talk to me. They don't know my language. What do you mean you don't know my language? I can hear you.—They said they were trying to help me. I don't think they're trying to help me. They have me held down. That's not helping me. (Defiantly.) Why are they putting a probe up my nose to my brain? (Upset) You want me to do that to you?

D: *Tell Loretta why that is happening. Explain it to her. She will not fear if you explain it to her. Humans like to have things explained.*

L: Tweaking the pituitary... tweaking?

D: *Why does it need to be tweaked?*

L: Not big enough... more knowledge.
D: *Do you want her to be able to retrieve some of that knowledge she had before?*
L: Yes. Help people.

They explained that they were not the ones who would send her the knowledge. It would come from somewhere else, but the pituitary had to be big enough to receive it. She then became upset again. "They poked something up my vagina. Eggs? You want eggs?"

D: *Why do you want the eggs?*
L: Embryo... save... for her?—They're saving it for me?
D: *Why do they have to be saved for Loretta?*
L: Different life. Future... future life.
D: *Why do they have to be saved for that life?*
L: Biology now important.
D: *What do you mean? In the future life, won't she be able to produce her own eggs?*
L: Not like this.
D: *What's different about it?*
L: Things changing... mutating... transmuting... mutating.
D: *Do you mean they are now, or they will or what?*
L: Now... things different now. Eggs are different now.
D: *They're changing?* (Yes) *And you want to preserve them?*
L: Yes. I might not get back to this state.
D: *Are they changing for the good or are they becoming worse or what?*
L: Not worse... just different. They will be used later.
D: *So in the future they won't make the eggs like this?*
L: No, not like this.
D: *What is causing the eggs to change?*
L: Vibration.
D: *I know the vibrations are making the body change.* (Yes) *But it's also making the eggs change?*
L: Yes... DNA changing.

D: *But she can no longer have children. Does that make any difference?*

L: In this lifetime she's not having children.

D: *But the eggs are still viable?*

L: Must be.

D: *So the eggs have to be taken and saved? Is that what you mean?* (Yes) *So they can be implanted in her in a future life?* (Yes) *What will be wrong with the eggs in the future life?*

L: Not wrong... just different. This seems to be a special time of carrying really high vibrations. It makes things change... makes things hold their power more.

D: *But in the future the eggs won't have that high of a vibration?*

L: Not for her. She's not going to manufacture eggs in the future.

D: *Will people stop manufacturing eggs or is it just her?*

L: I can't really tell. She won't. She has something different to do in the future, and children will be different... different process, not like here on Earth. So she's saving the eggs to work with them later in the new process.

D: *In that time will she understand?*

L: Yes, she will understand. She will know in that time.

D: *Will she have a physical body?*

L: Probably not.

D: *Will the eggs be used to produce other human beings?*

L: Other hybrids... not human. It would be a very high vibration hybrid. Maybe on the new Earth!

D: *It sounds like it will be very important.*

L: Yes. There is a team doing things like this. She's part of it... a team.

Parting Message: Love yourself. Love yourself. We do.

CHAPTER THIRTY

BARRAGE OF INFORMATION

E velyn was a nurse working with dying patients. She displayed great compassion and enjoyed doing this type of work. However, she wanted to know about a suspected UFO incident. She had a memory of being visited in her room and that was what she wanted to explore during the session. She also had irrational memories of seeing aliens in an incubator and suspended animation setting. When she was in trance I took her back to her house on the supposed date of the incident, just before going to bed. (What I call the "backdoor" approach.)

She described her small apartment and said her kitty and her little dog liked to sleep with her in her big bed. "We got the doggie (a cockapoo) from the shelter, and the kitty was homeless. I've had him for years now. They have a good home. They're spoiled." On this night she was restless and was having difficulty falling asleep, even though it was after midnight. Then something began to happen that made this night different. "This figure came down through the ceiling. I am surprised. The animals see it, but there's nothing they can do." I asked for a description, and now she described two beings, "They have long arms... human kind of arms... they have clothes... black suits on... and black shirts... black shoes."

D: *They blend in with the darkened room, don't they? What do their faces look like?*

E: Almost human, but they're not human... big black eyes and round, like a human, but they're bigger. No emotions. They don't talk. They don't smile. They don't look angry. They don't look anything... just a face... short dark hair.

D: *What happens?*

E: Pulled my arm... my right arm, but he grabbed it in the wrong spot or something. It hurts. (I gave suggestions that it would not bother her.) Strong... he's very strong. He's pulling me by my arms. The one on the other side is more cautious, I guess, but the right one, he pulled my arm... plus I'm heavy.—We went up through the roof.

D: *They must be strong if they can do that.*

E: They don't have to be strong. It works in other ways. It has something to do with gravity. They know how to do that.

D: *So you're going up toward the ceiling?*

E: No, we're already up over the roof.

D: *What did that feel like to go through the roof?*

E: Funny. Going through it, you become one with the roof. You can feel all the roofing it's made out of, and they look like air bubbles or something. The ceiling becomes different. Almost like a painting and not existing really.

There were several similar cases reported in *Custodians*. At first it was confusing to people to discover that they were able to do this. The ETs explained that the person's molecular structure was broken down to match the structure of the object they were passing through. In each of these cases the person was accompanied by two beings, one on each side. As though that is necessary to help them pass through solid objects and go to the craft.

E: That surprised me. We just went right through it. Now I'm outside and looking down on the building. It happens too fast. I don't even know what to think.

D: *Where are you going? Can you see?*

E: No... upward someplace, but I can't see. It happens very fast.

D: *What's the next thing you see?*

E: It's a room. It's dark. It has light in it, but it's still dark. No windows... no doors.

D: *Are these two beings still with you?*

E: Yes. They're standing right behind me.—I'm thinking this is not happening.

D: *What do you mean?*

E: This is a ship. This is a space ship, and those two guys behind me are not human. So my logical conclusion tells me that somebody just picked me up for a ride.

D: *How do you know it's a space ship?*

E: How do I know? I just know.

D: *What happens next?*

E: Nothing. We're just standing there waiting for something.

I had no way of knowing how long this would take, so I had her condense time so she would see whatever it was they were waiting for. She then saw lights come on in a long hallway and a creature approached her. "This creature is very, very tall. He's very pleasant, but I don't remember seeing anything like that before. His face is shaped like a pear... no hair and no chin, and he's very intelligent, smart. I think he's some type of leader. His skin is very different than ours. It's almost like he is solid skin, no clothing, no shoes or anything."

D: *What do you mean by solid skin?*

E: No pores breathing on the skin like humans would have. But it's soft. It's very, very soft... thin, very, very long fingers.

D: *How many fingers?*

E: Four fingers, but they're almost the same length. It seems like there's a thumb, but I think those are not really located the same way, and it is just closer to each other.

D: *Does he have eyes, nose and mouth like we do?*

E: Yes, but he's not using them.   They don't have a function really.   He's not using his nose to breathe.   And he's not using his mouth to eat or drink.   And he doesn't have teeth or a tongue, either.   It's just there for, I don't know, decoration or something.

D: *What about his eyes?*

E;   They're long, oval shaped... very pretty.   I never saw those colors before.   Just like mine... greenish blue... same color as mine.   He doesn't need to use the eyes the way we do.   He sees, but he does everything in his mind.   He doesn't use them for reading or any of the functions we do, but they're also very sensitive eyes... very soft.

At this point Evelyn began to cough and had a difficult time stopping.   I gave her suggestions to relieve it so we could continue and it wouldn't distract her.

E: He's telling me something about my lungs.   Polluted... too polluted.

D: *Can he see your lungs?*

E: Yes.   In his mind.

D: *He can see inside your body?*

E: He doesn't need to see.   He can sense it.   He just knows everything.

D: *Is there anything he can do about the lungs, or is that what he does?*

E: He does many things.   He does everything.   He says our whole environment is polluted.

Evelyn was still having trouble coughing, so I had to give more suggestions.

E: He said that the pollution has almost reached a breaking point, so it needs to be cleaned.   The climate itself... he

406

showed me that big winds need to come and blow all the pollution away.

D: *Is it possible to do that?*

E: Anything is possible, you know. He tries to tell me in words I can understand, saying if the big winds come on the surface and go around the Earth clockwise, with some kind of elements or energies in it, it just takes all the dark, gray poison. The pollution is not only air pollution, it is all the human and negative emotions that are polluting. It's all connected. He is showing it's all combined... it's all one.

D: *But if they have a strong wind come and try to blow this away, will that affect the people?*

About this point I could tell that Evelyn was no longer acting as the observer receiving answers from the entity. As usually happens the entity took over and began to answer the questions directly. Or it might have been the SC because it began using the same terminology and phrasing that I am familiar with. At any rate, Evelyn was removed from the conversation. When this happens I can get answers directly without going through the person's censoring mind filter.

E: It wouldn't have to kill the people because the combination of the wind would have energy particles in it like energy forces built into this wind. Hundreds and hundreds of different particles into it. It not only would clean the air, but it would clear the vibrations. It would blow through the human body like an energy wave, cleaning it and all the mountains, rivers and animals, so it's not just a wind. It has many different hundreds of components. He said I wouldn't understand.

D: *So it's not like a hurricane or that kind of wind?*

E: Very strong wind, but it also contains energy. It just blows over the whole planet.

D: *We always think of strong winds as being destructive.*

E: This is the simulation where it would rotate clockwise around the planet like a wind, a fog in the wind. It's a strong wind, but it won't have a hurricane kind of damage. It's like a foggy, clean, clear energy. It will have a lot of neutralizing energy. They are going to neutralize energies, bad energies, poison, misery, depressions, money... none of these things would even matter. When this wind goes through the planet, people would forget things that happened in the past. Amnesia, they would have amnesia. These particles would clear a lot of things.

D: *What do you mean, they would forget things that happened in the past?*

E: They will have a new beginning.

D: *You mean they will forget the things they were holding on to?*

E: No. Whatever they had, they will have, but they will see things much differently now... a different perspective, a different view, a different understanding, a different consciousness. That's the only way we can clean this planet. There's so much damage done.

D: *Do you think it will affect all the people here?*

E: Oh, yes... the whole planet. It has to. We can't just do half and not the other half.

D: *But some people are so deep in negativity.*

E: Doesn't matter. They grow stronger. It will give them amnesia of the bad things, and they need to move on with the good things... a lot of light and love. It will mostly put an end to time and we just have a new page. No question about your past. Many are looking forward to this. They know that something is coming.

D: *They know it is time to let go of the past?*

E: Yes, and work with a guide light... work with the universe.

D: *But by doing this, are you going against their free will?*

E: No, because time doesn't exist, so we just put an end to this time. And they can pick it up next time whenever they went to another place. Just postpone it, if you want to look at time, just postpone it.

D: *But I was thinking free will is so very important. I thought they were not allowed to interfere with free will.*

E: We understand what you're saying, but we will have more time to explain it. Let's put it this way. Priority... you have priority. Our priority is... no, that's not a good explanation.—We are one. We are God... with God... energy. You've been playing your games for many, many millions of years. You are in a little playpen and we watch you all the time practicing your games. But you are doing damage to the playpen, and we don't want this disease to spread to others who are still in the learning process.

D: *By others, do you mean other planets?*

E: Other planets... other beings who are still sort of standing back in a sandbox playing.

D: *Aren't we all in different learning stages?*

E: You learn what you choose to learn, but you know it already. You really don't have anything to learn. You are God. You are the all-knowing of all light. We are all light.

D: *But you know when we come to Earth, we forget all these things.*

E: Because you choose to play in your play box in your free will. And you can do as you wish, so it's really not interfering because you cannot interfere with the God as one. It is just a choice. You play in the play box and we are watching you, and we want to make sure that your play doesn't get out of hand like little kids. It's getting out of hand, so we have let you play with time, and now we just clean out the play box. That's all. Just postpone things.

D: *So when we move into this new time, as you said, will something happen to the old Earth? We talked about the winds, but is anything else going to happen?*

E: Water... rising waters... broken levies, oceans and very big waves. It's not only that the wind is going to clear our surface, but it will also help the planet once it goes through the planet as well, not only the surface, the whole planet inside and outside. Inside... outside.

D: *I know there are cities under the planet, aren't there?*

E: Yes... for them to clean up their play box too... some of them. So let's do the job anyway. They're not all perfect, and some are even playing dirtier games than those on the surface. So let's clean all of them. You are thinking they all have to die. It doesn't mean that. It's just that these wind vibrations will brush through inside and outside.

D: *I was thinking water would be a cleansing, too.*

E: Oh, it takes much more than water to clean out the sandbox. Every single thing is going to change on your planet. I'm sorry I can't explain the details, but every single thing is going to change from what you are experiencing today. *We* have the knowledge we have today because we never did actually go to play. We did not choose that. Many did, which is fine, that's what they do. We stayed in the light. At all human times, we did not choose to, but it does not mean we don't know what's going on on your planet or other planets. The vibration of the planet will be higher. Although they will not be able to gain yet the vibration that we carry, there will still be significant change. The frequencies are changing. Like radio waves frequencies... energy bodies, energies.

D: *Will we keep our physical bodies?*

E: Many can, absolutely, yes, with some changes. Changes will come from the light, from the food supplies. People will be living more in peace with the environment and with their bodies. They will understand that the purpose of this body is for serving the purpose of the game. And so they will be ordered to align this body to accommodate whatever game they are playing. They will be more conscious—if that's the right word—more conscious of their body, more conscious of the mind, and more alert and awakened to the game.

D: *How will the bodies change?*

E: They're going to be bubblier... more vibrational.

D: *Will we still consume food?*

E: Well, you're going to stop killing animals to eat them because eating the vibrations of a creature will now make you very, very sick. You will eat more watery things, and when you plant your food, you're going to plant not with a quantity, but a quality of love. And it will bring in the higher vibrations when you plant your trees, and the fruits are going to be higher vibrational, so you don't need to eat as much anymore.

D: *We won't really need the food?*

E: Not really... just minimal to sustain the liquid part of it. It contains more liquid than solid. Anything you plant will have other vibrations. The roots of the plant you put in the ground, you plant in a higher vibration because your hands and your thoughts, your mind, mentally higher vibration, go into planting so everything is aligning with a higher vibration.

During the interview Evelyn had mentioned (and it was one of her questions) that she was now nauseated from eating food. I wondered whether this was causing it. "Raising her vibrations too fast. She's very stubborn and now food makes her sick."

D: *Why is that happening?*

E: She wants to raise the vibration faster, and so the body is not compliant with the information she knows subconsciously. We don't understand why. We can't synchronize the body properly. For some reason, it's not crystallizing the body. We had some problems in the physical body to crystallize it to bring in the highest vibration... her original vibration. We see her thoughts that she likes food, which is giving up what she will miss, but we need to do it faster.

D: *But you know she has to eat to stay alive.*

E: She stays alive with her good liquids and crystal needs purity. In order to raise the vibration in the body, you need to crystallize and purify the body from poisonings in the body. It needs a faster process. The more we work on the body, the more poisoned by the Earth it becomes so it's one step forward, two steps backwards... one forward... two backwards... can't keep up with that for some reason. We do a lot of tunings and do many other things with the physical body.

D: *Do you mean she is resisting it for some reason, or is that the right word?*

E: Much sadness for her not knowing what she was supposed to do, and the level of resistance... the sadness of it.

D: *Where does the sadness come from?*

E: Loneliness in the Earth, very, very lonely. We understand that she wants to come home. We know that and it makes her very, very sad... very lonely... isolation... isolates herself.

D: *She doesn't want to be hurt. She's been hurt a great deal.*

E: See, the problem here is the mind. It's thinking. Her other mind that *we* think with, your higher mind... she knows what she is. She knows who she is... she knows.

D: *We don't know these things consciously. That's the thing.*

E: We don't really understand why we have to say everything in words to you people.

D: *I understand. (Laugh) I work with you a lot. We do it the slow way.*

E: Yes, but because we know everything because we tune into the counselor, the God knowledge, the light that will blind you if you say that. It does not blind you.

It's just an expression of it. I never liked being in this body before. I never had physical fingers, okay? So, I guess in some ways, we really don't understand that part. We don't understand, if you're coming from home, where *you're* coming from, where *she* came from, how you don't know this? She knows, but she doesn't know. What does that mean? How can you know and not know at the same time? See, if you have a cover or something over your eyes, then you remove it, or whatever expression you use. Your minds are not connected? We understand that, but why do you need to ask all these questions when you already know who you are and what you are?

Evelyn began to ramble during this part, and it didn't make any sense, so I have eliminated some of it. I tried to stick with what seemed to be the most important.

E: That goes back to her sadness. She needs to remove all conscious, remove it because you can function without it, believe it or not. No, that's not true because we see you need to speak language, do mathematics and drive a car. (Laugh)

D: *Because we need the consciousness to live in this world.*

E: Yes, we understand that now. We are teaching each other. Okay? So we need to bring her out of that dimension a little more and allow her to understand a little more, allow her to see a little more, so her other mind, her conscious mind will be at ease and allow us to do the frequency exchange to get the vibrations much higher.

D: *But that night we started out examining, she thinks this is the first time she went to the craft and met you. (Evelyn laughed.) I work with you enough, I know it probably wasn't her first time. (We both laughed.) Why was she brought there that night?*

413

E: To remind her consciously. That's why we allowed her to remember every detail so that she can take over curiosity and ask more questions instead of just going, "Oh, yeah, whatever."

D: *That was part of her curiosity, what else happened that night?*

E: What happened is that the top of her head was symbolically removed. This is symbolically, not physically. We don't chop her head off. (Laugh)

D: *(Laugh) Yes, I know that.*

E: And allow her to fully experience the fullness of the light. So she wants everything put into words. Well, we don't have fifty million years to put everything into words. (Laugh) So it's very hard. You can't put it into words. There's not enough time in the universe. It's just annoying.

D: *I know. I've been told this many times, that the words were inefficient.*

E: We don't even have words. It's annoying. One night she will remember the light.

D: *Why did you want her to remember that?*

E: The light? It's her origin. It was always there. It was just covered up. We want her to fully remember and know... the full knowing... no words. That's why this is the missing time she cannot explain because there was no time in the all-knowing. To have a full memory and to not worry about other things and questioning things. "Is it true or not true?" It just is. There's no explanation. God is light, the energy. The one you call God... it just is... no words.

D: *Do you think this memory will help her life?*

E: Yes. Then as she brings energy into the conscious mind, she will also spread it all around. See, this is part of the wind. That knowing and the particles that she spreads is part of the wind. It's not like a body will blow up and go into a million pieces. The energy of it, even if it doesn't project it from the whole body, but

414

from the mind, that will be part of the wind. But spreading this is a full knowing and it goes from your third eye part mainly as well. You bring that in, what I see now. You know what I see now? (What?) Nothing. There is nothing. No words, no thoughts, no nothing and at the same time, it's everything. Once you project that, that knowing, everything and nothing becomes part of the wind.

D: *Yet you do exist on this craft also as this being, don't you?*

E: The blue-eyed one? No.

D: *I'm not sure who I'm communicating with here.*

E: The original blue-eyed one. But I'm not a body. I'm a light. The image I project is a projection. It's like a movie. It's just for the eye to see... to relate, but it's not really me... no. It is for the eye to see and to remember... a tangible. You need to give humans pictures. So she can tell you the story that "I saw a tall man." Because if she said she saw the light... nobody would know what she was saying.

D: *I would because I work with this.*

E: But they do not. Impatient. She has this impatience. Now that she's been shown the knowing she expects everyone else to know it, and it is contributing to another baggage in the body. Because every negative emotion, impatience, frustrations, all of these will be just another obstacle that we probably can override at this time because she consciously needs to get rid of it. It needs to be aligned.—You know it's sad—what are the words?—the more you know, the more you don't understand the others. The more you understand something you cannot even put into words, the less patience you have toward others. How come they don't understand the light when they all came from the origin? How can you forget this? How can you be so—I don't want to say the word she uses. It starts with "S"—(Whispers: stupid.) How can you not understand? How can you not know and just have something in you to trigger something of goodness and unconditional pure love? She does not want a whole person... this light being. She wants just one microscopic light in everyone to trigger. She has the ability to trigger these and yet at the same time, she does damage to herself because of no patience, not understanding. They do not understand and in some ways, on a conscious level, she doesn't understand either. So which is better? Know less or know more? How do we balance this equally?—How did you figure out that I had no body?

D: *I have talked to your kind of beings before, that are light. And many of them do project an image that is easier for humans to understand.*

E: Oh, absolutely. And we are familiar with people who came here to work with the light as a person. It's just very hard to explain things. But we trick people to give them an image of the body, so now you have hundreds of bodies. (Laugh) Confusing, huh? This is a nice joke for you.

D: *People always think of you as being negative, and I know that's not what it's about.*

E: We don't even understand what negative is. (Laugh) We can't even comprehend it.

D: But the ones who don't understand say you are negative.

E: That is because they don't see the light and they are afraid. The fear. And we're going to wash that away too. At least significantly filter it.

D: *She wanted to know if she will be able to have communication with you more often?*

E: Yes, that's part of her sadness. You know, we always have the link. I don't know how to explain this, but you know we all have the link. It was always there from day one when she came to this planet in this life. The very second before birth, we had the link. So we probably will just show her the light more often. Like now, it is so bright and so brilliant and this is the only place she finds peace. Not in her worldly activities. Nothing ever made her feel anything, only when we were able to connect fully in the light.

D: *But she had so many negative things happen to her as a child that naturally she forgot. She became human.*

E: Very busy, yes, very busy with life. Very busy because we needed to clear up some environment around her. We needed to spread some of that light and to trigger it, and then, like now, you said free will. Some complied and some didn't. And anytime she had very bad times, she didn't know that she was always here with us. We brought her home. That way she was able to move on and on and on... one day at a time. That's why so-called "self-destruction" doesn't happen; doesn't exist but in the physical body. It is not allowed, but she was here with us. She was home.

D: *What about this tone she hears in her ear every once in a while?*

E: We tried to make a vibration higher by tuning the bodies. We are trying to adjust it. It's not a physical chip, implanting—it just is. I don't know how to explain it. So she needs to pay attention to it and to know to make some changes.

D: *When Evelyn does meditations she projects herself back to this craft, and she sometimes sees herself in an incubator. Can you tell her about that?*

E: That's her physical body. We not only help with physical particles, the atoms and the third dimensional manifestation, but also each time we do a little more vibrational tuning to the frequencies. It's like a tuning tube.

D: *You mean at that time the physical body of Evelyn is being worked on?*

E: Yes, the physical body also needs to be tuned. The tube is like a tuning device, but it not only helps the physical body to heal. At the same time you come home and spend your time with us in the light, it's of the physical body. When you remove the soul, the body is multidimensional. We can't see through it, so I wouldn't say multidimensional, but it's holographic. Images... so these particles, when we project a certain light into the frequencies, these holographic images pick that up and carry it through it, like you are tuning these machines or something.

D: *She wakes up in time to see that she's in some kind of container.*

E: That's some of the knowing that we allow her to know and see. So she can actually say, "I'm not crazy." I touched it. I saw it and the body lays in there, and then due to machinery, lights and things, the holographic. But at the same time she is able to come into the light and rejuvenate fully, and so when she returns back to the planet, everything is different. Everything is perfect. Nothing happened. Everything is bearable. Everything is just different.

D: *She also saw thousands of other people in other containers, so this means it's happening to others?*

E: Thousands... millions. We need many of them now to help. We need to regenerate or generate. Not all of them are entities like her. We also take other entities who might or might not carry physical bodies, and we don't discriminate. We are all one and we try to tune as many physical bodies as possible so they can carry the higher vibrations, able to survive it, able to spread it, and able to participate in it.

D: *But everyone is not able to do this?*

E: Not everyone, no. But we are doing pretty good now... pretty good. It's going to make a major difference. This is a corporation thing, you know. You have to change the holographic images to adjust to the human body on this Earth because nothing else will be tolerated. So the original body—which they can have physical bodies—is maintaining lower vibrational frequencies from us, but it's high enough... this is complicated, isn't it? (Yes) But anyway, they have the ability to project the human body or to shadow over it, too, like you would put a film on top of a film. – This body is taken out to the ship to the incubator, and imagine the physical body as nothing but holographic images occupied by the light being inside.

D: *I would say that once the spark of life is gone, then the body deteriorates?*

E: No, because the holographic images are the ones we are working on because that's what she is using in this life.

D: *I mean that what we call "death" occurs when the spark of life leaves the body, and then the body deteriorates.*

E: The holographic images deteriorate, yes, because the mind does not hold the thought patterns any longer.

I have had other cases (which are reported in my other books) where the person saw their *alien* body being preserved and tended in a type of cylinder or container. In some of these cases that other body is being kept alive in some form of suspended animation while the soul journeys to Earth to experience the human body. It is kept there so that when the temporary life on Earth is finished, the soul can return to the craft and continue its life there. I have had many clients observe this and feel an identification with the body in the cylinder.

The soul (or ET) has agreed to come and help the Earth in time of need, but it doesn't want to stay here. It really wants to continue its life on the craft because that is how far it has advanced. Besides, Earth is a hectic place to live, and they do not wish to stay. Another reason for being protected so they will not accumulate karma because karma would require that they remain in the Earth cycle. It is very courageous and brave for a pure or advanced soul to volunteer to come because it is exposing itself to a very real danger of being trapped here.

This would explain why the energy of the soul must be adjusted (and the energy of the mother) before the soul can enter. Sometimes only a small portion of the soul can enter at the beginning because it would be too much for the body. This often causes spontaneous abortion of the fetus because the energy is too strong. As the child grows, more bits of the entire soul can be allowed to integrate. Thus the body of the Volunteer is put to sleep and monitored as it awaits the completion of its mission. A silver cord has been seen connecting the soul to the body in the cylinder. I know that we have a cord that connects us to this physical body, and this cord severs at death. So this would mean that because we have many bodies all living at the same time (all our simultaneous lives: past, present and future), we must have multiple silver cords connecting the splinters (many bodies) back to the main soul. In some of my other books this has been seen as a main source with something resembling tentacles going in all directions. The ET body on the craft is intended to stay alive so the soul can return. Sometimes life support has been seen going through tubes which look like pulsing lights (energy).

It is also a way of passing the abilities of the ET in suspended animation into our time frame.

Other ETs have been observed going about their work on spacecrafts (and not put into suspended animation) while a splinter or part of them journeys to the Earth as a volunteer and lives life in a human body. This type can continue its life and is essentially in two places at once. This goes along with the idea that we are living many lifetimes simultaneously. Yet each part is not consciously aware of the other. Since they understand more about what is going on in this process they are aware of that part of their soul that is living on Earth, although the Earthly counterpart is unaware. It was thought that the human especially should not be aware because the concepts are too difficult for the human mind to assimilate. Yet as the veil is thinning, more knowledge is seeping in, and they are being allowed to glimpse what the SC thinks they are able to handle. Gets complicated, doesn't it?

I wanted to concentrate on Evelyn's physical problems. Headaches since childhood had been a real problem. It was difficult for this entity to understand and reduce to our terms of understanding because it saw everything as holographic images that were not real anyway. I had to explain to it that these were real to Evelyn because they were creating problems, so I wanted to do my best to alleviate them. It really had to come down to basics that I could understand in order to explain this.

E: It's almost like trying to fill up this bottle and you're overfilling it with energy and with more original stuff. It's actually very tricky to downsize. Do you know what I mean, to downsize the energies? (Yes) The light we have, why do we downsize it so low? It's much harder technology if you take it like that, harder to decrease it. I think increasing it would be much easier to learn, the way we see it, than to downsize it.

D: *Is this also causing the blood pressure problem?*

E: Absolutely, that's a major cause of the frequencies right now. To help her with these problems, we need more alignment. We need to sweep the body more and align it more with higher vibrations. Do you understand that?

D: *Can you do this while she's onboard the craft?*

E: That's what we do. I'm looking at it right now. There's left side pressure on the brain. I'm looking at the holographic images right now. We need to increase the vibration patterns of all the arteries and veins patterns in her heart and all the organs. So that's how we'll do it.

D: *It won't do any harm?*

E: No, no harm. Sometimes when you balance the holographic images with the images inside the holographic images, we're going to balance all of them out nicely.

D: *So this will release the pressure?*

E: When you're putting too many different quantum particles together, it has to be perfectly aligned so you have to raise the vibration here... lower it there. You know I do graphs and stuff, so we will work with the veins and arteries in the heart, and it's a healthy body. She has a lot of energy. That's why she says she can't sleep.

D: *I was wondering about that, too.*

E: That's why she can't sleep because when we were doing this, one hour sleep equals to many for you, you see?

D: *Yes, and we want to bring the body into balance.*

E: Yes, and not only bring it into balance, but we're raising it to a higher vibration.

They talked more about food and suggested for her to stay away from solid food and to go over to more liquids. I asked about soup, and they said that was okay as long as it was solid soups. "No big chucks of things in your soup. Make it all mushy. Make solid things in your soup liquidy. It takes much less energy to digest." I remarked that we often eat at restaurants and sometimes we can't avoid eating solids.

E: In the future you will. When all these things happen, many things will change. Right now, yes, it is harder, but when you start drinking solid juices, it will go through your digestive system very easily. It doesn't have that extra work from the liver or gall bladder to release certain kinds of stuff because the liquid is easier to move without pressuring the organs as much. We just let them nicely, smoothly go through it and then whatever energy we don't use in digesting, we use on other things.

D: *But occasionally we can have solid food right now.*

E: Oh, yes, but this will be not only in the future in your lifetime, it could be hundreds of years from now... fifty years maybe... that's what it will be.

I think he was referring that this will be the normal way of eating that far into the future. "Right now this is to get her used to more solid liquids for her to use less energy. We don't waste energy to digest."

I have had clients who said when they were born, they didn't want to nurse. They had to remain in the hospital and be fed intravenously until they began to suck. The SC said they had come from places where the body did not require food. Of course, they had to adapt in order to survive here.

I encouraged the SC to continue working on the physical problems while Evelyn was meditating or sleeping, or in the incubator. I said, "That's my job to try to help her in the best way we can. You see it in a different way, but I have to try to help the people in the physical while we're living here right now."

E: Yes, and that's one of the tricky things to do. Your job is harder than my job.
D: (That was a surprise.) *You think so?*
E: Yes because you need to make them understand what they can't even comprehend.
D: *Yes, but you have so much power, so I would think that's easier to do.*
E: No because I understand the process of it. I understand the program, the holographic, the thoughts. I know the program and you are living inside the program, so actually, to be realistic, as you say, it's harder for you to first realize you are in a real program. And then break out of the program and then try to make others believe they are in a program, you see?
D: *Yes. You have told me many times it's an illusion.*
E: It doesn't have any existence whatsoever. That's why it's so funny for us.
D: *It's a game. It's a play.*

E: Yes, it's a movie. It's not even a movie because it's so simple.

D: *But you know when we're involved in it, it's so real. That's the hard part.*

E: That's the design. It's purposely designed like that.

D: *To make it seem real and alive.*

E: Yes. And as soon as you leave, you will realize that you were in a program. But while you're in it, you can't even imagine—not that there are other programs—but that there is only one program and that is the God program. Every game has to feel real so you will interact with each other. You know, interact? (Yes) And so what happens is, you come here. And as a light being we are looking at you like, "Oh, look at those babies. Look how they play. They're so cute." (We laughed.) We really don't comprehend your pain and agony because we know how the program works. But we also know that it's only a program so we need to live in this program in order to realize it, just like you do. But nevertheless, there is nothing to learn if you are going back to the origin of all. With it or without the program, there is only one. I would say it like this: you got too bored, so you created a program. You know, there are some ways to explain it... just something to do.

D: *Hopefully we're learning something.*

E: Because the program is a program within the program, see what I mean. A learning experience program, but you started an original before the program ever came, or afterward the program will be closed off. Whatever way you're looking at it. The program can go on forever, yet the beginning and the end is just the One.

D: *Then did the Source... the God Source design it or did we do it?*

E: There is no God Source. There is only one. He is it.

D: *Did He design this program, or did we do it ourselves?*

E: Okay, we need to go back to the original Source, right? You cannot comprehend that this Source is one. You're breaking it down into individualities. I don't know if this is going to be a good explanation. In this one entity which will be called your God, it has gazillions and billions of thought patterns, games, matrix and all kinds of things. It's never been separated from anything. It was always one and always will be one. This is the best way maybe I can assimilate. I can have five billion things, but it's still my head. See what I mean now? Is it easier to understand? I have one head, but I have millions and millions of thought patterns in that one single head. I can have good things. I can have many things. I could have what I would want, but it still remains one. That one head never exploded into many other heads. It always was, so... we play in my head. Would that be good? *(Yes)*

My head was spinning trying to understand the barrage of words and analogies coming from this entity. Yet I knew I had kept Evelyn in trance far longer than usual, so I would have to interrupt and bring her back to consciousness. And release this entity to go back to wherever it came from.

E: Information is common for you?
D: *I get it from many people. Most people don't understand it, but I write about it and I spread the information to people. You want me to have the information so I can tell other people.*
E: Yes, it's very important to spread the light and news. You have the spark. I mean, you know what you know when you know it. That's so good.
D: *Well, I am still learning.*
E: You see, you already know everything. You just need to remove those little sunglasses and see the absolute light and then you'll know. It's a hard understanding to

make them understand, then you'll know. We can't make them understand what it means, but they'll know when they know.

Parting message: Do not look for my body. I could project myself as anything. Do not look for imagery in similarities, but just look to the light where it is. And that's where all the answers of all time will come. Instead of being occupied in looking for shifts and looking for particular entities, just look into the light, and the answer will come. Instead of occupying the dinner table. Human's way of understanding and that's the only way of communicating, and that's not so. I can occupy any image, any colors of eyes on any ships, or any imagery that I can create. It's not consistent. We have no body, so I have to project something. That's why I picked up on her eyes. I looked into her eyes and blue it is. It's just easier for her to relate to.

I told the SC that it was time to go. It said, "I would say, 'God be with you,' but we are all God and we are all one, so we are all together all the time."

So what began as a typical UFO case expanded and took many twists and turns and turned into something quite different. It appears that when the person remembers the event they are only remembering what they can handle and assimilate within their conscious mind. And even that limited version is distorted, so it is impossible to know what is real and what is illusion. The deeper we probe past the conscious and venture into the SC we find answers that boggle the mind. For this reason, is it better to leave it alone and only accept the superficial meaning? To accept only what our minds and the society in general can handle? Or to dig deeper and search for much more complicated explanations that just might reveal the truth when our minds are ready to accept it. And as "they" say, What is truth anyway?

CHAPTER THIRTY-ONE

THE KEEPERS OF THE GRID

This session with Joan has nothing to do with ETs or light beings, but it is so important that I wanted to include it in this book. But where to put it? It is a departure from the other types of volunteers that I have been describing because it introduces another group that have come at this time with a very special purpose. I feel others will also identify with this group although they are fewer in number. There are probably many other groups of special beings that I have yet to discover. One of Joan's questions dealt with her fascination with crystals. This interest was so great that she has a store that sold crystals. She wanted to know where this overwhelming interest came from.

Joan came into a desert-like scene: sand, no vegetation. She could see a very large pyramid, and also saw many people dressed in very simple tunics going about their business, carts and oxen, etc. Then she noticed a bearded man that stood out because he was dressed differently: a green caftan with his black hair covered by a white scarf. When she looked at herself she saw that she was also dressed in a different fashion: red soft and flowing silken robes. She was a young woman in her late twenties with long black hair and brown skin. She also saw that she was wearing much gold jewelry: rings and bangles and necklaces and adornments. She liked the feel of the gold.

As the man walked towards her she unexpectedly became emotional and started crying. Part of it was from seeing him again, "I've missed this place a lot."

D: *Do you think you live there somewhere?*

J: Yes. I want to say, the palace. It's off further to the left and it has steps rising... wide, wide, wide steps to an entrance with columns. I think that I was born there. Everything is made of stone and it's very smooth and cool and comfortable to me... spaciousness. There seems to be women who take care of my needs, and take care of the children.

I asked if there was anything that she did with the majority of her time, and she became emotional again. "I have a sense of being in the healing temples."

D: *Why does it make you cry?*

J: Oh... because I'm sorry for all that's been lost.

D: *You think it's been lost? But now you're seeing it and it's all there. Where is the healing temple? Is it at the palace?*

J: Yes. There are different pyramids of different colors. They are very near the palace. These are light pyramids and I spent my time there.

D: *And they are different colors?*

J: Yes, different light frequencies.

D: *How do they color the pyramid? I'm curious about what you mean by colors.*

J: You can generate frequencies by using the crystals to generate different light frequencies and... that's what we do.

D: *It makes the pyramids a different color?*

J: Yes. Depending on what's needed at the time. You can adjust refractions with crystals to generate different healing frequencies. We do this through intentions.

D: *Do you have to go into the pyramid, or do you do it from the outside?*

J: You do it from the outside. It's hard to explain, because it's both in a way. You're inside the pyramid, but you're outside of the color pyramids that are being created to the frequencies.

D: *I'm trying to understand. These color pyramids are separate from the large pyramid?*

J: The color pyramids are etheric. They're etheric energies that are generated through the manipulation of the crystals. I am in the lower right corner of the pyramid, on a flat platform of a spacious room. I feel like I'm at controls... almost like how you'd imagine airplane controls or ship controls or electronic controls. Something physical.

D: *Mechanical?*

J: A little bit, but it's different than that. It's not mechanical in that sense. It's more about placing your hands on it and generating intentions from that kind of level. And communicating with the crystals to generate the etheric frequencies that manifest the etheric pyramid.

D: *Where are the crystals?*

J: Some of the crystals are also etheric. But the floor of this space is a crystal. The whole room is a crystal on a crystal. The controls are in this lower right hand corner, and it's a huge floor that is a crystal. And on that big smooth floor is where you generate the etheric crystal pyramids. The entire room is crystal.

D: *It's like a sacred space.* (Yes) *Did someone teach you how to do this?*

J: I was born to do it. I just always knew it. I didn't have to be taught.

D: *Once you generate the etheric colored pyramids, and set your intentions, what do you do with that?*

J: You can heal or create or grow anything. You could use it to heal anything... a planet or thought forms or....

D: *This is where the intention comes in?*

J: Yes. You can use it to create whatever you want. We can grow food and enhance the crops.

D: *How do you use it to direct these things?*

J: It seems like things occur within it. I'm seeing right now the green colored pyramid where you can grow the food. Perhaps if we were talking about Earth life, tuning into the crystals with the Earth to activate the green frequency of growth. And energetically set this up in the etheric areas where there are gardens or any plant structure.

D: *What color are the other etheric pyramids?*

J: I am seeing too that you could probably heal the oceans with the blue rays. And when we first approached, I was very aware of the yellow pyramid and the blue pyramid. But then when we talked about the plants, the green one became evident.

D: *What would you use the yellow pyramid for?*

J: For making gold. (She began crying.)

D: *Why is that making you emotional?*

J: I'm not sure why because it is so deep within. It's so deep. The pain comes from what's been lost.

D: *You help the people a lot, don't you?*

J: Yes, but the people that I saw are very simple people. And it's almost as if we're a different species living here in this palace. They're so simple, and we deal in etheric and manifestation, and it's almost like we're being the creator gods.

D: *They wouldn't be able to understand what you do, would they?*

J: No, they couldn't.

D: *Were your family like the creator gods? (Yes) Then what are you doing there among the simple people? Did anyone ever tell you the story of where you came from, and how you came to be there?*

J: Yes. I have a sense of it being like the stories that we hear of the Annunaki, having come from another place to be here to work with the Earth energies and create.

D: *And to help the people?*

J: You know, I want to say yes, but it doesn't really feel so much that it's about those simple people. It feels more like we're helping the creator gods.

D: *What is the work of the creator gods?*

J: Working with the DNA of the planet... that's what it's about.

D: *The entire planet?* (Yes, yes.)

In my other cases we have heard of working with the DNA of the human body because it is being changed at the present time. I had never thought of the DNA of a planet.

J: It doesn't feel like we're from here. I've always been there. I must have been born there, but my father didn't come from there. I wonder about my mother. I don't know what she is. She's like I am.

D: *Do you like the work you're doing, working with the crystals and creating the energy?*

J: And working with the light frequencies and working with the frequencies of the energies. It is important to make manifest and to create. It's about creating the grids and creating the grid work. It's the planetary grids... the mind and the heart, the purity of the heart... the integrity of the mind.

I thought we had learned enough about this mysterious woman and her work. So I moved her ahead to an important day. She began to cry, as she exclaimed, "The grids are gone! The grids are collapsing! The etheric grids are collapsing and it's creating destruction, so these beautiful light frequencies are being lost. The light frequencies create the grids, but as the grid collapses, it destroys the crystal pyramids of the light frequencies. And I have a sense of a crack, a big crack. It's like concrete almost, but it's not concrete. It's like the grayness of destruction swallowing up the technology and the etheric creation."

D: *Did something happen to cause the grids to collapse?*

J: It seems to be all about the crack in the Earth mantle because that's what I sense. I sense a deep abyss and there's a fissure. There's a crack. What caused it? I don't know. Something must be out of balance. Something got out of balance. And it made the grids collapse

D: *So they are all connected?* (Yes) *Can you see what got out of balance? Was it something done by people or something else?*

J: Well, we hear stories, and what's the truth? But I sense that it is because of the need of purity of intent. That it was the frequencies of greed and such that caused the imbalance. I don't know what they were doing. It wasn't my group.

D: *Because you had the pure intention?* (Yes) *So it wasn't caused at the place you are?*

J: No, but it destroyed it all.

D: *No wonder you're upset. Is there anything your group can do about it because you have power with your mind?*

J: We can't stop it. We're just salvaging off what technology we can. And we'll get the crystals and retrieve them later.

D: *How do you do that?*

J: It's in the timelines. You just record the memories into the timelines in the crystals. This is the technology.

D: *You place the memories into the crystals?*

J: The memories and the frequencies.

D: *And the crystals can remember these things?*

J: Yes, the crystals know everything, but we can then access the information that we place into the crystals.

D: *So you do this with your minds... bring back the information you put into the crystals?*

J: Yes, with the light frequencies, with the mind, with the intention. We can salvage the information.

D: *Are these large crystals that you're putting it into?*

432

J: No, they don't seem to be. They seem to be your typical quartz crystal. You record the information. (To herself.) What did we record?... It's downloaded... all the information. The use of computer tech thought that all that knowledge, all that was transferred to the grids by... it must have been our minds. Before the collapse, all the frequencies, all the geometry, all the patterns of creation were placed into them. Like placing them into the DNA of the crystal.

D: *It sounds complicated, but then this can be accessed further in time?*

J: Yes, yes, the timelines are in the crystals.

D: *Is this one certain crystal?*

J: No, not one crystal. There are many, many, many crystals that hold the information.

D: *In the future when you access this, would you have to find this certain kind of crystal?*

J: I can access the information from most crystals. You know, it's kind of like now, there are those crystals that are like common people and then there are crystals who are like me. That have more knowledge.

D: *So all of them don't have this knowledge.* (No.) *If you were to hold a crystal, how can you sense whether it has any information?*

J: I can just tell if there's information there. It's in the feeling. It's all in the frequency that they hold. It's in the timelines. In this life and in future lives I need to access the information to restore the grids. (She was becoming emotional again.)

D: *Wouldn't that be complicated to be able to restore the grids?*

J: Not complicated. It's more about merging your DNA with the DNA of the crystal... just accessing and intending and awakening the keys. Once you access it into the crystal, then you're linked into it. And you can activate the Earth grids through the crystals because the crystal veins run throughout the Earth. And so if you touch one, the key, the keys, the portals... portals is a word, but that's not as true. As they're keys and they hold energy frequencies and if you activate the keys, then the grids will realign and reassemble.

D: *Before it was grids in the etheric, and this time there's to be grids in the Earth?*

J: Yes, they're to be, the Earth is more etheric now.

D: *And you said it was like portals?*

J: Yes, but keys is a better word than portals. It's like unlocking a lock. There are different places in the Earth where the grids are locked. Crystals have the information like a key to open the gridlocks. I never thought of that word "gridlock."

D: *It does fit, doesn't it?* (Yes, yes.) *But you said some of these are locked in the Earth. What caused some of these grids to be locked?*

J: We had to shut down information before people were too destructive. We had to withdraw our technology because of the disrespect of life. The only way to stop it was to destroy it.

D: *That must have been a very difficult decision.* (She became emotional: Yes.) *Because you were afraid the people would use it in a wrong way?*

J: They *were* using it in a wrong way. They could have destroyed the universe! (Upset.)

D: *What happened at that time that you decided to lock the grids?*

J: That's why I realize if we hadn't stopped it on the Earth, it would have collapsed the universe.

D: *The whole thing?* (Yes) *Explain what you mean.*

J: It just would have been a complete replication in the micro, in the macro cosmic in that order. Like pulling out the key pin. It would have been a collapse; it would have just been all swallowed into oblivion.

D: *Because one was building on top of the other?* (Yes) *So this was caused by these people using it for the wrong reasons and bringing it out of harmony?* (Yes,

yes.) *So you had to destroy the grids in the Earth or lock them or what?*

J: We had to destroy—I want to say "Atlantis." We had to destroy the continent in order to stop the abuse.

D: *I thought it was a desire for power and the people brought the destruction upon themselves.*

J: No. It had to be stopped because there would have been a replication throughout all space and time... all the grids. And we had to collapse this in order to stop it here.

D: *Would it have caused like a domino effect? Leading from Earth?* (Yes) *The Earth would have just collapsed?*

J: Yes. It was just a small thing compared to what would have happened in the cosmos.

D: *So it would have reverberated out?*

J: Yes. It would have been a replication from the micro to the macro, and macro to the micro... both directions. It would have destroyed everything.

D: *That was when it was decided to destroy the continent instead?* (Yes) *And stop it right there?*

J: Yes, to collapse the grid. That's what we did. (She began to cry loudly and emotionally.)

D: *But you had to do it.* (Yes) *It would have been much worse.* (Yes) *Yet it was not all lost because you said you preserved the knowledge in the crystals.* (Yes, yes.) *In that lifetime were you destroyed whenever the continent was destroyed? What happened to you?*

J: No, we just went off planet. With our intention we just left.

D: *You didn't need a vehicle or anything?*

J: No, I don't sense a vehicle. We were just a consciousness.

D: *Where did you go when you left the planet?*

J: Back to the All. There was no other option.

D: *Well, from that position you can see everything about that life. Where did you come from when you went to Atlantis? You had gained this great knowledge.*

J: From another dimension of time and space. We chose Earth as a perfect place to go.

D: *What was your intention on coming to Earth originally?*

J.   To create healing, to evolve consciousness, to expand light and love, expansion of consciousness.

D: *You said the people that were there were pretty common people.*

J: Yes, they are... they are.

D: *Were you expanding consciousness?*

J: Yes... expanding consciousness of the All.

D: *And it was working until somehow this other interference changed things?* (Yes) *Did you ever find out where the other interference came from?*

J: There were deceptions within the group. There were people who had other agendas. They were there for personal power and their explorations had taken a dark turn.

D: *What were they exploring?*

J: Dark matter... power and Dark Matter. It's opposite of light. It caused the imbalance. They were tapping into the Dark Matter.

D: *What did they hope to accomplish by tapping into the Dark Matter?*

J: I get the sense of wormholes or traveling. Or it's almost like they wanted to use the Dark Matter to create their own universe.

D: *Could they have done that?* (No) *But they thought they could?* (Yes) *Because they were not the creator beings, were they?* (No) *Were they using crystals in their exploration?*

J: It doesn't feel like crystals... no. It's the opposite. It's like light expands and dark contracts. They were using contracted energy. They found how to tap in.

D: *Did they have any logic behind it, or were they just wanting to see what they could do?*

J: Their own power and greed, control, manipulation and distortion. My thoughts are that curiosity killed the cat. More likely the cat was just curious about what death was like. That's how they were.

D: *They didn't really know what was going to happen. (No... no... no.) But it could have really been out of control?*

J: It *would* have.

D: *This whole universe could have been destroyed.* (Yes, yes.) *Because they were not successful in creating their own.* (No) *They just created power that was a negative power.* (Yes) *But you were able to stabilize it?*

J: Yes, in the collapse of the grids.

D: *And the knowledge was not lost.* (True) *This way the knowledge can be accessed in the future?*

J: Yes, we can access it now.

D: *That's what I'm thinking... this future time from where we're speaking now.—Over the years I have received much information about the destruction of Atlantis, but I have never heard this story before.*

J: That's because we have never told anyone before now. We think it is now time for it to be known. It must not happen again.

Was it merely a coincidence that this information came through in 2010 at the same time that a controversy was raging about the Collider Experiment? The similarity of the information is disturbing. The Large Hadron Collider (LHC) is located underground just outside Geneva, Switzerland and is described as one of the most profound scientific projects ever conceived. Built by the European Organization for Nuclear Research (CERN) it is the most expensive scientific instrument ever built. It is the largest machine in the world where the scientists are experimenting with anti-matter, "dark matter" and "dark energy" in space. It has been said that they are attempting to create a wormhole, or even their own universe. It is complicated, but the collider will shoot proton or lead ion beams from opposite directions. The two beams colliding doubles the energy released to an equivalent of 100,000 times the heat at the center of the Sun! Skeptics are saying they could unleash a tremendous power that they would not be able to control. The scientists say they are just experimenting with unknown energy that is readily available in the cosmos. My research said, "In a nutshell, the Large Hadron Collider experiment is a huge scientific effort to sneak a glimpse into the Mind of God at the moment of creation." To me it sounds like the same type of experimentation the scientists were preforming when they discovered atomic power. They also at that time had no idea what they were playing with. Also reminiscent of the HAARP experiments being conducted in Alaska to control the weather by shooting beams into the atmosphere. (More information about these experiments are found in my other books.) Many times when I have been given information about the downfall of Atlantis "they" have said, "You must know this because your civilization is going down the same dangerous path." I find it too similar to be coincidence and I think our scientists are walking a tightrope over a fire pit. They may unleash the same damaging power that collapsed the grids and almost destroyed the entire universe. The Collider experiments are now operating at half-power. It is not expected to be running at full power until 2014.

D: *Do I need to call in the subconscious or can you keep answering the questions? You're doing a great job.*

J: What are the questions? I'll see. (We both laughed.)

D: *One of the things Joan wants to know is, how can she get information from the crystals? Can she access this information that she put there herself?*

J: She accesses it every day.

Joan has a crystal store so she is constantly surrounded by crystals of all shapes and sizes.

J: She doesn't know that she's doing it, but there's a bigger plan to be enacted. It's to begin to work consciously with the grids and to identify and activate those portals and key nodes on energy grids and re-stimulate their activation. This can be done through placing crystals or working with intention.

D: *Do crystals have to be placed in a certain place?*

J: Yes, people have done this in this Earth life, going around and placing crystals. I could really see going around the planet and reactivating the grid work.

D: *Does Joan have to physically travel around the planet or can it be done in a different way?*

J: Yes, that's what she's been doing when she went to St. Croix and Alaska. It's the mending of the grids and following the lines.

D: *What do you want her to do now? Will she continue to work with the crystals?*

J: Yes. To tap into the Earth crystals, the big crystals and reactivate the grids.

This sounded like something Joan would want to do, but being human we need to have a process or instructions. I asked if there was anything specific that they wanted her to do so she could unlock the information that is in the crystals.

J: Purify the Earth vessel... drink plenty of water. Plant your feet on the earth and hold the crystal, and ask for others to assist. And in activating the grids the crystals will act as an intermediary between the etheric grids which have been established and the Earth grids that we're attempting to reactivate. So by holding the crystals while anchored to the earth, the human vessel becomes the link between the etheric grid and the Earth grids that we're trying to repair.

D: *Can she do this by herself or would it be better to do it with other people?*

J: It's better to do it in numbers. Three, six, nine... any of the factors of threes are the key for activating the grids... triangulations of energies.

D: *They operate on threes?*

J: Yes, to triangulate. Within the DNA of themselves in the planet. They should do this outside near water. They will work with the others in the etheric. The ones holding the etheric grid in place. They are beings of consciousness and light.

D: *And it's their job to maintain the grids of the Earth?*

J: Yes. The grid keepers.

D: *That would be a good name to call them, the "Grid Keepers," and to call them in to help.*

J: Yes, to repair the grids.

D: *And they can use the human body's energy and the crystal energy?*

J: Yes, and to triangulate off of all the different points in the Earth.

D: *That way she wouldn't have to physically go to these places, would she?*

J: No. It would be a triangulation between the Earth team, the Grid team and the activation point. The grid key.

D: *Do they know which activation point they are focusing on?*

J: Yes. It will be the one that becomes evident in their awareness. They'll just know. It will come into their mind, and into their consciousness. They could douse the different places to work on a world map, and it's evident by the natural disasters that occur, if you look to dominate quake zones. Look what's going on in the gulf now.

This session was conducted the beginning of May 2010 when the oil spill in the Gulf of Mexico was dominating the news.

J: There is discord of energy. The maximum discord is indicative of the keys that are needing to be "tweaked" or aligned or opened. The volcanoes, the hurricanes, the oil spill currently, the earthquakes, the war... all of these are indications.

D: *Of disturbances in the grid?*

J: The grids, yes. And also some of the volcanoes, that isn't imbalance in the grid. That is actually a balance in the grid.

D: *Bringing it back into balance?*

J: Yes, and that's a good thing. A release of energy.

D: *And these grid beings will give them the knowledge?*

J: Yes, the Keepers know because they have the overview.

D: *Can she also use this information about the crystals for healing?*

J: Well, this is the Earth healing, and so it is using it for healing. If you bring a system back into balance, the result is healing.

D: *So that is more important than working on an individual healing?*

J: Yes, yes. To work with the Earth grids and the energy grids. It's more important to heal the ocean than to heal an individual.

D: *We are getting more new information that we're moving into a New Earth. Is that tied in with this healing?*

J: It's as if concern for the child. We heal the mother so that the child will be well. We heal the mother so she can birth the New Earth. In order to make it the new Earth.

This is why we have to heal the Old Earth.

441

D: *She put the information into the crystals, so she ought to be able to get it back.*

J: Yes, and there is timing to that... everything in its appropriate time. It's like the petals of a flower unfolding, and you can't rush the bud or you'll wreck the bloom. I sense it's all in divine time and unfolding as it should be. We can restore the grids. That's the first step... to heal the planet.

D: *You told me before that you don't want to destroy a whole civilization again. It takes too long to build it back.*

J: Yes, and there's so much lost.

D: *You have told me that every people or civilization has free will, and you are not allowed to interfere in free will. You said you were not allowed to interfere in the development in civilizations because of free will.*

J: That's true, yes.

D: *But people have asked us why was Atlantis destroyed because wasn't it allowed to have free will to do these things? I think you've answered it.*

J: Good, yes. (Laugh)

D: *Because even free will can have its boundaries.*

J: Yes, but if someone doesn't know what they're doing....

D: *Like a child playing with fire.* (Yes) *You've said before the only time you could step in would be if we were going to destroy the world because it would cause reverberations.* (Yes, yes.) *So maybe you've given me the missing piece that I didn't have in my story. It makes a whole lot more sense and it's clearer now. So that's very important. You're like "Watchers," too.* (Yes) *And Joan was a Watcher when she was taking care of the planet?*

J: Yes, she was.

When our human life was created on this planet it was decided to give this beautiful place a creature with intelligence and free will. To see what he would do with it. There are very few planets in the universe that were allowed free will. I have explored some of these in my other books. But another rule was the prime directive of non-interference. This is often spoken of in the "Star Trek" series, but it is not fiction. It is very real and is carefully followed by all the space people. This means they are not allowed to interfere with the development of a civilization. They have said that there was only one exception to this rule, and that was if the civilization were to get to the point that it could destroy this planet. Then they were allowed to step in and stop it because if we were to do something like that it could have reverberations throughout the galaxy. Who would think that such a small planet as Earth would have that type of influence? We *are* a small planet, and we are deliberately isolated and quarantined here in our little corner of the solar system. They are afraid of *us*, afraid of what we could do with our violence. This is the main reason they have been watching us for so many eons. The reverberations could spread throughout the solar system, the galaxy and even into other dimensions where we would be interfering and destroying other civilizations unknown to us. The consequences would be horrifying. We now know this was the reason for sending pure souls as volunteers to help Earth at this time, to keep this from happening.

I now know through my work that many civilizations down through time have been destroyed. "They" have told me that each time they had reached the peak of intellectual knowledge and had perfected their minds to the point that they could do marvelous things. But in each circumstance (including Atlantis) the people had abused their powers and began to do things that were for greed and power rather than the betterment of the people. In the case of Atlantis we know they had been using the crystals for extreme power. They were also going against the laws of nature by using genetic manipulation to combine and create half-man/half-animal beings. They were definitely overstepping their boundaries. But, as my daughter, Julia, observed, they were still just exercising their free will. It didn't make sense to her that "they" had to destroy that civilization. She said, "After all, a rule is a rule is a rule." She is very strict about obeying the rules, and knows they were made for a reason. So the Atlanteans were doing things they should not have done, but they had not put the planet in danger of blowing up. True, the crystals were powerful and not being used correctly, but where was the dangerous threat that made "them" decide to take down the entire civilization? That was the missing piece that I had not thought of, until she brought it up. Now it became obvious. The Atlanteans had reached the same point we are at right now in our time. They were experimenting with Dark Matter and they did not know that the repercussions could backfire and destroy this entire planet. So this was why "they" had to go against the prime directive. This had been done so many times throughout the history of our Earth that they didn't want to have to do it again. Each time the abilities had to be taken away and civilization had to be rebuilt from a primitive state, and much time and technology was lost, as mankind climbed back up. This present time they didn't want to go down that route again. So in order to keep it from happening again, the call went out for the volunteers to come and help the planet Earth.

D: *Has Joan had other lifetimes on Earth?* (This was one of her questions.)

J: Just a smattering in a physical form. Most of her lives have been in the light realms.

D: *But Joan is not the only one doing this, is she?* (No) *It would be too big of a job.*

J: I hear the number: ten thousand of us. Scattered throughout the planet.

D: *All doing the same job of restoring the grids?*

J: Yes... subtle variances, but all with the same intention. We all know why we're here. Some more consciously

444

than others. Perhaps that's a piece of it, to awaken others.

D: *So they can heal Mother Earth?*

J: Yes. It's also to do with the DNA. The DNA is like the bridge of life and awakening the keys is like awakening the packets in the DNA that have been dormant.

D: *The human DNA?*

J: The human DNA... it's all DNA of everything. It's the cosmic ladder that accesses everything. That links everything so human DNA, the planetary DNA is all the same thing.

D: *So all of these have to be activated or changed?*

J: To awaken the packets of DNA that were shut down when we collapsed the grids.

D: *So when you collapsed the grids, you also shut down parts of the DNA?* (Yes, yes.) *Was that for a reason?*

J: Yes, for slowing it down... slowing it down. To deactivate those parts where the knowledge was in the DNA. It is now time to stimulate them.

D: *I've also been told the psychic abilities are coming back.* (Yes) *Is that part of the awakening of the DNA?*

J: Yes... access to the life codes.

D: *How is this being activated?*

J: With light frequencies. Increasing our light frequencies.

D: *Within the body?*

J: Yes. It comes from outside through the cosmic rays that enter into our planetary system. It stimulates the DNA packets that have been lying dormant, so we activate the light codes.

D: *That affects the human and also the planet?*

J: Yes, the planet and all of life or light.

D: *The light is very important. It is the ALL really. It's all there is.* (Yes)—*What about the people who are negative? The ones who are not in the light? Is their DNA also going to be activated?*

J: It feels like they'll just continue to sleep. It's rather like they are souls that are asleep. That's how I see it. They're sleeping. I get a sense of a "folding in," like a sleeping, a curling in... a folding in of energy. But that doesn't mean that at some other point... you know, we're talking about this as a time node *now*. At other time nodes it will be time for their codes to be awakened. It's not a bad thing to be left behind. Eventually everyone's codes will be activated, but you know, if you're not awake it's fine. That's not your time. Once again it's about the timing... the time lines. It's like seeds. You can't have every seed sprout all at once. (Laugh)

D: *What did you mean by "time nodes"?*

J: A time node is a contained energy of light and space. We exist in time nodes and so does this current Earth. We would say Earth in 2010 is a time node.

D: *Okay. But I want to clarify some things I've heard. Will there eventually become two separate Earths, when we move into the new Earth and leave the old Earth behind?*

J: I don't think so. I don't sense that that's like a new Earth. I'm sensing that there's just an expansion, a dimension or an expansion. Like you have a point. If you connect that to another point you have a line. Well, did that first point disappear when it became a line? It's the same thing. It's just that it will be a dimensional shift. Three D will still exist, but we will become also more expanded into the light frequencies.

D: *So it's like two separate Earths... one in the other dimension?*

J: Not separate. Is that point separate from the line? I guess that's how I question. That point still exists and that point is still that point. But the line is something else, just like the Earth will be something else. The old Earth will still exist. The new Earth will exist, but it will be in that analogy of the point and the line.

446

D: *In another dimension... in another frequency?*

J: Another expanded frequency... a frequency of expansion.

D: *So those that are light, their frequency is changing the DNA, and will go with that other, I guess.*

J: Yes. As if there's a simultaneous existence. It's just a dimensional shift.

D: *That's what is hard for people to understand. We are existing anyway in other dimensions.*

J: Yes. We don't have our awareness, and we don't have our DNA awakened to be conscious of it.

D: *This time we will be conscious?* (Yes) *We will be aware of our old Earth, the one where people are asleep?*

J: It won't be our concern.

D: *We will move on.* (Yes) *Every time I get a bit more information it makes it clearer because I have people asking so many questions when I lecture about this.— You told me one time that you don't even know what's really going to happen.* (Laugh)

J: No, we don't.

D: *Because it's the first time it's ever happened. That's what I've been told.*

J: The first time it's happened on Earth. (Laugh) Many planets have gone through dimensional shiftings.

D: *Because Earth is alive and has to evolve?* (Yes) *But this is the first time this has happened in this part of the universe?* (Yes)

Joan had been experimenting with lasers and thought she would be able to use them some way in healing.

J: I'm seeing that the laser lights can be used to connect the grid points, the etheric grid points to the Earth grids. That's what she is supposed to use the lasers for.

447

D: *But you said that would be for in the future.* (Yes) *How do you want her to use the laser?*

J: Just shining them out into the cosmos and triangulating off defining points and triangulating them using the light to anchor the etheric grids into the Earth grid.

D: *As well as the crystals?*

J: Yes, that must be a piece of it. The light anchors into the crystal.

We answered the rest of her questions, and the SC did the healing of the physical body.

Parting message: Don't be afraid of failure. They're just more opportunities.

So now after many years of working on this I had discovered the Three Waves of Volunteers who have come to help the Earth during these very important and essential times. But during this session I discovered another group that have come: 10,000 Keepers of the Grid. They are here for a different purpose, to restore the damage done to the grids of the Earth by the destruction of Atlantis. To bring them back into balance. They are also here to discover and access the hidden knowledge that was placed within the crystals. It is very valuable knowledge that has been waiting for this special time to be revealed once again. Let's use it correctly this time!

PART THREE

THE NEW EARTH

THE NEW EARTH

This entire book has focused on the volunteers who have come to Earth at this time to participate in the shifting into the New Earth. Just what is this New Earth that they are all talking about? How will we know when we get there? Will we notice any difference?

The information about the New Earth has come forth gradually over the past five or more years. I have accumulated the bits and pieces from hundreds of clients, and it took a long time to see a pattern emerging. It has been sprinkled throughout some of my other books (most notably *The Convoluted Universe* series). Many people at my lectures and through email correspondence have suggested that I put all the information about the New Earth into one book. So I am taking it from those books and putting it all together here. In the sessions in this book there are more bits and pieces. The amazing thing is that none of it conflicts. All of my clients are saying the same things, just using different wording. This adds validity because it all compliments each other. The following is information from my other books.

CHAPTER THIRTY-TWO

THE NEW EARTH

A

ll of our lives when we attended church, we heard the following verses from the Bible: *"I saw a new heaven and a new earth; for the first heaven and the first earth were passed away ... And I John saw the holy city, new Jerusalem, coming down from God out of heavens ... And I heard a great voice out of heaven saying, Behold, the tabernacle of God is with men, and he will dwell with them, and they shall be his people, and God himself shall be with them, and be their God. And God shall wipe away all tears from their eyes, and there shall be no more death, neither sorrow, nor crying, neither shall there be any more pain: for the former things are passed away. ... Behold, I make all things new. And he said unto me, Write: for these words are true and faithful. ... And the (new) city had no need of the sun, neither of the moon, to shine in it: for the glory of God did lighten it ... And there shall in no wise enter into it any thing that defileth, neither whatsoever, worketh abomination, or maketh a lie. ... And there shall be no night there; and they need no candle, neither light of the sun; for the Lord God giveth them light; and they shall reign for ever and ever."* (Rev. 21-22)

Many different explanations have been offered by the Church since the writing of the Bible. But the book of Revelation has remained enigmatic, *until now*. The explanations in this book that have been brought forth through many people while in deep trance, seem to hold the answers. They have described the Kingdom of God, many times, as a place of light where they have great joy being reunited with the Creator, the Source. At that time, every one of them have become beings of light, and there is no desire to return to the earthly physical form. This explains some of the meanings of the verses, but what about the prophecy of the New *Earth*? Again, the answer seems to come through many of my subjects during my sessions It was only as I was putting the book together that the similarity to the Bible became apparent. We are all talking about the same thing. John, who wrote the book of Revelation, put his vision in the words that he could find in his time period and his vocabulary. It is the same today. My subjects had to use the terminology they were familiar with. I know therefore, that we are only seeing a small portion of the total picture of the new world that is coming, but it was the best they could do. It at least gives us a glimpse of this wonderful and perfect place.

During my work, I have heard much about everything being composed of energy and the shape and form is only determined by the frequency and vibration. Energy never dies, it only changes form. I have been told that the Earth itself is changing its vibration and frequency, and it is preparing to raise itself into a new dimension. There are countless dimensions surrounding us all the time. We cannot see them because as the vibration speeds up, they are invisible to our eyes, but they still exist, nonetheless. In my book *The Custodians,* I explained how the extraterrestrials utilize this and travel by raising and lowering the vibrations of their craft. Sometimes, we also go to other dimensions and return and are not aware of this. This was written about in *The Legend of Starcrash.* So, I have touched on the subject over the years, but I did not understand the full meaning of it until I began receiving more and more information about it. "They" want us to know more because it is coming soon. And it will be a momentous event. Of course, even in the Bible, it was described as coming "soon." But now we can see and feel the effects all around us as the world prepares to shift into a new dimension.

"They" said that we will notice the physical effects more as the frequencies and vibrations increase. Many of us can sense on another level of our being that something is happening. With the changes subtly going on around us, our physical bodies must also change in order to adjust. Some of these physical symptoms are unpleasant and cause concern. "You will see and notice that as the frequency of the planet continues to raise in terms of its vibration, you will have less difficulty with symptoms of energy blockages."

Throughout my work, my subjects are being told that they must change their diet in order to make the adjustment into the new world. Our bodies must become lighter, and this means the elimination of heavy foods. During the sessions, my clients are warned repeatedly to stop eating meats (beef and pork especially), mainly because of the additives and chemicals that are being fed to the animals. They said they deposit chemicals and artificial components in our organs that will remain there for as long as six months. It is extremely difficult to filter and remove them from the body. We were especially cautioned against eating animal protein, and fried foods which act as an irritant to the body. "These act as aggravators to your system after many years of misuse. We do not mean to be judgmental, but the body is built for a certain type of vehicular traffic. The body cannot ascend in frequency to higher dimensional realms if the density and the toxins are polluting the environment of the human body."

Of course, if you are lucky enough to find organic meats that do not contain toxins, that would be safe, in moderation. They said chicken was better, and fish because they are lighter meats, but the best of all was "live" fruits and vegetables. This means those that are eaten raw rather than cooked. We were also cautioned about the elimination of sugar, and the consumption of more pure, bottled water and fruit juices that contain no sugar. Eventually, as the frequency and vibration continues to increase, we will adapt to a liquid diet. The body must become lighter in order to make the ascension. "As the energies on the planet continue to become heightened and more rarified, your body needs to shift with it." Of course, none of this is new. We have been told for many years about these facts of nutrition. But it seems to be necessary now to pay extra attention to our diet as everything is beginning to change.

In 2001 "they" stepped in to drastically get my attention and cause me to change my diet and lifestyle. During the sessions they would literally yell at me to get their message across. In 2001, I had problems with dehydration while in Florida and was experiencing unpleasant physical effects. "They" reprimanded me and made me give up my standard drink, "Pepsi," which I had indulged in for many years. They completely turned my eating and drinking habits around, and changed my diet for the better. By 2002, I had cleared a great deal of the toxins from my system and I was noticing the difference. It took several more months before I was "detoxified," so to speak. Every time they get a chance, they let me know that they are still monitoring me and I am scolded when they see me slipping back into old habits. During a session in England they said, "To understand the new energies in which you will be working, the body is being taught how to deal with this. One must never forget that there are energies out there that are not going to work with you. At this point, maybe these energies are not to be thrown away and pushed away from you. Because they are not familiar to you, you are thinking, 'They are not correct.' They are to be drawn into you and asked, 'What are they?' In fact, they are new energies. Maybe they are readjusting your body, and in so doing, they are removing toxins. Your kidneys especially will be working with a nonaccepted energy of the past. Just accept that the cleansing process is and will occur."

I was then given a process to energize the water we drink, to help in the detoxification process. "Water, in the basis of seventy percent of yourself, and seventy percent of the planet, is so far beyond importance, it is unbelievable. So therefore the resonance of the water you bring into your body is so very important. When you drink water, energize it with the knowledge you have. Send that knowledge. Spiral it in. Imagine the water spiraling, creating a vortex, in a both clockwise and anticlockwise direction. Creating the positive and negative key. You must move it out of balance. Imagine an energy entering the water and spiraling and creating a vortex. That is all it has to do. The thought will then energize the water. That will then reintroduce life force back into the water, which is the life force acceptance of the planet. All fluid on this planet, whether it is rock or whether it is fluid liquid, is liquid in a slower or faster motion. Everything has the resonance and memory of what it is. Humanity has lost the resonance and memory of what it is, but water can re-energize. Man's human thought format processes back into and helps work with its resonance. You must bear in mind that this energization of a bottle of water may only last a few hours. You may need to reintroduce it. So the formula may be, before you drink any liquid, do the same process. You can also do the same with food. Food simply being liquid in a slower motion. This will help with the body. This will also help clarify and create a place called "clarity" within your mind thought format because you have started losing some of the clarity. This clarity will come back."

From an email sent to me from an unknown source:
Time is actually speeding up (or collapsing). For thousands of years the Schumann Resonance or pulse (heartbeat) of Earth has been 7.83 cycles per second. The military have used this as a very reliable reference. However, since 1980 this resonance has been slowly rising. It is now over 12 cycles per second! This means there is the equivalent of less than 16 hours per day instead of the old 24 hours.

One of the indications that the frequency and vibration is occurring, is the speeding up and shortening of time.

Client: Starting in 2003, there will be an influx of energy that is going to really propel the Earth. There is going to be a greater schism between the group of people that are going to be staying behind, and the people that are going forward. The outcome will be a higher vibrational increase in Earth. This is affecting the whole universe. This is not just the Earth. This is galactic.

CHAPTER THIRTY-THREE

THE OLD EARTH

Anne said she wanted to go home, and experience what home was like, so at this point in the session, "they" gave her a glimpse of it and she became emotional. "Tell me what you're showing her. What does it look like?"

A: (Very softly) Energy. (She was openly weeping now.) It's like they're charging me with energy or something. (Whispering) I can feel it all over.... (Crying) It's like love.

I let Anne cry for a while, then I calmed her down so the other entity would be able to return and answer the questions and give information unemotionally. "We love her very much."

D: *I know it took a lot of courage to leave that beautiful place and volunteer to come here at this time.*
A: She feels that she's not fulfilling her purpose. That is her major, biggest frustration – that she is not doing what she came to do. She wants to finish. She has many abilities and talents, and she feels she should be using them in a certain way. And she cannot do this by herself.
D: *You said she volunteered to come to be here during the changes. Are these the changes I've been told about? (Yes) Do you want to talk about that part?*

A: Many changes. What are the things you have been working on?

D: *That we're moving to new frequencies and vibrations?*

A: That is correct. Do you have questions?

D: *I've been told a great deal of information, that everything is speeding up, and the vibrations and frequencies of our whole dimension are changing. Is that correct?*

A: Turbulence, much turbulence coming very soon. And there is the need to be very grounded. Much turmoil. There will be need for your stability and all of those who are here because people will be lost and confused and in much pain. Do you understand?

D: *By turbulence, do you mean more of the violent Earth changes that have been happening?*

A: Situations caused by humans, and situations caused by the Earth changes. And the coming through of new energies and beings that humans are not accustomed to seeing. This will cause a great deal of chaos, that only those who are understanding what is transpiring, will keep calm and be a reassurance to those in confusion. Remember and just be prepared for that because it's very easy to theorize until the situation is in the physical. Then the physical body needs to be prepared to handle the shifts of energy, and the shock that comes with the process of change. It is one thing to feel you can understand what is happening. But it is another to be in the midst of chaos and keep yourself calm when it's happening.

D: *That's difficult for humans, isn't it?*

A: It is difficult. And that is a crucial and practical area to focus on at this time because it is in the physical that you are helping. There are other levels that are helping, but you are in the physical as she is, and other beings are. So in the physical, they could transmit that calm that will be necessary during times of chaos.

D: *But will they listen to us?*

A: It is not up to you to decide. It is up to you to make sure you have the tranquility and grounded energy for those who want to listen to you. That alone requires much work in the physical to keep those energies in place because that's what you came to do. Anne is very trained because her life experiences have required her to maintain a level of calm in the midst of madness.

Anne had lived a childhood with abusive and unstable parents, and then a chaotic marriage.

A: That has been a good training ground for her, so that when the time comes, it is not so difficult for her to maintain that calm in the physical. Do you understand?
D: *Yes, I do. I've been told that these changes are going to cause a separation into two Earths. The old Earth and the new Earth, as the vibrations and the frequencies increase. Is that correct?*
A: That is correct. There is a different world, if you will, which some souls will remain or choose to live in after the changes. The world that keeps that level of vibration they wish to stay in, and that will be where they remain, or move into. But the new energies will only be livable for those who have worked their own energy up to that vibration.
D: *But the turbulence you spoke of, will that be on the old Earth?*
A: It is now as we go through these changes. This is the time of transformation in the next few years, and the outcome has been prophesied by many. I don't have much to add to that, other than, those who are here now need to remember the important role they are playing in the physical before the changes happen, or before the final changes happen. In the midst of the process, there's a need for those who are here to give the assistance. To line up, if you will, as if it were in the military. It's time for them to show up and be aware

that they are being called to be very present and ready. And maintain their ground because there might be situations in which a soul might be in a crucial point where they could go either/or, vibrational wise. And you may be able to make a difference at that time.

D: *What do you mean by either/or?*

A: Their spiritual growth may be in a grey area where they may qualify to step up to a higher vibration, if only they have the courage to jump. Or else they may choose not to, and that is their choice. But your role, if you keep your energy, may be crucial for someone in that situation because you may be the hand that extends for them to jump.

D: *Make the jump into the higher vibration.* (Yes) *But the higher vibration, the new Earth, will not experience this turbulence?* (No) *It seems as though right now, we are in this part that is experiencing the turbulence.*

A: It is just the beginning. It has begun, but the chaos has not begun. The chaos, the madness of people running around in confusion because all of their illusions have been shattered. That will be the time of the test of the strength that needs to come forth for those of you who are here to help in the process. There will be a time when people are running in the streets confused and in fear, not unlike the hurricane in Louisiana.

D: *That's what I was thinking of, the tsunami and the hurricanes.*

A: But that multiplied worldwide in most cities is a very different scenario.

D: *Are there going to be similar disasters in many cities?*

A: Some caused by natural, some caused by those in power who are making every effort to keep things the way they are. They are aware of the changes. They refuse to accept. It's like a child who doesn't want to hear the truth. And they refuse to admit they are no longer in charge. So they continue to cling to these ways and may cause more confusion. They feel they may be able to slow down the process and maintain a low vibration by keeping fear on the surface.

D: *They're trying to instill fear in people.*

A: Fear has always been in people because that's how most, if not all, the societies of this world have functioned for many years. Fear is the way they have maintained power, and almost everyone in this world is in fear. There are different levels of fear, but these changes and the technology that has allowed everyone to communicate freely, have caused a great deal of concern for those in power because now the fear is vanishing. Many things that are occurring, even the catastrophes, act as a catalyst to bring fear out so it is dealt with. And so it is a cleansing in a way. But those in power don't want this process to occur, and they prefer to keep a level of fear under the water, if you will. And like a desperate child, they try every tactic they can think of at this time to not let that fear dissipate, because that is what is happening. The fear is dissipating despite what the surface seems to show.

D: *People are beginning to think for themselves.*

A: They are. They are confronting their own demons, if you will because life is taking them places where they have to see things that other times they haven't had to deal with. Therefore, their fears, although they are very present, are at least coming to the surface, whereas before, they were not. Therefore, it is a cleansing that, as it continues, will only liberate more and more, which is a process that those in power are very aware of. They want to slow it down, thinking there might be a way to prevent it. So they will push and push to every extreme they can until things get very difficult. And many people will not be prepared for that edge they are pushing for.

D: *Is the war one of the things?*

A: The war, absolutely the wars, also their diseases that they scare people with.

D: *These diseases are not really there, are they?*

A: They can be if people choose to allow those energies to enter into their body. But for the most part, they are only in the energetic fields. And like anything else that is talked about, or thought about, it can become reality in the physical.

D: *Yes, if enough people accept it as their reality.*

A: But the diseases are extremely blown out of proportion, and they are not epidemics as they are portrayed to be. The media and the movies are showing you their desperation as they insist in presenting to the masses information that is completely negative and fear-based. Subject matter such as murder, death and betrayal, attacks and such that keep the consciousness focused on these matters, as opposed to portraying in the media images of hope and inspiration. But nevertheless, there are enough of those positive messages being broadcast at this time, that like a domino effect, they are no longer stoppable.

D: *Another fear the government is trying to promote is terrorism.*

A: Yes. It is just another tool, like the diseases, to find excuses to give people a reason to be afraid and not unify, but to trust that the government will solve their problems. They are imaginary problems, and in the subconscious, many people are becoming aware of this. They are no longer believing, although many are in the masses. But on their subconscious level, they are beginning to awaken, and the power knows this. That is the reason they are resorting to ridiculous stories that only those who wish to believe, believe in them because anybody with a logical and reasonable mind could not believe them.

D: *Yes, anybody who thinks for themselves.*

A: So they are presenting the masses the opportunity to choose because they are pushing for an edge. And in that way, they are serving a purpose by pushing the edge, so that everybody makes a choice because this is a time of choice. This is no longer a time of middle ground and neutrality.

D: *You said earlier that we would be here whenever the chaos breaks out. Would this be caused by many of these disasters?*

A: Disasters and the breakdown of the structures of government. And the breakdown of the safety net that most people feel they are part of. Such as their Social Security, and their paychecks, and their jobs, and their religious beliefs. Especially if and when ships and/or other things like that begin to become part of the consciousness that many are not prepared for. Therefore, they may run around in shock and confusion, unsure as to what's real and what's not. The structure of government is breaking, and will break even more to a point of chaos. Like a domino effect, like a crumbling.

D: *If the ships arrive, what would be their purpose for coming?*

A: They are always here. It is only a time for them to become visible as the permissions open up, because it is a time of, not only free will as there is now, but also a time for others to claim their place in the new world. Not just the humans, but others who also belong here, but are in a different vibration. So partly, it is not that they choose to become visible, it is partly that the energies make them visible.

D: *I am aware they've been here. I've been working with them. I know they're positive. I've had no problems with them.*

A: But by them becoming visible and part of the consciousness of the people, and the governments crumbling, and chaos, and natural disasters, you can see how the majority of people would be completely shocked. And their religions and their idea of a structured life would be brought down. So now, they would have nothing to cling to. This causes a great deal of fear for those who have not stepped out of their own house. That fear could lead to madness or schizophrenia or other types of reactions. And it is at that time, and that kind of reaction, that will leave people most vulnerable, where you can be of most service.

D. *Then others like myself and Anne are some of the ones who are here to help?*

A: The ones who are prepared to see these changes and not crumble in fear will be the pillars on which others will lean when nothing makes sense to them. It doesn't mean you will provide the truth to them, it just means you are not falling down like they are.

D: *Because, I was thinking, what can we do when everyone is in chaos?*

A: When you are not losing your mind and you are calm, it doesn't matter what you do. People will see that in you and seek that in you because they don't know what to make out of what they're seeing. And you may not know what to make out of what you're seeing, but you have been prepared. Therefore, you will know and have some sense of trust that things will be okay. You are not crazy.

D: *Where the others won't have any preparation at all.*

A: Exactly.

D: *You know that I've had many, many people coming to me for the last two years who are either healers or they're being told by you, the subconscious part, that they are to be healers. We keep wondering why the world would need so many healers?*

A: Do you know the population of the planet?

D: *Yes, it's quite large.*

A: That might be one reason why. Also, it is a time that's very precious for many souls because of the learning lessons available, as it is an unusual time that this planet has not experienced. Therefore, it is an opportunity to experience a very one of a kind soul journey. And it's an opportunity to step up in the soul level, experience-wise because of the challenges it presents. Therefore, many advanced souls are interested in the opportunity for themselves.

D: *I was thinking if structures do break down, the medical profession would definitely be one of them. Maybe that would be one reason to have healers that can use energy and natural healing.*

A: There is a time coming when the energy will be high enough that disease will not be as you know it today. And though the help of those healers is definitely needed, there will be a time when those diseases are not going to be anymore. Therefore, the healing is only temporary. The healers will heal when there is a need. If there are no hospitals because everybody has left the city, for example, or maybe it's drowned (is she referring to the city inundated?), then there are healers available to help. But that is not the only reason they are here. They are here for their own learning purpose, as their own soul is interested in experiencing this shift.

D: *That's why we all chose to be here at this time?*

A: A big reason.

D: *I've also been told that our DNA is being altered so we can adjust to these changes. Is that true?*

A: There are many groups that are participating in the acceleration of energies, and they have their own technology. From our perspective, we would say that through the infusion of higher vibrations on the planet, it reflects back on the people. So it is not their DNA that's being adjusted, at least from our perspective. It is the higher vibrations that are naturally affecting their DNA, which is dormant in some areas. And therefore, it is being activated.

D: *I've heard this is the reason for many physical symptoms people are experiencing at this time.*

A: Areas of blockage in the body, whether they are karmic issues, or their own diseases caused by their lack of self-discipline with their eating habits, or other things, independently of the cause of the disease. But they're basically areas of blockages that are being brought to the surface with these new energies, whereas before, they might have been laying dormant. It is being brought to the surface much like the karmic issues that are being brought to the surface. These energies are forcing these areas to deal with the dark negativity so the energy can flow freely, that those blockages need to be cleared up. In order for that to happen, the issues that are causing these diseases need to be attended to, which requires a level of participation from the people who are suffering. And that is their choice whether they attend to these things or not.

D: *What I have heard is that many of these physical symptoms people are experiencing are being caused by the change in the vibration as the human body adjusts to it.*

A: That is correct.

D: *If the chaos belongs to the old world, will this be happening at the same time the two worlds are separated? I don't know if I'm wording it right. The new Earth is supposed to be going into a new vibration and a new dimension. And it was described as separating, becoming two worlds. Does that make any sense?*

A: There are many theories. Depending on the perspective, it is a matter of energetic vibration. And one vibration is visible, and some vibrations are not visible to each other. Therefore, if one vibration – the lower, or slower vibration—remains, it's not that it becomes a separate world, it is simply no longer visible. It's the new world that is basically a split-off because of the higher vibration.

D: *But in the new world, things are different than the old world. Isn't that true?* (Yes) *They won't be experiencing the chaos?*

A: No, the chaos is mostly a breaking down of the belief systems. The chaos is caused by the belief systems being challenged and brought down to a place of a complete blank slate, or clean slate. And that is the chaos for many. Those who go on to the new world are comfortable with new belief systems, and therefore, will no longer struggle the way those struggle now. It's not that it's a transformation where all of a sudden people become something they are not. It is just the changes. It's either people can move on from there, from them, or not.

D: *That's what I've been trying to understand. I've been told the new world would be beautiful, we wouldn't have these problems. And they said, don't look back. You don't want to see what's happening to the old world.*

A: It is basically a deterrent to look back. It's not that you cannot look back, it's just that you cannot change other people's choices. And therefore, if you're looking back and it is causing you grief, it is only slowing you down.

D: *But you said we're supposed to be involved with these people.*

A: We are here during the time of changes. We are here to keep our energy grounded. It is not so much to be with those with a higher vibration because they can fend for themselves. And it is not for those who are in deep negativity that we must be next to either. It is for those who are in the midst of confusion, but are perhaps ready to make a jump, that we are most helpful to.

D: *Does that mean we have to stay with the old world as workers?*

A: You will only stay until it's time for you to go. And during the time that you stay, you can do your service. When it's time for you to go, you will know, and then you will no longer be available to those. It is not a matter of, "How long should I stay?" That is a question that is answered eventually. It's a matter of knowing what to do while you are here.

D: *I have thought we would be separate from those experiencing the chaos. We would be in a different beautiful world.*

A. For a while, through the process of transformation, not necessarily separate. It's not like one day to the other there is a new world that you are part of, and the old world goes away. There is a process. Eventually, things will change. But in the small process, whether it lasts one month or five years, it is a process that you are still part of, as you are now. You are of it, now. So long as you are here, it is your job to keep the grounded energy for those who are in confusion. Once the actual shift happens, even if you wanted to be here, you couldn't.

D: *Those who have raised their vibrations will go on.*

A: That's correct.

This answered a question I was asked while giving a lecture at the Ashram in the Bahamas. A young woman said that she would like to stay with the Old Earth to help those who would be left behind. I told her that was noble, but I didn't think it could happen. Now, here was the answer. It has to do with vibrations, and once your vibrations have reached the correct frequency you just automatically go to the next level. As they said, "Even if you wanted to stay, you couldn't." Your intent doesn't matter. This is bigger than we are.

D: *And so we're trying to help those who are still trying to decide and make up their minds?* (Yes) *That's why I was trying to get clarification. I've heard it from many people, but sometimes it's a little confusing.*

A: It is confusing from the vantage point of a human.

D: *Then you do see more turbulence happening.*

A: Yes, absolutely. This is the beginning, as those in power are not near done with their strategies. They will cause many more events. And there will be other events, natural causes. So the chaos is much larger than we envision in isolated cases. But of course, all of those things could change, as there is no set future.

D: *I've been told that age is not important anymore.*

A: Age is an illusion. It will be more apparent as we move along in the process of evolution.

D: *I've also heard that whenever the transition happens, we would be allowed to take our physical bodies with us if we want to. Is that correct?*

A: That is true, but it will only be for a short time. There will be another transition very shortly thereafter.

D: *What will happen at that time?*

A: Mankind will become pure energy.

D: *The ones that make the ascension.*

A: That is correct.

D: *I've also heard not everyone will make the transition.*

A: Everyone will be given the opportunity. Whether they can hold that vibration or not is up to them individually. There will be no judgment made on them. They will simply be able to hold the energy, or not. But none will be destroyed as the comments have been heard. They will be placed in an appropriate space for the vibration they are emitting.

D: *And that's what they mean when they say they will be left behind.*

A: In God's plan all will return to God.

D: *Just at different intervals.*

During another session, I was speaking to the subconscious.

D: *You keep saying things are changing.*
S: They're accelerating changes, and your scientists don't have a handle on it.   This global warming, it's devastating to the ecology   It's happening so much faster than the scientists are saying.
D: *They don't really believe it?*
S: They believe it, but they think the danger is decades away. It's not; it's here! The danger is at our doorstep. There will be some safe places in the U.S.
D: *What's causing the global warming?*
S: You know, accelerants.   I mean the aerosols, gas, everything that pollutes the environment— environmental pollution.   It's what man is doing. That's why our summers are so hot. And there will be more storms. Many, many, many more. Unbelievable. You aren't going to believe what's coming. The coasts are going to be in for a fun time. The increasing storms and tsunamis are going to accelerate it. The timetable is changing.
D: *Originally there was a different timetable?*
S: Yes. It's moving forward.   It's sooner than it was meant to be. Unfortunately because of what mankind is doing.

From another session a subject saw a terrible future scenario:

D: *One last question that Janice wants to know about. She wanted to be allowed to go forward in time to the year 2325. Twenty-three twenty-five. And see if she will be in the physical at that time, or whether she will be in the spiritual. Can you take her forward to that time, and show her a scene or a picture?*

She went immediately to a scene and began reporting what she was seeing.

J: I'm an instructor. I'm instructing people about how to grow the coogies (Phonetic). (Chuckle)

D: How to grow what?

J: Coogies. The coogies. You know, they're a plant that's grown for the food on the Earth. It's like brussel sprouts almost. It grows in a huge base. And people touch the metal edge of the container that this plant is in. It causes vibration so the plant grows.

D: Why do you have to grow this kind of plant for food?

J: Nothing can grow on Earth. It's grown in outer space, on ships. With the vines leading up over the sides of the walls. Through mesh, to supply oxygen to the plants, to the room, to the ship. I call it "coogies." That's a funny name, coogies. The workers travel in spacesuits on tethers that are connected to the ground. And they travel up the tether, like an elevator, to the spacestations to tend to these plants. And I'm having a class. I'm the one who supervises this work. It's important.

D: What has happened to the Earth that it can't grow food?

J: The dummies screwed it up! They ruined the ecology of the Earth. Earth is still healing itself at this time.

D: What did the dummies do to the Earth to destroy the ecology?

J: Fighting. Hatreds. Neglect. Misuse. Wastefulness. The ecology, they just ruined it. They ruined the animals, the people, until they themselves could no longer live there.

D: Where do the people live?

J: They're hybrided peoples. They're peoples of remnants of the Earthlings, and of another spiritual planet. They're hybrided in order to accept the dimensions that are coming. From when we're talking now to that time period. Those bodies are used. The greys hybrided.

D: *Are the people living on the Earth?*

J: Yes, they live on the Earth, but they live in suits. Fires. Some of the Earth is shooting fire up through the ground. By the year 2030 there are fires coming out of the ground in the area that's Arizona. Twenty-five, fifty feet, shooting high like geysers. And people fighting. Traveling on the ground in suits that protect them from the heat, but fighting each other. There's a war between Mexico and the United States. They're coming up and fighting through this land. It's useless. They can't exist down there.

D: *Why are they fighting with the Americans?*

J: Possession of land. Certain lands are still livable, but not very many.

D: *Do you mean that by that time there will be large parts of the land that are not livable?*

J: Yes. That already is now coming, destruction.

D: *And this will cause some of the land to be not livable?*

J: It will cause all of the land to be nonlivable, according to the way the human body lives. In the year 2001 we're already becoming... it's harder to breathe and harder to live now.

D: *But what has happened to the Earth to cause the land to be unusable?*

J: Vibrations. When they did the very first thing to ruin the ecology of Earth, it set off a chain reaction. And those vibrations continue one after the other. First one animal, then another species, then another species. A chain reaction. The first time they ever set off the atomic bomb, it made a chain reaction. In nature vibrations, like circles when you drop a rock into the water. Less concentric circles have already faded a whole lot. The first time they ever did away with a species it actually molded the trigger for extinction. The bombs that they set off cause repercussions that they never even could imagine. Even in their own spirits. Vibrations that shake up the very creation.

D: *I was wondering if it was a war that caused the land to be depleted. But you think it's just people.*

J: It's all war. Every time you do anything negative, it's war. Killing each other is real, what they call "war," it's already too late. I mean, when you do something, you cannot change what you do. It causes the circles. It causes repercussions you don't even dream about. And it causes the disruption of nature. When we disrupt nature it's like a dead-end street because it cannot go on to be whole with integrity as nature intended. As God intended.

D: *Is this part of what the ones we call the ETs are here in 2001 to try to help with?*

J: They're so full of love. And they're so kind. Light beings. The energy that comes through them. The greys I'm talking about, and the others, too. They're just on different levels. Even the reptilians. They're all helping in their own ways. But the greys especially are emissaries from their people. Sent with more love than the others, I think. I might be just partial to that particular light, but they have more love.

D: *But in this future life that Janice was being shown, much of this has affected the Earth, and she is helping to grow food to feed the people.*

J: It takes very little to sustain a physical body, but people don't realize it. You can live more on love and oxygen and osmosis than you can on food. Food is hard on the body.

D: *But people don't understand that. They like food.*

J: They will understand when they become hybrided. And they're fighting that. They don't want it. They think that the greys are taking the world over, and... how scary!

(Chuckle) What are they giving up? They're giving up the wars, and their hatreds, and their dark sides. Goals? (Laugh)

D: *But they'll understand whenever the body is corrected to where it can take care of itself. But these are the things we're headed for anyway.*

Again, this is not the first time I have heard and written about this condition occurring to our planet Earth. In *Legacy From the Stars*, I end the book with a session where the woman subject went into the future instead of going into the past. She was living in an ant-farm tunnel existence beneath the surface of the Earth. The surface had been contaminated to the point that nothing would grow there. The atmosphere had been changed to a poisonous gas that they could not exist in. The only way they could go to the surface was by wearing a type of suit, and they couldn't remain there very long. This future being had evolved because of living in underground conditions into something that did not resemble present-day human beings. They looked like the familiar little ETs called "greys," which brings up the theory that they are possibly us in the future. And maybe they have come back into our time period to warn us about what will happen if we continue on our present course. There may also be the desire to change their own dismal future time period.

Also I have found this same scenario when I do my group regressions all over the world. This is a workshop I do where I put the entire audience into trance at the same time. It is a fun workshop, and I have them journey back in time to a past life to discover information that will help them in their present life. I also have other parts to this workshop, including one where I have them journey into the future to see what their lives might be. I know they could be seeing probable futures which may or may not become reality, so this part of the workshop is not to be taken seriously. But for my own information as a curious reporter I am amazed to see how many times they repeat the same possible scenarios. Some see themselves living onboard orbiting spaceships where they grow food in hydroponic conditions in the absence of gravity. They do this because the Earth needs food, and it will not grow on the surface anymore. Some have seen themselves in an underwater laboratory where they harvest food from the sea, so the people of Earth can have food. These are dismal probable futures resembling what Janice saw. It is not the type of future I would wish on my descendants, but it does show the amazing resiliency and innovation of the human race to survive.

CHAPTER THIRTY-FOUR

AN EARLIER SHIFT

I have been receiving a great deal of information about the coming shift. Much of this has already been written about in *Book Two* of the Convoluted Universe series. And yet the information continues to come. This is our destiny, our future. In this session, I was given another missing part of the story. This has happened on Earth before. Groups of people in the past have been able to shift en masse into another dimension. These are usually groups that are surrounded in mystery because they simply disappeared, leaving no clues as to what happened to their civilizations. There has been much speculation, and various theories have been brought forward by the so-called "experts." But few have considered the fact that they simply walked off this Earth, and entered a different dimension, leaving no trace behind. The Mayans are a prime example, also some North American Indian tribes. I had been told through my work that these groups had become very advanced in their development, and had chosen to change vibrations and shift en masse. I was told this was one of the most logical explanations for the Mayan calendar stopping at the year 2012. If they, in their advanced state, had been able to accomplish this, they were able to see that in the future, the entire planet would follow and accomplish the same feat. This would be an even greater event than what they had accomplished. So they marked in on their calendars as the time the entire planet and everything on it changed frequency and moved into the other dimension, taking every living thing with it. I had been told these things, and it sounded reasonable to me. However, I was not expecting to have a regression where someone went back to a lifetime when they actually experienced such an event. This woman was able to report something that we can only speculate about at this time. It was another piece of the puzzle given by a voice from the past. "They" were making sure I was given all the pieces. My job was to organize them and put them together into a coherent story.

After experiencing death from an accident in Roman times, Suzanne looked down and saw the road she had been walking on as a spiral. "It seems to be the road, but it's also symbolic. Almost like these shells that they cut in half. That's a good example of it. It's like, by looking at the spiral, you're getting some insight into the Universe, and deeper understanding of what makes things tick. Seeing your place on the spiral, seeing how the spiral fits into the Universe, fits into time."

I then moved her away from the death scene, and told her to go to something else, either forward or backward, something that was appropriate for her to see. "I came in on a wooden stairway with wooden railings that were descending from the left. Some kind of log structure straight ahead, and there is no one there. Almost as if you were in a fort or something, and you were looking out through the structure. So it's built in the side of a mountain, but they've cleverly dug into the mountain. That's where the main part of the building is. It is built into the stone of the mountain. This is a Native American place. And I'm getting that this is on the etheric, or something in the astral somewhere. Or it could be fifth dimensional now, but it's no longer 3-D."

D: Not physical?
S: It seems to be physical, but just not of the Earth plane. It feels like the Earth is vibrating somewhere else. As if there's an overlay of the dimension over the Earth, this would be in the overlay. It might have been at one time 3-D and it increased in vibration. And it's now

almost like a parallel in that universe or something related to the Earth, but not the third dimensional Earth.

D: *Does this place feel familiar to you?*

S: It's home to me.

D: *That dimension?*

S: Yes, and it's very much like Earth in that there are stones and trees. And this is definitely in the mountains. It's more like our southwest. It's very comfortable here. My interests and my work are with spiritual things, and with healing.

D: *How do you perceive your body?*

S: I feel like I am a male, and I'm young—not an old person yet, maybe around thirty. Experienced. I'm doing my work, I'm still very fit.

D: *How are you dressed?*

S: Very simply. Some kind of woven material. It's very functional, sort of like a tunic. Very simple.

D: *But you said you don't feel you're on the Earth.*

S: No, it's not the Earth, but it's related to the Earth.

D: *But you have a physical body?* (Yes) *Then how are you able to go to this place if it is not of the Earth? You can look at it and understand how it happens.*

S: Now it seems that it's all very natural, not unlike the Earth. People were born and raised. But I was trying to see if maybe at one time we were of the Earth, and changed somehow. That may have been how it was.

D: *You said it was related to the Earth in some way. What do you mean by that?*

S: I think we have consciousness of the Earth, almost like we're in another dimension. So either we can perceive it from where we are, or we were once of the Earth and moved off somehow.

D: *So if you moved off the Earth, then you took this physical place with you?*

S: It seems like what might have happened was the band of people—I said "band" because it's not like there are many, many people around. And somehow, we've reached a point of changing frequencies, as if we all went on a similar experience. When people do things as a group. But it was like that whole society was able to transcend.

D: *Was this an intentional thing?* (Yes) *Was it something that was talked about?*

S: Talked about and worked for. People aspired to this.

D: *So not everyone did this, just a certain group of your people?*

S: It was all the known people then. We were an Indian tribe, and we knew there were other tribes around, but they weren't part of our world, Earth society. We were just by ourselves. We only cared about what happened to us.

D: *How were you able to do this? Were you taught?*

S: There were teachers for some generations, the wise people. And we were taught with meditation. It was all of us. Maybe we're only a few hundred people, but that was our whole world. I think we experienced it before we moved in. We would go and come individually and in groups. The frequency was raised and we experienced that, and shifted back.

D: *How did they know this would happen?*

S: I was just wondering about that. It's like the people just knew. I don't know if at one time someone might have told them. I'm sensing now that maybe we were not from the Earth altogether, but we came to Earth, establishing a colony. But we knew mentally we could transport ourselves and move.

D: *Why did you want to do that?*

S: I think it was exploration. Just to see if it could be done. We did the 3-D experience, and then shifting, we moved to just another dimension.

D: *So there wasn't any reason to leave the Earth, the 3-D experience?*

S: No, not imminent danger.

D: *I was thinking that if you were happy where you were in the 3-D experience, or Earth, you wouldn't have any need or desire to move, to shift.*

S: It makes me smile. It's like a spiritual nature is always to learn. So even if things are good, it's like, "Hmm, what's around the corner, and what's to explore?"

D: *In the 3-D world, were you a spiritual group?*

S: Very much. We had great respect for the Earth, and the forces within it.

D: *But you had no desire to stay there. (No) So it was decided that you would all do this at once? (Yes) You said you did go back and forth.*

S: At first, yes. It was like trying to get out at first. And as we became practiced in that, then we could all make a shift. I'm seeing a blue stone, lapis lazuli. It seems connected to where we come from, and it's symbolic of that. Like turquoise would be to the southwestern Indians, and to the Tibetans. Lapis lazuli is associated with these people somehow. It seems they're from somewhere else in the cosmos.

D: *So they weren't originally of the Earth?*

S: I think it was done before our time, but not before the grandparents' generation.

D: *Did they tell you stories of what happened?*

S: They must have, but I don't remember them.

D: *Maybe that's what made it easier for you to move to the other dimension?*

S: Perhaps. Certainly the knowledge. But I also want to say that people are smarter than they think. Everyone knows how to do this. They may not know they do.

D: *And your people took their physical body and surroundings with them. Is that right?*

S: I'm not sure about that. I think either they manifested similar surroundings where they went, or they moved into another dimension that already had that there.

D: *Do you like it there?*

S: It's more the excitement of learning things. The "there" doesn't matter. The excitement is with learning. I'm very active in my thinking.

D: *Do you have to eat there? Do you have to consume anything?*

S: We do eat, but it seems like the food is lighter, more vibrational. It lasts longer in us, for us. The requirements aren't so great.

D: *And you don't want to go back to the Earth?*

S: We have moved on. It seems the next step of the evolution of us.

I moved him forward to see if anything happened there that was important. It seemed like such an idyllic place, what could he find that would be significant?

S: I see that we're being asked to come back. And I have tears now. We're being asked to come back to the Earth.

D: *The whole group?*

S: Some of us. We know some things that would be of help to the people. And we have great compassion for the people.

D: *But you don't want to go?*

S: Yes and no. It's like taking that first trip for the exploration. Yes, you want to go, but you're torn. It's sad to leave home. We are people who are very loving, very compassionate. And we wish to share this with others.

D: *But this place is not like the spirit side, is it?*

S: Not totally. It seems to be another physical, but less dense, existence. Not totally spirit, I don't think.

D: *It's not like the spirit place where you go when you die and leave the body.*

S: I don't know. We seem to be pretty eternal. We've moved off the physical where we might have died, to some place or frequency where it's not necessary to die.

I think we actually pulled it off. Kind of a transition of even the molecular structure of our bodies. I think we became spirit somehow.

D: *You mean it changed in some way?*

S: Yes, it was some transformation when we left. I think we took our bodies with us when we left. I think we took the physical bodies that changed, and we took it with us.

D: *You said it changed the molecular structure?*

S: Yes, totally. Yes.

D: *This was the only way you could make the change?*

S: I think we could have died, but we couldn't have done it en masse. I mean, we could have died en masse. But this was an experiment of sorts. It was the melding of a group mind from the 3-D. It was the forerunner of where we can go now, I see.

D: *So it was a group that experimented at first.*

S: Yes. I think there were others trying different ways. This was our way.

D: *You weren't dissatisfied with the Earth. You just wanted to try something different, more spiritual.*

S: Both are equally spiritual, but it seems like we have less restrictions beyond the 3-D. There are advantages.

D: *So someone is telling you, you have to come back?*

S: Not have to. It's like there's a call, there's a need. There's an opportunity.

D: *How do you know this?*

S: It's been talked about. More mental telepathy, but it's communicated, it's known. It's like things have gotten much worse on the Earth since we left, since we moved off. Things have changed.

D: *So you have a way of knowing what's happening on the Earth.*

S: Yes, very much. That's why I say we're connected. We can know these things. There are like holographic thought processes that happen. Any one of us can tune in, or most everyone can tune in to what they want.

And there's some relationship between our people and the people who have remained on Earth. It's like someone has this idea. Someone recognized a need there that all of us have information about. But it's the time now.

D: *You have done it so you know how to experience it.*

S: Yes. Oh, there's great advantage to having heavy Earth experience.

D: *So what do you want to do?*

S: Oh, definitely go. I think I can be helpful there, yes.

D: *You don't mind leaving that beautiful place?*

S: Yes, I do. (Laugh) But you can't be here and there at the same time.

D: *How are you going to do this? Do you know?*

S: It's coming in as a baby somehow. I can't see whether we're being ensouled, or if it's a merger of consciousness somehow. But it's a real experience. So somewhere, you join with a fetus. It feels like our whole active consciousness goes.

D: *So what happens to your body there?*

S: I'm not so sure it was a body, now—or just consciousness, vibrational consciousness. Energy.

D: *So then your consciousness comes back into a baby?*

S: It seems that way, yes.

D: *That means starting all over again, doesn't it?*

S: Yes. Well, almost.

D: *But it's important. Do you think the same thing is going to happen to the Earth again?*

S: Same thing being?

D: *You said you were here to show them how.*

S: Things are in sad shape in some ways here. People have forgotten, or didn't learn, basic stuff. I think it's more that they need to learn about love and forgiveness. It doesn't matter what dimension you're in, the lesson always seems to be the same. That we are love, and sourced by the One Creator. People get caught up in survival at so many levels.

D: *But when you come back as a baby, are you going to remember what you're supposed to do?*

S: It's programmed. It feels like there are programs that will go off. Yes, we forget. There's a cloud that way. But there are somehow programs that can be activated. It seems like it's a time release thing. Some of it is triggered by associations with people or events. Earthquakes, volcanic eruptions, severe storms. I feel that all through my body. There's some call that happens.

D: *So when Earth events happen, it triggers things?*

S: That's one of the things, yes. I feel that all through my body with great energy.

D: *So when these Earthly things happen, they trigger the program that is in the humans?* (Yes) *The ones who have come in for this mission?*

S: Yes, who have that program. Participating in ceremonies from antiquity are also big triggers.

I decided it was time to call in the subconscious to answer the questions and explain things more fully. Although this other part of Suzanne was doing a good job, it also suggested calling forth the subconscious, "Although it's probably all one anyway." I asked it why it picked that lifetime for her to see.

S: She needs to understand that she is an explorer first, and will always go into new situations. And that this time on Earth is a time for exploration. It's not a done deal.

D: *Where she was, it appeared to be a different dimension.*

S: That is correct.

D: *She had the feeling this group came from somewhere off of the planet. Do you know anything about that?*

S: Yes, they came from the Source.

D: *Directly?* (Yes.) *As a group?*

S: It's not really a group. It's a mind trying to have experiences, so it's splintered. It's the same soul. Suzanne understands that souls splinter, go off. These are probabilities that have their own life. That is that. And it's okay. The joke is, we are all one.

D: *Why did they want to live on Earth?*

S: Earth is pretty special. There is much that can be learned.

D: *But then they decided to shift frequencies.*

S: By coming and taking on the physical and being forerunners. It's very important to create a mold, to create a track. People can entrain to what has happened. The first ones, it's more difficult, then it becomes easier. You have a term for that: the hundredth monkey, or whatever. You make it easier for others if you've made the path. And time is all one. So it's always been known there would be a time for the need for ascension of sorts, of shift, of transformation, of transcendence.

D: *Did something happen that they wanted to leave and try this experiment?*

S: They were exploring how to change dimensions and forms. They were exploring how to be genuinely 3-D, physical, and then to take that body and make a shift.

D: *And take the body with you.*

S: In this case, to take the body with you and that was what was done.

D: *That was why it was an experiment.*

S: Yes, and that template is here. That knowledge is available.

D: *Was it easier for them because they came directly from the Source?*

S: Yes, they had greater skills, I suppose, and in Earth terms that happened very quickly. But it took some doing.

D: *They weren't here long enough to be contaminated. Would that be correct?*

S: I don't know contamination.

D: *You know how Earth does contaminate people. They get stuck.*

S: The Earth is pure goodness.

D: *So it was easier for them, I guess because they had not interacted with other humans that much?*

S: Just with themselves, which was really one mind. So it was, yes, taking the luster off our great accomplishment. (Laugh)

D: *She said it was an Indian group?*

S: It was like an Indian group, it was of that time. It was ancient time.

D: *We have stories of Indian tribes that just disappeared. People have always wondered what happened. Was that one of the examples?* (Yes) *So they took their bodies with them into another dimension where they created what they wanted it to look like? Or was it a dimension where these things existed?*

S: In the experience of going, first becoming 3-D, and then never losing connection to Source. So knowing the other was possible, and shifting back and forth, back and forth, back and forth, making a path. They experimented because they allowed themselves to be really dense. But they had the advantage of knowing always Source in spirit, always. So then it became an experiment of trying to change the 3-D. How to raise the frequency, how to shift dimensions, how to do this with the physical, how to take the physical. So in all of these comings and goings, sometimes there were already things in place in the other dimension. And in some ways, sometimes they made things when they went to the other dimension.

D: *They made it resemble where they came from.* (Yes) *But then she said they were called to come back?*

S: Yes. It was part of the plan. First you explore, you make a path that others will follow. Some others will follow, many others will follow. It will be useful, but somebody has to come back and again show the way. Do it, take the path that they once built, unbeknownst to them. She has returned to help others so they can make this transition.

D: *But Suzanne didn't realize this consciously.*

S: Not coming in, no. But always she knew Source.

She was told she was to travel to the Southwestern part of the United States. "In the canyons, in the rocks, where it's dry, where it's high. Then her mission will be clearer. There is memory in the stone, and in the bone. There is memory." This was the area where the tribe lived before it made the shift.

Suzanne had been doing extensive traveling to all parts of the world. I wanted to know the spiritual significance of that. "She was leaving a vibrational trail when she went that spiraled up. This is the significance of the spiral that spirals up. (See the part about the spiral at the beginning of this chapter.) And as she walked, she left the imprint, so it encodes for people who walk that way, who come in contact with her. It activates and teaches how they too can ascend up the spiral way. She doesn't have to tell people. It is transferred energetically. She influences hundreds, hundreds, hundreds, hundreds of people just by being there. Every continent she went to, she left her imprint. We want her to follow the spiral way. She knows this, and every cell in her body, and it will be made clear to her. It's an energy spiral."

I wonder if this applies to me also. When I first began my work, I was told that I would travel extensively all over the world, even though at that time I had only traveled to some conferences in the United States. I was told that everywhere I went, some of my energy would remain. That this would not deplete my own energy, it would just remain in the area, and would affect many people. They said that all I had to do was think about the place I had visited and my energy would immediately return there. Their prediction certainly came true because I have now lectured on almost every continent in the world, and my books are now translated into twenty languages.

So the energy is certainly capable of spreading and influencing. And we are totally unaware of what is happening when we are in these places.

CHAPTER THIRTY-FIVE

PHYSICAL EFFECTS
AS THE BODY CHANGES

I have received much information about the physical symptoms that people are experiencing as their bodies adjust to these frequency and vibrational changes. Many of these include: headaches, tiredness, depression, dizziness, irregular heart rhythms, high blood pressure, muscle aches and pains in the joints. These do not all occur at the same time. A person may have one or two for a few days, and then it will taper off and not come back for a few months. These are caused by the body adjusting to the raising of the vibrations, and the body has to have time to adapt. "They" have said that the body could not suddenly change vibration. The energy would be too strong for the body to handle, and it would be destroyed. So it has to occur in gradual steps that the body can adapt to. One symptom that is persistent and that can last for a longer period of time is ringing or tones in the ears. It is not harmful to the body, but it certainly can be aggravating. This has been explained by the body trying to adjust to the increase of energy. One way to help with this is to visualize a dial, and to mentally adjust it up or down until the desirable frequency is matched. And to say to yourself, "I want my body to move up, up, up until it matches this higher frequency." With all of these symptoms the people have gone to their doctors, only to be told there is nothing wrong with them. The doctors cannot find any cause for the complaints. However, their solution is to put the person on medication anyway, which does no good because they are not aware of the cause.

I have had a few clients that have experienced more radical symptoms that confounded their doctors. One was Denise, a registered nurse in a large hospital, who came to see me in August of 2005. She had complaints of having seizures and numbness in some parts of her body, but the doctors said it was not a stroke. She also passed out one day at work. When they performed the MRIs, the X-rays, they saw what looked like Christmas tree lights, all over the brain. They called these "nodules." When they took chest X-rays, they found the same thing, nodules throughout the lungs. She also had abnormal enzyme activity in her liver. The doctor couldn't figure out what was going on. In subsequent MRIs and X-rays of the brain, the lights had moved to different areas, appearing more or less as a band, instead of being all over the entire brain. They had a difficult time finding any diagnosis that would fit, but finally came up with an idea of what the *disease* was: sarcodoisis. But one of the doctors said, "I don't think it could possibly be that. On the one hand, it is so very, very, very, very rare. And on the other hand, she couldn't possibly have gotten this where she lives in the desert, where the air is very dry." This disease was supposed to occur where there was dampness and molds. But they were unable to diagnose it any further than that. So they put her on steroids which caused diabetes.

When we did the session, the subconscious said there was no disease. No harm had been done to the body. They were rewiring the brain so it could handle the changes of what is to come. And the same with the lungs and the other parts of the body. It was an adjustment of the energy in the body so it can handle the raising of the higher frequencies and vibrations. I asked, "Then why did it appear like little dots and lights all over her brain?" And they just said, "Connect the dots!" The seizures and numbness were because a lot had to be done quickly. Normally, they don't want to overload the body, so these changes, these adjustments, are happening very gradually. But in some cases—I guess because time is speeding up and the changes are becoming eminent—they have to adjust the body faster. So it was too much, and this created the seizures and the numbness. The time she fainted was an over load on the system. But they said she didn't have to worry, it wouldn't happen again. There wasn't anything wrong with the brain. And now, if she has another MRI, it wouldn't show anything because that phase has ended. The next phase was the adjustment of the chemistry of the body, which will not produce these kinds of effects.

When the doctor told her she had this strange disease, he said she had less than six months to live. And she kept saying, "I don't think so." When she went back for her checkup, the doctor just kept staring at her, and saying, "I just don't understand why you look so well." She was picking up, without him saying it, that he meant, "Because you're supposed to be dying!" Denise is a nurse in intensive care. And she said, "I see people who are dying all the time. I knew I wasn't dying. So I didn't know what they were talking about."

The subconscious saw her doing wonderful things during the shift, and in the next ten, twenty years she's going to have a big part to play in all of this. I wanted to know more about the steroids. I knew they could be dangerous, especially if they caused the diabetes. They said the diabetes would be phased away. It was only a test to teach her about body lessons. She wouldn't need it now. They said not to worry about the steroids. Even though it was a powerful medicine, they could neutralize it so that it would not affect the body in a negative way. It is flushed out of the system as a harmless byproduct. They have the ability to do this. To neutralize any medication that is not needed and flush it out of the system.

MORE FROM OTHER CLIENTS

Patsy came to me complaining of allergies to dust and pollens. The SC said, "These are physical reactions to being on this planet. I'm feeling that she can live with that. It's also a reminder of who she is. That she's living in an element that's not home." She also had problems in her colon area, and an unexplained rash that she wanted to find out about. "I keep getting 'manufacturing,' and I can't explain it any other way. But something is being manufactured in there. It's almost like a necessary element is being made that's having the reaction in the colon and on the skin. The mucous is a byproduct of the changes that are being made in the body, which is a reaction on the skin. It has to do with what is occurring on the Earth at this time. She has known for a long time that her body is being changed. It just doesn't happen in a way that you can understand when you're in a physical body, but there are many changes going on. Doctors cannot help on this level. They don't understand the changes that are taking place."

Patsy also always had very low blood pressure. "That's normal for her. She doesn't need to be like the rest of the people. And for her to operate with that in the body she's in, is all that's required of her. That's one reason we influence her not to go to the doctors because they try and find something wrong. She doesn't need to be part of that."

D: *They want everybody to be the same.*
P: Yes, they do. That way they're easier to control and medicate. There are many that aren't the same. There is no harm to come to her body.
D: *I get many people who are in fear if they don't understand something.*
P: They're learning. Fear is destructive, very destructive.

Carol had gone through a past life which is not relevant to this book. The subconscious was talking about healing her body. They dissolved a tumor located in her pelvic area, and it would be passed from the body safely. This is how the SC deals with growths of this type. There was no need for the surgery that the doctors were planning. It had been caused by her exposure to other's negative emotions. "Anger, resentment, fear. Fear. She takes in other people's fears and transmutes them. In some situations it is necessary, but in her case it is destructive to the body." She was one of the volunteers who had never been on Earth before, so she could not handle strong emotions. The first and second wave do not understand emotions, and they can be paralyzing in some cases.

C: It is time to stop the pain and suffering, and to move on. We will also need to work on the blood and the changes in the blood, and the changes of consistency in blood. There's an intuition; there's a wisdom of the blood cells and the bone marrow, and the formation and deformation of cells and material. The changes are being created. And she needs to understand how those changes are being created because the physical body is going to change. And so she needs to understand that process so the physical body doesn't die and give out because of the changes and the transitions that are down the road in the future within ten years.

D: *You said the body is changing?*

C: Yes. The physical body is changing in vibration.

D: *How is this affecting the blood?*

C: The blood is changing in consistency. And sometimes there's a "glumping," and sometimes there's a thinning. And so as the changes occur in the vibration of the whole body, the cells will be functioning differently. So some of the old functions are being cast away, and some cells are taking on new functions. I'm not sure what the wordage is, but there's....

D: *Having to learn something new?* (Yes) *It's something these other cells haven't done before.*

C: Correct.

D: *And this is what you meant, she has to learn how to adjust it; otherwise, the body can't handle it?*

C: Correct.

D: *Is this happening to other people around the world right now?* (Yes) *I've heard of many different symptoms.* (Yes) *So each person is having to learn to adjust?*

C: Every single person won't, but people who will be instrumental in helping others, in teaching others, and in guiding groups. It's about bringing through frequencies that can make massive changes very quickly in the physical body.

D: *Changes that would normally have taken many generations. Is that what you mean?*

C: Yes. It's about compressing time. There is no space and there is no time, but in the Earth plane there *is* time and space. So for spontaneous healings to occur in the Earth plane, there has to be a compression of time that occurs as the cells get new instructions, and let go of the old instructions.

D: *Oh! And this is difficult in some people's bodies. I guess this would create physical symptoms the doctors wouldn't understand. Is that true?*

C: That is correct. They do not have the technology to understand it. There are some who have advanced minds that can deal with that. But the medical field in general is very archaic in terms of what it needs to know, or what it needs to have available. And that is really not workable. That will fall away. The mind is being utilized for change, but also people have to be able to change their minds to let go of their distorted beliefs and come into truth.

D: *We have to get away from the brainwashing we've had all our lives that tell us we must depend on outside sources. We don't really need to do that.*

C: That is correct.

D: *Carol has had a lifetime of being the victim, and being betrayed.* (Yes) *Why did she have a life like that? What was the purpose?*

C: It is necessary for her to understand victimization because there will be masses of people who will be victimized rather quickly, and in large groups. And so all of it will be important to be able to work with them simultaneously. There will be an instant knowing so many steps can be bypassed, by knowing the ins and outs, if you will, of victimization, so it won't be necessary to deal with victimizations. It will be necessary to spontaneously fix what needs to be fixed to shift—it's about the shift....

D: *She'll be instrumental in working with some of these people.* (Yes) *Because she can identify with them and understand.*

C: Yes. And she will be working with healers.

Nancy defied several attempts to take her back to a past life. Her conscious mind was also very active and kept interjecting saying she was making everything up anyway. Finally after using several methods that did not produce results, I decided to call forth the SC and let it handle the situation.

D: *Is there an important past life that Nancy needs to see that will help her in her present life?*

N: Yes and no. The plus sides are important for karmic lessons. However, we're moving it to the non-karmic necessity. So that's why we give a yes or no answer.

D: *Then she doesn't need to see her past lives?*

N: Not necessarily. They don't matter.

D: *What about karma?*

N: Karma is virtually cancelled as we move to the new Universe.

D: *Then that means she doesn't have karma to worry about?*

N: No, she does have karma, but it's not going to be important. It's not necessary to fulfill the mission of this life or to move into the next life.

D: *That's why Nancy was not allowed to see any of her other lives?*

N: It's not that it wasn't allowed. It's just that it wasn't necessary. It would cause confusion. The human mind would get hung up on what it was seeing. But it couldn't release or relinquish the judgment in what you wanted her to see, or what you normally would show.

D: *Many people relate to things that happened in other lives so they can move forward.*

N: But because we're in this pinnacle of—going to go this way all —this doesn't matter anymore. Because there will no longer be reincarnating into the Earth the way that we know it. To look at other lives would only be more confusing because ideas and tools that were necessary and helpful in the old world are not going to be needed in the new world.

D: *I still have many clients whose problems come from other lifetimes.*

N: But all that is discharged. Your work is important because there are some energy tools that need to be released in this lifetime. Energy tools of more or less health issues. It's things of the now that are not related to moving forward because the moment you move forward, that will all be discharged and relinquished. We never know when the new Earth will appear, but it is coming. It's going to be here. It's just a question of when the vibration and energy will reach the level to almost... *pop* and create the second world. So you help people with their physical ailments, so they don't have to be uncomfortable till whenever this is going to occur. It's important because we don't know when it's going to occur—more sooner than not. So if these people come to you, then I guess they have a discomfort that there's no reason for anyone to have.

Nancy wanted to know her purpose (just as everyone else who comes to see me). The SC answered, "This isn't the answer she wants, but her purpose is not revealed as yet because the new Universe has not been created. Everything is still in planning, moving, facilitation stages, and it can still all change. We can see a plan, a big picture, but it still can change."

D: *Can't you give her any idea of what she's supposed to do because she wants to plan.*

N: Almost instantaneously the thought will come.

D: *Is there anything you want her to work on to get ready?*

N: None of it's necessary at this point. She's going to go to the new Earth, and will immediately know what it is she will be doing because the new energy and vibration will be higher. The effort is needed here, but it's already crossed the marker where you're either going or you're not going.

D: *I've heard it's already been decided because the vibrations can't change that quickly.*

N: No. Once you've crossed the marker and you're going, then it's almost like a respite period. And when you get there, it will just be so different that all the things we think we need to do now, and were appropriate in the not so distant past, will not be needed in the new world.

D: *She said she wants to make a difference in other people's lives, and to help the world.*

N: Which would have been necessary if the Earth had stayed in the same vibrational dimension that it is now, but it's almost like you're waiting for it to happen. It's going to happen, but you won't know what it will look like until it happens because it's a group participation and a joint effect. And all we can say is, it *is* going to happen.

D: *I've heard that some people won't even realize that anything has happened.*

N: I think that thought is even changing, and most definitely the ones that move forward will know what's happening. The ones that are left behind, it's still not determined—devastation's not an appropriate word to use, but I can't think of another one—who will really realize it or not realize it. It's still changing.

D: *But she's wanting to do something to help now. She has studied healing and Reiki, and studied working with angels.*

N: But everyone will have the same gifts and tools and the new energy.

D: *Everyone will be doing the same thing?*

N: Well, not the same things, but it just will not be necessary. The reason why we do all these things is to bring the energy up to that level. But when you're immediately all on that level, there's no need for healing because we'll all be healed. You can still continue working with people and helping them until the transition. But when everyone transitions, it's almost like you're all at the same rate. You're all on the same page and your veil is lifted, so it's the big "ah-hah!" moment.

D: *There are still people out there that need her, aren't there?*

N: Right. There are people that, minute to minute, you're pulling over to the new world. They're almost in a holding pattern, but they're pulled over and they're waiting. They'll be waiting there to move forward.

D: *So she will never know who those people are, among those she comes in contact with.*

N: No, nor will they. She should always focus her energy on a sanction of all the energies of everyone on Earth to move forward. And as each person increases their vibration, it's a chain reaction, and it resonates and bounces off the next person to the next, to the next. Until it's an entire huge crescendo that becomes the vibration of Earth in total. If everyone stopped doing what they're doing, it would just become a dim hum. But because we all go and move forward and we're all working at our own pace, it just raises it higher and higher until it's just going to disperse into the cosmos. So you can't really say not to do any work. Just keep doing what you're doing, but the focus is changed. To be bored is great because it will just instantaneously create all knowledge, all the things we strive for here. But, "Give me Reiki, so I feel better" or "Take away this," it won't be necessary. Everyone will have the tools. And once you have the tools, you don't have the aches or the pains. It's almost like a "human clause" that will no longer be in effect. It's always good in human form to, as you say, have goals and dreams and aspirations. It's very difficult to put into words because we think it's coming more quickly than you think, and you are spending a waste of time. But that doesn't sound right either, a waste of time. But I think the best thing that anyone could do is have a good intent. Always express your willingness to help, and never turn anyone away that comes to you. Any lessons she needs to be learning now, have to do with the karmic wheel, and it's going to be dispensed soon. Once your vibration gets to a certain level, you're beyond the, "Have to pay karma back." That's why it's not important to pursue questions about past lives. That's her human mind, and all the human minds having a curiosity about things. It's almost child-like. "Why? Why? Why? How come?" So you could just feel guaranteed, or rest assured that if you have awakened, you will move into the new Earth.

Later in the session, Nancy's body was being worked on to remove the desire to smoke and then with compulsive eating so she could lose weight. She could feel them scanning and readjusting, especially in the right side of her brain. Then she felt vibrations throughout her body. "They're just scanning and removing impulses."

D: *Trust them. They know what they're doing. They're removing the impulse to overeat.*
N: Yes, and things that have become habitual. The body's designed to basically handle anything, but the problem is with portion control and quantity. The body is a miracle and the body can dispose of or handle anything in small doses. The favorable food would be anything with less additives, less preservatives. Less is best. Even smaller portion sizes, but just to rid the body of chemical additives, preservatives. So the trend is to go to healthier, leaner, less toxic things for the body. The body will last longer when it doesn't have to work as hard. We have given her the impulses to take and readjust, readjust and program. She will love this. The taste buds are already changing. It's beginning to happen.

They always emphasize smaller portions and several small meals during the day (they called it "grazing"), instead of huge meals. Eventually, we will move into an all liquid diet.

Then, after we move to the New Earth, there is the possibility of not eating at all. At that point, we will be living off pure energy and light. The same as many of the ETs I have spoken to.

At the beginning of 2011 while this book was being put together some unusual events happened that made it clear that the shift was becoming closer. It showed that the changes in the frequencies and vibrations are not only affecting humans, but also animals of all kinds. No one is immune from the changes that are occurring around us and becoming more evident.

Portions of two sessions during January 2011:

L: You know the realities are shifting now. What you have called the new earth, is the new earth, is becoming manifest. The energy is there. The heavier energies that create harm, disharmony, and imbalance are not moving to the new earth. They won't be part of it. Their energy does not resonate. Those that resonate with that old energy will stay in that old energy. And they can pull themselves free of it at any moment that they choose to be free of it, but they have to be willing.

D: *I vowed when I got you again that I have a question I want to ask. Something has been going on here in the world in Arkansas. They are talking about all the birds just dropping out of the sky.*

This made the news when it happened on New Year's Eve, 2010. It was mostly redwinged blackbirds, and thousands of them were discovered. The same night there was also a big fish kill in the Arkansas River. Then it was reported in Sweden, and a few days later in Kentucky and Tennessee. When the birds were examined there was no obvious cause, except blunt trauma. Of course, there was blunt trauma, the birds fell out of the sky and hit the ground! The official explanation was that there were fireworks on that night and this must have frightened the birds. If this was true, then why aren't bird kills reported on the 4th of July? The only unusual weather phenomenon was a terrible electrical storm that produced unusual winter tornadoes in the Arkansas area.

L: The symbology is that it's a shift in energy because the birds, the cows, the fish, the whales, the turtles, the

505

bees, are all representations of the change in energy and they were stuck. They didn't shift fast enough.

D: *We are all shifting, our vibrations and frequencies. They are smaller, and they couldn't shift fast enough?*

L: Animals are on a different energy level than humans and are much more sensitive to the shifts. And some of this was manmade, man interfered with.

D: *What do you mean?*

L: There is a shifting of energy of the planet as the new earth is taking form. There is some movement between old and new energies. There is separation going on, but there is energy feeding both. Sometimes the birds, the animals, bees, even the plants, and humans. If they are tuned a certain way they will respond some way to that shifting energy, and their physical body is not able to withstand. Their indwelling spirit has to move with the energy.

D: *That's what I've been told, if the energy was shifted all at once, it would destroy the human body.*

L: It would, and so the human body is being changed.

D: *A gradual adapting of the frequencies and vibrations.*

L: Which is why there is sickness because sickness is another form of the body adapting.

D: *I have been told that the ones who cannot adapt or change their vibrations and frequencies to adapt, they will just leave the planet.*

L: They cannot keep their soul and their physical body together. The Mobius Strip becomes unraveled. It falls apart.

I had never heard the term "Mobius Strip," so I had to do research. I then found it is a mathematics term, also called the twisted cylinder. Math has always been my worst subject, so I had to try to break this down so I could roughly understand it, so I could convey it to the reader. A sphere has two sides. A thin sheet of paper lying on a desk also has two sides. A Mobius Strip has a one-sided surface: only one side and only one edge. A simple way to make one is to start with a strip of paper. Twist one end 180 degrees (half turn) and glue the ends together. For comparison, if you glue the ends without twisting the result would look like a cylinder or a ring. The Mobius Strip is known for its unusual properties. A bug crawling along the center of the loop will continue going in the same direction. I'm sure there is much more to this and there are probably readers who could explain it much better. So forgive me for my limited understanding. We all have our limitations.

The SC is saying here: "They cannot keep their soul and their physical body together. The Mobius Strip becomes unraveled. It falls apart." I think it is comparing the soul energizing force to a continuous Mobius Strip. When the Strip falls apart, it becomes a simple strip of paper again with no unusual properties. Maybe the same thing is occurring with the birds and the animals. They are receiving too much energy, a burst that is more than their bodies can handle, and this causes their matrix to unravel or come apart. "They" have said many times that if the body receives more energy than it can handle it would destroy the body.

D: *So these birds are doing the same thing?*

L: It's the same thing.

D: *It was happening here in Arkansas, but also all the way over in Sweden.*

L: It's happened all over the world, even in East Texas, birds falling.

D: *They just didn't put it on the news.*

L: No, there's talk in the community. There was some discussion among various people. It's reported, but it is not reported.

D: *It was interesting that it happened on New Year's Eve.*

L: There are those who use this as a means to manipulate to a negative apocalyptic vision. But it's not—well, it depends—are you mostly negative or are you mostly positive? If you're mostly positive then it's an indication of the shifting energies between the old and the new. And what is frightening the scientists and sandbox players is that they know they have no control over that. They cannot camouflage it. They can suppress it, deny it, but they cannot change it. They cannot stop it and it tells them that this shifting is increasing. The animals still have their soul. All living things have souls.

D: *You cannot kill the souls.*

L: No. The soul is fine, but the physical body, whether it is bird or whale, gets left behind in the shift and it's not into the new. The old energy was where it belonged. It couldn't transmute to the new energy, so it was left with the old. Shifting energy. The new earth already exists, but it is becoming more in form, stronger, more created, moment to moment.

D: *And to our reality.*

L: Yes, into your time and space.

D: *So the Old Earth will still exist as the New Earth is formed. We thought at first it was like a splitting.*

L: No, it's like a Phoenix from the ashes. (Laugh) Only that's too frightening for some people because they think the Phoenix arises from ashes means, of course, the planet has to be ash.

D: *And it has to be a catastrophe. All of the negativity, the different cataclysms will be with the Old Earth. (Right.) We're all moving to the other one.*

L: Right. We're all having growing pains.

D: *They said we won't even be able to tell the difference. It won't just be all of a sudden... POW, we're there.*

L: No. You will know by how you feel. If life feels softer, gentler, sweeter, happier. If it feels more joyful, you will know.

D: *We're moving into the New Earth?*

L: Yes, it's been going on for many years. We're here... have been. The last thing you want to do is unhinge the psychic mind... you want the mind to travel with the body. If you unhinge it, then everything falls apart. So

508

this shift allows everyone to adapt gently, as a gentle adaptation.

D: *I have been told that the other ones will stay with what they've created, and it's all right.*

L: Yes. It's all right because it's all learning. How do you know what you appreciate? How do you know what joy feels like if you have never known pain? It's a concept until you feel it, but no, you don't have to keep feeling it over and over. Enough is enough.

D: *What about the New Earth?*

J: I see layers. It's layers and layers and layers and layers and layers, like onion layers. And you can see through them, and you can pick any layer you want. And the further out, the lighter it is. The further in, the closer to the core, that is the dense. That's the very dense and that's the one that will appear very similar. That's where a lot of the emotions are, and I see it's looking red, like it's red hot. And then as it goes out, it gets lighter and lighter and lighter and they're more translucent. It's just lighter and you can move so easily. It's just like floating.

D: *Are there really two Earths... the Old Earth and the New Earth? They keep saying they are going to separate.*

J: It separates in the sense that this one is so light. It moves away and everything that's on it is just so light. And it's floating and easy, and it's a whole different concept and thought structure. There are emotions, but it's a different range of emotions. I mean, it's not anger. There are not those heavy, dense emotions. There's the light. It's a separation in that way. You have a separation of emotions and when you separate those emotions, it separates who you are. It separates how you feel and that makes you a lighter person, which takes you to this lighter place. It's separation that way and the two are not together anymore. But it's like all these different layers. There are layers in-between too, so you have extremes. You have the very outer one, which is probably the epitome of this light, light, light, light Earth and then you have the center, which is probably the epitome of the old Earth. You just have this very red hot—it keeps looking red hot—it's anger and heavy emotions, heavy thoughts, heavy feelings and things like that, where this other is light. But you have all these layers in-between that you can choose. You move in with them... in among them and then at some point you just keep choosing. "Ah, there's a choosing... choices." You make choices and that moves you through these layers. And as you keep choosing one way or another, that's what keeps pulling them apart.

D: *Is that where the separation is coming in?*

J: That's the separation. You keep choosing and when you choose light, you go that way. You keep moving in that direction. You choose heavy thoughts, you choose heavy emotions, you choose those things and you will move in that direction. Though there's quite a while that you keep moving back and forth among layers. It's to show you that you do have choices here. This isn't a "do or die," or make a "right or wrong," or a "now or never" kind of thing. You are moving among these things to see that it's within you to make the choice. It's within you to have this happen. It's within you to make *your* New Earth or *your* Old Earth. It's to make your reality any way you want it.

D: *They keep saying this is the first time this has happened in the history of the Universe, that an entire planet is going to move into a different dimension.*

J: It's very beautiful. This is different. Civilizations have done it before. People, single people, have done it before.

D: *They say the first time for the planet.*

J: This is because the planet is participating. She is a being also. She wants to do this and so she's created all these layers so these are layers that She is working through as well, so these are choices She is making. She's doing the very same thing that we, with her, are doing. We're all doing this and that's why there are all these different layers of Earth because She is doing this as well. It's not just this one *BOOF!* It's a movement and there are these layers and as the people move around with their emotions, then that moves through the different layers of these different levels. And so as we keep choosing light, joy, ease, smooth... then that moves us, too. It keeps moving us ever closer. As you choose, you start thinking, "You know, I like the feeling of this better than that." And so then you start making choices that move you more in that direction. You have to keep testing it. You may take two steps this way and then you take a step back and then think, "Oh, I don't like the feeling of this. Let's go this way." That's your layers. That's why it's gradual. And you start realizing how much control you have within the whole thing, and that's what this is about, to show you that you have control. It's all your control. It's all your creation. It's all your reality. It's all what you are creating, whatever you want to create, and so you move within there, and each person is having this experience. The more aware you are with it, the more fun you can have with it because you can move with consciousness and be aware of what you're doing.

D: *We've had a mystery lately with the birds. They said they were falling out of the sky. And I was told at another session that it was happening all over the*

511

world, not just here in Arkansas. Do you have anything to say about that?

J: What I'm seeing when you said that is that there's a movement of the Earth. It's like it did a... (hand motions) It's almost like a jerk, but it's nothing that we felt on Earth. But it was like a jerk and when it did that, it's in these outer layers. It was a shift there. It shifted and when it did that, it created this kind of—how do you describe that?

D: *A shockwave of some kind?*

J: Something like that. It's almost like a jolt in the atmosphere. It's almost like an earthquake in the air.

D: *Reverberation?*

J: It's more of a vibration. A rift! It moved here, but it didn't move in another place, and so that created something like an earthquake. So anything in that layer or in that part, anything that was sensitive... yes, they are very sensitive. It's like the canaries in the mines. That's your warning. That's your signal that something's happening because animals are very sensitive. They're in touch all the time.

D: *We were told that it was the energy, and because they're smaller they can't handle the shifts of energy. But then I had a question. Yes, it affected the birds, but it didn't kill all of the birds, just certain ones in certain places.*

J: Maybe it was just that certain birds are more sensitive... that particular kind was more sensitive at that time.

D: *To certain kinds of vibrations?* (Yes) *But it didn't kill all of the birds of that type.*

J: No. I think it had to do with where they were. So it's like an earthquake. It's going to do something right there. And that's where that was, that layer, that level, where it was happening was affecting certain places. It didn't happen completely around the globe. It happened in a section so that section was connected to certain areas and those areas were affected.

CHAPTER THIRTY-SIX

THE NEW BODIES

Here is some of the information about the New Earth that came from various clients, taken from the *Convoluted Universe* series:

The entity speaking through V. had a deep, gravelly voice:

V: The whole idea is, we have to get people to expand just a little bit. And we have to get this level raised just a little bit. And when we do, we can make that change, and make it easier for them. It will be the ones that we can't get to change that are going to be left behind. It's going to be horrible. We can't get them to see. We can't get them to love.

D: *Then the others, the ones that will change, will go into another world? Another Earth?*

V: It's like it's going to expand into another dimension. Let me see how I can explain this to you. It's like a raising, if you can understand, like we're going to raise into a different vibration. They'll be able to see what's going on, but we can't help them anymore.

D: *Is it like a separation? Like two Earths, is that what you mean?*

V: Oh no, no. It's a changing of dimension. We're going to go from here to here. And those that can't change will be left behind.

D: *When we go into the other dimension, will it be a physical Earth?*

V: It will be just like we are right now.

D: *That's what I meant by two Earths.*

V: Yes, yes. But they're not going to be aware of us. God help them, God help them. It's going to be so terrible for them.

D: *They won't know what has happened?*

V: No, they will know. That's the whole idea. They will know, but it will be too late for them to change their vibrations. They can't change it in a second. They have to change it over a period of time. We've been working on this for awhile. It has to seep in and work on your body, and it has to slowly change and raise your vibrations. And when it happens, it's going to be too late for them, but they will see it, though. They will die, but they will see it and they will learn from that.

D: *That world will still exist, but it will be different?*

V: Not very well, no, not very well. There won't be much left in that world. Not much.

D: *Many people will die at that time?*

V: Yes. But I think much of their death will be painless. I think they will live just long enough to see what's happening. And I think God will spare them the horrible traumatic pain. I pray that's what will happen.

D: *But the others that do shift into the new vibration, with an identical physical world....*

V: (Interrupted.) Yes, but some won't even be aware that they've made the change. Some will. Those that have been working towards it will know.

D: *Will they know about the people being left behind?*

V: I don't think so. There will be an awareness of a change that took place. I'm not sure if it's going to be a conscious awareness. Let me think about that. (Pause) We'll go into this dimension and we'll know. Some won't know though. They'll feel something. They'll feel a difference. Almost like a cleanness, a clearness. A crispness, a difference. I know what it is. They'll feel the difference. They'll feel the love.

514

D: *So, even if they haven't been working toward it, they will be carried along with it.*

V: Yes, because they're ready for it.

D: *And the other ones won't be....*

V: They're not, they're not.

D: *So, they're left in the negativity? You said the whole world is going to be changed at that time.*

V: Yes, those that can go on, that can move into this, will move. And those that can't, won't. And it'll be horrible for them.

D: *And it will be like two worlds.*

V: Yes, two worlds existing at the same time, but not always aware of each other.

D: *I know when you're in a different dimension, you're not always aware of the other one. But that's the message you want to get across is that we should spread this information about love while we still can, to bring as many as possible along.*

V: Love is the key. Because God is love. And love is God. And love is the supreme power. And that's what we need to feel in our lives. What we need to give to each other and feel for each other.

D: *Yes, love has always been the key. So, they're trying to tell as many people, so they can bring them along. That's what the urgency is.*

V: The urgency is that we've run out of time. Just be prepared. Uh, what? Tell her what?

She was listening to someone else. There were mumbling sounds, then the deep gravelly voice returned.

V: Tell you... ready. Ready for the change coming soon. Soon now. Ready... She's not a good vehicle. She's not done this before. I can't get my ideas through her to convey to you. I must work on it. Let's cleanse this vehicle. Oh, yes! Uh... there. That's better.

D: *What is it you want to tell me?*

V: Must help all mankind. Tell them what is to come soon. Changes, dimensional shift. Those that can hear you will hear you. They'll be ready for that dimensional shift. (Her normal voice returned.) Those that can't, will not accept it anyway, so (Laugh) they'll think we're crazy. But the others, they may not know it, but it will touch a spark in them. When it happens, they'll be ready and they can make that shift. They may not know it's coming, but something inside will be ready for it and they'll be able to make it. It's those that don't know it's coming, but if we tell them, it's inside them. Then when it happens, it'll come out and they'll be ready for it.

D: *Those of us that do make the shift, will we continue to live our lives the way we have?*

V: No, no, better. Different. Longer.

D: *Will we continue physical lives?*

V: Oh, physical in that dimension, yes. But physical in this dimension, no.

D: *But I mean, if we make the shift, will we....*

V: (Interrupted) You mean, will you live or die?

D: *Will we continue lives as we know it?*

V: Yes, some will not even be aware. You see, that little thing that we plant in their head, will help them make the dimensional shift and they may not even know it. But they'll know there's destruction. They'll see destruction. They'll see what's taking place and they'll see the dead bodies, but they won't know that they've made that shift. They won't be aware of the fact that the reason they're not down there dead is because they made that shift and that change didn't affect them.

D: *You said something about the things that are put in the head. Do you mean the implants?*

V: No, no, no. I mean a seed, a thought. They don't know it consciously, but inside, that will help them. It's like a spark that, when the time comes, their mind would have accepted it subconsciously, already.

D: *I have heard that we will live longer?*
V: Longer, better. Learn. Things will be so much better. People will learn more, after a little while. They'll know more. They'll become more aware of things. The way things are. They may not know when they make the shift, but then they'll learn about it. They'll realize after awhile what's happened.
D: *And the ones that are not ready will be left on the other Earth.*
V: Yes, they'll be gone.
D: *And many on both places won't even realize that something dramatic has occurred.*
V: The ones on the other place will. They'll be dead. But they'll know because that's the lesson they've learned. Once they die, they will know. They will see the truth. And they will see what opportunity they missed, but they will learn from that.
D: *I have also been told that when they reincarnate, if they have negativity, karma, to repay, they will no longer come to Earth because the Earth will have changed so much.*
V: They will not be allowed to come back here until they've made the switch. They've made the change.
D: *I've heard they will go somewhere else to work out their karma because they have missed the opportunity.*
V: Yes. Some will. And some may be given an opportunity to come back. But it will be awhile, a long, long while.
D: *But in the meantime, we will be going forward and learning new things and making progress in a whole new world.*
V: What a beautiful world. A world of light and peace. Where people can live together and love one another.
D: *But it will still be a physical world with our families and houses like we have now.*
V: Just a smarter world.
D: *(Laugh) That, I can understand.*

Another subject who was experiencing unexplained physical symptoms, described the new body in this way:

S: She is identifying more with her future body. It's not really settled in yet, but it's there. And this future body takes her essence, or portions of her. And merges it or pulls it up so she will get used to this future body.

D: *Will the body physically change?*

S: Some, yes. It will be stronger, and younger. This body that she is in now, it could be healed and redone, but she needs the future body. It will be lighter. More capable. She is feeling this now, her essence has been merging with this future body and pulled up.

D: *So this body she has now will be changed?*

S: It will be essentially left behind. It's going to be transformed and parts of it that aren't needed will be dropped away.

D: *So it's not like leaving one body and going into another.*

S: No. Gradually the newer body and the older body will be mostly merged together. But there will be certain parts of the older body that won't be necessary, so they will be left behind. It will just disintegrate.

It will probably be so gradual that we will not even notice the difference. Except for the physical symptoms that some are experiencing as the body makes the adjustments. I have been told that the older generation may be more aware that something is happening in the body. Yet it does no good to worry about it, since it is a natural process that is occurring now to everyone as part of the evolution of the new Earth.

More from another subject in Australia:

C: It's like a car. Imagine a car that has an old body. It's just the same old car you've been driving. And then you put a new engine in it. And suddenly that car begins to perform differently, even though it looks the same. And then you get another engine, and you replace it. And the car keeps getting faster and faster, and brighter and smarter. And then before you know it, the car is doing such good things, that the body starts to change. It's like the energy of the new engine starts to reform the body. And before you know it, the chap has turned into a sport's car. A beautiful, glossy, attractive vehicle. And that's what this is about. The energies that are coming in have the ability to transform the vehicle. And it will start to be different. It's going to look different. It's going to look... well, *younger* comes to mind. It's going to look smarter and younger. The cells of the body, the vibration of the body is changing, and is matching the vibration of the incoming energy. And the physical changes will be next.

D: *What will those physical changes be?*

C: Oh! The body's going to change to be *lighter*. And I'm getting that it will look *taller*. It's not that it's going to *be* taller. But the energy from within is somehow going to become visible on the outside. And it will make the body seem taller, elongated, slimmer. And more transparent.

D: *Transparent?*

C: Yes. It's a pioneering thing.

D: *Is this the way the people on Earth will be evolving?* (Yes) *Will everyone make the changes?*

C: Yes, because the people have all been given that choice. If they want to evolve with the Earth, they will evolve into this new human being. It will look different. And that's what this experiment is about. That's why Christine and others are moving the ones who don't want to evolve with the Earth. They are going to leave. (Almost crying) And bring a lot of pain to their families. But the people who are staying must hold the light. That's a big job. To get divorced and separated from these things that are happening *now*. And these things are going to continue to happen until the cleansing is complete. Those who are here to stay, are taking this race of people into a very new and different civilization. Those people are being tested now, to see if they can hold the light when there is disaster, and not be sucked in. They're the people who will move ahead with this planet.

D: *Almost like a last test?*

C: Yes. The testing is going on right now. Whatever each being needs to test them, to see what they're capable of giving back to this program; how firm their commitment is. How willing they are to serve. That is all being tested now.

D: *So each one is having their own individual test?*

C: Yes. And the people who are finding it tough now are the ones who are staying. They're the ones who are going through the tests. But some of them are not coming through.

D: *They're not passing the test.*

C: No. There are some who are not.

D: *This is what I was told by other people, that some would be left behind. (Yes) And I thought that sounded cruel.*

C: No, it's not cruel because each soul is given the choice. And if they are not moving and evolving, it's because they are choosing not to. And they will reincarnate into another place of their choice. And it's all right. Because it's only a game. They'll stay in the Old Earth. The New Earth is so beautiful. You will see colors and animals and flowers you never imagined possible. You'll see fruit that is perfect food. It doesn't have to be cooked. It's just eaten as it is. And everything that the being needs to nourish them will be there. These new fruits are developing now with the help of the Star People.

D: *Are these fruits and vegetables we don't have on the Earth now?*

C: We don't have them. They're mutations in some ways. I'm seeing a custard apple as an example of what happened. We will have a fruit called a "custard apple." And it doesn't look like an apple. It has a rough exterior, and it's about the size of two oranges put together. And then you open it. It's like custard inside. So that's a fruit, but a food. It's not just a fruit, but another food has been introduced to it, like custard. That's an example of one of the future foods. So these foods will be delights to the senses. And nutritious and sustaining for the—I keep being stopped when I start to say "body." And I am being told to say "being." They'll be nutritious for the being. And things we now have to cook—like you'd cook custard—will be incorporated into these fruits. And it has to do with helping the planet, and cutting down on the use of electricity and energy. So the fruits are going to provide us with what we need.

D: *I've heard man has done many things to the food that is not healthy for the body.*

C: That's right. The organic foods are coming onto the Earth, and those organic farmers are moving with the Earth evolution program. That's why they're there. And that's why consciousness is being raised about this because people need to know how to grow properly. And the Rudolph Steiner schools are teaching children this. So, the children who are going to be with the new Earth will know this. And those children are now teaching in universities and in institutions, and they're spreading the word. So when the cleansing of the Earth occurs, much of that toxicity is going to be pushed away. You see, the new Earth is not this dimension.

The new Earth is another dimension. And we will move into that new dimension. And in that new dimension, there'll be these trees that have purple and orange in their *trunks*. And there will be beautiful rivers and waterfalls. And the energy will be brought back. There will be energy in the streams and the water that goes over rocks and sandbanks. And it *hits* the Earth. It creates energy and will be straightened out in this world. Many of these streams have been changed and straightened out to make them navigable and nice. That's taking away the energy from the Earth. The Earth is going to be cleansed. I'm seeing water.

D: *Does this have to occur before the Earth shifts and evolves into the new dimension?*

C: I'm seeing us stepping through. (Startled) Oh! What I'm seeing is that the people who are going to the new dimensions will step through into this new world.

D: *While the other one is being cleansed?*

C: Yes, yes.

D: *What do you see about the water that will happen with the cleansing?*

C: (A big sigh) It's not going to be shown to me.

D: *They don't want you to see it?*

C: No, they won't show me that. What they're showing me is... an opening? And we step through. We step into, what *looks* like this Earth, but it's different colors. It's different textures. At *first* it looks the same. At first only. And then as we look around, we start to see that it's not. It's changing before our eyes. And it's so beautiful.

D: *But this is not the spirit side? Because the spirit side is described as being very beautiful also.*

C: No, it's the new Earth. It's not the spirit side. It's the fifth dimensional Earth. Some people will pass through before others. I'm being told to tell you now that Christine has been there several times. There's a group going to go through now. And she'll be bringing more through. And they'll be coming and going a bit until they go for good.

D: *Then the others will be left on the old Earth?*

C: Yes, the ones that are choosing to stay will stay.

D: *They'll be undergoing a lot of hardships, won't they?*

C: Yes, the whole planet. (Startled) I just saw the whole planet explode. That's horrible, isn't it?

D: *What do you think that means?*

C: I don't know. I just saw it explode. But I saw the new Earth. There's this beautiful fifth dimensional place with harmony and peace.

D: *When they showed you the planet exploding, is that just symbolic? As though that Earth will no longer exist for the ones who cross over?*

C: Well, the people who have crossed over are watching what's happening. They can see. Now, is it going to explode? They're saying to me, "Don't get caught up with what's going to happen because you've got to focus on the light." And that's the challenge for these people who are going to be in the new Earth. The challenge for them is to not get caught up in anything that's going to happen because that's what pulls us back into the third dimension. And that's what's happened to many people who were on a path forward. They've been pulled back because they got caught up in the fear and the sadness and regret and the black stuff. So they're saying, "You don't need to know because it wouldn't serve anybody if it were known." So really what they are saying is, "Focus on the good stuff." Focus on the fact that there is going to be this beautiful new existence, new dimension, that many people on the Earth are going to be moving into. Who are already moving into.

D: *I was told whenever you cross over, you will be in the same physical body that you have now. You will just be changed.*

C: Yes, you will still be in the same body, but it is going to change.

D: *So it can be done without dying or leaving the body. It's a different thing altogether.*

C: Yes, we just walk across. Christine's done it before, and she knows how to do it. She's done it and understands it.

D: *But it will be and because there will be so many people that won't understand what's happening. It's so hard with so many—I want to say "ordinary"—people who have no idea of anything except the religion they've been taught. They don't know that this other is possible.*

C: Yes, but they're not ordinary. They only seem ordinary. It's a mask they're wearing. They're changing.

D: *But there still are many people who haven't even thought about these things.*

C: Yes, but they'll be choosing not to awaken, and that is their choice. We have to respect that. They have been given the choice like everybody on the Earth, and they have made that choice. And that's okay. It's all right. It's fine.

D: *So, if they have to go to another place to work out the negative karma, that's part of their evolvement. (Yes.) But do you see a majority of people evolving to the next dimension?*

C: No. Not the majority. And the numbers, to some extent, are not important because what will be, will be. And the *more* people that can awaken and take that journey, the more people there'll be. That's why so many of you are doing this work. To help people open up to the journey, and let go of the fear. And step into that void where anything is possible. Where the *blackness* is residing. That's what you people are all doing. And you need to do it. And everybody you speak to, then goes out and does it as well. You may not be aware of it, but you're acting like Christ. Everyone you speak to becomes a disciple, and they go out, and they in turn awaken other people. So it's working. And it's soon. It's all happening soon.

D: *Do you have any idea of a time period?*

C: The next few years will be the—I'm getting the word "decision point." It will be the "cut-off" point. I think it means that those who have not decided by then, will be left behind. It's critical.

D: *But there are some entire countries in the world that are not ready for this. That's why I am thinking there are many people that won't make the crossover.*

C: There's more happening than people know about. I'm seeing some countries where people are being persecuted. The reason that's happening is to awaken spirituality because persecution causes it. When people are persecuted or when they're facing death, or when they're facing huge human feats. That is a trigger that awakens people. And that's the purpose of much of the persecution that's occurring at the moment; to make sure that these people are awakened. So that's the positive side of it.

D: *Is there something that triggers it or precipitates it?*

C: It's like the curtain drops. And I'm not allowed to see. I'm just being told that it will be the end of one and the beginning of another.

D: *They're trying to lead us into war at this time. (2002) Do you think it has something to do with that?*

C: (Big sigh) I'm afraid that's the test. I said that many people were being tested. And I didn't realize it then, but I do now, that's all part of the test, if we can keep ourselves separated from that. It's like we have to create our own... it's like each one of us is the universe. All parts of the universe are held *here* (placed her hand on her body). And if we keep this universe here....

D: *This body?*

C: Yes. If we keep it at peace, and we keep it in balance, then we are passing the test. Then we can withstand anything. And those things that are happening in the world are really to test the whole; all of us.

D: *You mean to not get caught up into the fear.*

C: Yes. Turn the TV off. Don't listen to it. Don't read the paper. Don't get caught up in it. Your *world* is what you create here. (Touched her body again.)

D: *In your own body.*

C: Yes. In your own space here. This is your own universe here. If every person creates peace and harmony in their own universe, then that's the universe they're creating in that fifth dimensional Earth. The more people who can create peace and harmony in this body universe, the more people who will be in that fifth dimensional new Earth. The ones who can't create peace and harmony in this body universe, are not passing the test. That's the test.

D: *We're trying to do this to keep the war from happening, or to lessen it anyway.*

C: I'm being told that it doesn't matter what happens because it's all a game. It's all a play. And the things that are happening are there for a reason. And the reason at the moment is to test each human being to find out where they are in their own evolution. And so if we hold peace and light here (the body), we don't have to worry about whether there's a war or not. It's only an illusion anyway.

D: *But right now it seems very real, and it could have some very disastrous consequences.*

C: Yes, but that's fear for each individual. Our job is to help each individual find peace *here* (the body). And then, of course, as you bring more people together, who have peace and harmony within their own body universe, then instead of the blackness spreading, that spreads. And that creates this whole new world. If you'd been given all that information back in the beginning of your work, you would have been overloaded. It's the same reason why they're saying,

"We're not going to tell you exactly what's going to happen." We don't *know* exactly what's going to happen. But we're not going to tell you what we know because you don't need to know. All you need to do is focus here (the body) creating your heaven on Earth. Each human being creating their own heaven on Earth. That's all you have to do. And coming together with others who are creating their own heaven on Earth. And then expanding that energy *out*. And before you know it, you've changed the world. You don't even think about the world. What you focus on is what you create. Think about peace. The main thing people have to understand is that, what they focus on expands. So if they focus on, if they can replace predictions with something that is wonderful that they want, and expand that. Then they can create their own heaven on Earth. And I'm being shown in your book *The Convoluted Universe* (*Book One*), you give a description of thought. I'm being told to remind you about this. You talk about an energy ball the size of a grapefruit. And that ball has energy strands. And I'm changing this as I go. Energy strands which go over each other and transverse each other. And those energy strands can do anything they like. They can split, and they can become four energy strands. They can weave. They can multiply. They can go backwards. They can zip up. They can do absolutely anything. And this is the ball of possibility. When you think a thought, it doesn't just disappear. It becomes an energy strand. It becomes energy. It moves into that ball of possibility. So, imagine your thought becoming energy. And the *more* energy you give it, the stronger that becomes. And then it manifests, and it becomes *real*. It becomes physical. If you send a thought out that there's going to be peace. And then you follow it with, "Oh, but that war is getting worse," or "Those politicians are making a mistake." You weaken the energy: the positive strand you brought out. So we have to teach people to send out the positive thought, and then to reinforce it with *more* positive thoughts, and more positive thoughts. And we have to teach them that when one of those negative thoughts comes into their mind, not to just let it go, but to replace it with a positive thought. So that they're adding to that energy ball of possibility. They're contributing to it. We have to teach them to do that. They do not know how to do that. And I'm being told to tell you to reinforce that the illusion- I don't know why I'm being told to tell you this. But they're saying that if we could get people to think of this conflict that's occurring in the Middle East as a movie, it would help people. The other thing I'm being told to tell you is that for every action, they can make an opposite reaction. Where there's birth, there's death. And everybody *must* let go of any greed, any domination, materialism. Any of those issues that are stopping them from doing this work, must be let go. Because these issues are not going to serve anybody in the new Earth. There's not going to be the need for money, as such. So why would you bother about it? Those who are working for the Earth, for the universe, are being provided for, and will continue to be. What you need will come to you. So it's time now to let go of that ethic of working to get the money. You're working to change the Earth. You're working to save this situation. That's where the driving force must be. It must come from love and service. And that's the only way we will maximize this effort. It must come from love and service, not from greed.

D: *I've been told love is the most powerful emotion.*

C: Yes, love heals.

People at my lectures are always asking me what do they have to do in order to move to the New Earth? "They" have said there are two important things you have to let go of. One, as just explained, is fear. Fear is an illusion, yet it is the strongest emotion that a human has. It must be released or it will hold you to the old Earth. I tell people to ask lots and lots of questions. Don't believe everything you hear or read. Think for yourself. Don't give your power away to anyone. Make up your own mind and discover your own truth. It may not be *my* truth, but it will be yours because you have discovered it. And then don't be surprised if that truth changes. We are constantly learning. Stay flexible. Don't let fear cloud your judgment so that you can't think for yourself.

The second thing you must let go of is karma. We accumulate karma through living many, many lifetimes on Earth, often with the same people repeating the same mistakes. This is why it is called "The Wheel of Karma." It just goes round and round and holds you to the pattern. I call karma the "baggage and the garbage" that we carry around with us. You must get rid of the "junk" so you can ascend. We all have bad things that happen in our lives. That's what life is all about. I have found that we agree to these events and things in order to learn from them. I ask people when they tell me about their bad experiences, "Did you learn anything from it?" If you learned even one thing from it then that was the reason you experienced it. If they say they did not learn anything from it. Guess what? They will have to experience it all over again until they understand what it was trying to tell them. They have to repeat that grade in school. You can't go from kindergarten to college. So go over your life. What are you holding on to? What haven't you let go of? It no longer matters if you were mistreated or abused as a child. What did you learn? It doesn't matter if you had a horrible marriage. Let it go!! Some of my clients have said, "I can't let it go. You don't know what they did to me!" It is not hurting anyone but yourself by holding onto karma, and creating more by not releasing it. In order to ascend into the New Earth you have to let it go. You have to forgive, or you will have to stay with the old Earth and go through it all again. That is how the law of karma works. Is that what you want?

During my lectures I give the people an exercise that they can use to release karma. You can't speak to the person face to face. That is too difficult to do. Besides, sometimes the person you are angry at has died and it is impossible to face them. You have to do it mentally. Remember that when you were on the spirit side you made a plan of what you *hoped* to accomplish in this life. You made contracts with various souls to play various parts in your scenario on Earth. Some of your greatest enemies or challenges during your life were your greatest friends on the spirit side. They volunteered to come and play the villain in your Earthly scenario. And some of them play their parts *very well!*

So picture the person in your mind standing in front of you. Say to them, "We tried. We really tried. It's not working. I am tearing up the contract." And see yourself tearing up the contract and throwing it away. Then say to them, "I forgive you. I release you. I let you go. You go your way with love, and I'll go mine. We don't have to be connected anymore." And see it happening. The key here is that you have to really mean it. You have to believe it. Once you have done that they will have no power over you anymore. Then you have to forgive yourself. Remember, it always takes two people to create the situation. None of this is easy, but it is essential and imperative, if you want to get off the Wheel and ascend into the New Earth. It's up to you!

* * *

This was part of a longer session in 2002 where the subject had a connection with extraterrestrials. They were supplying information about many things, including what they could do (or are allowed to do) to correct the damage mankind has done to the Earth.

P: They're moving me... forward into the future. They're moving my body. Oh, my god, I'm getting dizzy.

I gave calming suggestions so she would not have any physical effects. She calmed down and stabilized. The feeling of motion dissipated. This experience has also happened to other subjects I have worked with, when they are moved too quickly through time and space.

D: *What are they showing you now?*

P: All I see is light. It's just a brilliant explosion of light. The planet is being bombarded with a special light and it contains different colors. And these different colors affect the consciousness of people in different ways, but it not only affects people. It affects plants and animals and rocks and water and everything. It's a certain type of white light, and it has all types of colors in it. And it changes and moves and it permeates the very core of the planet. I see it's coming from the core of the planet. They shoot it down from, I guess, the ships, and it touches the core of the planet and it bounces out from the core and affects everything from an inward to an outward movement. If you were standing on the planet, you would feel the energies coming through your feet and coming out through the top of your head.

D: *The opposite of what it usually does.*

P: This is different. It's coming from the ships to the core of the planet and then it's bouncing back up. And it's affecting the whole planet. They don't want us to blow ourselves up.

D: *Is this something that is happening in 2002, or is it happening in the future?*

P: This is the future. They're going to do it! To correct the alignment in the planet to keep anything bad from happening. 2006.

D: *2006. Will we have gotten the planet more out of alignment by this time?*

P: Yes, yes. Oh, there are people on the planet and they're praying, but it's not enough because it's so messed up.

It's going to get out of its orbit. And that will affect the rest of the cosmos. So by them directing these energies to the core of the planet, it's going to come back up, and that will correct the alignment. And when it corrects the alignment, it will also correct many other things on the planet. It will help the flooding, the droughts and things like that, that man has brought upon the planet. There's not going to be an annihilation of this planet. The council makes sure that it won't happen. The beings are down here on the planet watching, and they know what's going on and they know who's doing it and they can affect them. It's not that we *can't* intervene, we're not *allowed* to intervene.

D: *Because there are some things you can't do.*

P: That's right, but we can watch. And we know who's doing it.

D: *But whenever the planet gets to the point that man has damaged it so much, that's when you can help?*

P: That's when we're going to send these... I see multi-colored lights. It's like multi-colored shafts of energy and they're being shot down into the core of the planet. And then they bounce back out and it affects the whole planet and it will keep the planet in alignment.

D: *Is this being done by many ships?*

P: It's a confederation. I see many. I see different levels or classifications of beings affecting the planet. We're involved in that. There are many, many beings.

D: *So it's a massive job.*

P: A confederation. Yes, yes.

D: *But isn't it dangerous to shoot things at the core of the planet. Hasn't something gone wrong before when that happened?*

I was thinking of the destruction of Atlantis. This was partially caused by scientists focusing the energy from the giant crystals downward to the center of the Earth. Too much energy was created, and contributed to the earthquakes and gigantic tidal waves.

P: This is not what you think. This is pure light energy. And the only effect it will have on the planet is good. It will not harm the planet.

D: *I was thinking of what they did in Atlantis.*

P: This is not the same thing. It's hard for me to explain. This is done on a soul level. It's like pure divine energy. It's not the energy in Atlantis. The energy in Atlantis was done through atomic power. This is energy that the divine has created that is done through light. It's not done through the separation through molecular structures. This is something we have created, and we send it from the Source. Anything that's from the Source is good and it's not going to harm the planet. It's going to do what we want it to do. And we've been allowed to do this. It is because the planet has caused this that we are taking this action. It's necessary.

D: *Isn't this interference?*

P: No! We cannot interfere with the people here. We can't come down and bully them and tell them what to do. But we can bring our ships and we can point this energy at the core of the Earth. We can do things like this. This is actually on a soul level. So therefore, we are not interfering with the karmic structure of the people here. Everyone here has a karmic purpose, and we are not interfering with that. We're not allowed to. We don't do that.

D: *Do the people on Earth see this when it happens?*

P: They feel it. In other words, they'll go through the transformation. And they won't realize what's happened to them. Some of them will realize. Those who are sensitive will know that something has happened. But many on the planet will just go on in their normal lives, and they will be lifted up and they will be changed and the Earth will be changed. The rocks and the water, but they'll just go on existing because we are not affecting the karmic pattern. We can't do that. We're doing this on a soul level, but it's not affecting their Earth lives as far as karmic patterns go. We're not bothering that.

D: *But the Earth has to get to a certain point before you're allowed to do this.*

P: 2006. It's getting bad. It's already very, very bad right now. If it's allowed to continue, the air will harm very many people And the reason we're involved is, there are people in their physical embodiments breathing this atmosphere with all this pollution and it's changing their genetic heritage. We cannot let that happen and we *will* not let that happen! We gave people of this planet their genetic heritage. And now they have messed up their drinking water, their food, their planet. Everything here is polluted. Man has destroyed his genetic heritage and we're going to repair it because they are not going to mess up our experiment! This is a divine experiment and they can't mess it up. We're going to change it.

To find out more about the grand experiment that mankind has been involved in since its beginning, see my books, *Keepers of the Garden* and *The Custodians.*

P: We have to do this. The whole planet was destroyed many times. You know about Atlantis; there have been many other explosions, floods. This is something that we can't allow to happen at this time because it's going to affect the rest of the cosmos. And the Earth is coming a little more out of alignment. And we will be putting the planet, not only back in alignment, but we will also help cleanse and clear the genetic structure of everything and everyone on the planet. And this has been put forth, and it's been agreed upon, and it will be done. Because mankind has reached the point that it will not be cleaned up soon enough before it destroys the genetic makeup that we created.

D: *So it only has to get out of alignment just a little before it will affect the other....*

P: It's already affected other—not only civilizations in a physical realm that you know, but also on higher planes. That's why we're going to do this.

The various universes are so interwoven and interconnected that if the rotation or trajectory of one is disturbed, it affects all the others. In the extreme case, this could cause all the universes to collapse on themselves and disintegrate. This is one of the reasons for the monitoring of planet Earth by ETs. To detect any problems caused by our negative influences and alert the other galaxies and universes so countermeasures can be initiated. They have to know what the Earth is up to, so the rest of the universes, galaxies, and dimensions can protect themselves and survive.

D: *I thought if you were going to have a massive project like that on Earth, people would be able to see all these ships.*

P: Ohh, you typical Earthling! No, you can't see our ships. We're in different dimensions. There are many different vibrational rates. You won't even be able to see the light, but it's there. At some time, your scientists will be able to measure this type of energy. At some point, the scientists will be able to determine that we are in the atmosphere, and they'll see our ships. They will have machines and devices so they can determine where our ships are. But they don't have that technology right now because we've moved across the veil and we're in—shall we call it—an astral realm. It's a higher level than that, but it's a finer level. And your eyes can't see them, but in the future they will have machines that can see it.

D: *But they will know something is happening to the energy levels. That something is changing.*

P: It will change, and the people will change, but they're not going to be aware of what has happened. It's going to be a big event, but they're not going to be able to discern it on a physical level. On a soul level, they can tell. Subconscious level they'll know, but not on a conscious level because you're thinking of a physical energy. This is not physical energy, this is energy from God. This is soul energy. And it operates within a different dimension than you're thinking. It's very different.

D: *So the people will feel it, but they won't see it. They'll just know that something is happening in their bodies.*

P: Some will know. Those that are sensitive will know that something has happened, but they won't know what. And that's what we want. We don't want to disrupt anything.

D: *How will this affect the human body?*

P: It will prevent the decay of the genetic material DNA within the body. Like I said, it's becoming damaged and we can't have that. We can't have a whole race of people damaged. The energy will change the DNA genetic structure of the humans so that it will be more perfect. That's what we really want. We want the humans on the planet to be in perfect harmony. Not only with themselves, but with us and the rest of the cosmos. They're not in that right now.

D: *So when the DNA structure is changed, how will the body be different?*

P: When the DNA is changed, the body will be what we wanted it to be many millennia ago. We tried this in Atlantis, it failed! The reason it failed was because the energies were used in a negative way by the beings in Atlantis. We tried to bring forth a more feminine energy back in the days of Atlantis, which would raise up and cause a union between the divine male and

536

divine female. It failed. Therefore, the planet Earth went through many, many, many thousands of years with women being subjugated and the feminine energies being suppressed. Now, this is the time that both will be equal. The male and female divine energies will join and this will make for a perfect being... like Christ. Everyone here will realize they can be a perfect Christ, when these energies are in balance. The energies have not been in balance; they've been out of balance for thousands of years. That's why there are so many problems on the planet. So when the DNA structure is altered, the divine energies, the male/female, the yin and the yang, of the God energies can unite and there will be perfection upon the planet. Perfection within the bodies. And this planet will be something that we can show to the rest of the worlds, the rest of the cosmos. That this is our experiment, and this is what we have done and it has succeeded. The light has succeeded because it will be perfect as we have wanted it to be for thousands of years. When we first came here, it was perfect. You've probably been told that. It was altered. You know the meteorite came, disease came. Everything was messed up. We're going to have it perfect again. And this is part of that alignment that we'll be doing to make it perfect again. And this is perfectly normal.—This is all part of genetics, but the reason that happened, was that humans have not been in balance. The divine energies have not been balanced within the psyche or even within the physical mind, but the psyche that comes into the body manifests physically. These have been out of alignment. This causes disease within the body. When the bacteria landed here on the meteorite, had the bodies at that time been in total perfect alignment, it wouldn't have mattered. The disease wouldn't have gotten in there. But the bodies had already begun to change when it hit, so there was nothing we could do.

She was referring to the same thing that was mentioned in my book *Keepers of the Garden,* which explained that disease was introduced to Earth and spoiled the grand experiment by a meteorite that struck the Earth when the fledgling species were still developing. This caused a great deal of sorrow in the council in charge of developing life on Earth because they knew their experiment of creating the perfect human being could not happen under these circumstances. They had to make the decision whether to stop the experiment and start over again, or allow the developing humans to continue, knowing that it would never be the perfect species it was intended to be. It was decided that so much time and effort had been expended in developing humans, that they should be allowed to continue. The hope was that maybe some time in the future, the species could develop into the perfect human being with no disease. This is the main reason for the sampling and testing done by the ETs that people misinterpret as negative. They are concerned with the effects of pollutants in the air and chemical contamination of our food on the human body. And they are attempting to alter its effects.

The ET continued: "We didn't want to not do the experiment. We couldn't just throw the planet away. We couldn't just let all these lifeforms, all these souls be forever altered. We had to step in and we've been coming here for ages and ages. This is the culmination of many, many years of work. Millions of years. And it's coming very soon and we're pleased because mankind has reached the point to where this can be brought forth again upon the planet. As I said, we tried it back many, many thousands of years ago and it *failed,* but we expect it to succeed this time. It's already beginning to succeed. And we're very happy about that."

D: *Will all of the people of Earth experience this?*
P: As I said before, everyone will be affected. It's just that there are those who will be sensitive, who will pick up that it has been done. Some people will not realize on a

conscious level that it's been done. It's been done on a soul level. If you were to put them in trance as you have this person now, they would know they have been affected, and they could explain to you what it has done to their genetics. But on a conscious level, they haven't a clue. They don't know. And that's what we want.

D: *I was thinking of negative people (Murderers, rapists, beings of that sort.) Will they be affected in a different way?*

P: *Everyone* will be affected. They will know on a subconscious level what has happened. As the subconscious changes, and becomes aware of this, and is activated, yes.

D: *They still have karma.*

P: This will also be affected, because this planet in the future is not going to have karma. That is something that won't be allowed here. It will be a planet of Light and Peace and will be our grand experiment that succeeded.

D: *I've been told this is why many in the universe are watching.*

P: Yes, that's right. We're here to do that. And it will be safe.

One final piece of information came through a client at my office in 2004. I believed one part of all of this was still unclear: How could some people be aware that they had made the shift into the New Earth, and others would not be? How would it be possible to move an entire population with only a minority knowing anything had happened? "They" must have been aware that I was struggling with this lingering thought, so they supplied it. After all, how could I write about it, and lecture about it if I didn't have all the pieces?

Bob: Most planets, but especially this one was only designed originally for five hundred and fifty thousand people. Half a million people. That was as large as it was supposed to go. More people are reincarnating here to experience all these major changes. And the Earth has been damaged and changed beyond the capability to repair it. This planet has been unfortunately changed in such ways that there's no sense of return whatsoever to its original pristine condition. But now because of the prime directive from the Creator, this has to accelerate. Because it's been too long. There are two ways to do this. You can cause the planet to rotate and the Earth crust to shift. And you literally, when that happens, start all over again from ground zero. That's what touched off the Ice Age and killed all the dinosaurs. It doesn't matter how it happened, but basically it did the same thing. A civilization disappears, and you start off with the Ice Age and Neanderthal Man and all that kind of good stuff all happens again. You lose control of your entire civilization, and you end up as a legend like Atlantis and Lemuria. This has all happened many times before. But that's not what's going to happen this time. This time you shift as a planet. And *basically* as a universe. You shift the whole dimension. The dimension changes. You go from 3 point 6 (3.6) which we are now, to five. And you say, "Well, what happens to four?" Well, four is sort of here in a way, but it's just going to *jump* it. You're going to end up as five. When the dimensional *change* comes, you will literally *jump* that. There's a lot of complications with this. This is why it's being watched so carefully. Many people who are spiritually ready will be able to make the transition very easily. Others are literally going to be taken off planet. In the flick of an eyelid they won't even know it's happened, most of them. And they will end up on another planet that's pristine, ready and waiting for this to happen. And your capabilities will be far beyond what they are now. You have basically five primary senses. You'll have many more than that when the transition goes through. You will become automatically telepathic. They'll wake up in their little lives the next day—or what can be done, depending on how it's shifted.—It has happened before, by the way.—We will simply shut down. It's like going into suspended animation. We suspend it. It may take two or three days to transfer the populace.

D: *The entire world, or just the....*

B: Yes. All the people that are spiritually ready to make this transition. They'll all be shifted off. And when they wake up on this other planet, they won't even realize it's happened. There was a shift like this a few years ago on this planet, with all of us. And not many people knew about it. It just *was*. It was like a whole week passed by in the course of a night. It *has* happened that way.

D: *Why did that happen at that time?*

B: We needed to shift the sun, technically, and we needed to be able to adjust it. And if anybody could see it, they would all know what happened. That wasn't a very practical way of doing it. So we just kind of shut everybody down.

D: *So they wouldn't know it?*

B: Yes. You went to sleep that night, and you slept like you thought it was a twelve hour period. And you woke up. And your watch was still running the same. But in fact you had literally gone through a whole week.

D: *Everyone was put into suspended animation?*

B: Yes. You shut down the whole thing all at the same time.

D: *While the world moved?*

B: Oh, yes. The planet moves. You have the so-called "night and day." But we actually adjusted it. It was a really interesting trick to do it. But it does work. This planetary adjustment that's coming up. This frequency change thing that is coming up. You can't merely *do* this with everybody awake. Because you're going to have all sorts of strange reactions in people. So they *think* they're all awake. But yet we can shut them down. It's a bit of a trick. It's very technically involved.

D: *So they would think they were having dreams if they did see anything,*

B: Yes, yes, precisely. But they might not have conscious remembrance of it because don't forget, most people *don't* have conscious remembrance of what they dream anyway. And you can change things in dreams very easily, too.

D: *You said this was done a few years ago.*

B: Yes, it was. We had to make an adjustment in the sun's frequency.

So apparently that would be the answer. The entire population of the world would be shut down and put into suspended animation while the transfer was made.

This is also found in the Bible: *"In that day, he who is on the housetop, and his goods are in the house, let him not come down to take them away. And likewise, the one who is in the field, let him not turn back. I tell you, in that **night**, there will be two men in one bed: the one will be taken and the other will be left. Two women will be grinding together: the one will be taken and the other left. Two men will be in the field: the one will be taken and the other left. And they answered and said to Him, "Where Lord?" So He said to them, "Wherever the body is, there the eagles will be gathered together."* (Luke 17:31-37)

I have been asked many times about the Mayan calendar ending at 2012. People think that is the date for the end of the world if the Mayans could not see beyond that. I have been told that the Mayans evolved spiritually to this point where their civilization shifted en masse to the next dimension. They stopped the calendar at 2012 because they could see this would be the time of the next major event: the shifting of the entire world into the next dimension.

We will ascend to the other dimension by raising our consciousness, the vibration and frequency of our body. At first, you can continue in a physical body for a while. Then as you gradually discover it is no longer necessary, the physical body dissolves into Light, and you live with a body made of light or pure energy. This sounds very similar to several cases in my books where the subject saw a being that glowed and was composed of pure energy. They have evolved beyond the need for a physical limiting body, and we will do this also when we reach that stage. So in many cases, when the being ascends, they take the physical body with them. But this is only a temporary situation and the shedding and letting go of the body depends on the level of understanding the being has reached. We do tend to hold on to the familiar, but eventually see that even though we were able to take it with us, the body is too limiting and confining for the new reality in the new dimension. When we reach this new dimension, the new body of light or energy will never die. This is what the Bible meant when it referred to "Eternal Life."

The spirit side or the in-between lives state, where I have found that we go when we die in this lifetime, is like a recycling center. It leads back to another life on Earth because there is still karma to be worked out, or something that needs to be attended to. People keep returning because they have not completed their lessons or their cycles. By raising the consciousness, the frequency and vibration, there is no need to return to that place (the in-between state). It can be transcended by going to the place where everyone is eternal, and there is no reason for recycling. We can remain there forever. This is probably the place many of my subjects refer to as "home." The place they deeply miss and desire to return to. When they see it during the regressions they become very emotional because they have been deeply longing for it, yet not consciously knowing it existed.

CHAPTER THIRTY-SEVEN

THOSE LEFT BEHIND

lsewhere in this book and in the *Convoluted Universe* series I covered the stories of individuals who witnessed the destruction of their home planet. They were new to Earth, and some said they were only sent to Earth during crucial times. The destruction had been a personal experience, and they would be extremely valuable during this time to make sure it didn't happen again here on Earth. This was another such individual who had seen an entire planet destroyed.

D: *Why did Jean decide to come back now? You said she'd been here at other pivotal points in Earth's history.*

J: This is the big one. This is the great one. This is happening now. And many are remembering who they really are, and are being contacted. The new children are being brought in, and she loves the children. So she's helping others to balance the energies. It's being a bridge. Bridging the energies now. *You* are a bridge. Of course, you are. So there are those of you that came in to help bridge the information, to be the ambassadors.

D: *To help these people wake up to who they are?*

J: Absolutely. And to be okay. To accept any of them who have experiences that they filed away. It's a big time on your planet because this is the big one. This is where you, as a planet, awaken out of the dream of thinking you're alone. That you're all that is. Your

Earth is evolving. You are all evolving. All eyes are on Earth right now, anyway. This is the big one. Many fought to be here. Even children that come in, even for hours. You'll all carry that, the badge of having been here.

D: *Even for a few hours?*

J: Absolutely. To have been on this planet at a time of this kind of evolution. No planet has ever quite evolved this way before, this uniquely. If you were going to have the option to carry the identification of having been on a planet that will be known through the multiverse, even if you can be here for a few hours, that you could say, "I was on Earth at the time of evolution." Why not?

D: *Is this what I call the New Earth?* (Yes) *That there will be an old and a new, and then a separation.* (Yes.) *And that some won't make the evolution?* (Yes. Yes.) *I'm still trying to understand that.*

J: It is difficult for many humans to understand this concept.

D: *I'm still trying to clarify this to myself, so I can explain it to other people.*

J: All right. We will give you this piece. For those that choose to stay in karma, they have to live that out somewhere. So, do they stay with the old Earth? Do they get taken to some foreign planet? No, they stay where they created.

D: *I see. And those are the ones that will not go on in the evolution?*

J: Not at this time. No. Eventually. Not at this time. But that will be difficult.

D: *Then the old Earth will continue to exist?*

J: Yes. This one.

D: *Will the people in the old Earth be aware that anything has happened when the evolution occurs?*

J: All right. We will take you back to the time of Atlantis. In your history, Atlantis had several destructions, and people perceived that others died.

D: *You mean there was more than one destruction?*

J: Yes. There is an Atlantis that went on, and exists in time and space. Therefore, from that perspective, that Atlantis exists now in another dimension.

So there will be those on the old Earth that will experience it because they buy into the fear of the death and destruction and devastation of Earth, and they will be there. In their mind, they may perceive that all of you are dead or gone, or whatever. And likewise, you may perceive them as gone, but either way, there will be two experiences. So think of this as already there. The orchestration to create this experience is so much bigger than any human can perceive at this time. This is a big orchestration, not just occurring on your Earth, but with the help of so many. So many. And no other planets have done this before.

D: *I've been told that the whole universe is watching.*

J: More than just the universe. There are those even from *other* universes that are watching.

D: *Because they said this had never happened before, where an entire planet moves into another dimension.*

J: Never. Ever. Also look at the fact that, as a consciousness, you see yourselves as separate. Consciousness on this planet was created in a unique way to be able to experience itself as separate. Most other races do not see that. Regardless of where they are, they don't experience themselves as separate from their Source. Your planet has.

D: *So the ones who are part of the councils, and work on the ships, know their Source, and know where they come from?*

J: Of course. And they love you humans. You don't even know what you've done. They recognize there are primitive behaviors on the planet, but to reach the level that you have, based on the restrictions that you've had to work within. It's amazing. Your capacity to love is deep. Your capacity of fear is deep. That's the power of control that gets everybody in trouble. Fostered by the fear.

D: *I know Earth was created with free will. But it was also created with the idea of not knowing it was part of the Source?*

J: Yes. It was an interesting construct of consciousness, in that it experienced itself as separate. Where else could there be more growth than in a situation where you actually saw yourself as separate from your Source?

D: *But you said the other races know they are all part of the Source.*

J: Yes, they do. So can there be more soul growth on Earth? Yes.

D: *If we thought we were alone, and then had to discover this all by ourselves.*

J: Yes. They have to discover the truth of who they are on their own. Yes.

D: *With nothing else to help them. I can see what you mean.*

J: You have density here. You have the beauty. You have the senses. You have much going on here, but you also have not understanding. Look where you are.

D: *I've had many people have sessions where they go back to the Source. They see how beautiful it is, and they don't want to leave it again.*

J: When you connect with the Source, it is the most beautiful experience. So your question is what? Are the sessions happening for them to connect with that Source?

D: *Yes. Why is it happening? So they will know what it's like, or to remind them or....?*

J: For those that need to have that experience, yes. For some, it would be too great, and they wouldn't be able

548

to go on. They would just as soon leave. It's different for each one of you. Every person is different in terms of what they can and cannot experience. And what it will trigger within their subconscious because each one of you is a unique and individual fingerprint on the planet. There are no two of you really alike. Think what a genius is the mastery of that. Think of the beauty and the wonder of that. And there are many of you, other lifetimes now, working on the other side, and they are all participating in this as well. You are never alone, any of you.

D: *We have to rediscover where we came from, and why we're here. But there was one question people have asked me, and I think you have answered part of it. That if some are taken, and some are left behind, wouldn't those that go on to the new world notice the other members of their family were gone? These are some things I'm still trying to clarify, in our way of thinking. I have to be able to explain it to people.*

J: We understand. We understand. We understand. We will give you this explanation. We hope this helps. People are going to start falling out of people's lives. They're going to start noticing them falling away. Quite rapidly, now. In other words, people, family members, whoever they have been close to, just falling away, disappearing. It will not all happen overnight. So by the time the shift happens, some of those people will already have fallen out of their life, will separate. Will just disappear. Not be around. So and so moved over here, left town, did this. Do you understand?

D: *Yes, but we could go to the police and try to find the person, or....*

J: It won't happen that way. It will be them moving away, something happened, distancing, distancing, distancing. By the time it actually occurs, the distance will be there. Haven't you had people fall out of your life lately?

D: Yes. Of course, we could always contact them if we needed to.

J: But you won't. That's our point. You won't contact them. It will just be a natural falling away. The frequencies and vibrations will no longer match, and therefore, they will fall out of your mind. The need to contact them won't be there.

D: And this means they are either staying with the old Earth, or they're going on to the new one?

J: In some cases, there have been those that have left early, and are working on the other side of the veil. You're aware of that. But some of those that disappear, after a period of time, you think, "I wonder what happened to this person?" But you don't have the urge to contact them like you would normally. You don't have that driving urge, "Oh, I'm concerned, I must call. I must reach out." It's not the same. You find that your need to connect with them just isn't there. It just falls away. You forget.

D: I've been told that at first, those who enter the new world will have physical bodies. So we won't know when we have actually made the shift, the separation. Is that correct?

J: That may be too simplistic of a description. For those of you that came in to bridge this... we'll explain it this way. As you do your work, you facilitate. You help people to awaken, to open up to more of who they are. To raise their vibration, their frequency, to be able to resonate at the higher cycles per second so they can make the shift. Does that make sense to you?

D: Yes. That's what I'm trying to help people to do.

J: Exactly, what you're helping people to do. Yes. It will happen. It's not going to happen in the way that people think, where there'll be a cataclysm or this or that or the other thing. No. It will just be like you wake up one morning, and you think everything's normal, and you're going on, and you will be there. You will notice a difference in resonance, but you will already be there because your resonance is increasing every day already, as it is. And so, all of a sudden, one day, you will reach the prerequisite cycles per second to take you from here to there. Let's explain it this way. If somebody came back right now from the eighteen hundreds to see you, you would glow to them. You've already reached those cycles per second that would glow to a human form of, say, the eighteen hundreds. So in essence, your cycles per second are raising.

Comment: Could this be one reason why when John and the others went to visit Nostradamus (*Conversations With Nostradamus* trilogy*)*, he saw them as glowing energy spirits of the future? Was this because they were actually vibrating at a faster frequency that made them glow? That is something to think about.

J: That's the reason you're a bridge to help others to raise their cycles per second so they can make the shift. And the faster you raise more people, they activate other people with their frequencies and vibrations. So what you are doing is activating more and more people on the planet, which activates others, which raises the frequency of the planet. Do you understand? It's all cyclic. Everything affects everything else. You have people that come to Earth and don't have to do anything, they are just strictly activators. Their energy fields activate everybody else's. [See examples in this book.] You have those that are working very hard and diligently, that are like broadcasters. They broadcast out over the planet, like a microwave signal.

D: *This makes sense to me. This is why I've been told age won't make any difference.*

J: That's exactly right.

D: *We'll be functioning at a different level, different vibrations.*

J: Different vibration, different cycles per second.

D: *This is the way some of the other races (ETs, aliens) function, don't they?*

J: Yes. They age at a totally different rate. The goal for humans is a longer life expectancy. Much longer. And also, creating the bridge of understanding. And if you begin with health, you are able to reach people in a non-invasive, non-threatening way.

D: *In this new world, where age won't matter, will the body eventually die? The way we consider it on Earth now, in our reality.*

J: There will be some of you that will have the option not to die at all. Just to make your transition, just to cross over. But not everybody's going to be at exactly the same frequency at the same time. Remember that.

D: *Yes. I was thinking maybe the body would get to the point that it could just maintain itself until the soul was ready to leave.*

J: That's exactly right. Not for everyone, though. If you have many people making this transition, and let's say that the frequency has to be approximately 44,000 cycles per second in order to make that frequency shift. Not everyone is going to be at that frequency shift at the same time. You're going to have different variables in the frequency shift. There will still be those of you that are on that front line, on that cutting edge, even on the other side. Even in the new world. You understand? Because there always will be. Because there always are on every level. Every race always has those that are out there on the cutting edge. A little further out, going a little further because that's evolution.

D: *I was thinking that was the way it would be. We'd have a lot more time to do our work, and to help reach people.*

J: Of course.

D: *We wouldn't have to worry about the limitations of the body.*

J: Oh, the limitations of the body. No. Well, look at your whole. You are already changing. You are going through cellular changes. They are making adjustments on you.

D: *I've been told they were doing it on me.*

J: Yes, they are. (Laugh) And because you're a spokesperson, again, a bridge, who is more important to look good than you?

D: *I guess. Well, if I hear it from enough people, maybe I'm going to believe it, anyway.*

J: You need to believe it.

D: *I've also been told that not everyone will make this shift into the new world.*

J: This is correct. When the Earth is going to make a shift, there's the idea that many souls are allowed in for experience because, as you say, you experience many things in your growth as a soul. And so, there have been many, let's say, beginners coming into the planet. Sometimes being in a class with advanced students can be helpful. As you know, the old country schoolhouses? *(Yes)* So you might have levels of students all in the same room, and they all benefit from that. But there finally comes a time when the students need to move on. And that means that those who are left behind will have to find their own planet. They will be put in other schools, other places.

D: *I always thought it sounded cruel to leave them behind.*

J: Oh, no. They won't be left behind. They will be taken to a place where they can grow.

D: *That's the way I've understood it, too. It would be like a separation.*

J: It's more natural. It's like when you leave your body, you go to another dimension and you grow in that dimension, and you may or may *not* come in as another body here. You may go somewhere else. And if the whole Universe is a body, there are many, many galaxies and planets where they can go.

* * *

More information about how our bodies and the entire world will go through the dimensional shift process, and it will be undetected by those around who do not make the shift or change:

"Our bodies and everything around us are now increasing their vibratory rate and adjusting to a new frequency. Every cell of the body begins to vibrate at such a fast rate that it turns into light. When this begins, the temperature of the body increases and the body starts to glow with light. When every cell is vibrating at a very high rate, you will disappear from normal vision and move into a higher dimensional reality. This is because the body has moved in vibration beyond the third dimension and is now vibrating on a much higher dimensional level. This then means that you will not go through the death process, as you will then have a Light Body. Aging will not exist for you, and you will have stepped into the next dimensional reality. You can then access the next stage of spiritual evolution."

"They" have emphasized that this has happened down through time to certain individuals and small groups of people. But what makes it unique now, is that it will be the first time that an entire planet will make the shift into another dimension. This will be the new Earth and the new world. This is described in the Bible as the new heaven and the new Earth. The others who are not ready, will be left behind (just as it says in the Bible) to continue to live out their karma. They will not even be aware that anything has happened. Those who have not become enlightened, will have to return to another, denser planet that is still involved with negativity, to work out their remaining karma. They will not be allowed to come to the "new Earth" because their vibration will not match.

The Earth is a living being. She has been evolving just as we are, albeit at a much slower rate. She is now preparing to move into her next incarnation, which will happen when she raises her vibrations and frequencies to take her into another higher dimension. She has tolerated humans living on her since the beginning, and it doesn't matter to her whether we go with her or not. She is moving regardless, and if we choose to go, it is our decision. We have created such a nuisance that she would rather we didn't go with her. We are like fleas on a dog, and it is obvious that we have caused great damage and distress to this beautiful planet. So if we want to go with her on this next adventure then we have to make changes in ourselves. Our frequency and vibration must be raised, or we will be left behind.

❧ —·· ·◆❥❖—❍—◆❄•——◆❄—◖❦❧◗·· ·—❍

Several years ago, I was on a panel at a conference with Annie Kirkwood, the author of *Mary's Message to the World*. She told about a vision she had that seems to portray the evolution of the New Earth. She saw the Earth as it is viewed from outer space. Then it started looking like two Earths, one superimposed on the other. There were little lines of flashing lights going between both the Earths. Then as she watched, she saw it begin to pull apart; the way a cell does when it is dividing to produce another cell. One Earth went off in one direction, and the other one went in the other direction. On the one Earth she and others were exclaiming, "Yes, yes, it really happened! We did it! We really *are* a new Earth!" And on the other Earth she heard her sister's voice, "That girl was so crazy! She was out there telling everybody all these crazy things. And nothing happened! She just died!" So it appears that when the final event occurs, there will be some people that will not even be aware that anything has occurred. This will be the separation of those who go on with the New Earth and those who are left behind on the Old Earth which will still be steeped in negativity.

Later during a lecture I explained this vision, and afterwards a man came up to me. He said, "I want you to know that I am a businessman. I usually don't have experiences that I can't explain logically. But whenever you were describing the two Earths separating this auditorium suddenly disappeared, and I found myself in outer space. As I watched, I saw it happen exactly the way you described." He said the scene was still very vividly in his mind. He went home and created the picture below on his computer, and gave permission to use it in this book. It is much more impressive in color, but the New Earth is the glowing orb superimposed over the old Earth.

Created by Michael R. Taylor (MT)

At a lecture in Chicago in 2006, I was discussing the evolution of the New Earth. I was describing the vision that Annie Kirkwood had about the Earth splitting into two Earths. How, as the one divided into two separate Earths the people on each would not be aware of what was happening on the other. Those who had raised their frequency and vibration would ascend into the New Earth as it evolved and lifted into a different dimension. Thus becoming invisible to the ones "left behind." There have been several things about this concept that bothered me. I always like to have the answers; I guess because of my great curiosity. I have felt there are gaps or holes that needed to be filled. Pieces that needed to be explained. Someone in the audience asked the question about how this could happen, and those on one Earth not be aware of what was happening on the other one. Suddenly I had a revelation. A thought came to me that might be the glimmering of an understandable explanation. It is always wise to trust these flashes of intuition and knowledge because often they are coming from our guides. In this case, it might have been coming from the same source that gives me all of the information through my clients. I suddenly said, "A possible explanation just came to me."

Earlier in the lecture I had talked briefly about the theory of parallel universes and lives that are created by our thoughts and decisions. In *Book One,* I wrote about a theory I had never heard of, and that gave me a headache trying to understand. In brief it says that: Any time an individual has to make a decision they usually have more than one choice. This is what I call, "Coming to a crossroad." They have to decide to go one way or another. It could be a decision about a marriage, a divorce, a job, anything. They ponder each choice and put a great deal of energy into deciding which path to take. Then they make a decision. We have all experienced these "crossroads." We know that had we chosen to go the other path, our lives would be totally different. We decide to go one direction. But what happens to the energy that we have sent into the other decision that was not chosen? *It also becomes a reality!* Another universe or dimension is instantly created to act out the other decision, and another "you" is also created to be the player in that scenario. This was the *simple* explanation because it does not only happen when we are faced by major decisions. It can happen each and every time we are faced with choices, no matter how big or small. Each time we make a decision, another universe or dimension is instantly created so the other choice can also become a reality, and another "you" splits off to play that part. They are all just as *real* as the present life we are focused on. We are not aware of these other parts of us, and it is wise that we are not. Our human minds would never be able to handle it all. I was told that the problem is not with the brain, it is with the mind. There are simply no concepts within our human mind to allow us to comprehend all the complexities of it. That is why we will never be allowed to have all the answers. There is no way we could understand. So they (in their wisdom) choose what small pieces to give us during this time of awakening, so we will have some expanded information. And as our minds expand to encompass new ideas and theories, they will give us some more small morsels. I personally am grateful for the bits and pieces I am being given. It shows that our minds are awakening. This is the only way we are going to be able to handle the concept of our Earth changing frequency and vibration in order to shift into a different dimension. The information I am receiving now I could never have even begun to understand when I started my work over thirty years ago. So I know I have grown, and I can see this reflected in the books I have written over these years.

The revelation that came to me during the lecture in Chicago was that perhaps the reason the people on each Earth will not be aware of each other, and what is happening, might be that it will be similar to the concept of the creation of parallel universes and dimensions. Only on a much grander scale. If we are not aware of these other parts of ourselves acting out the other decisions we have created by the energy we have focused on them, then the people on the two Earths would be unaware of each other. One Earth would be going in the direction of one decision or choice, and the other Earth would be going in another direction. Each acting out an alternate decision. It is up to the people on Earth at the present time to each make their personal decision of which path they want to follow. The energy is present and becoming stronger. It is physically affecting our bodies. Our own frequency and vibration is being altered. But I believe it is still up to us what we decide, which Earth we gravitate toward because of our free will. The main difference here is that "they" said this has never happened on such a grand scale before. Never in the history of the universe has an entire planet changed its frequency and vibration to shift into another dimension. That is why it is said to be the greatest show in the universe, and everyone from many different galaxies and dimensions are watching to see what is going to happen. Are we going to be able to do it? Are we going to be able to pull it off?

The train is leaving the station. It is taking us to a great adventure that has never been experienced on this scale before. It is up to each individual whether they get onboard or remain standing on the platform. The volunteers who have fulfilled their purpose are ready to go "home." All aboard!! And remember, you are never alone.

Author Page

Dolores Cannon, a regressive hypnotherapist and psychic researcher who records "Lost" knowledge, was born in 1931 in St. Louis, Missouri. She was educated and lived in St. Louis until her marriage in 1951 to a career Navy man. She spent the next 20 years traveling all over the world as a typical Navy wife, and raising her family. In 1970 her husband was discharged as a disabled veteran, and they retired to the hills of Arkansas. She then started her writing career and began selling her articles to various magazines and newspapers. She has been involved with hypnosis since 1968, and exclusively with past-life therapy and regression work since 1979. She has studied the various hypnosis methods and thus developed her own unique technique which enabled her to gain the most efficient release of information from her clients. Dolores is now teaching her unique technique of hypnosis all over the world.

In 1986 she expanded her investigations into the UFO field. She has done on-site studies of suspected UFO landings, and has investigated the Crop Circles in England. The majority of her work in this field has been the accumulation of evidence from suspected abductees through hypnosis.

Dolores is an international speaker who has lectured on all the continents of the world. Her fifteen books are translated into twenty languages. She has spoken to radio and television audiences worldwide. And articles about/by Dolores have appeared in several U.S. and international magazines and newspapers. Dolores was the first American and the first foreigner to receive the "Orpheus Award" in Bulgaria, for the highest advancement in the research of psychic phenomenon. She has received Outstanding Contribution and Lifetime Achievement awards from several hypnosis organizations.

Dolores has a very large family who keep her solidly balanced between the "real" world of her family and the "unseen" world of her work.

If you wish to correspond with Dolores about her work, private sessions or her training classes, please submit to the following address. (Please enclose a self addressed stamped envelope for her reply.) Dolores Cannon, P.O. Box 754, Huntsville, AR, 72740, USA
Or email her at decannon@msn.com or through our Website: www.ozarkmt.com

Other Books Published
by
Ozark Mountain Publishing, Inc.

Continue for more books by Ozark Mountain Publishing, Inc.

For more information about any of the above titles, soon to be released titles, or
other items in our catalog, write or visit our website:

OZARK
MOUNTAIN
PUBLISHING

PO Box 754
Huntsville, AR 72740
www.ozarkmt.com
1-800-935-0045/479-738-2348
Wholesale Inquiries Welcome